Study Guide

for use with

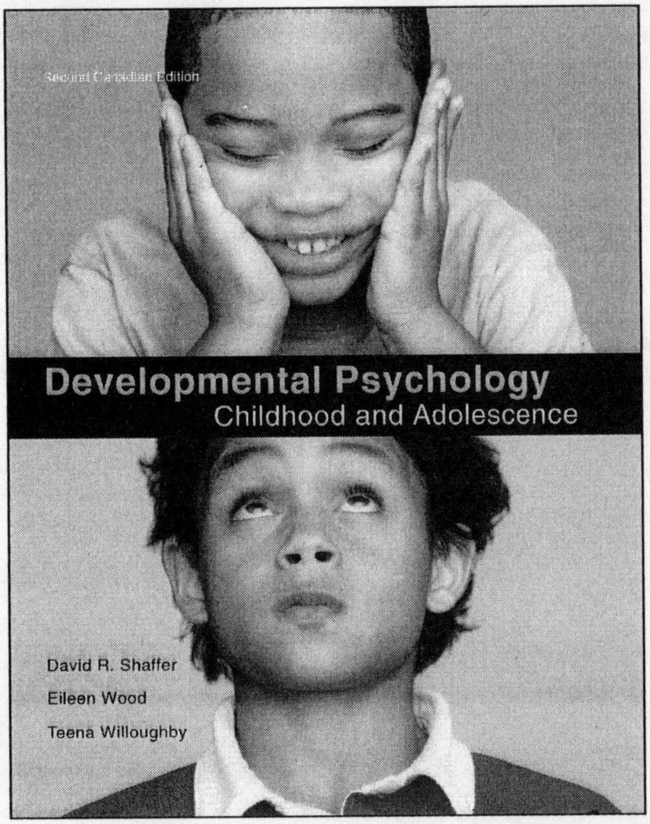

Prepared by
S. A. HENSCH
University of Wisconsin

GILLIAN R. WARK
Simon Fraser University

THOMSON
NELSON

Australia Canada Mexico Singapore Spain United Kingdom United States

THOMSON
NELSON

Study Guide for use with
Developmental Psychology: Childhood and Adolescence,
Second Canadian Edition

By David R. Shaffer, Elleen Wood and Teena Willoughby

Prepared by S. A. Hensch and Gillian R. Wark

Associate Vice-President and Editorial Director:
Evelyn Veitch

Publisher:
Joanna Cotton

Senior Marketing Manager:
Murray Moman

Senior Developmental Editor:
Edward Ikeda

Production Editor:
Carrie McGregor

Senior Production Coordinator:
Hedy Sellers

Creative Director:
Angela Cluer

Cover Design:
Maria Castelli

Printer:
Webcom

Printed and bound in Canada
2 3 4 07 06

For more information contact Nelson, 1120 Birchmount Road, Toronto, Ontario, M1K 5G4. Or you can visit our Internet site at http://www.nelson.com

ISBN-13: 978-0-17-640655-4
ISBN-10: 0-17-640655-7

National Library of Canada Cataloguing in Publication Data

Hensch, Shirley-Anne, 1955-
Study guide for use with Developmental psychology: childhood and adolescence, second Canadian edition / S.A. Hensch, Gillian R. Wark.

ISBN 0-17-640655-7

1. Child psychology–Problems, exercises, etc. 2. Adolescent psychology–Problems, exercises, etc. I. Wark, Gillian R., 1966– II. Title.

BF721.S4688 2004 Suppl. 1
155.4 C2004-905661-1

Dedication: Special thanks go to Jeff Bisanz for helping me contact Canadian researchers through DPNet, and to Anoosha Aghakhani for helping me locate Canadian articles. Warmest thanks go to my husband, Rene Pantoja, for his support in putting together this second Canadian edition of the study guide, and to Isabella Rose, my daughter, and to Hunter John, my son, for inspiration.

Gillian R. Wark

CONTENTS

To the Student: About Your Study Guide ..... *v*

List of Activities ..... *vii*

Chapter 1 Introduction to Developmental Psychology and Its Research Strategies 1

Chapter 2 Theories of Human Development 17

Chapter 3 Hereditary Influences on Development 36

Chapter 4 Prenatal Development, Birth, and Newborns' Readiness for Life 58

Chapter 5 The Physical Self: Development of the Brain, the Body, and Motor Skills 78

Chapter 6 Early Cognitive Foundations: Sensation, Perception, and Learning 97

Chapter 7 Cognitive Development: Piaget's Theory, Case's Neo-Piagetian Theory, and Vygotsky's Sociocultural Viewpoint 116

Chapter 8 Cognitive Development: Information-Processing Perspectives and Connectionism 152

Chapter 9 Intelligence: Measuring Mental Performance 178

Chapter 10 Development of Language and Communication Skills 198

Chapter 11 Emotional Development and the Establishment of Intimate Relationships 221

Chapter 12 Development of the Self and Social Cognition 243

Chapter 13 Sex Differences and Similarities, Gender-Role Development, and Sexual Behaviour 263

Chapter 14 Aggression, Altruism, and Moral Development 282

Chapter 15 The Family 307

Chapter 16 Extrafamilial Influences: Television, Computers, Schools, and Peers 332

ABOUT YOUR STUDY GUIDE

PLEASE READ BEFORE USING YOUR STUDY GUIDE

This study guide was developed to accompany *Developmental Psychology: Childhood and Adolescence, Second Canadian Edition*, by David Shaffer, Eileen Wood, and Teena Willoughby. It presents several ways to help you master the material, ways that other students have found enhanced their learning. In addition, the Study Guide presents a series of activities that are designed to either help master the material, to personalize it, or to allow for first-hand observation of children. Your instructor may assign some of the activities to bring to class for discussion or to turn in for credit.

Each chapter of the Study Guide contains the following:

LEARNING OBJECTIVES: A set of learning objectives is provided at the beginning of each chapter. These learning objectives indicate the key concepts included in each chapter, and the skills and abilities you should master by the time you have completed each chapter. To meet these learning objectives you will need to do more than simply read your textbook. The activities contained in this Study Guide are designed to help you master the learning objectives for each chapter.

CHAPTER OUTLINE AND SUMMARY: The chapter summary from the text has been integrated with an outline (based on chapter headings) to provide you with an overview before reading the text chapter and to provide you with a summary after reading the chapter. You should find that after reading the chapter, the outline will trigger associations that it did not before. If a heading fails to elicit any associations, take it as a cue to re-read that section.

VOCABULARY SELF-TEST: The text author provides a running glossary in the text margins of each chapter. The vocabulary self-test for each chapter is based on those margin definitions. The first part of the self-test presents definitions and asks you to recall the appropriate term; the second part of the self-test presents terms and asks you to recall the appropriate definition. Once you have completed this portion of the Study Guide for each chapter, you can further test yourself. Cover the cues that are provided and use your answers to recall the appropriate definition in Part I, or the appropriate term in Part II.

SHORT-ANSWER STUDY QUESTIONS (to use as a processing tool or self-test): Short-answer study questions are provided for each chapter. These questions relate to the learning objectives for each chapter and they are designed to help you become more actively engaged in the material, rather than passively absorbing it as you read. It is well established that active processing facilitates learning. One way to utilize the study questions is to read and answer each question as you read the chapter. Doing so will help you focus on the material and extract the main points for each section of material. The study questions and answers you have completed can then be reviewed to prepare for exams. The chapters are perforated so that you can tear out each Study Guide chapter if you wish.

Cooperative study groups. Many students find it useful to plan time to go over any study questions that were troublesome for them with a fellow student. The discussion that occurs while coming to an agreement on the answer is a form of active learning that fosters cognitive growth since each student is forced to justify his or her response. Keep in mind, however, that it is important to also allow time for independent review and study of the study questions and your answers, the text, vocabulary, and lecture notes. Group study sessions should be used to supplement/complement rather than to totally replace individual study time. It is best to have each member of the group complete all questions independently before meeting as a group; much of the learning occurs in the answering process.

MULTIPLE-CHOICE SELF-TEST: A set of multiple-choice questions is included for each chapter to further help you test your mastery of the material. These questions do not exhaustively test all the material from the chapter, but they do test broadly across the full range of material. In completing the multiple-choice self-test you should consider each of the alternatives, and decide why each alternative is correct or incorrect, rather than simply trying to pick the "correct" answer. The answers to these questions are presented at the end of each chapter, along with a rationale for the answer that specifies *why* the selected answer is correct, *and why the other alternatives are incorrect.* In mastering the material in any course it is important to know why certain answers or solutions are inappropriate, in addition to knowing why a particular answer or solution is appropriate.

ACTIVITIES: The Study Guide also includes one or more activities/projects for each chapter that your instructor may choose to assign. An introduction, instructions, related references (when appropriate), and references and websites of interest (when appropriate) for each chapter's activities are presented after the multiple-choice self-test in each Study Guide chapter. The activities are of five types:

(a) activities to facilitate mastery of some part of the material presented in a chapter

(b) activities using the media

(c) self-report activities designed to personalize the material, thereby making it more meaningful and memorable to you

(d) activities that give you the opportunity to work with a child

(e) activities that involve interviewing other college students or describing other people.

Note on activities involving children: One type of project involves observing a child respond to a task or questions that you present. Most students find that it is possible to find access to one or more children if assigned a project that involves working with a child. Possibilities include a niece or nephew, someone you babysit, the child of a friend or neighbour, a child at the campus daycare, etc. You may need to plan to complete the project when you are home on a weekend if your hometown is where you have access to children. **For any activity involving a child you must obtain parental permission before working with the child and follow the guidelines for ethical research described in Chapter 1 of your text.**

LIST OF ACTIVITIES
(grouped by type)

ACTIVITIES TO FACILITATE MASTERY

1-1 Assumptions about children: How they affect treatment/practice

1-2 Practice in identifying research designs and methods for studying developmental change

2-1 Assumptions made by major theories

2-2 Assumptions about children: How do we explain aggression?

3-2 Create a zygote

3-3 Understanding genetic transmission

4-1 Giving advice on prenatal and postnatal care—you be the expert

4-3 Giving advice on prenatal and postnatal care—you be the expert

5-1b My looks and my self-esteem

6-3 To circumcise or not to circumcise?

7-4 Examples of three formal-operational acquisitions

7-5 Constructing classroom settings

9-1 Ways in which home environment supports intellectual development

10-3 Bilingualism and education

11-2 Working mothers and daycare

14-2 Temper tantrums and discipline

ACTIVITIES USING THE MEDIA

13-1 Media (ads, television, films) as a potential influence on sex typing and self-concept

13-2 Media (children's television programs) as a potential influence on children's gender stereotypes

16-1 Television aggression

SELF-REPORT ACTIVITIES THAT PERSONALIZE THE MATERIAL

3-1 Determinants of similarities and differences

3-4 Scarr and McCartney's passive, evocative, and active genotype/environment correlations

4-2 Everyday medications and their teratogenic effects

5-1a My looks and my physical capabilities

5-2 Puberty: Its timing, how it is experienced, and its relation to body image, dieting, and body building

6-1 Verbal comments as consequences affecting behaviour

7-4 Examples of three formal-operational acquisitions

12-1 Who am I?

12-2 Who am I to be?

15-2 Your family as a complex social system

ACTIVITIES WITH CHILDREN (suggested ages in parentheses)

6-2 Evidence for operant conditioning and memory in young infants: Piaget's secondary circular reactions
(1 child, 2–6 months of age)

7-1 Conservation of number
(2 children, 3–9 years of age)

7-2 Animism and anthropomorphism
(2 children, 3–9 years of age)

7-3 Children's use of imagined spatial coordinates in drawing chimneys, trees, and water level
(2 children, 4–12 years of age)

8-1 Development of systematic attentional/search strategies
(2 children, 3–8 years of age)

10-1 Children's understanding of nonliteral language
(3 children, 4–14 years of age)

10-2 "Where ball?," "no wet," "ghetti," and other early utterances
(2 children, 18 months to 3 years of age)

11-1 Synchronous interaction between baby and adult
(1 child, 1–12 months of age)

INTERVIEWS OR DESCRIPTIONS OF OTHER PEOPLE

3-5 Positive versus negative eugenics: Changing attitudes

4-4 Research local birthing practices

9-2 Who is intelligent?

13-3 Gender roles: Past and present

14-1A Family variables associated with aggression: One case

14-1B Family variables associated with nonaggression: One case

14-3 Kohlberg's stages of moral development

15-1 The impact of divorce from the child's perspective

15-3 Teenage employment during the school year

Chapter One

Introduction to Developmental Psychology and Its Research Strategies

Learning Objectives

By the time you have finished this chapter you should be able to:

1. Describe what is meant by developmental change and discuss two general ways in which developmental changes can occur.
2. Describe three goals of developmentalists and distinguish between normative development and ideographic development.
3. Outline four general observations about the character of human development.
4. Briefly trace the history of the concept of childhood.
5. Compare and contrast the views of the philosophers Hobbes, Rousseau, and Locke toward children.
6. Discuss the roles of G. Stanley Hall and Sigmund Freud in the emergence of developmental psychology.
7. Differentiate between the terms "theory" and "hypothesis."
8. Discuss the two qualities that scientific measures must have if they are to be useful.
9. Discuss the strengths and weaknesses of interviews and questionnaires as methods of investigating developmental change.
10. Contrast the clinical method of gathering data with standard interviewing techniques.
11. Discuss some of the steps researchers can take to ensure data gathered using observational methods is unbiased, and outline the types of situations in which researchers might use structured observation.
12. Explain how case studies are compiled and discuss two major shortcomings in using case studies to investigate developmental change.
13. Discuss the main uses of ethnography in the study of development and outline the main limitations associated with this research method.
14. Discuss the main uses of psychophysiological methods in the study of development and outline the main limitations associated with these types of measures.
15. Explain how a correlation coefficient can be used to assess the strength and direction of the relationship between two variables, and identify the major limitation of correlational research designs.
16. Differentiate between the independent and dependent variables in an experimental study and explain why researchers use techniques such as random assignment when conducting experiments.
17. Explain the main differences between natural (quasi-) experiments and laboratory experiments.
18. Compare and contrast cross-sectional, longitudinal, and sequential research designs, and note the strengths and weaknesses of each design.
19. Explain the role of cross-cultural research studies in understanding human development.
20. Outline the ethical standards that apply to psychological research.

Chapter Outline and Summary

1. What is development?

Development refers to systematic continuities and changes in individuals between the time of conception and death.

a. *What causes us to develop?*

Maturation refers to the biological unfolding of an individual's genetic plan. Learning refers to relatively permanent changes in feelings, thoughts, and behaviours as a result of experiences. Most developmental changes are the product of both maturation and learning.

b. *What goals do developmentalists pursue?*

Three major goals are description, explanation, and optimization of development. In pursuing these goals developmentalists need to consider typical patterns of change (normative development) and individual variations (ideographic development).

c. *Some basic observations about the character of development*

Human development is a continual and cumulative process. In addition, people are physical, cognitive, and social beings, and each of these components of development is affected, in part, by changes taking place in the other areas. There is also plasticity in human development. Finally, development is shaped by its historical and cultural context.

2. Human development in historical perspective

a. *Childhood in premodern times*

In the early days of recorded history children had few, if any, rights and their lives were not always valued. However, it is almost certainly an overstatement to conclude that medieval societies had absolutely no concept of childhood and merely treated children as miniature adults.

b. *Toward modern-day views on childhood*

Thomas Hobbes' doctrine of original sin held that children are inherently selfish egoists who must be restrained by society. Jean Jacques Rousseau's doctrine of innate purity suggested that children are born with an intuitive sense of right and wrong that is often corrupted by society. John Locke believed that the mind of an infant is a *tabula rasa,* or "blank slate," and children are neither inherently good nor inherently bad.

c. *Development of children's rights in Canada*

Historical changes in the development of the concept of childhood are reflected in historical changes in Canadian policy regarding children's rights.

d. *Origins of a science of development*

Baby biographies published in the late 19th century implied that human development was a topic worthy of scientific scrutiny.

The person who is most often cited as the founder of developmental psychology is G. Stanley Hall. However, Sigmund Freud's psychoanalytic theory also generated new research into early childhood development.

A theory is a set of concepts and propositions that describes and explains some aspect of experience. In addition, good theories generate testable predictions called hypotheses.

3. Research methods in developmental psychology

a. The scientific method

The scientific method dictates that investigators must be objective.

b. Gathering data: Basic fact-finding strategies

Scientifically useful measures must be reliable, which means they yield consistent information over time and across observers, and valid, which means they measure what they are designed to measure.

With a structured interview or questionnaire all the individuals who participate in a study are asked the same questions, in the same order. Interviews and questionnaires cannot be used with children who are too young to read or comprehend speech well. Also, answers to questions from interviews or questionnaires may be inaccurate for a number of reasons. However, structured interviews and questionnaires can be excellent methods for obtaining large amounts of information in a short period of time.

With the clinical method, each participant's answers determine what he or she will be asked next. However, this nonstandardized treatment of participants raises the possibility that examiner bias may affect the questions asked and the interpretations provided.

Naturalistic observation involves observing individuals in their common, everyday surroundings. One way to observe children is with a time-sampling procedure in which the investigator records behavioural events displayed by individuals during a particular time interval. Unfortunately, infrequent or socially undesirable behaviours are unlikely to be witnessed. Also, in natural settings a number of events are usually occurring at one time, and this makes it difficult to accurately identify causes for actions. Finally, the presence of the observer may cause individuals to act differently than they normally would.

When structured observations are collected, each participant is exposed to a setting that may cue the behaviour being studied, and then he or she is observed using a hidden camera or a one-way mirror.

Any or all of the data collection methods mentioned above can be used to compile a case study of individual development. However, case studies are often difficult to compare across individuals and may lack generalizability.

Ethnographers live within the cultural or subcultural community they are studying and prepare extensive descriptions that can be useful in understanding cultural traditions and value systems.

Psychophysiological methods can be useful for interpreting the mental and emotional experiences of infants and toddlers who cannot report such events. However, changes in physiological responses may reflect mood swings, fatigue, or reactions to the recording equipment, rather than changes in attention or emotional reactions.

4. Detecting Relationships: Correlational and experimental designs

a. The correlational design

In a correlational design the investigator gathers information to determine whether two or more variables are meaningfully related. The correlation coefficient that is calculated provides an estimate of the strength and direction of the relationship between the variables. The absolute value of the correlation coefficient indicates the strength of the relationship; the sign of the correlation coefficient indicates the direction of the relationship.

When the sign for a correlation coefficient is positive it indicates that the variables under investigation tend to move in the same direction; when the sign is negative it indicates that the variables being investigated tend to move in opposite directions. The major limitation of correlational research designs is that they cannot be used to unambiguously establish the nature of cause-and-effect relationships.

b. *The experimental design*

In experimental research participants are exposed to different treatments and the reactions to the different treatments is observed. The different treatment conditions represent the independent variable, or the variable that is changed by the researcher. The reactions that are observed represent the dependent variable, or the variable that is measured as part of the investigation.

Confounding variables are variables that unintentionally differ between the treatment conditions. The effects of such variables are reduced through experimental control. One aspect of experimental control is random assignment of participants to the various treatment conditions of the experiment.

The greatest strength of the experimental method is its ability to unambiguously establish the nature of cause-and-effect relationships.

c. *The natural (or quasi-) experiment*

In some situations an experimental design cannot be used for ethical reasons. Under these circumstances it is sometimes possible to conduct a natural or quasi-experiment. In this type of study the consequences of a natural event are observed. However, because participants are not randomly assigned to the treatment conditions, it can be difficult to determine precisely which factor is responsible for any differences that are found between the various groups in the study.

5. Designs for studying development

a. *The cross-sectional design*

With cross-sectional research designs people who differ in age are studied at the same point in time. The people who are being compared in designs of this type are from different cohorts, and differences that are found in cross-sectional studies may represent cohort effects. Also, cross-sectional studies cannot provide answers about individual development over time.

b. *The longitudinal design*

With longitudinal research designs the same participants are observed repeatedly over a period of time. Practice effects may threaten the validity of the results obtained from longitudinal studies, and selective attrition may produce a nonrepresentative sample. Finally, cross-generational changes in the environment may limit the conclusions from longitudinal studies to those participants who were growing up while the study was taking place.

c. *The sequential design*

Sequential designs combine the most desirable features of cross-sectional and longitudinal studies. Participants of different ages are selected and each of these cohorts is followed over time.

6. Cross-cultural comparisons

Cross-cultural studies are those in which participants from different cultural or subcultural backgrounds are observed, tested, and compared. Such investigations help guard against the overgeneralization of research findings and even challenge our assumptions about how developmental research should be reported.

7. Ethical considerations in developmental research

Investigators who work with children may not use any research procedures that may harm the child physically or psychologically. The informed consent of parents or other responsible adults must be obtained, in addition to the consent of the child. Researchers must keep all information obtained from research participants in the strictest of confidence. Finally, at the end of the study children must be fully debriefed, and they have the right to be informed of the results of the research study.

Vocabulary Self-Test

Part I: For each of the following definitions provide the appropriate term. (Answers to this portion of the self-test are provided at the end of the chapter.)

1. independent variable — The aspect of the environment that an experimenter modifies or manipulates in order to measure its impact on behaviour

2. normative development MATURATION — Developmental changes in the body or in behaviour that result from the aging process rather than from learning, injury, illness, or some other life experience

3. reliability — The extent to which a measuring instrument yields consistent results, both over time and across observers

4. selective attrition — Nonrandom loss of participants during a study that results in a nonrepresentative sample

5. correlational design PSYCHOPHYSIOLOGICAL METHODS — Methods that measure the relationships between physiological processes and aspects of children's physical, cognitive, or emotional behaviour/development

6. ideographic development — Individual variations in the rate, extent, or direction of development

7. clinical method — A type of interview in which a participant's response to each successive question or problem determines what the investigator will ask next

8. cross-sectional design — A research design in which subjects from different age groups are studied at the same point in time

9. tabula rasa — The idea that the mind of an infant is a "blank slate" and that all knowledge, abilities, behaviours, and motives are acquired through experience

10. correlational design — A type of research design that indicates the strength of association among variables

11. time-sampling — Procedure in which the investigator records the frequencies with which individuals display particular behaviours during the brief time intervals that each participant is observed

12. random assignment — A control technique in which participants are assigned to experimental conditions through an unbiased procedure so that the members of the groups are not systematically different from one another

13. original sin — The idea that children are inherently negative creatures who must be taught to rechannel their selfish interests into socially acceptable outlets

14. hypothesis — A theoretical prediction about some aspect of experience

15. natural observation — A method in which the scientist tests hypotheses by observing people as they engage in everyday activities in their natural habitats

Part II: For each of the following terms provide the definition.

Experimental Design: ______________________________

____

Longitudinal Design: ______________________________

____

Innate Purity: ______________________________

____

Learning: ______________________________

____

Confidentiality: ______________________________

____

Validity: ______________________________

____

Sequential Design: ______________________________

____

Dependent Variable: ______________________________

____

Normative Development: ______________________________

____

Cohort Effect: ______________________________

____

Structured Interview: ______________________________

____

Informed Consent: ______________________________

____

Natural (or Quaşi-) Experiment: ______________________________

____

Practice Effects: ______________________________

____

Ethnography: ______________________________

____

Short-Answer Study Questions

WHAT IS DEVELOPMENT?

1. Identify the two general ways in which developmental changes can occur and provide examples that illustrate each of these processes.

   a.

   b.

2. List three goals of developmentalists.

   a.

   b.

   c.

3. Provide one example of normative development and one example of ideographic development.

   a.

   b.

4. List four general observations concerning the nature of human development.

   a.

   b.

   c.

   d.

HUMAN DEVELOPMENT IN HISTORICAL PERSPECTIVE

5. List three child-rearing practices from premodern times that would support the position that the concept of childhood may have been very different than it is now.

   a.

   b.

   c.

6. What conclusion does the text author reach in Box 1-1 regarding the impact of culture and historical era on the course of human development?

7. Briefly outline the views of the philosophers Hobbes, Rousseau, and Locke with respect to the inherent tendencies of children.

   Hobbes:

   Rousseau:

   Locke:

8. What method of studying children did G. Stanley Hall and Sigmund Freud each use in learning about development?

   Hall:

   Freud:

9. How have our changing conceptions of childhood influenced Canadian policy and the development of children's rights?

RESEARCH METHODS IN DEVELOPMENTAL PSYCHOLOGY

10. Identify the two qualities that scientific measures must have if they are to be useful, and briefly explain what is meant by each of these terms.

    a.

    b.

11. Identify three potential shortcomings of structured interviews and questionnaires in obtaining information about development.

a.

b.

c.

12. Explain how the clinical method of gathering data differs from a structured interview or questionnaire.

13. List two ways that researchers can attempt to minimize observer influences during naturalistic observation.

a.

b.

14. Briefly describe the research method known as "structured observation" and explain when this method might be used.

15. Identify two potential drawbacks in using case studies to obtain information about development.

a.

b.

16. Identify one key strength and one weakness of ethnography as a method of research.

Key strength:

Weakness:

17. Identify one key strength and one weakness of psychophysiological methods of research.

Key strength:

Weakness:

DETECTING RELATIONSHIPS: CORRELATIONAL AND EXPERIMENTAL DESIGNS

18. From the following correlation coefficients select the correlation coefficient that indicates the strongest relationship and the weakest relationship. Also, for each correlation coefficient indicate whether the values for the two variables would tend to move in the same direction or in opposite directions.

    +0.79 –0.85 +0.50 –0.21 +0.01 –0.46

19. What is the major limitation of the correlational method of research?

20. During an experiment the researcher changes one of the variables and measures the impact of that change.

    The variable that the researcher changes is called the:

    The variable that the researcher measures is called the:

21. During an experiment the researcher will often use random assignment to place participants in each of the treatment conditions. Why is this necessary?

22. Identify the main differences between natural or quasi-experiments and laboratory experiments.

DESIGNS FOR STUDYING DEVELOPMENT

23. Describe the procedure used by each of the three designs for studying developmental change listed below. Also, for each design identify the key strengths and weaknesses.

    Cross-sectional design

    Procedure:

    Key strengths:

    Weaknesses:

Longitudinal design

Procedure:

Key strengths:

Weaknesses:

Sequential design

Procedure:

Key strengths:

Weaknesses:

24. Explain what is meant by the term "cohort effects," and identify the research design that is most likely to confound age effects and cohort effects.

    Cohort effects are:

    Research design most likely to confound age effects and cohort effects:

CROSS-CULTURAL COMPARISONS

25. Explain how cross-cultural studies are carried out and identify why these studies are important in fully understanding human development. To illustrate your points, refer to the historical and cultural changes in our conceptions of childhood and adolescence discussed in the text.

ETHICAL CONSIDERATIONS IN DEVELOPMENTAL RESEARCH

26. Identify the four main ethical guidelines that have been adopted to protect the rights of children who take part in research studies.

    a.

    b.

    c.

    d.

Multiple-Choice Self-Test

For each of the following questions select the best alternative. (Answers and explanations for this self-test are provided at the end of the chapter.) Once you have selected your answer, provide a brief explanation for why the answer you selected is the best choice and why the remaining answers would not be correct.

1. The holistic perspective of development is a dominant view or theme today, one around which the text is organized. This view emphasizes:

    a. the active role of the child/individual in her own development
    b. that development is a lifelong process that is continual and cumulative
    c. the interdependent way in which all components of the self (physical, cognitive, social, emotional, etc.) determine outcomes
    d. the belief that all the members of the family influence each other

Rationale: ______________________________

____

2. John Locke's notion that the mind of an infant is a *tabula rasa* means that he believed children are:

    a. blank slates ready to learn from experience
    b. inherently evil or sinful
    c. innately good
    d. not capable of learning

Rationale: ______________________________

____

3. A set of concepts and propositions designed to organize, describe, and explain an existing set of observations is known as:

    a. a hypothesis
    b. a theory
    c. an observation
    d. an experiment

Rationale: ______________________________

____

4. If a measure consistently shows the same results, it is said to be:

    a. valid
    b. reliable
    c. objective
    d. generative

Rationale: ______________________________

____

5. An interview technique in which a child's response to each successive question determines what the investigator will ask next is called:

   a. the experimental method
   b. a case study
   c. the correlational method
   d. the clinical method

Rationale: ____

____

6. If there is a strong negative correlation between amount of time spent playing video games and physical fitness, the correlation most consistent with these findings is:

   a. .00
   b. +.40
   c. –.10
   d. –.80

Rationale: ____

____

7. Researchers studying the effects of alcohol consumption tested the physical coordination skills of 21-year-old men who were first assigned to drink a beverage with either 4, 2, or 0 ounces of alcohol in the laboratory. In this study, the dependent variable would be:

   a. the age of the research participants
   b. the amount of alcohol consumed
   c. the length of time that elapses between drinking the alcohol and taking the coordination test
   d. the physical coordination skills of the research participants

Rationale: ____

____

8. Blair is interested in understanding how children's academic performance changes over long periods of time as a result of the number of friends they have. Blair's best choice of research design and method would be a:

   a. cross-sectional, experimental study
   b. longitudinal, experimental study
   c. longitudinal, observational study
   d. cross-sectional, observational study

Rationale: ____

____

Activities and Projects Related to this Chapter

ACTIVITY 1-1

ASSUMPTIONS ABOUT CHILDREN: HOW THEY AFFECT TREATMENT/PRACTICE

INTRODUCTION: This activity builds on the material presented in Chapter 1 that deals with the concept of development and the changes in views and treatment of children over the centuries. It is also preparation for the section on research methods, where, in effect, you are reading about ways to determine whether the assumptions we make about children (assumptions that guide our practices) are valid. In addition, this activity provides some preparation for the material presented in Chapter 2 that deals with the major controversies about the nature of children and developmental change.

INSTRUCTIONS: Identify the assumption(s) about children and the nature of their development that underlie each of the following practices.

Practice A: Having ratings on movies or television programs (F, G, PG, PG-13, AA, R)

Practice B: Historical changes in Canadian policy regarding corporal punishment

WEBSITES OF INTEREST

For more information on Canadian research, visit the Human Early Learning Partnership web page: www.earlylearning.ubc.ca

REFERENCES OF INTEREST

Flagel, D.C. (2000). Children as research subjects: New guidelines for Canadian IRBs. *IRB: A review of human subjects research, 22(5),* 1–3.

Hertzman, C., McLean, S., Kohen, D., Dunn, J., & Evans, T. (2004). Early child development in Vancouver. *Horizons, 6(4),* 44–47.

Hertzman, C., McLean, S., Kohen, D., Dunn, J., & Evans, T. (2002). Early development in Vancouver: Report of the Community Asset Mapping Project (CAMP). Final report prepared for the Vancouver Richmond Health Board.

Hertzman, C., & Kohen, D. (2003). Neighborhoods matter for child development. *Transitions,* Autumn, 3–5.

Hesson, K., Bakal, D., Dobson, K.S. (1993). Legal and ethical issues concerning children's rights of consent. *Canadian Psychology, 34(3),* 317–328.

Kohen, D.E., Brooks-Gunn, J., Leventhal, T., & Hertzman, C. (2002). Neighborhood income and physical and social disorder in Canada: Associations with young children's competencies. *Child Development, 73(6)*, 1844–1860.

PRACTICE IN IDENTIFYING RESEARCH DESIGNS AND METHODS FOR STUDYING DEVELOPMENTAL CHANGE

INTRODUCTION: This activity is related to the material presented in Chapter 1 on the characteristics of experiments. It will provide you with practice in applying what you have learned about research methods.

INSTRUCTIONS: Research questions for four potential studies are presented. For each study do the following:

1. Decide which of the following strategies you would use for assessing developmental change:
   a. longitudinal
   b. cross-sectional
   c. sequential
   d. none of the above; developmental change would not be studied
2. Indicate the type of research design that you would use and why.
   a. laboratory experiment
   b. natural (or quasi-) experiment
   c. correlational study
   d. case study
   e. clinical interview
   f. naturalistic observation
   g. structured observation
   h. none of the above; a different research methodology was utilized
3. How would you operationally define your variables, and how would you measure them?
4. Specify what type of conclusion could be drawn.
   a. causal (variable X caused variable Y to change)
   b. relational (variable X is related to variable Y, but did not necessarily cause a change to occur)
5. Specify any possible confounding factors that could limit interpretation (e.g., nonrandom assignment).

Research question #1: Does birth order have an affect on children's academic performance?

Research question #2: Does the number and quality of friendships change with age for boys and girls?

Research question #3: Are there differences in attention span between children whose mothers smoked during pregnancy and children whose mothers did not smoke?

Research question #4: Does playing violent video games affect boys' and girls' social behaviour?

ANSWERS TO SELF-TESTS

VOCABULARY SELF-TEST (The answers may be found on the pages in parentheses.)

1. independent variable (p. 20)
2. maturation (p. 2)
3. reliability (p. 12)
4. selective attrition (p. 27)
5. psychophysiological methods (p. 17)
6. ideographic development (p. 3)
7. clinical method (p. 13)
8. cross-sectional design (pp. 24–25)
9. tabula rasa (p. 9)
10. correlational design (p. 19)
11. time sampling (p. 15)
12. random assignment (p. 21)
13. original sin (p. 8)
14. hypothesis (p. 11)
15. naturalistic observation (p. 14)

MULTIPLE-CHOICE SELF-TEST (The answers may be found on the pages in parentheses.)

1. **c** (p. 5) The holistic view recognizes that changes in one area of development often affect other areas of development. Activity/passivity (a) is the issue of whether individuals are shaped by their environment, or whether they shape their environments. The view that development is cumulative (b) suggests that early outcomes impact later development. Family members (d) are only one component in the overall development process (the holistic view considers all the components in the process).

2. **a** (p. 9) The term *tabula rasa* means blank slate. The view that children are inherently evil (b) would be consistent with Hobbes' view of original sin. The view that children are innately good (c) would be consistent with Rousseau's view of innate purity. No major development theory suggests that children are incapable of learning (d).

3. **b** (p. 11) Theories organize and explain observations. A hypothesis (a) is a prediction that is based on a theory. Observations (c) are the data that are used to develop theories. Experiments (d) are one of the methods that can be used to test predictions generated by theories.

4. **b** (p. 12) Reliability refers to whether or not similar results will be obtained in the future, in other words, the consistency of a measure. When measures are accurate they are valid (a). Objectivity (c) refers to whether the measure is observable and free from bias. Generativity (d) is a characteristic of theories; generative theories foster further research.

5. **d** (p. 13) With the clinical method an interview is used, but the interview changes based on the individual's responses to questions. With the experimental method (a) one variable is changed and changes in a second variable are measured. With the case study method (b) individuals are studied in depth. With the correlational method (c) observations are made of two factors to determine if the factors are systematically related.

6. **d** (pp. 19–20) Because physical fitness decreases as the amount of time spent playing video games increases, the correlation coefficient must have a negative sign, and it must be greater than 0.00 (no correlation). Alternative (a) would indicate the two factors are not related. Alternative (b) would indicate a positive relationship. Alternatives (c) and (d) are negative, but the relationship was described as strong and alternative (d) is a stronger relationship than alternative (c).

7. **d** (pp. 20–21) The dependent variable is the factor that is measured during the study, and these researchers are measuring physical coordination. Answers (a) and (c) both refer to factors that don't change across the study so they are controlled (or unchanging) variables. The amount of alcohol (b) is the factor that is manipulated, or changed by the researcher; it would be the independent variable in the study.

8. **c** (pp. 26–28) To study how children's academic performance changes over time a longitudinal study would be most appropriate, so the answer cannot be (a) or (d). It would be unethical to randomly assign children to either have friends or no friends; therefore an experiment (b) would not be possible.

Chapter Two

Theories of Human Development

Learning Objectives

By the time you have finished this chapter you should be able to:

1. Describe three characteristics of a good theory.
2. Identify three central issues in the study of human development.
3. Describe the three personality structures proposed by Freud.
4. Outline the five stages in Freud's psychosexual theory of personality development.
5. Identify three lasting contributions of Freud's psychoanalytic theory.
6. Outline two main differences between Erikson's and Freud's theories of personality development.
7. Identify each of the eight stages in Erikson's psychosocial theory of personality development and describe the significant events and influences associated with each stage.
8. Explain how neo-Freudian views differ from Freud's original views and identify the contributions of three prominent neo-Freudian theorists.
9. Describe the learning viewpoint of development.
10. Outline the key components of operant conditioning.
11. Explain how observational learning highlights Bandura's emphasis on the cognitive processes involved in learning.
12. Explain what is meant by reciprocal determinism.
13. Identify the key contributions and chief criticism of the learning approach to development.
14. Describe the basic ideas in Piaget's theory of cognitive development, focusing on the processes of assimilation and accommodation.
15. Outline the main characteristics associated with each of Piaget's four stages of cognitive development.
16. Identify two lasting contributions of Piaget's cognitive theory.
17. Describe Vygotsky's sociocultural perspective of development.
18. Outline the main differences between Vygotsky's sociocultural perspective and Piaget's theory of cognitive development.
19. Outline the main differences between the information-processing view and Piaget's theory of cognitive development.
20. Identify the basic assumptions that underlie the ethological approach and explain what ethologists mean by sensitive periods in development.
21. Evaluate some of the key criticisms that have been raised concerning the application of the ethological approach to understanding human development.
22. Describe the five subsystems that form the foundation of Bronfenbrenner's ecological systems theory.
23. Describe three different world views and categorize the main developmental theories from the chapter according to the world view it represents.

Chapter Outline and Summary

1. The nature of scientific theories

A theory is a set of concepts and propositions that describe, organize, and explain a set of observations. Good theories are parsimonious, falsifiable, and heuristic. Parsimony means good theories are concise and can explain a broad range of phenomena with a few principles or assumptions. Falsifiability means that good theories can be tested, and the results that are obtained will either support or refute the theory. A theory has heuristic value if it does not limit itself to simply explaining existing phenomena, but allows new predictions to be made.

2. Questions and controversies about human development

a. *The nature/nurture issue*

The nature/nurture issue centres on the debate as to whether human development occurs primarily as the result of biological forces (nature) or environmental forces (nurture). This is a restatement of the two processes that can produce developmental change: maturation (biological unfolding of an individual's genetic plan) and learning (changes in feelings, thoughts, and behaviours as a result of experience). Contemporary researchers stress that all complex human attributes result from an interplay between biological predispositions and environmental forces.

b. *The active/passive issue*

The active/passive issue centres on the debate about human nature. The active side of the debate suggests that people are active creatures who, to a large extent, determine how they will be treated by others. The passive side of the debate suggests that people are passive creatures who are shaped by social forces they encounter.

c. *The continuity/discontinuity issue*

The continuity/discontinuity issue centres on the course of human development. The continuity side of the debate suggests that human development is an additive process that occurs gradually. Changes that do occur are largely quantitative changes that build on previous developments. The discontinuity side of the debate suggests that human development is often stage-like, with abrupt changes or "steps." When change occurs it is often a qualitative change that makes the individual fundamentally different than he or she was at the previous stage of development.

3. The psychoanalytic viewpoint

a. *Freud's psychosexual theory*

Freud's theory states that the human personality consists of three components that develop over five stages of psychosexual growth. The three components of personality are the id, the ego, and the superego. The function of the id is to satisfy inborn biological instincts as soon as possible. The function of the ego is to find realistic means of gratifying the instincts of the id. The function of the superego is to enforce moral values and standards, and to ensure that the ego finds socially acceptable means of meeting the impulses generated by the id.

These personality components emerge across five stages of psychosexual development. From birth to age 1 children are in the oral stage of development and derive pleasure from sucking, chewing, and biting. From ages 1 to 3 children are in the anal stage of development. During this stage toilet training can be a source of conflict between parents and children. From ages 3 to 6 children are in the phallic stage of development. Freud suggested that during this stage children develop a desire for their opposite-sex parent. This emerges as the Oedipus complex in boys and the Electra complex in girls.

From ages 6 to 11 children are in the latency stage and psychosexual conflicts are repressed. Once children reach puberty they enter the genital stage. Adolescents must now learn to express psychosexual urges in socially acceptable ways.

b. *Contributions and criticisms of Freud's theory*

There is not much evidence that an individual's later personality can be reliably predicted on the basis of the developmental conflicts that Freud outlined. However, Freud introduced the concept of unconscious motivation to mainstream psychology, and he deserves credit for focusing attention on the impact that early experiences can have on later developmental outcomes. Also, Freud studied a side of development that has often been overlooked by developmentalists who focus on behaviour and rational thought processes; Freud investigated the emotional side of development.

c. *Erikson's theory of psychosocial development*

Erikson also developed a theory of personality development that portrayed development as a stage-like progression. However, in Erikson's theory children are active explorers who adapt to their environments, not passive beings who are moulded primarily by their parents. Also, Erikson's theory places much more emphasis on cultural influences in development, and far less emphasis on psychosexual urges.

Erikson suggests that during our lifetimes we pass through eight stages of psychosocial development. From birth to age 1 the crisis that is being resolved is basic trust versus mistrust. During this time the mother or primary caregiver is the key social agent. From ages 1 to 3 the crisis that is being resolved is autonomy versus shame and doubt. During this time the parents continue to be the key social agents. From ages 3 to 6 the crisis that is being resolved is initiative versus guilt. During this time the family is the key social agent. From ages 6 to 12 the crisis that is being resolved is industry versus inferiority. During this time teachers and peers emerge as significant social agents. From ages 12 to 20 the crisis that is being resolved is identity versus role confusion. During this time the key social agents are peers. During the early adult years (20 to 40) the crisis that is being resolved is intimacy versus isolation. The primary task during this stage is to achieve a sense of love and companionship with another person. During the middle adult years (40 to 65) the crisis that is being resolved is generativity versus stagnation. The primary task during this stage is to become productive in work and raise a family. During the late adult years (65+) the crisis that is being resolved is ego integrity versus despair. At this point the individual reflects back over his or her life. A meaningful, productive life produces a sense of integrity; an unfulfilled life with unrealized goals produces a sense of despair.

d. *Contributions and criticisms of Erikson's theory*

Erikson's theory has had a lasting impact in the study of topics such as emotional development during infancy, the growth of self-concept and the identity issues that face adolescents, and the influence of friends and playmates in social development. However, his theory is vague when it comes to specifying causes for developmental change. Consequently, his theory is more of a descriptive overview of human social and emotional development, rather than an adequate explanation for how and why this development occurs.

e. *Psychoanalytic theory today*

Neo-Freudians place more emphasis on the social aspects of development and less emphasis on the role of sexual instincts in development. Karen Horney is a neo-Freudian who has made contributions in understanding the psychology of women; Alfred Adler was one of the first to suggest that siblings are an important influence on development. Harry Stack Sullivan wrote extensively about how same-sex friendships during middle childhood set the stage for intimate relationships in later life.

4. The learning viewpoint

a. *Watson's behaviourism*

In the behavioural perspective, development is viewed as a continuous process of behavioural change that is shaped by a person's unique environment. Consequently, development can differ dramatically from person to person.

b. Skinner's operant learning theory (radical behaviourism)

Skinner's operant learning theory claims that development depends on external stimuli, rather than on internal forces such as instincts, or biological maturation. Two important forces in the environment are reinforcers, which strengthen behaviour and make the behaviour more probable in the future, and punishers, which suppress behaviour and make it less likely the behaviour will occur again in the future.

c. Bandura's cognitive social learning theory

Bandura agreed that operant conditioning is an important type of learning, but he stressed that humans are cognitive creatures who think about the relationship between their behaviour and the consequences that follow their behaviour. This cognitive emphasis is one of the clearest distinctions between social learning theory and operant learning theory. This cognitive emphasis is clear in Bandura's conceptualization of observational learning. With observational learning individuals learn from watching others. To learn in this way it is necessary to attend to the behaviour, encode what is observed, and store the information in memory. Without the execution of these cognitive processes, we would not be able to later imitate the behaviour we had observed.

d. Social learning as reciprocal determinism

One key component in Bandura's social learning theory is reciprocal determinism. He suggests that human development reflects a complex interaction among an active person, that person's behaviour, and the environment. In other words, the situations or environments that an individual experiences will affect that person, but the individual's behaviour will also affect and shape the environment. Therefore, human development is a continuous, reciprocal interaction between individuals and their environments.

e. Contributions and criticisms of learning theories

The learning perspective has contributed substantially to our knowledge of a variety of aspects of human development. And the emphasis on the immediate causes of behaviours has produced a number of practical applications. However, many view the learning approach as an overly simplified account of human development.

5. The cognitive-developmental viewpoint

a. Piaget's view of intelligence and intellectual growth

In Piaget's view of cognitive development, knowledge consists of cognitive structures or schemes. A scheme is an organized pattern of thought or action that can be used to cope with or explain some aspect of an individual's experiences. As children mature these schemes become more complex. The two main processes involved in the construction and modification of cognitive schemes are assimilation and accommodation. When an individual assimilates a new experience he or she interprets the experience in terms of existing cognitive structures; the new information "fits" into existing schemes. When new information doesn't "fit" into existing schemes, old cognitive structures must be altered or new cognitive structures must be created. This is the process that Piaget termed "accommodation." Piaget believed that, throughout our lifespan, we continually rely on the complementary processes of assimilation and accommodation to adapt to our environments.

Piaget also proposed that cognitive development occurs across four major stages or periods. Young infants (from birth to age 2) are in the sensorimotor stage of cognitive development. They try to understand the world using sensory and motor capabilities, and during this time they develop an initial sense of self and an understanding of object permanence. From 2 to 7 children are in the preoperational stage of development. Now they are able to use language and images to represent and understand their environment. From 7 to 11 children are in the concrete operational stage. During this stage children acquire cognitive operations, but they lack abstract reasoning skills. These abstract reasoning skills will emerge during the final stage of development, formal operations (from age 11 on).

b. *Contributions and criticisms of Piaget's viewpoint*

Piaget's early work contributed to a new area of developmental research known as social cognition. His theory has also had a large impact on education. However, many of his ideas have been challenged, and it appears that Piaget consistently underestimated the intellectual capabilities of infants, preschoolers, and elementary-school children.

c. *Vygotsky's sociocultural perspective*

Vygotsky viewed cognitive growth as a socially mediated activity. In the sociocultural perspective, the transmission of cultural beliefs, values, traditions, and social skills from generation to generation is emphasized. In contrast to Piaget, who depicted children as independent explorers, Vygotsky focused on the influence of cooperative dialogues on children's cognitive growth. Children learn through social interactions, and they learn best when instruction from more competent others is geared to match their zone of proximal development —the difference between what children can do by themselves and what they can potentially do with the assistance of others.

d. *Contributions and criticisms of Vygotsky's viewpoint*

Vygotsky's attention to social and cultural aspects of cognitive development suggests that cognitive development will vary across cultures. Although his theory has been criticized as placing too heavy an emphasis on the role of verbal dialogue in instruction, his emphasis on the influence of socially mediated activities on cognitive development has expanded our understanding of cognitive development and has implications for applied directions.

e. *The information-processing viewpoint*

Information-processing theorists acknowledge that biological maturation is an important contributor to cognitive growth, but they are also aware that the strategies children develop for attending to and processing information are influenced by the experiences they have. Also, the information-processing approach views cognitive growth and development as a continuous process involving quantitative changes in information-processing abilities. This contrasts sharply with Piaget's discontinuous, stage-like view that focuses on qualitative changes in cognitive skills and abilities.

f. *Contributions and criticisms of the information-processing viewpoint*

The research methods employed by information-processing researchers have enabled them to identify how children approach problems and why children make logical errors in solving problems. One key criticism of the information-processing approach is that humans are not just information-processing "machines" that function like computers; people dream, reflect on their experiences, and show creativity.

6. The ethological (or evolutionary) viewpoint

a. *Assumptions of classical ethology*

Ethologists assume that members of all animal species are born with "biologically programmed" behaviours that are products of evolution. These characteristics are thought to have evolved as a result of natural selection because they are adaptive and promote survival.

b. *Ethology and human development*

Human ethologists believe that children display a wide variety of preprogrammed behaviours and that each of these behaviours aids the individual in surviving and developing. However, ethologists are also aware that development could not progress very far without learning. Many ethologists think that human development is marked by sensitive periods, which are times that are optimal for the emergence of particular competencies or behaviours. During these times the individual is particularly sensitive to environmental influences.

c. *Contributions and criticisms of the ethological viewpoint*

Ethologists have contributed to the field of developmental psychology by focusing on adaptive, genetically programmed characteristics that ultimately influence the course of development. They have also contributed to the methodology of the field by studying human development in normal, everyday settings, and by comparing human development to development in other species. Our understanding of altruism and empathy, for example, has been advanced by the ethological viewpoint. However, evolutionary approaches are difficult to test and some theorists suggest that cultural learning experiences quickly overshadow innate evolutionary mechanisms.

7. The ecological systems viewpoint

In his bioecological theory, Uri Bronfenbrenner assumes that natural environments are major influences on development. Each person is embedded in several environmental systems and these systems interact with each other to influence development.

a. *Bronfenbrenner's contexts for development*

The microsystem is Bronfenbrenner's innermost layer and it refers to the activities and interactions that occur in an individual's immediate surroundings. Microsystems are dynamic contexts in which each person influences and is influenced by all the other people in the system.

The mesosystem is the second of Bronfenbrenner's layers and it refers to the connections or interrelationships among a number of microsystems such as home, school, and peer groups. Nonsupportive links between microsystems can undermine optimal development.

The third of Bronfenbrenner's environmental layers is the exosystem, which consists of contexts that children and adolescents are not a part of, but which may nevertheless influence their development. The exosystem includes factors such as the mass media, government and government agencies, and local school boards.

The macrosystem is the cultural, subcultural, or social class context in which the microsystems, mesosystems, and exosystems are imbedded.

Bronfenbrenner's model also includes the concept of a chronosystem, which adds a temporal dimension to his model. Age-related changes in the child can affect the direction of development, and the age of the child can also influence the impact of changes within the other systems.

b. *Contributions and criticisms of the ecological systems theory*

Bronfenbrenner's detailed analyses of environmental influences on development have suggested a number of ways to optimize developmental outcomes. The emphasis on complex transactions between developing persons and their dynamic environments is both a strength and a weakness of the theory. Specifically, the ecological systems theory is not able to provide normative patterns of development or a complete account of human development. It has little to say about specific biological contributions to development.

8. Theories and world views

The mechanistic model views human beings as machines. It is a structuralist model that suggests we can understand human behaviour if we understand all the component parts. It also sees individuals as passive entities who change in response to outside influences. In this model development is a continuous, gradual process.

The organismic model takes an opposing position in each of these areas. It is a holistic model that suggests organisms cannot be understood as a simple collection of parts. In addition, in this model individuals are viewed as active entities who change under the guidance of internal forces in distinct, discontinuous stages.

Learning theories are primarily mechanistic theories, although Bandura's social learning theory does reflect the organismic assumption that people actively influence their environment. Psychoanalytic theories and cognitive-developmental theories are primarily organismic theories.

A third world view, known as the contextual model, has emerged. In this view development is the product of a dynamic interplay between the person and his or her environment; people and the environment are both active in the developmental process. Also, the potential exists for both qualitative (discontinuous) change and quantitative (continuous) change. So, this world view is a blending of the mechanistic and organismic models.

The theories that come closest to adopting this view of development are information-processing theories, ethological theories, and Bronfenbrenner's ecological systems theory.

Vocabulary Self-Test

Part I: For each of the following definitions provide the appropriate term. (Answers to this portion of the self-test are provided at the end of the chapter.)

1. parsimonius The quality of a theory that uses relatively few explanatory principles to explain a broad set of observations

* 2. behaviourism A school of thinking in psychology that holds that conclusions about human development should be based on controlled observations of overt behaviour

X 3. QUALITATIVE CHANGE Changes in kind that make individuals fundamentally different than they were before

4. assimilation The process by which children interpret new experiences by incorporating them into their existing schemes

5. ego Psychoanalytic term for the component of the personality that is rational

* 6. reciprocal determinism The notion that the flow of influence between children and their environments is a two-way street

X 7. ORGANISMIC MODEL The view of children as active entities whose developmental paths are primarily determined by forces within themselves

8. theory A set of concepts and propositions that describe, organize, and explain a set of observations

9. microsystem MESOSYSTEM The interconnections among an individual's immediate settings, or microsystems

X 10. COGNITIVE DEVELOPMENT Age-related changes that occur in mental activities such as attending, perceiving, learning, thinking, and remembering

X 11. CONTEXTUAL MODEL The view of children as active entities whose developmental paths represent a continuous, dynamic interplay between internal forces and external influences

12. psychosexual theory Freud's theory that states that maturation of the sex instinct underlies stages of personality development

13. punishment Any consequence of an act that suppresses that act and/or decreases the probability that it will recur

14. continuity/discontinuity issue A debate among developmental theorists about whether developmental changes are quantitative or qualitative

15. CHRONOSYSTEM In ecological systems theory, changes in the individual or the environment that occur over time and influence the direction of development

Part II: For each of the following terms provide the definition.

Accommodation: ____

____

Reinforcer: ____

____

Macrosystem: ____

____

Id: ____

____

Scheme: ____

____

Heuristic Value: ____

____

Information-Processing Theory: ____

____

Quantitative Change: ____

____

Ethology: ____

____

Mechanistic Model: ____

____

Sensitive Period: ____

____

Nature/Nurture Issue: ____

____

Falsifiability: ____

____

Exosystem: ____

____

Superego: ____

____

Short-Answer Study Questions

THE NATURE OF SCIENTIFIC THEORIES

1. Identify three characteristics of good theories and explain what is meant by each of these characteristics.

   a.

   b.

   c.

QUESTIONS AND CONTROVERSIES ABOUT HUMAN DEVELOPMENT

2. Describe the nature/nurture issue as it applies to developmental psychology and explain the contemporary view regarding this issue.

3. Describe the active/passive issue as it applies to developmental change.

4. The continuity/discontinuity issue centres on the course of human development. Explain how a theorist from the continuity side of the issue would view development, and contrast that with the view of a theorist who took a discontinuous view of development.

   a.

   b.

THE PSYCHOANALYTIC VIEWPOINT

5. Identify the three personality structures proposed by Freud and briefly describe each of these structures.

   a.

   b.

   c.

6. List each of Freud's five stages of psychosexual development, noting the ages when each stage occurs, and provide a brief description of each stage.

Stage	Age	Description

a.

b.

c.

d.

e.

7. Identify three major contributions that Freud's psychoanalytic theory has made to the field of developmental psychology.

a.

b.

c.

8. Identify two main differences between Erikson's psychosocial theory and Freud's psychosexual theory of development.

a.

b.

9. List the first five stages in Erikson's theory of personality development, noting the ages when each stage occurs, and provide a brief description of each stage.

Stage	Age	Description

a.

b.

c.

d.

e.

10. List three prominent neo-Freudian theorists and identify the developmental area each individual has been most extensively involved with.

   a.

   b.

   c.

THE LEARNING VIEWPOINT

11. Referring to the three developmental issues identified at the start of the chapter, outline the learning view of human development.

12. Explain how reinforcers and punishers affect behavioural tendencies.

   Reinforcers:

   Punishers:

13. Identify one key difference between Bandura's cognitive social learning theory and Skinner's operant learning theory.

14. Provide an example that illustrates Bandura's concept of observational learning.

15. Reciprocal determinism suggests that human development reflects an interaction among three key elements. Identify these three elements and provide an example that illustrates the notion of reciprocal determinism in development.

   The three interacting elements are:

   Example of reciprocal determinism:

COGNITIVE-DEVELOPMENTAL VIEWPOINT

16. Piaget believed that children develop intellectually through the complementary processes of assimilation and accommodation. Use an appropriate example to illustrate each of these two processes.

    Assimilation:

    Accommodation:

17. List each of Piaget's four stages of cognitive development, noting the ages when each stage occurs, and the primary types of schemes associated with each stage.

	Stage	Age	Primary schemes
a.			
b.			
c.			
d.			

18. Identify two lasting contributions Piaget's cognitive theory has made to the field of developmental psychology.

    a.

    b.

19. Describe Vygotsky's sociocultural model and compare it to Piaget's model of cognitive development.

20. Use the three developmental issues identified at the start of the chapter to contrast the information-processing view of cognitive development with Piaget's view.

THE ETHOLOGICAL (OR EVOLUTIONARY) VIEWPOINT

21. Explain what ethologists mean by a "sensitive period," and provide one example of a characteristic that shows evidence of having a "sensitive period."

    Sensitive period refers to:

    An example illustrating a sensitive period in development would be:

THE ECOLOGICAL SYSTEMS VIEWPOINT

22. List the five subsystems that make up Bronfenbrenner's ecological systems theory and explain what is included in each subsystem.

    a.

    b.

    c.

    d.

    e.

THEORIES AND WORLD VIEWS

23. List the key characteristics of the mechanistic, organismic, and contextual models, and identify the developmental theories that match these different world views.

Mechanistic Model:

a.

b.

c.

Theories that match this view:

Organismic Model:

a.

b.

c.

Theories that match this view:

Contextual Model:

a.

b.

c.

Theories that match this view:

Multiple-Choice Self-Test

For each of the following questions select the best alternative. (Answers and explanations for this self-test are provided at the end of the chapter.) Once you have selected your answer, provide a brief explanation for why the answer you selected is the best choice and why the remaining answers would not be correct.

1. A good theory is one that builds on existing knowledge by allowing for the formation of new testable hypotheses, meaning the theory is:

   a. parsimonious
   b. heuristic
   c. falsifiable
   d. discontinuous

   Rationale: ______________________________

   ____

2. A person taking the position that development is discontinuous would characterize developmental changes as:

   stagelike, abrupt

   a. abrupt, qualitative, and often unconnected over time
   b. primarily a product of maturation
   c. gradual, quantitative, and connected over time
   d. arising from the child's active role more than from the influence of external forces

   Rationale: ______________________________

   ____

3. According to Freud, the aspect of personality that is the conscious, rational component is the:

   a. superego
   b. ego
   c. id
   d. collective unconscious

   Rationale: ______________________________

   ____

4. Chris smokes heavily, needs a lot of reassurance from his wife that she still loves him, and overeats. Based on Freud's theory, we might expect to find that Chris had some type of trauma during the:

   a. genital stage of psychosexual development
   b. anal stage of psychosexual development
   c. phallic stage of psychosexual development
   d. oral stage of psychosexual development

   Rationale: ______________________________

   ____

5. Yolanda has just celebrated her second birthday. According to Erikson's theory, the life crisis that is likely to be most relevant to Yolanda in the next couple of years would be:

a. autonomy versus shame and doubt
b. intimacy versus isolation
c. basic trust versus mistrust
d. industry versus inferiority

Rationale: ______________________________

____

6. The notion of reciprocal determinism held by cognitive social learning theorists emphasizes the role of:

a. unconscious motivation in human development
b. human–environment interactions in human development
c. adaptive schemes in human development
d. evolutionary forces in human development

Rationale: ______________________________

____

7. According to Piaget's theory of cognitive development, children acquire new knowledge through:

a. actively constructing new understanding based on their experiences
b. observational learning
c. adult instruction, e.g., demonstrations and explanations
d. punishment and reward

Rationale: ______________________________

____

8. Of the theories described in the text, the theory that most clearly reflects a mechanistic world view would be:

a. Freud's psychoanalytic theory
b. Bronfenbrenner's ecological systems theory
c. Skinner's learning theory
d. Piaget's cognitive developmental theory

Rationale: ______________________________

____

Activities and Projects Related to this Chapter

ACTIVITY 2-1

ASSUMPTIONS MADE BY MAJOR THEORIES

INSTRUCTIONS: Below are each of the major theories discussed in Chapter 2. For each theory indicate with a check mark on the appropriate line what assumption that theory makes about (1) the major determinant of behaviour (nature, nurture), (2) the role of the child in her own development (active, passive), and (3) the nature of developmental change (continuous, discontinuous). If a particular theory seems to be "middle of the road" on an assumption, put the check mark between the lines.

THEORY	(1) MAJOR DETERMINANT OF BEHAVIOUR		
	NATURE	NURTURE	BOTH
Freud's Psychoanalytic	______	______	______
Erikson's Psychosocial	______	______	______
Skinner's Behaviourism	______	______	______
Bandura's Social Learning	______	______	______
Piaget's Cognitive-Developmental	______	______	______
Ethological (e.g., Bowlby)	______	______	______
Bronfenbrenner's Ecological Systems	______	______	______

THEORY	(2) ROLE OF CHILD IN OWN DEVELOPMENT	
	ACTIVE	PASSIVE
Freud's Psychoanalytic	______	______
Erikson's Psychosocial	______	______
Skinner's Behaviourism	______	______
Bandura's Social Learning	______	______
Piaget's Cognitive-Developmental	______	______
Ethological (e.g., Bowlby)	______	______
Bronfenbrenner's Ecological Systems	______	______

THEORY	(3) NATURE OF DEVELOPMENTAL CHANGE	
	CONTINUOUS (small increments)	**DISCONTINUOUS** (stages)
Freud's Psychoanalytic	______	______
Erikson's Psychosocial	______	______
Skinner's Behaviourism	______	______
Bandura's Social Learning	______	______
Piaget's Cognitive-Developmental	______	______
Ethological (e.g., Bowlby)	______	______
Bronfenbrenner's Ecological Systems	______	______

ACTIVITY 2-2

ASSUMPTIONS ABOUT CHILDREN: HOW DO WE EXPLAIN AGGRESSION?

INTRODUCTION: This activity builds on the material presented in Chapter 1 and 2 that deals with the concept of development and the different major theories in developmental psychology. This activity should give you good experience viewing a particular developmental issue from different perspectives. It also should show you how integrating theories may be helpful in understanding the complete picture of certain childhood behaviours.

INSTRUCTIONS: Choose three different major theories (at least one identifying external sources of behaviour and one identifying internal sources of behaviour). From each perspective, explain the development of aggression in children. How are the explanations different or similar? What implications can you think of for potential intervention research? How might each perspective suggest changes in childhood aggression and, ultimately, in Canadian policy or parenting practices?

ANSWERS TO SELF-TESTS

VOCABULARY SELF-TEST (The answers may be found on the pages in parentheses.)

1. parsimony (p. 38)
2. behaviourism (p. 47)
3. qualitative change (pp.40–41)
4. assimilation (p. 53)
5. ego (p. 42)
6. reciprocal determinism (p. 50)
7. organismic model (p. 65)
8. theory (p. 37)
9. mesosystem (p. 63)
10. cognitive development (pp. 51–52)
11. contextual model (pp. 65–66)
12. psychosexual theory (pp. 41–42)
13. punisher (p. 48)
14. continuity/discontinuity issue (p. 40)
15. chronosystem (p. 64)

MULTIPLE-CHOICE SELF-TEST (The answers may be found on the pages in parentheses.)

1. **b** (pp. 37–38) When a theory has heuristic value it means that the theory continues to generate hypotheses. Parsimony (a) refers to the conciseness of a theory. Falsifiability (c) would indicate a theory could be disproved by testing its assumptions. Discontinuity (d) refers to assumptions about human nature; it is not a characteristic of theories.

2. **a** (pp. 40–41) A discontinuous view of development sees changes as abrupt, qualitative, and often unconnected over time. In contrast, a continuous view of development sees changes as gradual, quantitative, and connected (c). A view that development was primarily a product of maturation (b) would reflect a "nature" position with respect to development. Focusing on the child's role, either active or passive, (d) relates to the active/passive assumption, rather than the continuity/discontinuity assumption.

3. **b** (pp. 42–43) In Freud's view the ego is the conscious, rational component of personality. The superego is the moral component of personality (a). The id (c) is the biological component. The collective unconscious (d) is not part of Freud's theory of personality.

4. **d** (p. 43) Chris is smoking and overeating, both forms of oral gratification. Fixation at the genital stage (a) would not produce any obvious behavioural problems. Fixation at the anal stage (b) might result in messiness or wastefulness. Fixation at the phallic stage (c) might produce problems in sexual orientation (same-sex/other-sex).

5. **a** (p. 45) At the age of 2 the stage that a child is in is called autonomy versus shame and doubt. The stage of industry versus inferiority is entered around the age of 6 (d). Basic trust versus mistrust (c) occurs earlier (birth to 1 year). The stage of intimacy versus isolation (b) occurs later, during early adulthood.

6. **b** (p. 50) Reciprocal determinism suggests that the environment affects people, and that people affect their environment. Unconscious motivation (a) is the focus of psychoanalytic theories. Adaptive schemes (c) form part of cognitive theories of development, in particular Piaget's theory. Evolutionary forces (d) are the focus in ethological theories.

7. **a** (pp. 52–53) Piaget focuses on the active interactions between the individual and the environment as a key source of cognitive development. Observational learning (b) is a major component in Bandura's social learning theory. Adult instruction (c) is a key aspect in Vygotsky's theory of cognitive development. Punishment and reward (d) are aspects of learning theories, such as those proposed by Watson and Skinner.

8. **c** (p. 65) Mechanistic theories see people as passive and changing continuously as behaviour patterns are added or subtracted. This is most clearly reflected in Skinner's learning theory. Freud's theory (a) and Piaget's theory (d) are both stage theories, which fit more closely with an organismic world view. Bronfenbrenner's theory (b) views people as playing an active role and takes a more contextual world view with respect to development.

Chapter Three

Hereditary Influences on Development

Learning Objectives

By the time you have finished this chapter you should be able to:

1. Describe the basic structure of chromosomes and genes.
2. Compare and contrast the processes of mitosis and meiosis and explain how crossing-over creates unique genetic patterns during meiosis.
3. Describe the process that will result in monozygotic twins and explain how this differs from the process that will result in dizygotic twins.
4. Explain how an individual's sex is determined by the pairing of chromosomes at site #23.
5. Explain what is meant by dominant and recessive genes, and trace genetic transmission patterns in heterozygous and homozygous individuals.
6. Discuss what is meant by codominance of genetic traits.
7. Explain what is meant by genetic imprinting and identify two disorders that show this pattern of transmission.
8. Explain what is meant by a sex-linked characteristic, and discuss how these characteristics increase the genetic vulnerability of males.
9. Discuss what is meant by polygenic transmission of traits.
10. Describe the major sex-chromosome disorders.
11. Identify the cause of Down syndrome and describe the typical characteristics associated with this disorder.
12. Identify some of the major gene-based abnormalities and describe the disorders that result from these abnormalities.
13. Describe three methods used for detecting genetic disorders during the prenatal period.
14. Describe some of the treatments that have been developed to optimize the development of individuals with hereditary disorders.
15. Discuss the heredity–environment issue and the key concepts involved in behavioural genetics.
16. Explain how studying twins and adopted children can help to separate the contributions of heredity and the environment.
17. Explain what information is provided by a heritability coefficient.
18. Discuss what is meant by nonshared environmental influences and shared environmental influences.
19. Discuss what is known about the role of heredity in intellectual performance, personality, and mental illness.
20. Describe how heredity and the environment can interact using the canalization principle and the range-of-reaction principle.
21. Discuss the three types of genotype/environment correlations identified by Scarr and McCartney and explain how these genotype/environment correlations influence development.

Chapter Outline and Summary

1. Principles of hereditary transmission

An individual's genotype is determined by the genes he or she inherits. An individual's phenotype is the outward expression of the genotype and consists of a person's observable or measurable characteristics.

a. The genetic code

The new cell that is formed when a sperm cell fertilizes an egg cell is called a zygote. The zygote contains the genetic code that will change the single cell into a human being. There are 46 chromosomes in the nucleus of the zygote, each of which consists of thousands of genes. With the exception of the sex chromosomes, chromosomes exist as matching pairs, one derived from the mother's egg cell and one derived from the father's sperm cell. Genes are made up of deoxyribonucleic acid (DNA). DNA molecules are able to replicate themselves, and this process permits the one-cell zygote to grow into a complex human being.

b. Growth of the zygote and production of body cells

Mitosis is the process of cell division in which a cell duplicates its 46 chromosomes, and then splits into two daughter cells, each of which is a duplicate of the original cell. The process of mitosis continues throughout the lifespan. It generates new cells that enable the individual to grow, and it also replaces old cells that become damaged.

c. The germ (or sex) cells

Germ cells are the special cells in the body that produce gamete cells. In males the gamete cells are called sperm cells and in females they are called egg cells. Gamete cells are produced through a process called meiosis. During meiosis the germ cell duplicates its 46 chromosomes. The pairs of duplicated chromosomes segregate into two parent cells, which then divide again. This process results in 4 daughter cells that each contain 23 unpaired chromosomes. An event called crossing-over often occurs just after the germ cell duplicates its chromosomes. During crossing-over adjacent chromosomes can exchange segments of genetic material.

When the chromosomes segregate into the daughter cells, each chromosome pair segregates independently of all the other pairs. This process results in more than 8 million possible genetic combinations from a single germ cell. In addition, the crossing-over process that can occur during the early phases of meiosis actually alters the genetic composition of the chromosomes, and as a result the number of possible variations exceeds the variations that would occur if there were no exchange of genetic information.

d. Multiple births

Occasionally a zygote will begin to duplicate, and then separate into two separate but identical cells. These cells each develop into separate individuals. The resulting twins are called monozygotic (identical) twins because they developed from a single zygote and share the same genotype.

More frequently two egg cells are released and fertilized by two different sperm cells. The resulting zygotes each develop into separate individuals. These twins are called dizygotic (fraternal) twins because they developed from two different zygotes. They do not share a common genotype and are no more similar in terms of their genetic make-up than non-twin siblings.

In Canada, the incidence of multiple births has increased dramatically over the last couple of decades.

e. Male or female?

Human chromosomes occur in pairs, and 22 of the 23 pairs are called autosomes. In the autosomes each member of the gene pair is similar. In contrast, the 23rd pair of chromosomes may be either X or Y chromosomes. The pairing of chromosomes at this location determines what the individual's sex will be. When an X chromosome and a Y chromosome are paired the person will be male, when two X chromosomes are paired the person will be female. Because females have only X chromosomes at this location, egg cells always contain an X chromosome. Therefore it is not possible to have two Y chromosomes paired at this location.

f. What do genes do?

At the most basic level, genes call for the production of enzymes and other proteins that are necessary for the formation and functioning of new cells. Genes also guide cell differentiation, ensuring that some cells develop specialized functions (such as neurons, bone cells, and muscle cells). Finally, some genes regulate the pace and timing of development by "turning on" or "turning off" other genes at different points during the lifespan. However, environmental factors can influence the way in which the messages coded in the genes are carried out. Consequently, an individual's phenotype is partially the result of his or her underlying genotype, and partially the result of environmental factors that influence the way in which that genotype is expressed.

g. How are genes expressed?

Many human characteristics are influenced by a single pair of genes (also called alleles) that follow a simple dominant-recessive pattern of inheritance. A dominant allele is a relatively powerful gene that is expressed in the individual's phenotype and that masks the effect of less powerful genes. A recessive allele is a less powerful gene that is not expressed in the individual's phenotype if it is paired with a dominant allele.

People who have two alleles of the same type for a given characteristic are said to be homozygous for that characteristic; individuals who have different alleles for a given characteristic are said to be heterozygous for that characteristic. Homozygous individuals will express the trait that matches their genotype; they will display the dominant trait if both alleles are dominant, and they will display the recessive trait if both alleles are recessive. Heterozygous individuals will express the trait associated with the dominant allele, but can pass the recessive allele to their offspring. The only time the recessive trait will be displayed is if an individual inherits a recessive allele from both parents.

Some genes do not follow the simple dominant-recessive pattern and instead show a pattern called codominance. When this occurs the trait that is displayed in the individual's phenotype is a compromise or blend of the traits carried by the two alleles. Codominance is also evident when one allele is "stronger" but fails to completely mask the effects of the "weaker" allele. Therefore, the stronger allele shows incomplete dominance. An example of this pattern of transmission is seen in sickle-cell anemia. In individuals who are heterozygous for sickle-cell anemia most of the red blood cells are normal, but some of the red blood cells will assume an unusual sickle shape.

Some traits are called sex-linked characteristics because they are determined by genes located on the sex chromosomes. The majority of sex-linked disorders are produced by recessive genes located on the X chromosome. Because males inherit only a single X chromosome, they have no corresponding genes on the Y chromosome to mask the effects of the recessive characteristic. Consequently, if a male inherits an X-linked trait from his mother, the trait will be displayed in his phenotype. In contrast, females all have two X chromosomes and therefore will display only X-linked traits in their phenotype if they inherit the recessive gene from both their mother and their father.

Genetic imprinting is a process in which particular gene pairs are biochemically marked so that only one parent's allele (either the mother's or the father's) is expressed, regardless of its composition. Two traits that follow this pattern of inheritance are diabetes (which is more likely to develop if the disease is present in the father) and Angelman syndrome (which is more likely to develop if the syndrome is present in the mother). At present, the causes of genetic imprinting are poorly understood and its evolutionary significance is not clear.

Most important human characteristics are influenced by many pairs of alleles, rather than by a single pair. These traits are called polygenic (many genes) traits. When a trait is influenced by multiple genes many different phenotypes appear; many people are near the average, with a few individuals showing extreme variations of the trait in question. Examples of polygenic traits include height, weight, intelligence, skin colour, temperament, and susceptibility to cancer.

2. Chromosomal and genetic abnormalities

Approximately 5% of newborn infants have a congenital problem of some type. Congenital defects are conditions that are present at birth, although they may not be detectable when the child is born. Congenital problems may result from chromosomal abnormalities, genetic abnormalities, harmful conditions that the embryo or fetus is exposed to during prenatal development, or complications that arise during the birth process.

a. Chromosomal abnormalities

During the process of meiosis the final segregation of the chromosomes among the gamete cells is sometimes uneven. Some gametes have too few chromosomes and some have too many. In the majority of cases, a zygote that is formed from the union of an abnormal and normal gamete cell will fail to develop, or will be spontaneously aborted. However, approximately 1 child in 200 is born with 45 or 47 chromosomes, instead of 46.

Many chromosomal abnormalities involve the 23rd pair of chromosomes. Males who are born with an extra X chromosome have Klinefelter's syndrome; males born with an extra Y chromosome have Supermale syndrome. Females who are born with an extra X chromosome have Poly-X syndrome; females born with only a single X chromosome have Turner's syndrome. Individuals can also inherit an X chromosome that is brittle or may have broken into two or more pieces. This results in a condition known as Fragile-X syndrome.

The most common autosome abnormality is trisomy-21 or Down syndrome. Children with Down syndrome have some degree of mental retardation and may have congenital eye, ear, and heart defects. They also typically show a number of distinctive physical characteristics, including a sloping forehead, a protruding tongue, and almond-shaped eyes.

Most chromosomal abnormalities result from the uneven segregation of chromosomes during the process of meiosis. However, this is not the only cause of chromosomal abnormalities. Chromosomal abnormalities increase dramatically among children born to older mothers. One possible explanation is the "aging ova hypothesis." Because a female is born with all her ova already present in the ovaries, over time the ova may deteriorate. This may be due to the normal aging process, or due to prolonged exposure to environmental toxins. Recent research suggests that some mothers who have a genetic condition that hinders metabolism of folic acid and/or a diet low in folic acid may be at elevated risk of delivering a Down syndrome baby. The risk of chromosomal abnormalities is also increased if a father has been exposed to environmental hazards that can damage his chromosomes.

b. Genetic abnormalities

Most genetic abnormalities result from the pairing of recessive alleles. If both parents are heterozygous for the trait in question, the dominant allele will mask the recessive trait in their phenotype. However, it is possible for the parents to pass the recessive allele to their offspring. On average, one out of four children who are born to parents who are both heterozygous for a trait will inherit two recessive alleles for that trait. This individual will display the trait in question, even though neither parent displayed the trait.

One exception to this pattern is sex-linked traits. These traits will be expressed in males if the recessive allele appears on the X chromosome he inherits from his mother. On average, one out of two male children born to a mother who is heterozygous for a sex-linked trait will inherit the recessive allele. This individual will display the trait in question, even though his mother does not display the trait. Females will display only sex-linked traits if they inherit the recessive allele from both their mothers and their fathers.

Finally, genetic abnormalities may also result from mutations. Mutations are changes in the chemical structure of one or more genes that have the effect of producing a new phenotype. Mutations may occur spontaneously, or they may be induced by exposure to environmental hazards.

3. Applications: Genetic counselling, prenatal detection, and treatment of hereditary disorders

Services such as genetic counselling and prenatal diagnosis allow parents who are at risk for having a child with a hereditary disorder to make reasoned decisions about conceiving a child or carrying a pregnancy to term.

a. Genetic counselling

Genetic counselling is a service that helps prospective parents assess their likelihood of having children who are free from hereditary defects. This type of service is particularly helpful for couples who have relatives with hereditary disorders or for parents who already have a child with a hereditary disorder.

b. Prenatal detection of hereditary abnormalities

One procedure that can be used to detect the presence of hereditary disorders in a developing fetus is amniocentesis. A sample of the amniotic fluid is extracted from the mother's uterus. This fluid can then be analyzed. The results will indicate the sex of the fetus, the presence of chromosomal abnormalities (such as Down syndrome), or the presence of a variety of genetic disorders. One disadvantage of amniocentesis is that it cannot be performed during the first trimester of the pregnancy because there is insufficient amniotic fluid. It will take up to an additional two weeks to obtain the results from the procedure, so parents face a second-trimester abortion, if the fetus has a serious defect and abortion is their choice.

An alternative procedure has been developed called chorionic villus sampling (CVS). A sample of the chorion is extracted and the cells from this sample are analyzed. The results will provide the same information as that obtained from amniocentesis, but the procedure can be performed as early as the 8th week of the pregnancy, and the results are typically available within 24 hours. This can give parents more time to carefully consider whether the pregnancy should be terminated, in the event the fetus has a serious defect. However, CVS has a greater risk of miscarriage and in rare instances the procedure has been linked to limb deformities in the fetus. A much safer screening technique involving DNA analysis of fetal cells from the mother's bloodstream with no risk to the fetus should become available in the near future.

Another very common and safe prenatal diagnostic procedure is ultrasound. This procedure is most useful after the 14th week of pregnancy. It can be used to detect multiple pregnancies, detect obvious physical abnormalities, and determine the sex and age of the fetus.

c. Treating hereditary disorders

Some hereditary disorders can be effectively treated, either after a baby is born or while the fetus is still in the uterus. Phenylketonuria (PKU) is a metabolic disorder that causes degeneration of the nervous system when it goes untreated. In the mid-1950s scientists developed a diet low in phenylalanine that could prevent the harmful consequences of this formerly incurable disorder. In addition, there is now a simple blood test that can detect PKU. This blood screening is now routine for newborn infants, and babies who are found to have PKU are immediately placed on the special diet.

New medical techniques have also been developed that make it possible to treat some hereditary disorders by delivering drugs or hormones to the unborn fetus. Also, new surgical techniques have been developed that have allowed surgeons to perform bone marrow transplants and repair heart, neural tube, and urinary tract defects in the developing fetus.

Gene replacement therapy has been tested as a potential treatment for cystic fibrosis and adenosine deaminase deficiency. This type of therapy does not cure the underlying disorder, but it is capable of lessening the symptoms that individuals experience.

Finally, germline gene therapy is a process in which harmful genes are altered or replaced by healthy genes in the early embryonic stage. This approach has successfully corrected certain genetic disorders in animals, but ethical issues may prevent its use with humans for some time to come.

4. Hereditary influences on behaviour

Behavioural genetics is the scientific study of how genotype interacts with the environment to determine behavioural attributes such as intelligence, personality, and mental health.

a. *Methods of studying hereditary influences*

Selective breeding and family studies are the two major strategies that can be used to assess hereditary contributions to behaviour. Selective breeding involves deliberately manipulating the genetic makeup of animals to study hereditary influences on behaviour. This method can be used to assess the heritability of various attributes in animals, but it cannot be utilized in studies involving people (for obvious ethical reasons).

Family studies typically involve either twin studies or adoption studies. In twin studies researchers compare monozygotic twins who are reared together with dizygotic twins who are reared together. If genes affect the attribute being studied, then the monozygotic twins should be more similar than the dizygotic twins with respect to that attribute.

Adoption studies focus on adoptees who are genetically unrelated to other members of their adoptive families. If adopted children are more similar to their biological parents than to their adoptive parents with respect to a given attribute, it indicates that genes must be influential in the determination of that attribute.

Finally, in some instances it is possible to compare sets of identical twins who were reared together with sets of identical twins who were separated in infancy and reared in separate homes. If identical twins reared together are more alike on an attribute than identical twins reared apart, we can infer that environment plays a role in determining the way in which the attribute will be displayed.

Behavioural geneticists rely on mathematical calculations to tell them whether or not a trait is influenced by genetics and the degree to which heredity and the environment interact to account for individual differences in that trait. For traits that are either present or absent in a given individual, researchers calculate concordance rates. This is a measure of how often both members of a given pair display the trait if one member has it. For traits that can assume many values, researchers calculate correlation coefficients.

The amount of variation in a trait that can be attributed to genetic factors is called the heritability coefficient. The heritability coefficient is equal to two times the difference between the correlation coefficients obtained for monozygotic twins reared together and dizygotic twins reared together.

Two sources of environmental influence can also be estimated. Nonshared environmental influences (NSE) are experiences that are unique to specific individuals and are not shared by other members of the family. Nonshared environmental influences are equal to one minus the correlation coefficient for monozygotic twins reared together. Shared environmental influences (SE) are experiences that are common to individuals who share the same home environment. Shared environmental influences are the influences that remain once heritability and NSE influences have been taken into account. These influences can be estimated by adding together the heritability ratio and the NSE influences and subtracting that total from one.

b. *Hereditary influences on intellectual performance*

Genes account for about half the total variation in people's IQ scores, meaning that IQ is a moderately heritable attribute. However, as children mature, it appears that genes contribute more to individual differences in IQ. What appears to happen, based on information from both twin and adoption studies, is that the influence of shared environment on intellectual performance declines with age, while the influence of both genes and nonshared environment becomes increasingly stronger.

c. *Hereditary contributions to personality*

Family studies and other longitudinal projects reveal that many core dimensions of personality are genetically influenced. Introversion-extroversion shows about the same moderate level of heritability as IQ does, and empathic concern also appears to be genetically influenced. The aspects of the environment that appear to contribute most heavily to personality are nonshared environmental influences. When NSE influences are estimated for personality, these effects appear to be at least as important as genetic influences in determining personality.

d. *Hereditary contributions to behaviour disorders and mental illness*

Identical twins are usually discordant with respect to mental illnesses and behavioural disorders, which means environment must be a very important contributor to these conditions. However, for disorders such as schizophrenia, manic-depressive psychosis, and a number of neurotic disorders, the concordance rates among monozygotic twins are higher than the concordance rates among dizygotic twins. This is an indication that these disorders are influenced by genetics to some extent. It appears that people do not inherit behavioural disorders, but rather inherit a predisposition to develop the disorder. The environment that the individual encounters plays a large role in determining whether the disorder will be displayed.

5. Heredity and environment as developmental co-conspirators

a. The canalization principle

Our genes can operate so as to limit or restrict development to a small number of outcomes. Attributes that are genetically canalized simply unfold according to the maturational program in our genes. However, potent environmental influences can also limit, or canalize, development. The canalization principle suggests that there are multiple pathways for individual development, and that nature and nurture interact to determine the pathway each individual will follow. However, either genes or the environment may limit the extent to which the other factor will influence the final developmental outcome.

b. The range-of-reaction principle

Gottesman suggested that our genotype establishes a range of possible responses to different kinds of life experiences. This is our inherited range of reaction, and it sets boundaries on the range of possible phenotypes each individual might display in response to the environment. One important implication of the range-of-reaction principle is that because people differ genetically, no two individuals will respond in precisely the same way to the same environment.

c. Genotype/environment correlations

Many behavioural geneticists now believe that our genes may actually influence the types of environments we are likely to experience. The notion of passive genotype/environment correlations is based on the fact that the rearing environment that biological parents provide is influenced by the parents' own genes, and therefore is correlated with the child's own genotype. The notion of evocative genotype/environment correlations is based on the idea that a child's genetically influenced attributes will affect the behaviour of others and thus will influence the environment in which the child develops. The notion of active genotype/environment correlations is based on the assumption that children will prefer and seek out environments that are most compatible with their genetic predispositions.

According to Scarr and McCartney, the relative importance of these three influences will change over the course of childhood. During infancy passive genotype/environment correlations are particularly important. As children reach school age, active genotype/environment correlations become more important. Evocative genotype/environment correlations have an influence throughout the lifespan.

6. Contributions and criticisms of the behavioural genetics approach

Behavioural genetics has shown that many attributes that were previously thought to be shaped solely by the environment are, in fact, influenced by genetics. Research in this area has also helped to illustrate that genotypes and environments interact to produce developmental change and variations in developmental outcomes. However, the approach has been criticized as an incomplete theory that describes but does not explain how these two different components actually influence developmental outcomes.

Vocabulary Self-Test

Part I: For each of the following definitions provide the appropriate term. (Answers to this portion of the self-test are provided at the end of the chapter.)

1. ________________ Twins that result when a mother releases two ova at roughly the same time and each is fertilized by a different sperm, producing two zygotes that are genetically different

2. ________________ A method in which fetal cells are extracted from the chorion from a pregnant woman so that they can be tested for genetic defects

3. ________________ Genetic restriction of phenotype to a small number of developmental outcomes

4. ________________ A threadlike structure made up of genes and found in the nucleus of each body cell

5. ________________ Having inherited two alleles for an attribute that have different effects

6. ________________ The percentage of cases in which a particular attribute is present for both members of a twin pair if it is present for one member

7. ________________ A pattern of inheritance in which one allele dominates another so that only its phenotype is expressed

8. ________________ A problem that is present, but not necessarily apparent, at birth

9. ________________ The genetic endowment an individual inherits

10. ________________ Method of detecting gross physical abnormalities by scanning the womb with sound waves and producing a visual outline of the fetus

11. ________________ A relatively powerful gene that is expressed phenotypically and masks the effect of a less powerful gene

12. ________________ The amount of variability in a trait that can be attributed to hereditary factors

13. ________________ The process in which a germ cell divides, producing gametes that each contain half of the parent cell's original complement of chromosomes

14. ________________ Condition in which two heterozygous but equally powerful alleles produce a phenotype in which both genes are fully and equally expressed

15. ________________ The notion that our genotypes affect the types of environments we prefer and will seek out

Part II: For each of the following terms provide the definition.

Crossing-Over: ____

____

Sex-Linked Characteristic: ____

____

Amniocentesis: ____

____

Evocative Genotype/Environment Correlations: ____

____

Phenotype: ____

____

Fragile-X Syndrome: ____

____

Monozygotic Twins: ____

____

Polygenic Trait: ____

____

Zygote: ____

____

Heritability Coefficient: ____

____

Recessive Allele: ____

____

Mutation: ____

____

Mitosis: ____

____

Range-of-Reaction Principle: ____

____

Homozygous: ____

____

Short-Answer Study Questions

PRINCIPLES OF HEREDITARY TRANSMISSION

1. Differentiate between the terms genotype and phenotype.

   Genotype:

   Phenotype:

2. Sketch an illustration that depicts the differences between mitosis and meiosis.

   Mitosis: **Meiosis:**

3. Identify and describe the two processes that ensure the genetic uniqueness of each human gamete cell.

   a.

   b.

4. Identify two different types of twins and describe the way in which each type of twinning occurs.

   a.

   b.

5. Explain why an individual's sex is determined entirely by the genetic code contained in the father's sperm.

6. Imagine that Mr. and Mrs. H are each heterozygous with respect to a particular trait that follows a simple dominant-recessive transmission pattern. Identify all the potential genotypes that might emerge in this couple's offspring, and indicate what percentage of the time they could expect each genotype to occur.

7. The simple dominant-recessive pattern of genetic transmission is only one type of genetic transmission. Identify and describe four other patterns of genetic transmission, and give an example of a characteristic determined by each type of transmission.

   a. **Name of Pattern:**

      Description:

      Example of characteristic with this pattern:

   b. **Name of Pattern:**

      Description:

      Example of characteristic with this pattern:

   c. **Name of Pattern:**

      Description:

      Example of characteristic with this pattern:

   d. **Name of Pattern:**

      Description:

      Example of characteristic with this pattern:

8. Some women display recessive sex-linked traits such as colour blindness. When this occurs what can you infer about the genotype and phenotype for each of the parents?

   Father's genotype:

   Father's phenotype:

   Mother's genotype:

   Mother's phenotype:

CHROMOSOMAL AND GENETIC ABNORMALITIES

9. There are four chromosome disorders that result from an abnormal number of chromosomes at site #23. Identify each of these disorders and describe both the physical phenotype and the intellectual characteristics typically associated with each disorder.

   a. Disorder:
   Phenotypic Appearance:

   Intellectual Characteristics:

   b. Disorder:
   Phenotypic Appearance:

   Intellectual Characteristics:

   c. Disorder:
   Phenotypic Appearance:

   Intellectual Characteristics:

   d. Disorder:
   Phenotypic Appearance:

   Intellectual Characteristics:

10. Explain the chromosome abnormality associated with fragile-X syndrome and describe some of the characteristics found in individuals with this syndrome.

11. Explain the chromosome abnormality associated with Down syndrome and describe some of the characteristics found in individuals with this syndrome.

12. Identify three potential causes of chromosomal abnormalities.

    a.

    b.

    c.

13. List three examples of defects that are attributable to a single pair of genes, rather than to chromosomal abnormalities.

    a.

    b.

    c.

14. Explain why diseases such as Tay-Sachs continue to occur, given that this disease is always fatal during early childhood. (How can the genetic pattern continue to appear if all individuals who have the disorder die before they have a chance to have offspring of their own?)

15. We typically associate genetic mutations with maladaptive outcomes, but evolutionary theorists believe some of these mutations may actually be beneficial. Provide an example that supports the evolutionary position.

APPLICATIONS: GENETIC COUNSELLING, PRENATAL DETECTION, AND TREATMENT OF HEREDITARY DISORDERS

16. List three methods of prenatal testing and note the advantages and limitations associated with each procedure.

    a.

    b.

    c.

17. Describe gene replacement therapy and germline gene therapy and discuss the ethical issues associated with each of these forms of treatment.

HEREDITARY INFLUENCES ON BEHAVIOUR

18. Behavioural geneticists who study human behaviour usually rely on two types of family studies to determine the influence of heredity on a trait. Describe the rationale behind each of these research designs and also indicate the types of comparisons that can be made with each design.

    Twin design:

    Adoption design:

19. Give the formula for calculating the heritability coefficient for a trait, and explain what information this coefficient provides.

20. Discuss what nonshared environmental influences (NSE) are and explain how the overall impact of these influences can be estimated.

21. Discuss what shared environmental influences (SE) are and explain how the overall impact of these influences can be estimated.

22. Discuss the general conclusions behavioural geneticists have reached concerning the role of heredity in intellectual performance, personality, and mental illness.

    Intellectual performance:

    Personality:

    Mental Illness:

HEREDITY AND ENVIRONMENT AS DEVELOPMENTAL CO-CONSPIRATORS

23. Explain what is meant by the term "canalization" and provide examples of genetic canalization and environmental canalization in human development.

    Canalization:

    Example of genetic canalization:

    Example of environmental canalization:

24. Summarize the range-of-reaction principle using appropriate examples.

25. Summarize each of the genotype/environment correlations proposed by Scarr and McCartney (1983).

    a.

    b.

    c.

26. Use genotype/environment correlations to explain why fraternal twins and other nontwin siblings are likely to become increasingly dissimilar on many attributes as they mature.

27. Use genotype/environment correlations to explain why identical twins are likely to show a high similarity to one another, even when they are raised in different home environments.

Multiple-Choice Self-Test

For each of the following questions select the best alternative. (Answers and explanations for this self-test are provided at the end of the chapter.) Once you have selected your answer, provide a brief explanation for why the answer you selected is the best choice and why the remaining answers would not be correct.

1. As the zygote moves through the fallopian tube toward the uterus:

   a. it undergoes little change until after implantation
   b. it begins to reproduce itself through the process of meiosis
   c. it begins to reproduce itself through the process of mitosis
   d. it undergoes such rapid differentiation that by the time of implantation, it already looks quite human

   Rationale: ______________________________

   ____

2. The sex of an embryo is determined by the genetic contribution from:

   a. the father
   b. the mother
   c. the parent who contributes the dominant gene at site #23
   d. the parent who contributes the recessive gene at site #23

   Rationale: ______________________________

   ____

3. A person who carries one dominant and one recessive gene is said to be:

   a. heterozygous for that trait
   b. homozygous for that trait
   c. codominant for that trait
   d. corecessive for that trait

   Rationale: ______________________________

   ____

4. One trait that illustrates the principle of codominance is:

   a. AB blood type
   b. Down syndrome
   c. colour blindness
   d. diabetes

   Rationale: ______________________________

   ____

5. The factor common to the four chromosomal abnormalities (Turner's syndrome, Poly-X, Klinefelter's syndrome, and Supermale syndrome) is:

   a. brittle chromosomes that have broken apart
   b. an abnormal number of sex chromosomes (too many or too few)
   c. the presence of too many X chromosomes
   d. an extra 21st chromosome

   Rationale: ____

   ____

6. To test for possible chromosomal or genetic defects during pregnancy, a woman over 35 may consider having this procedure done:

   a. amniocentesis
   b. ultrasound
   c. germline gene therapy to correct the disorder during the embryonic stage of prenatal development
   d. postnatal genetic testing

   Rationale: ____

   ____

7. If the correlation on a trait were .75 for identical twins, .55 for siblings, .23 for cousins, and .11 for genetically unrelated adopted siblings, one could conclude that:

   a. heredity plays no role in that trait
   b. environment plays no role in that trait
   c. heredity is a prime contributor to that trait, but environment also plays a role
   d. environment is the prime contributor to that trait, with heredity making only a minor contribution

   Rationale: ____

   ____

8. Scarr and McCartney propose that the environments children prefer and seek out are ones compatible with their genetic predispositions, thereby augmenting the impact of heredity. They called this kind of influence:

   a. passive gene influence
   b. evocative gene influence
   c. canalization
   d. active gene influence

   Rationale: ____

   ____

Activities and Projects Related to this Chapter

ACTIVITY 3-1

DETERMINANTS OF SIMILARITIES AND DIFFERENCES

INTRODUCTION: This activity relates to the material in Chapter 3 on the interdependent role of heredity and environment in determining physical characteristics, personality, intelligence, etc. As a resource for this activity you are asked to tap what/who you know best—yourself. It is suggested that you complete this activity before reading the text material, and then look back over your responses after reading the text to see if you might have a different perspective on possible determinants.

INSTRUCTIONS:

1. Describe yourself in <u>two</u> of the following areas:

a. SOCIABILITY
b. AGGRESSION
c. PERSONALITY (e.g., introversion/extroversion, sociability, shyness, etc.)
d. TEMPERAMENT
e. INTELLIGENCE

2. Speculate about what factors (both environmental and hereditary) you think may have contributed to your being the way you are in those two areas.

ACTIVITY 3-2

CREATE A ZYGOTE

PROLOGUE: Your child has just begun its course of development. The egg has been fertilized and is at the one-cell zygote stage. That one cell carries all the genetic heritage from the mother and father in the form of ____________________ (chromosome, genes), which are carried on ____________________ (chromosomes, genes). That one cell will go through rapid division, a process called ____________________ (mitosis, meiosis), reproducing that genetic material in every new cell.

STEP 1: Decide what gender your child will be. (circle) Male Female

STEP 2: Draw a magnified picture of your child as a one-cell zygote. Show all the pairs of chromosomes. Use a different colour for those contributed by each parent. Indicate which pair is the sex chromosome pair with a line and label. See the text for ordered drawings of the chromosomes for a male and for a female. Place the chromosome pairs in the nucleus of the cell.

QUESTIONS TO PONDER AS YOU DRAW: How does the gene exert its influence? If my child is genetically predisposed to be socially withdrawn, does that mean my child is precluded from ever becoming socially adept and comfortable with social interaction? Why do two siblings often turn out so different when they have both some shared genes and have shared the same parents/home?

ACTIVITY 3-3

UNDERSTANDING GENETIC TRANSMISSION

INTRODUCTION: This activity relates to the text material on transmission of characteristics through single-gene pair inheritance. Below are two problems that will help you understand the possible outcomes that can occur from various parental genotypes.

PROBLEM 1: Sally and Joe Smith are both of above average intelligence. They were surprised when they gave birth to a PKU baby and were told that without dietary intervention their baby would be retarded. How could Sally, a woman without PKU and of normal intelligence, have carried a PKU baby?

Answer: Both Sally and Joe were heterozygous. The potential for two heterozygous individuals to produce a child who is different from either of the parents can be illustrated by completing the following diagram. Enter the possible resulting combinations of the dominant **N** (normal physiology and IQ) and recessive **pku** (abnormal physiology and potential for retardation) in Sally and Joe's offspring.

Joe's N-pku genotype

Sally's N-pku genotype		N	pku
	N		
	pku		

PROBLEM 2: Both Rachel and Jake have normal physiology, but they are concerned about whether any of their children might inherit cystic fibrosis. Rachel remembers the difficult time her little sister had in her struggle with cystic fibrosis. It is determined that Rachel is indeed a carrier of cystic fibrosis but that Jake is not. What is the likelihood that one of their offspring might be born with cystic fibrosis? They are assuming "none" since only one parent is heterozygous, but they aren't sure.

Answer: Check their conclusion by completing the following table.

Jake's homozygous genotype

Rachel's N-cf genotype		N	N
	N		
	cf		

ACTIVITY 3-4

SCARR AND McCARTNEY'S PASSIVE, EVOCATIVE, AND ACTIVE GENOTYPE/ENVIRONMENT CORRELATIONS

INTRODUCTION: This activity relates to Scarr and McCartney's theory of genotype/environment interactions.

INSTRUCTIONS:

PART 1: After reading about Scarr and McCartney's theory, generate one or two examples from your own life or from the lives of others that you know for each of the three types of genotype/environment correlation.

PASSIVE GENOTYPE/ENVIRONMENT CORRELATION

EVOCATIVE GENOTYPE/ENVIRONMENT CORRELATION

ACTIVE GENOTYPE/ENVIRONMENT CORRELATION

PART 2: The text presents curves depicting the hypothetical relationship of each type of genotype/ environment correlation with age. Look carefully at each developmental trend, one at a time. Then speculate about why one would expect to find the developmental trend depicted.

PASSIVE

EVOCATIVE

ACTIVE

PART 3: Did your examples (Part 1) follow the hypothesized developmental trends portrayed in the text? Speculate about why or why not.

ACTIVITY 3-5

POSITIVE VERSUS NEGATIVE EUGENICS: CHANGING ATTITUDES

INTRODUCTION: This activity relates to the material in Chapter 3 on the ethical issue of positive eugenics versus negative eugenics. Ask several people you know of different ages, sex, ethnicity, and education about their opinions or attitudes regarding gene replacement therapy and germline therapy. Make sure that they understand what each therapy involves. Be sensitive to others' responses and reactions as this is a controversial issue. Did you note any individual differences? If so, what might account for such differences?

REFERENCES OF INTEREST

Bane, A., Brown, L., & Carter, J. (2003). Life and death decisions: America's changing attitudes towards genetic engineering, genetic testing and abortion, 1972–98. *International Social Work, 46(2),* 209–219.

ANSWERS TO SELF-TESTS

VOCABULARY SELF-TEST (The answers may be found on the pages in parentheses.)

1. dizygotic twins (p. 74)
2. chorionic villus sampling (p. 86)
3. canalization (pp. 98–99)
4. chromosome (p. 71)
5. heterozygous (p. 76)
6. concordance rate (p. 91)
7. simple dominant-recessive inheritance (p. 76)
8. congenital defect (p. 80)
9. genotype (pp. 70–71)
10. ultrasound (pp. 86–87)
11. dominant allele (p. 76)
12. heritability (p. 89)
13. meiosis (p. 72)
14. codominance (p. 77)
15. active genotype/environment correlations (p. 101)

MULTIPLE-CHOICE SELF-TEST (The answers may be found on the pages in parentheses.)

1. **c** (p. 71) Mitosis is the normal process of genetic duplication that underlies growth and replacement of body cells. The zygote begins to change rapidly immediately following conception, forming into a blastocyst, which shows some cell differentiation by the time implantation begins (a). Meiosis (b) is the genetic process that produces the gamete cells. The embryo does not take on a human appearance until near the end of the embryonic stage at 8 weeks post-conception (d).

2. **a** (p. 74) The father can contribute either an X or a Y chromosome, thereby determining the sex of the embryo. The mother (b) always contributes an X chromosome, and therefore does not influence the sex of the embryo (all humans have at least one X chromosome at site #23, inherited from their mother). Sex is determined by a chromosome, not by a single gene pairing (c & d).

3. **a** (p. 76) An individual who was heterozygous would have one dominant and one recessive gene for the trait. Homozygous is the term used when two genes are the same (b). Codominance (c) is the term when an individual is heterozygous, and a blending of the traits is displayed in the phenotype. Corecessive (d) does not exist as a genetic pattern.

4. **a** (p. 77) AB blood type is the blending of two different genes, a gene for type A blood and a gene for type B blood, and both types are expressed equally. Down syndrome (b) is a chromosomal abnormality, not a trait determined by the pattern of a single gene pair. Colour blindness (c) is a sex-linked disorder. Diabetes (d) is a disorder that shows evidence of genetic imprinting.

5. **b** (p. 81) All these disorders occur when there are an abnormal number of chromosomes at site #23. When brittle chromosomes are present at site #23 (a) the disorder that is seen is called Fragile-X. Only two disorders involve too many X chromosomes (c); Turner's involves too few chromosomes and Supermale involves too many Y chromosomes. An extra chromosome at site #21 (d) would result in Down syndrome.

6. **a** (pp. 85–86) Amniocentesis can be performed during the second trimester (after the 14th week). Ultrasound (b) will not be able to detect chromosomal defects. Germline gene therapy (c) would not be able to correct a chromosome disorder, and the procedure is still experimental and not used with humans. Postnatal means after birth (d).

7. **c** (pp. 90–92) Because the coefficients decrease as kinship decreases it is apparent that heredity plays a role, but environment must also have an influence because the correlation between identical twins is not 1.00. Heredity must play a role (a) because the coefficients decrease as kinship decreases. Environment must play a role (b) because the correlation is not perfect between identical twins. The environment is not the prime contributor to the trait (d) because genetically unrelated adopted siblings are less similar than siblings.

8. **d** (p. 101) Active gene influences occur when individuals seek out environments that are compatible with their genetic predispositions. Passive influences (a) reflect the home environment. Evocative influences (b) reflect the behaviour of others toward the individual. Canalization (c) is not part of Scarr and McCartney's theory.

Chapter Four

Prenatal Development, Birth, and Newborns' Readiness for Life

Learning Objectives

By the time you have finished this chapter you should be able to:

1. Identify and describe the three stages of prenatal development, listing the characteristics and major events that occur during each stage.
2. Define the term "teratogen" and discuss some of the factors that can influence the overall developmental impact of teratogens.
3. Identify various maternal diseases that can have an impact on prenatal development, and describe the potential impact of these diseases at various times during the course of the pregnancy.
4. Identify various drugs and environmental hazards that can have an impact on prenatal development, and describe the potential impact of these teratogens.
5. Discuss how the mother's nutritional status, emotional well-being, and age can influence prenatal development.
6. Describe the main characteristics in each of the three stages of labour.
7. Describe the Apgar method for assessing newborns and know what the different scores mean.
8. Contrast the Apgar assessment method with the Brazelton Neonatal Behavioural Assessment.
9. Discuss the potential benefits and drawbacks to the use of obstetric medications during delivery.
10. Outline two alternative approaches to a hospital birth.
11. Discuss what research has shown with respect to the long-term impact of early emotional bonding between the newborn and the parents.
12. Describe postpartum depression and discuss the factors that are typically related to the development of postpartum depression.
13. Outline some basic complications that can occur during birth and discuss how these problems are usually dealt with.
14. Distinguish between preterm and small-for-gestational-age babies, and outline some of the potential short-term and long-term consequences for infants who are born preterm or small for gestational age.
15. Identify and describe the main reflexes found in newborns.
16. List six major infant states and discuss how these states change as the infant develops.
17. Outline some techniques parents might use to soothe a fussy baby.

Chapter Outline and Summary

1. From conception to birth

Prenatal development normally spans a period of approximately 266 days, lasting from the moment of conception to the time of birth. This time span can be divided into three major periods: the germinal period, the embryonic period, and the fetal period.

a. The germinal period

The germinal period normally lasts about 14 days, from conception until the developing blastocyst is firmly embedded in the uterine wall. As the zygote develops through the process of mitosis it is transformed into a blastocyst. Cell differentiation is already evident within the blastocyst; the inner layer is the embryo disk, which will develop into the embryo, and the outer layer of cells will become tissues that protect and nourish the embryo.

About 75% of all zygotes fail to implant properly in the uterine wall and therefore do not survive this first stage of prenatal development. When a blastocyst is implanted in the uterine wall the outer layer of cells rapidly begins to develop into the amnion, the chorion, the placenta, and the umbilical cord. The amnion is a watertight sac that fills with amniotic fluid. This fluid helps to protect the developing embryo. It cushions the embryo, regulates the temperature of the embryo, and provides a weightless environment that makes it easier for the embryo to move. The chorion eventually becomes the lining of the placenta, and the umbilical cord will connect the embryo to the placenta.

The placenta is a semipermeable structure that allows some substances to pass through but prevents the bloodstreams of the mother and the embryo from mixing. Within the placenta oxygen and nutrients pass from the mother's bloodstream into the embryo's bloodstream, while carbon dioxide and metabolic wastes pass from the infant's bloodstream into the mother's bloodstream.

b. The period of the embryo

The period of the embryo lasts from the third through the eighth weeks following conception. By the third week the embryonic disk is already differentiating into the ectoderm, mesoderm, and endoderm. The ectoderm will become the nervous system, skin, and hair; the mesoderm will become the muscles, bones, and circulatory system; the endoderm will become the digestive system, lungs, urinary tract, and other internal organs.

During the third week the ectoderm begins to fold and form a neural tube that will become the brain and spinal cord. By the end of the fourth week the heart has formed and begun to beat. During the second month the embryo becomes more human in appearance and is growing about one-ninth of a centimetre per day. By the fifth week the eyes have corneas and lenses, and by the seventh week the ears are well formed and a rudimentary skeleton has developed.

During the seventh and eighth weeks sexual differentiation occurs. The process begins when a genital ridge appears. If the embryo is a male, a gene on the Y chromosome will trigger a biochemical reaction that causes testes and male sex organs to develop. If the embryo is a female, no biochemical reaction is triggered and, in the absence of these biochemical signals, ovaries and female sex organs will develop.

By the end of the eighth week the embryo is just over 2.55 centimetres long and weighs less than 7 grams, and yet all the structures that will be present when the baby is finally born are already in place, in a rudimentary form.

c. The period of the fetus

The final seven months of the pregnancy are called the period of the fetus, and during this time it is appropriate to refer to the developing organism as a fetus, rather than as an embryo. During the third month the digestive and excretory systems are working and the fetus can swallow, digest nutrients, and urinate. By the end of the third month the sex of the fetus can be detected by ultrasound.

During the second trimester fetal kicks and other movements are strong enough to be felt by the mother. The fetal heartbeat can now be detected with a stethoscope and the hardening of the skeleton is evident on an ultrasound scan. At 20 weeks the fetus is covered by vernix and lanugo. Vernix protects the fetal skin from chapping and the lanugo helps the vernix stick to the skin. By the end of the second trimester the fetus is approximately 35 to 38 centimetres long and weighs about 1 kilogram.

During the final three months of the pregnancy all the organ systems mature rapidly. Somewhere between weeks 22 and 28 fetuses reach a point called the age of viability. This is the point at which survival outside the uterus is possible. However, many fetuses born this young require oxygen assistance because the air sacs in their lungs are too immature to inflate and exchange oxygen for carbon dioxide on their own.

2. Environmental influences on prenatal development

a. Teratogens

The term "teratogen" refers to any disease, drug, or other environmental agent that can harm a developing embryo or fetus. Teratogens have the largest impact on body structures or organ systems that are developing most rapidly when the teratogen is encountered. Susceptibility is influenced by the unborn child's genetic makeup, the mother's genetic makeup, and the overall quality of the prenatal environment. The same defect can be caused by a number of different teratogens, and a single teratogen can cause a variety of defects. The longer the exposure or the higher the "dose" of a teratogen, the more likely it is to cause serious defects. The father's exposure to teratogens prior to the time that the child was conceived may also affect the embryo or fetus, and the overall, long-term effects of teratogens are often influenced by the quality of the postnatal environment.

Each major organ system or body part has a sensitive period during prenatal development when it is most susceptible to teratogens. In general, the period of the embryo (from weeks 3 through 8) is when the unborn child is most vulnerable to the effects of various teratogens. However, some systems (such as the eyes, genitals, and nervous system) can be affected throughout the pregnancy.

Some disease agents are capable of crossing the placental barrier and can cause damage to the developing embryo or fetus. Rubella (German measles) has been associated with a variety of defects including blindness, deafness, cardiac abnormalities, and mental retardation. The disease is most dangerous during the first trimester. Between 60 and 85% of babies whose mothers contract rubella in the first eight weeks develop birth defects; this drops to 50% in the third month, and only 16% if the mother contracts the disease during weeks 13 through 20.

Toxoplasmosis is another infectious disease that can cause serious damage to a developing embryo or fetus. The disease is caused by a parasite found in undercooked meat and cat feces. The disease can cause severe eye and brain damage if exposure occurs during the first trimester, and it can induce a miscarriage if exposure occurs later in the pregnancy.

Unfortunately, sexually transmitted diseases (STDs) are extremely common and can produce serious birth defects. Syphilis cannot cross the placenta until midway through the second trimester, which means treatment early in the pregnancy can prevent harm to the developing fetus. However, when left untreated syphilis can cause serious eye, ear, bone, heart, or brain damage, and it greatly increases the risk of miscarrying the fetus. Genital herpes can cross the placenta, although most infections occur during birth. This incurable disease will kill one-third of all infected newborns, and another 20 to 25% will experience blindness, brain damage, and other serious neurological disorders as a result of the infection. Acquired immune deficiency syndrome (AIDS) is caused by the HIV virus, which can be transferred through bodily fluids. Transfer can occur across the placenta, during birth, or during breastfeeding. Although treatments are becoming more available, HIV-infected infants usually die by the time they reach adolescence.

About 60% of pregnant women take at least one prescription or over-the-counter medication at some point during their pregnancy. Unfortunately, some of the most commonly used medications, including aspirin and caffeine, have been linked to developmental complications in the embryo or fetus.

The use of alcohol during pregnancy can also disrupt prenatal development. Excessive consumption of alcohol over the course of the pregnancy can produce a disorder known as fetal alcohol syndrome (FAS). In Canada, 1 to 2 in 1000 babies are born with FAS. FAS produces defects such as microcephaly and malformations of the heart, limbs, joints, and face. Also, the majority of babies born with FAS score well below average in intelligence throughout childhood and adolescence. Social drinking during pregnancy can lead to a less serious set of problems called fetal alcohol effects (FAE). FAE produces minor physical abnormalities, attention difficulties, and subnormal intellectual functioning. Pregnant women need to be aware that there is no well-defined sensitive period for fetal alcohol effects; drinking late in the pregnancy can be just as risky as drinking during the first trimester. Health Canada recommends that pregnant women and women who are planning to become pregnant not consume alcohol.

Smoking during pregnancy introduces nicotine and carbon monoxide into both the mother's and the fetus's bloodstreams. This impairs the functioning of the placenta and increases the risk of the mother delivering a low-birth-weight baby. Approximately 1 in 5 children under the age of 3 in Canada had mothers who reported smoking during their pregnancy. Recent research suggests that the negative impact of maternal smoking on cognitive performance may be long term.

Most illicit drugs do not seem to produce physical abnormalities in the unborn baby, but there are often behavioural disturbances after the baby is born ranging from sleep disturbances to tremors. Mothers who take narcotic drugs or cocaine during their pregnancy are also more likely to miscarry or deliver prematurely.

Radiation disrupts prenatal development, and pregnant women should avoid X-rays unless the procedure is critical to their own survival. Finally, environmental toxins, in the form of chemicals and pollutants, can have teratogenic effects on developing fetuses and embryos. These same toxins can affect the reproductive system of either parent prior to the point when a child is conceived, and they may damage parental chromosomes, increasing the likelihood of genetic defects.

b. Maternal characteristics

The precise effects of malnutrition depend on when it occurs during the pregnancy. In the first trimester malnutrition can disrupt the formation of the spinal cord; during the third trimester it is more likely to result in low-birth-weight babies with an increased risk of early infant mortality. However, mothers who consume sufficient calories may still have diets that lack essential nutrients. Magnesium and zinc in the mother's diet improves the functioning of the placenta, and sufficient folic acid helps to prevent spina bifida and other neural tube defects.

Transient stressful events, such as a fall, have few if any harmful consequences for a mother or her fetus. However, prolonged, severe emotional stress is associated with premature delivery, low birth weight, and other birth complications. These stress-related complications are more likely to occur when the expectant mother is ambivalent or has negative feelings about her marriage or the pregnancy, and when she has few friends or little social support.

Teenage mothers are more likely to experience birth complications and are also more likely to deliver premature or low-birth-weight babies when compared to mothers in their twenties. This increased risk may partially result from the fact that teenage mothers are less likely to receive good prenatal care. After the age of 35 there is an increased risk for spontaneous abortion, or miscarriage. There is also an increased risk of complications during pregnancy and delivery among older mothers largely because, like adolescents, they are less likely to seek adequate prenatal care early in the pregnancy.

c. Prevention of birth defects

Parents can significantly reduce the likelihood of having a child with birth defects if they follow some simple steps. Parents should take advantage of genetic counselling if there is a family history of a specific disorder. The mother should seek good prenatal care as soon as possible. From the start of the pregnancy the mother should avoid exposure to contagious diseases. She should also avoid eating undercooked meat and avoid contact with cat feces. She should not take any drugs that are not absolutely essential. She should avoid smoking and drinking throughout the pregnancy. She should avoid radiation or X-ray treatments. Finally, she should ensure that she consumes sufficient calories and that her diet has all the essential vitamins and minerals.

3. Childbirth and the perinatal environment

a. The birth process

Childbirth consists of three separate stages. During the first stage the mother experiences uterine contractions that dilate the cervix so the head of the fetus can pass through. The second stage begins when the head of the fetus passes through the cervix and ends when the baby is born. During the third stage the placenta is expelled from the mother's body.

b. The baby's experience

Full-term newborns are typically about 51 centimetres long and weigh about 3.2 to 3.4 kilograms. In the first minutes after the baby is born his or her physical condition is assessed using the Apgar test. This test measures five characteristics: heart rate, respiratory effort, muscle tone, colour, and reflex irritability. A newborn can score 0, 1, or 2 points on each characteristic, and the total score indicates the newborn's overall condition. A score of 7 or higher indicates the newborn is in good physical condition; a score of 4 or lower often indicates the newborn requires immediate medical attention.

In contrast to the Apgar test, which measures physical well-being, the Neonatal Behavioural Assessment Scale (NBAS) provides a more sensitive measure of a baby's neurological well-being. This test is generally administered a few days after birth, and it assesses the strength of 20 inborn reflexes, as well as changes in state and reactions to social stimuli. Several studies suggest that parents who are educated about the NBAS may become more responsive to their infants' needs and behaviours.

c. Labour and delivery medication

Labour and delivery medications can cross the placenta and, in heavy doses, can make babies lethargic and inattentive. Some researchers fear that parents could fail to become involved with a sluggish, inattentive baby. In light of the uncertainties about the long-term consequences of medications used during labour and delivery, women and their doctors should carefully weigh the pros and cons of their use and seek to limit the use of these medications whenever possible.

d. Approaches to childbirth in Canada and Around the World

Natural, or prepared, childbirth is based on the philosophy that childbirth is a normal and natural part of living. The founders of this approach to childbirth claim that childbirth can be comfortable without the need for medication if women are taught to associate childbirth with pleasant feelings and ready themselves for the process by learning relaxation techniques that make childbirth easier. Research reveals there are many benefits to natural childbirth; one of the most important benefits is the social support mothers receive from their spouses and other close companions.

While the majority of Canadian births take place in hospitals, a small but growing number of families are opting to deliver their babies at home, with the aid of a certified nurse-midwife or doula. Women who deliver at home have shorter labours and use less medication than those who deliver in hospitals. Many hospitals now provide birthing rooms, or alternative birth centres, that create a home-like atmosphere, but still make medical technology available. The evidence suggests that giving birth in a well-run alternative birth centre is no more risky than a standard hospital delivery.

e. The social environment surrounding birth

The social environment surrounding a birth has changed significantly over the past 20 years. Many hospitals have altered their routines to allow extended early contact between the mother and her infant, which may help promote emotional bonding. In Canada, hospital procedures now encourage support personnel (nurses, doctors, and/or midwives) to provide continuity of care, flexibility of birthing positions, and more freedom to women to give birth as they choose.

Some mothers find themselves depressed, irritable, and even resentful of their babies shortly after birth. Mild forms of this condition are called the maternity blues; this mild depression is probably linked to hormonal changes following childbirth along with the stresses associated with being a new parent. However, slightly more than 10% of new mothers experience a more serious reaction called postpartum depression. Mothers who experience more than the maternity blues should seek professional help in overcoming their depression.

New fathers often display a sense of engrossment with their baby, and some studies have found that fathers who handle and help care for their babies in the hospital later spend more time with them at home. Other studies have not found these long-term effects but do suggest that early contact with a newborn can make fathers feel closer to their partners and more a part of the family.

4. Birth complications

a. Anoxia

Nearly 1% of newborns show signs of anoxia (oxygen deprivation). In some cases anoxia occurs because the umbilical cord becomes tangled or squeezed during childbirth; in other cases it can occur if the placenta separates prematurely. Permanent brain damage can occur if the newborn is deprived of oxygen for more than 3 to 4 minutes.

Anoxia can also occur in developing fetuses if there is an RH incompatibility between the fetus and the mother. RH-negative mothers who are exposed to RH-positive blood begin to produce RH antibodies. These antibodies can cross the placenta during pregnancy and destroy the fetus's red blood cells, depleting the fetus's oxygen supply. RH incompatibility affects only RH-negative mothers, and it usually does not affect a first pregnancy. Antibodies typically develop only following the birth of an RH-positive baby, which can put subsequent RH-positive fetuses at risk. However, RH incompatibility has become less of a concern since the development of rhogam, a vaccine that prevents RH antibodies from developing. RH-negative mothers routinely receive an injection of rhogam following childbirth to prevent RH antibodies from developing.

b. Low birth weight

About 6% of Canadian babies are born weighing less than 2500 grams. Preterm infants are babies who are born three or more weeks prior to their due date. Although these infants are small, the baby's weight is often appropriate for the baby's gestational age. Small-for-gestational-age babies have experienced slow growth as fetuses and are underweight for their gestational age. Small-for-gestational age infants are at greater risk for developing serious complications.

At least 50% of the babies who weigh less than 1000 grams at birth die at birth or shortly thereafter. Preterm infants often have very little sufactin, and this makes breathing difficult for these infants. Also, preterm infants are at risk of forming less secure emotional ties to their caregivers. Today, parents of preterm infants are encouraged to visit their baby often and to become actively involved with their infant during their visits. Babies in intensive care are more responsive and show quicker neurological and mental development if they are periodically massaged and soothed by the sound of a mother's voice. "Kangaroo mother care" provides skin-to-skin contact and has been shown to yield positive mental gains for the infants and positive parenting.

The long-term consequences for low-birth-weight babies depend to a large extent on their home environment. When mothers are well educated and knowledgeable about the factors that promote optimal development these infants often do well. Children from less stable or economically disadvantaged families are less likely to do well. The long-term prognosis for low-birth-weight children seems to depend critically on the postnatal environment in which they are raised.

c. Reproductive risk and capacity for recovery

Prenatal and birth complications can leave lasting scars, particularly if the complications are severe. However, in a supportive, stimulating home, the majority of these children eventually overcome their initial handicaps.

5. The newborn's readiness for life

a. Newborn reflexes

A reflex is an involuntary and automatic response to a stimulus. Some patterns of behaviour are called survival reflexes because they have clear adaptive value. Survival reflexes include the sucking and swallowing reflexes as well as the rooting reflex. Other reflexes are called primitive reflexes and are believed to be remnants of our evolutionary history. These include the Babinski, the swimming, the grasping, and the stepping reflex. These primitive reflexes normally disappear during the first few months of life.

b. Infant states

Newborns move in and out of six distinct states during a typical day. These states include two sleeping states: regular sleep, in which the baby is still and the breathing is slow and regular, and irregular sleep, in which the baby may jerk or grimace and breathing is often irregular. There are also two alert states: alert inactivity, where the infant is relatively quiet but the eyes are open and attentive, and alert activity, where the infant displays bursts of motor activity and may become fussy. The two remaining states are drowsiness and crying. Newborns typically spend about 70% of their time sleeping.

c. Developmental changes in infant states

As infants develop the amount of time they spend sleeping declines. Also, the proportion of time they spend in irregular sleep, or REM sleep, also declines. Newborns spend at least 50% of their sleeping hours in REM sleep, but by 6 months of age the proportion has decreased to only 25 to 30% of the total sleep time. Autostimulation theory is the most widely accepted explanation for why newborns spend so much of their time in REM sleep. According to this theory, REM sleep allows internal stimulation that promotes nervous system development. This theory is consistent with the finding that newborns who are actively stimulated while they are awake spend less time in REM sleep than infants who receive less stimulation while they are awake.

A baby's earliest cries are unlearned responses to discomfort. Babies cry most often during the first three months of life. After that the amount of crying decreases. Congenital problems are sometimes detectable by listening to an infant's cries. An analysis of crying during the first few weeks of life can be a meaningful diagnostic tool.

One concern that all new parents have is how to calm and soothe their newborn when he or she is fussy. Presenting a mild sucrose solution is often an effective means of calming a distressed newborn. Continuous, rhythmic stimulation will also often calm a restless or fussy baby. Finally, swaddling the baby in a blanket can also comfort a fussy infant.

Vocabulary Self-Test

Part I: For each of the following definitions provide the appropriate term. (Answers to this portion of the self-test are provided at the end of the chapter.)

1. ________________ Name given to the prenatal organism from the third through the eighth week after conception

2. ________________ The period of the birth process lasting from the first regular uterine contractions until the cervix is fully dilated

3. ________________ Inborn responses such as breathing, sucking, and swallowing that enable the newborn to adapt to the environment

4. ________________ External agents such as viruses, drugs, chemicals, and radiation that can harm a developing embryo or fetus

5. ________________ Term used to describe the strong affectionate ties that parents may feel toward their infant

6. ________________ B-complex vitamin that helps to prevent defects of the central nervous system

7. ________________ A lack of sufficient oxygen to the brain that may result in neurological damage or death

8. ________________ A theory proposing that REM sleep in infancy is a form of self-stimulation that helps the central nervous system to develop

9. ________________ The first phase of prenatal development, lasting from conception until the developing organism is firmly attached to the uterine wall

10. ________________ A synthetic hormone, formerly prescribed to prevent miscarriage, that can produce cervical cancer in adolescent female offspring and genital-tract abnormalities or sterility in males

11. ________________ Group of serious congenital problems commonly observed in the children of mothers who abuse alcohol during pregnancy

12. ________________ A blood protein that, when present in a fetus but not the mother, can cause the mother to produce antibodies

13. ________________ A newborn infant from birth to about 1 month of age

14. ________________ A quick assessment of the newborn's heart rate, respiration, colour, muscle tone, and reflexes that is used to gauge perinatal stress

15. ________________ A watertight membrane that develops from the trophoblast and surrounds the developing embryo, serving to regulate its temperature and cushion it against injuries

Part II: For each of the following terms provide the definition.

Age of Viability: ______________________________

____

Neonatal Behaviour Assessment Scale: ______________________________

____

Thalidomide: ______________________________

____

Period of the Embryo: ______________________________

____

Primitive Reflexes: ______________________________

____

Vernix: ______________________________

____

Cesarean Section: ______________________________

____

Preterm Baby: ______________________________

____

Second Stage of Labour: ______________________________

____

Respiratory Distress Syndrome: ______________________________

____

Chorion: ______________________________

____

Toxoplasmosis: ______________________________

____

Implantation: ______________________________

____

Placenta: ______________________________

____

Breech Birth: ______________________________

____

Short-Answer Study Questions

FROM CONCEPTION TO BIRTH

1. Identify the three stages of prenatal development, the major developmental milestones accomplished during each, and indicate the time span that each stage covers.

   a.

   b.

   c.

2. The outer layer of the blastocyst forms four major support structures that protect and nourish the developing embryo or fetus. Name each structure and explain its function.

   a.

   b.

   c.

   d.

3. The embryonic disk differentiates into three layers. Name each of these layers and state what each layer will eventually become.

   a.

   b.

   c.

4. Describe the process of sexual development that occurs during the prenatal period.

5. Describe fetal development during the second and third trimesters and explain what is meant by the term "age of viability."

ENVIRONMENTAL INFLUENCES ON PRENATAL DEVELOPMENT

6. Define the term "teratogen" and list seven generalizations about the effects of teratogens.

   A teratogen is:

   a.

   b.

   c.

   d.

   e.

   f.

   g.

7. Use the concept of sensitive period to explain why the developing baby is most vulnerable to the effects of teratogens during the embryonic stage of prenatal development.

8. Assume a pregnant woman is exposed to a teratogen during her pregnancy. For each time period listed, identify the structures that are most likely to be affected, and indicate the extent to which they are likely to be affected.

   Exposure during Week 3:

   Exposure during Week 5:

   Exposure during Week 8:

   Exposure during Week 16:

   Exposure during Week 25:

9. Alcoholic beverages now carry a government warning that states "Women should not drink alcoholic beverages during pregnancy because of the risk of birth defects." What types of defects have been associated with heavy alcohol consumption during pregnancy? What types of defects have been associated with social drinking during pregnancy?

   Heavy consumption:

   Social drinking:

10. Physicians now routinely advise pregnant women to stop smoking, at least during the pregnancy. What impact does exposure to cigarette smoke have on the developing embryo or fetus?

11. Maternal malnutrition can disrupt prenatal development. What is the likely developmental outcome if the mother is malnourished during the first trimester? What is the likely developmental outcome if the mother is malnourished during the third trimester?

   First trimester:

   Third trimester:

CHILDBIRTH AND THE PERINATAL ENVIRONMENT

12. Identify the three stages of childbirth and indicate what occurs during each stage.

   a.

   b.

   c.

13. Explain how the Neonatal Behavioural Assessment Scale (NBAS) differs from the Apgar test.

14. Explain how the Apgar test is used to assess a newborn's general physical condition and indicate the score that would be recorded for each of the following newborns.

    Apgar test:

    Baby P has no pulse and is not breathing. The infant is extremely pale and is limp. Apgar score:

    Baby R has a slow pulse and irregular breathing. The infant has weak muscle tone with no reflex response, and the extremities are blue. Apgar score:

    Baby H is crying and active. The baby is completely pink and the heart rate is 120 beats/minute. Apgar score:

15. What are the pros and cons associated with administering medications to the mother during the birth process?

16. Describe two alternatives to a standard hospital birth.

    a.

    b.

17. Discuss what research has shown with respect to the long-term impact of early emotional bonding between the newborn and the parents.

18. Describe postpartum depression and identify the factors that have been related to the development of postpartum depression.

BIRTH COMPLICATIONS

19. One potential birth complication is anoxia. Define anoxia and identify three conditions that might produce anoxia.

    Anoxia:

    a.

    b.

    c.

20. Explain the distinction between preterm and small-for-gestational-age infants.

21. Identify some of the short-term and long-term consequences of low birth weight.

THE NEWBORN'S READINESS FOR LIFE

22. Explain the difference between survival reflexes and primitive reflexes and identify two infant reflexes that would fall into each of these categories.

    a.

    b.

23. Identify the six states that occur in newborns and indicate approximately how many hours are spent in each state during a typical day.

    a.

    b.

    c.

    d.

    e.

    f.

24. Outline the developmental changes that occur in an infant's sleep patterns during the first six months.

Multiple-Choice Self-Test

For each of the following questions select the best alternative. (Answers and explanations for this self-test are provided at the end of the chapter.) Once you have selected your answer, provide a brief explanation for why the answer you selected is the best choice and why the remaining answers would not be correct.

1. Of the following, the substance that typically cannot pass through the placenta to the developing embryo is:

   a. oxygen
   b. maternal blood cells
   c. sugars, proteins, and fats
   d. viruses

   Rationale: ______________________________

   ____

2. The 24th week of pregnancy is often set as the legal upper limit for medical abortion. At this point in time, the milestone that is reached by the developing fetus is:

   a. the heart and circulatory system begin functioning.
   b. spontaneous movement is apparent for the first time
   c. sex differentiation and sex organ development is now completed
   d. the minimal age of viability has been reached

   Rationale: ______________________________

   ____

3. A preterm baby is:

   a. an infant who was born early
   b. an infant who is low birth weight
   c. a newborn to 1-month-old infant
   d. an infant who is about to be born

   Rationale: ______________________________

   ____

4. Teratogens are most likely to produce major structural abnormalities during:

   a. the first two weeks after conception
   b. the 2nd–8th weeks following conception
   c. the 12th–20th weeks following conception
   d. the last trimester of pregnancy

   Rationale: ______________________________

   ____

5. Sam and Nina are in the delivery room, waiting for the birth of their first child. The doctor tells them that Nina is 5 centimetres dilated. Nina is currently in:

   a. the first stage of labour
   b. the second stage of labour
   c. the third stage of labour
   d. the fourth stage of labour

   Rationale: ____

   ____

6. Margaret's newborn baby is crying loudly in the delivery room and has turned bright red all over. When a nurse attempts to extend the baby's leg the infant pulls away from the nurse. Based on this information it is likely that Margaret's newborn would score:

   a. 0 to 3 points on the Apgar scale
   b. 4 or 5 points on the Apgar scale
   c. 8 to 10 points on the Apgar scale
   d. 15 points (or more) on the Apgar scale

   Rationale: ____

   ____

7. Young infants will curl their toes under to a foot stroke. This reflexive reaction is an example of the:

   a. Moro reflex
   b. Babinski reflex
   c. rooting reflex
   d. palmar reflex

   Rationale: ____

   ____

8. Kashimira is lying in her crib. Her eyes open and close frequently, looking dull rather than bright when they are open. Kashimira's responses are generally slow, but when her father holds a bright red ball over the crib, she gets excited and becomes more active. Before Kashimira saw the ball, she was in a state of:

   a. alert activity
   b. alert inactivity
   c. irregular sleep
   d. drowsiness

   Rationale: ____

   ____

Activities and Projects Related to this Chapter

ACTIVITY 4-1

GIVING ADVICE ON PRENATAL AND POSTNATAL CARE—YOU BE THE EXPERT

INTRODUCTION: This activity relates to the material presented on factors influencing prenatal development, such as maternal diet, smoking, drug use, diseases, etc. Assume that you were asked to give a talk to a group of women over the age of 35. What advice could you give them regarding factors that might influence the course of their pregnancy? What advice would you give them regarding prenatal screening techniques? Try to think not just about what not to do, but also about how you can give advice that will help them make healthy choices for themselves and their babies.

RELATED REFERENCES

Aaronson, L. S., & MacNee, C. L. (1989). Tobacco, alcohol, and caffeine use during pregnancy. *Journal of Obstetrics, Gynecology, and Neonatal Nursing, 18,* 279–287.

Batstra, L., Neeleman, J., & Hadders-Algra, M. (2003). Can breast feeding modify the adverse effects of smoking during pregnancy on the child's cognitive development? *Journal of Epidemiology & Community Health, 57(6),* 403–404.

DiPietro, J.A. (2004). The role of prenatal maternal stress in child development. *Current Directions in Psychological Science, 13(2),* 71–74.

Einarson, A., Selby, P., & Koren, G. (2001). Abrupt discontinuation of psychotropic drugs during pregnancy: Fear of teratogenic risk and impact of counselling. *Journal of Psychiatry and Neuroscience, 26,* 44–48.

Fried, P.A., & Makin, J.E. (1987). Neonatal behavioural correlates of prenatal exposure to marijuana, cigarettes, and alcohol in a low risk population. *Neurotoxicology and Teratology, 9(1),* 1–7.

Kaemingk, K.L., Mulvaney, S., & Halverson, P.T. (2003). Learning following prenatal alcohol exposure: Performance on verbal and visual multitrial tasks. *Archives of Clinical Neuropsychology, 18(1),* 33–47.

Misri, S., Kostaras, D., & Kostaras, X. (2000). The use of selective serotonin reuptake inhibitors during pregnancy and lactation: Current knowledge. *Canadian Journal of Psychiatry, 45,* 285–287.

Moore, K. L. (1989). *Before we are born.* (3rd ed.). Philadelphia: Saunders.

Nelson, S., Lerner, E., & Needlman, R. (2004). Cocaine, anemia, and neurodevelopmental outcomes in children: A longitudinal study. *Journal of Developmental and Behavioral Pediatrics, 25(1),* 1–9.

O'Callaghan, F.V., O'Callaghan, M., & Najman, J.M. (2003). Maternal alcohol consumption during pregnancy and physical outcomes up to 5 years of age: A longitudinal study. *Early Human Development, 71(2),* 13–148.

Ornoy, A. (2002). The effects of alcohol and illicit drugs on the human embryo and fetus. *Israel Journal of Psychiatry and Related Sciences, 39(2),* 120–132.

Ramsay, M.C., & Reynolds, C.R. (2000). Does smoking by pregnant women influence IQ, birth weight, and developmental disabilities in their infants? A methodological review and multivariate analysis. *Neuropsychology Review, 10(1),* 1–40.

Weiss, S.J., Wilson, P., & Morrison, D. (2004). Maternal tactile stimulation and the neurodevelopment of low birth weight infants. *Infancy, 5(1),* 85–107.

ACTIVITY 4-2

EVERYDAY MEDICATIONS AND THEIR TERATOGENIC EFFECTS

INTRODUCTION: This activity relates to the material on the potentially harmful effects of over-the-counter and prescription medications on prenatal development. One purpose is to increase your awareness of the potential for harm to the fetus from a pregnant woman's ingestion of medications. Most gynecologists caution pregnant women to not take any kind of drug without first consulting them. Why? What's the big deal? How can a medication that is not harmful to the mother, but therapeutic, cause damage to a developing fetus? Reasons include:

1. The dose that is therapeutic for a 61-kilogram (135-pound) woman may be a massive overdose for a developing embryo or fetus.

2. The mother is not undergoing organogenesis (differentiation of the organ systems) but the fetus is.

3. The placenta and immature fetus may be unable to convert the medication into a harmless or therapeutic substance.

4. The mother's physiology may be altered, compromising the intrauterine environment.

INSTRUCTIONS: Go through your medicine cabinet and look for those drugs (prescription and non-prescription) that have a warning about taking them when pregnant or nursing. This warning may appear on the bottle, the package insert, or on the original box. Include such medications as aspirin, antibiotics, birth control pills, allergy medicines, cold or flu medications, acne medications, antidepressants, nicotine patches, diuretics, blood pressure medication, PMS drugs, etc. Write down each medication and its teratogenic effects. (Note—if you do not take any medications, visit a friend who does and ask to read the labels, or go to a drug store and read the labels on several over-the-counter drugs.) Put together a list of at least five medications and their teratogenic effects.

ACTIVITY 4-3

GIVING ADVICE ON PRENATAL AND POSTNATAL CARE—YOU BE THE EXPERT

INTRODUCTION: This activity relates to the material presented on Sudden Infant Death syndrome. Assume that you were asked to create an advertisement (such as a TV commercial or poster) aimed at educating caretakers on the factors influencing the incidence of SIDs. What information would you include in the advertisement? Do some research on available programs, such as the Back to Sleep program, and their sponsors. Have such programs been effective?

RELATED REFERENCES

Gordon, A.E., El Ahmer, O.R., & Chan, R. (2002). Why is smoking a risk factor for sudden infant death syndrome? *Child: Care, health & development, 28(suppl1),* 23–25.

Howard, L.M., & Hannam, S. (2003). Sudden infant death syndrome and psychiatric disorders. *British Journal of Psychiatry, 182(5),* 379–380.

Kelmanson, I.A., Groswasser, J., & Franco, P. (2003). Sighs during sleep in future victims of sudden infant deaths. *Sleep & Hypnosis, 5(2),* 83–88.

Riese, M.L. (2003). Newborn temperament and sudden infant death syndrome: A comparison of victims and their cotwins. *Journal of Applied Developmental Psychology, 23(6),* 643–653.

ACTIVITY 4-4

RESEARCH LOCAL BIRTHING PRACTICES

INTRODUCTION: This activity relates to the material presented on childbirth and alternative birthing practices. Contact a few maternity wards in local hospitals. Ask the nurses or associated prenatal instructors about the common practices of birth, birthing positions, medications, complications, etc. Determine if there are differences amongst hospitals or birthing centres. Secondly, you may even research the statistics on these practices across Canada through the Internet and see if they are affected by regional factors and, if so, why. A third method of collecting data would be to informally interview people of various ages and ethnicities and see if there are any historical or cultural differences. Document your findings and relate them to the information you have learned from your text and instructor.

ANSWERS TO SELF-TESTS

VOCABULARY SELF-TEST (The answers may be found on the pages in parentheses.)

1. embryo (p. 109)
2. first stage of labour (p. 127)
3. survival reflexes (pp. 140-141)
4. teratogens (p. 114)
5. emotional bonding (p. 133)
6. folic acid (p. 124)
7. anoxia (p. 135)
8. autostimulation theory (p. 143)
9. germinal period (p. 109)
10. diethylstilbestrol (DES) (p. 119)
11. fetal alcohol syndrome (p. 119)
12. RH factor (p. 135)
13. neonate (p. 125)
14. Apgar test (p. 129)
15. amnion (p. 110)

MULTIPLE-CHOICE SELF-TEST (The answers may be found on the pages in parentheses.)

1. **b** (p. 110) The bloodstreams of the mother and the embryo/fetus are separated by a semipermeable membrane in the placenta and they do not mix. Oxygen (a) and sugars, proteins, and fats (c) must cross the placenta if the embryo/fetus is to grow and develop properly. Viruses (d) can also cross the placenta, and when this occurs (especially early in the pregnancy) fetal development may be disrupted.

2. **d** (p. 113) Sometime after the 22nd week of pregnancy the fetus is sufficiently developed and it is possible for it to survive outside the uterus. The heart and circulatory system (a) begin functioning during the embryonic period. The fetus is moving (b), and the sex organs have developed (c) by the 12th week.

3. **a** (p. 136) An infant who is born early is called a preterm baby. Babies who are low birth weight (b) may be small-for-gestational-age babies if they are light for their gestational age. Neonate is the term used to refer to any newborn infant (less than 1 month old) (c). An infant who is about to be born (d) is called a fetus.

4. **b** (pp. 114–116) The developing embryo/fetus is most susceptible to the effects of teratogens when differentiation is occurring most rapidly (weeks 2–12). During the first two weeks (a) implantation has not yet occurred, therefore there is no placenta and teratogens cannot directly impact the blastocyst. Teratogens can still affect the developing embryo/fetus after the 12th week (c or d), but they are not likely to produce structural abnormalities since all the major structures have formed by the 12th week.

5. **a** (pp. 127–128) During the first stage, contractions cause the cervix to dilate to 10 cm (4 in). The baby travels along the birth canal during the second stage of labour (b). During the third stage (c) the placenta is expelled from the uterus. There is no fourth stage (d) in the delivery process.

6. **c** (p. 129) A baby who is crying, who is bright red, and who has good muscle tone is healthy and will probably score high on the Apgar scale. The baby is crying and has turned bright red all over, giving an Apgar score of at least 4 (eliminates alternative a). In addition, the infant pulls away, adding 2 more points (at least 6 points total) (this eliminates alternative b). The maximum score on the Apgar is 10 points (eliminating alternative d).

7. **b** (pp. 140–141) The Babinski reflex is evident when infants curl their toes under to a foot stroke. The Moro reflex is a startle reflex (a). The rooting reflex (c) occurs when infants turn their head and mouth toward a touch. The palmar reflex (d) occurs when infants reflexively close their fingers around an object placed in their palm.

8. **d** (p. 142) Opening and closing her eyes and an unfocused (dull) look in her eyes would indicate Kashimira is drowsy. With alert activity (a) her eyes would be bright and her arms and legs would likely be moving. With alert inactivity (b) her eyes would be bright and she would be scanning her environment, but not moving her extremities. Irregular sleep (c) is REM sleep, when an infant's eyes are closed and the eyes dart back and forth beneath the closed lids.

Chapter Five

The Physical Self: Development of the Brain, the Body, and Motor Skills

Learning Objectives

By the time you have finished this chapter you should be able to:

1. Outline the typical pattern of changes in height and weight from infancy through the late teens.
2. Describe the cephalocaudal and proximodistal trends in physical development and explain the typical pattern of growth when these trends temporarily reverse just before puberty.
3. Describe general skeletal and muscular development between infancy and adulthood.
4. Describe the development of the brain and nervous system in terms of neural and synaptic changes and myelinization.
5. Explain what is meant by plasticity of the brain and describe evidence for experiential effects on neural development.
6. Describe the developmental course of cerebral lateralization.
7. Compare and contrast three possible explanations for the sequencing and timing of early motor development.
8. Describe the course of the developmental changes that occur in voluntary reaching and manipulatory skills.
9. Describe the continuing developmental changes that occur in gross motor skills, fine motor coordination, and reaction times during childhood and adolescence.
10. Describe the physical changes associated with puberty.
11. Describe the general reactions of adolescents to the physical changes associated with puberty.
12. Discuss the nutritional problems that can become a concern during the adolescent years.
13. Discuss the psychological impact of early versus late maturation for both sexes.
14. Describe the impact of biological factors such as genotype, maturation, and hormones on physical growth and development.
15. Describe the impact of environmental factors such as nutrition, illness, and emotional stress on physical growth and development.

Chapter Outline and Summary

1. An overview of maturation and growth

a. Changes in height and weight

Babies double their birth weight in the first six months and triple it by the end of the first year. By the age of 2 infants are approximately half their final adult height and have quadrupled their birth weight. From age 2 until puberty children grow approximately 5 centimetres per year and gain approximately 3 kilograms per year. This slow, steady growth becomes a "growth spurt" when the child reaches puberty. During each year of the two- to three-year growth spurt the young adolescent will gain between about 4.5 and 7 kilograms and grow 5 to 10 centimetres in height.

b. Changes in body proportions

During childhood physical development follows two general trends: cephalocaudal and proximodistal. Cephalocaudal means that growth proceeds from the head down, with the top of the body initially growing more quickly than the legs. During the prenatal period the head grew most rapidly; over the first year the trunk will show the most rapid growth, and from the first birthday until adolescence the legs will grow most rapidly. Proximodistal means that growth proceeds from the centre of the body outward toward the extremities. Throughout infancy and childhood the arms and legs continue to grow faster than the hands and feet.

Both these growth trends reverse just before puberty. During adolescence the trunk again grows faster than the rest of the body, and the hands and feet reach adult proportions before the arms and legs or trunk reach their adult proportions.

c. Skeletal development

At birth, most of the bones are a source of blood cells. As well, most of the infant's bones are soft, pliable, and difficult to break. There are fewer bones in the feet and hands and the bones are less well connected than they will be in adolescence. Skeletal maturation shows the same cephalocaudal trend that was evident in general growth. The skull and hands mature before the legs and feet.

d. Muscular development

Infants are born with all the muscle fibres they will ever have, but the muscle fibres are immature and account for only 18 to 24% of the newborn's body weight. Muscular development also follows the cephalocaudal and proximodistal pattern of growth, and by the time individuals reach their mid-20s muscle tissue will account for 40% of total body weight in males and 24% of total body weight in females.

e. Variations in physical development

There are significant individual differences in the rate of growth and there are also meaningful cultural and subcultural variations in physical growth and development. Generally, individuals from Asia, South America, and Africa tend to be smaller than North Americans, Northern Europeans, and Australians. Also, Asian-American and African-American children tend to mature faster than European-American and European children.

2. Development of the brain

In newborns the brain weighs approximately 450 grams, 25% of its final adult weight; by the age of 2 the brain has increased to nearly 1350 grams, or 75% of its final adult weight.

a. Neural development and plasticity

Neurons are the basic cells that make up the brain and spinal cord. All the neurons a person will ever have are already formed by the end of the second trimester of the pregnancy.

The brain growth spurt that occurs during the last trimester of pregnancy and the first two years of life occurs because glial cells are developing and neurons are maturing, not because new neurons are being created. In young infants the brain shows a remarkable level of plasticity. This simply means that the brain is responsive to the effects of experience. During the first year of life the infant actually has more neurons and forms more neural connections than are found in the adult brain. Neurons that do not successfully connect to other neurons die, and synaptic connections that are not stimulated disappear through synaptic pruning. Differences in synaptic organization can be seen as a function of age. All this helps to make a more efficient system.

b. Brain differentiation and growth

At birth the most highly developed areas of the brain are the brain stem and midbrain, which control states of consciousness, reflexes, and vital biological functions. The first areas of the cerebrum to mature are the primary motor and sensory areas. By 6 months of age, the primary motor areas of the cerebral cortex have developed sufficiently to direct most of the infant's movements. Inborn reflexes such as the palmar grasp and the Babinski reflex disappear as the motor cortex develops and voluntary control of motor responses develops.

Myelinization involves the formation of a myelin sheath around axons. This waxy coating insulates the neuron and helps to speed the transmission of neural impulses. The pathways between the brain and the skeletal muscles myelinate following a cephalocaudal and proximodistal pattern. As the neurons are myelinated the child will become capable of increasingly complex motor activities. Myelinization proceeds rapidly in the first few years of life but some areas of the brain, such as the reticular formation and frontal cortex, are not fully myelinated until late adolescence or early adulthood.

The cerebrum consists of two hemispheres that are connected by the corpus callosum. The two hemispheres appear identical, but each hemisphere controls different specialized functions. This means that functions such as language and spatial processing are lateralized within the cortex. Cerebral lateralization also involves a preference for using one side of the body more than the other. The corpus callosum plays an important role in integrating these lateralized functions.

During adolescence myelinization of higher brain centres continues, which may increase attention span and speed of neural processing. In addition, reorganizations of neural circuits in the prefrontal cortex continue until at least the early adult years, bringing about increases in the ability to engage in strategic planning.

3. Motor development

Motor skills over the first two years evolve in a definite sequence. Although there is wide variability among children, the majority of children (more than 50%) can roll over at about 3 months of age, can sit without support at about 6 months of age, and walk without assistance just past their first birthday.

a. Basic trends in locomotor development

Motor skill development follows the same two trends as growth and myelinization: cephalocaudal and proximodistal. Children gain control of their arms before they have good control of their legs, and they use their entire hand for grasping before they learn to use their fingers for grasping.

There are three possible explanations for the sequencing and timing of early motor development. The maturational viewpoint suggests that motor development is the unfolding of a genetically programmed sequence of events. One supporting piece of evidence comes from cross-cultural studies that show infants from around the world progress through the major motor milestones in the same sequence. The experiential viewpoint suggests that opportunities to practise motor skills also play an important role in motor skill development. This view suggests that for the development of motor skills, maturation is necessary (skills won't emerge until the skeletal and muscle systems have matured sufficiently) but not sufficient (skills will not emerge in physically mature infants unless the opportunity to practise those skills is present). The dynamical systems theory suggests that motor skills emerge because goal-driven infants constantly recombine actions they have mastered into new and more complex action systems that help them achieve new objectives.

b. *Fine motor development*

Voluntary reaching begins with prereaching, which involves uncoordinated swipes at objects that are in the infant's visual field. In 2-month-old infants reaching skills appear to regress. This occurs because reflexive responses are disappearing; soon reaching will be under voluntary control. Three-month-old infants show voluntary reaching and are able to make corrections as they reach for an object in their visual field. Interestingly, 3-month-old infants are just as successful at reaching accurately for objects they can only hear (in the dark) as they are at reaching for objects they can see. By 5 months of age infants can successfully reach for and touch (1) stationary illuminated objects that darken until invisible as the infants reach for them, and (2) glowing objects moving in the dark, even though they are unable to see their own hand. This suggests that early reaching is guided by proprioceptive information rather than by vision.

By the age of 4 to 5 months infants have lost the reflexive palmar grasp and use an ulnar grasp to hold objects. This is a clumsy, claw-like grasp that uses the hand rather than the fingers to hold the object in question. Toward the end of the first year the pincer grasp emerges and infants are able to use their fingers to turn knobs and dials and to pick up tiny objects using only the thumb and forefinger.

c. *Psychological implications of early motor development*

As motor skills develop they permit the infant to engage in pleasurable forms of social interaction with others. Also, achieving various motor milestones may foster perceptual development. Mobile infants are better than infants of the same age who are not mobile at searching for hidden objects. Self-produced movement helps infants and toddlers to orient themselves in space and develop an understanding of distance and three-dimensional space.

d. *Beyond infancy: Motor development in childhood and adolescence*

Throughout the preschool years motor skills continue to develop. Three-year-old children are able to jump off the floor using both feet; 4-year-old children can hop on one foot and catch a large ball using both hands; and by 5 years of age children often have sufficient balance to ride a bicycle. Continuing through the school years, children run faster and throw balls farther with each passing year.

There are nearly no differences in physical abilities between boys and girls until puberty, at which point, in contrast to girls, boys continue to improve on tests of large-muscle activities. Research suggests that this sex difference may be partly attributable to differences in biology and partly to differences in socialization.

Eye–hand coordination is improving at the same time. Three-year-old children have difficulty buttoning buttons or tying laces; by age 5 these tasks are easy for the child to perform. As children mature reaction times will also become quicker.

4. Puberty: The physical transition from child to adult

a. *The adolescent growth spurt*

"Growth spurt" refers to the rapid gains in height and weight that occur at the beginning of adolescence. Girls typically experience their growth spurt between the ages of $10^1/_2$ and 13, with peak growth occurring at age 12. Boys typically experience their growth spurt between the ages of 13 and 16, with peak growth occurring at age 14. During this time girls will also experience a widening of their hips and boys will experience a noticeable broadening of the shoulders.

b. *Sexual maturation*

The reproductive system typically matures at the same time as the adolescent growth spurt. In females "breast buds" may be the first outward sign of puberty, followed by the appearance of pubic hair. As the height spurt occurs, the breasts grow rapidly and the sex organs begin to mature. At about the age of $12^1/_2$ girls in Western societies typically experience menarche. It may take 12 to 18 months after menarche for ovulation to begin. In the year following menarche, breasts complete their development and underarm hair appears.

In males enlargement of the testes may be the first outward sign of puberty, followed by the appearance of pubic hair. Spermarche occurs at about the age of 13.4 years. The penis will be fully developed by the age of $14^1/_2$ to 15, and at this point most boys are capable of fathering a child. Somewhat later, facial and body hair will appear.

Over the past 100 years there has been a secular trend toward earlier maturation. However, among industrialized nations this trend continues at a much slower rate, and the trend toward earlier maturation is now occurring in the more prosperous countries among nonindustrialized countries. The reasons for this secular trend seem to be better nutrition and advances in medical care.

5. The psychological effects of puberty

a. *General reactions to physical changes*

Girls are often concerned that they are growing too tall or too fat, and they may try dieting in an attempt to match the "feminine ideal" of slimness. Girls who perceive that they are fat or who have poor body esteem may have relatively low self-esteem. Boys typically have a more positive body image and are more likely to welcome the weight gains that accompany puberty.

b. *Social impacts of pubertal changes*

In many nonindustrialized societies puberty is taken as a sign that the child has become an adult, and the transition is often marked in formal rites of passage. In North American families parent–child conflicts may increase during puberty, although these conflicts generally decline during later adolescence.

c. *Does timing of puberty matter?*

Boys who mature early typically enjoy a number of social advantages over boys who mature late. Early-maturing males are likely to receive social recognition from adults and peers for their athletic capabilities. In addition, they may be granted increased privileges and responsibilities. On the other hand, late-maturing males are more likely to be anxious and feel somewhat socially inadequate. In adulthood, early-maturing males tend to remain more confident and sociable, but they also tend to be more rigid and conforming when compared to late-maturing males.

Girls who mature early tend to be less popular than their later-maturing classmates, and they are more likely to report symptoms of anxiety and depression. As young adults, early-maturing females are no less well-adjusted than their later-maturing peers.

6. Causes and correlates of physical development

a. *Biological mechanisms*

The unique combination of genes we inherit from our parents (our genotype) influences our physical growth and development. Our rate of maturation is also genetically influenced.

Hormones have an influence on development. Thyroxine is essential for proper development of the brain and nervous system. Growth hormone stimulates the rapid growth and development of body cells. At puberty, ovaries in females begin to produce more estrogen, and testes in males begin to produce more testosterone. Once these sex hormones reach a critical level, the pituitary gland begins to secrete more growth hormone and this increase seems to be responsible for the adolescent growth spurt. Finally, androgen plays a role in muscle and bone maturation in both sexes.

b. *Environmental influences*

Diet is one of the most important environmental influences on human growth and development. Children who experience short-term growth deficits due to malnutrition or undernutrition will typically experience a period of catch-up growth that returns them to their genetically programmed growth trajectory. However, prolonged undernutrition during the first five years of life can seriously retard brain growth and permanently stunt physical growth.

Marasmus and kwashiorkor are two nutritional diseases that children may experience if they are severely undernourished. Children who consume too few calories and too little protein may develop marasmus. They will become very frail, and as growth stops body tissues begin to waste away. If calorie consumption is sufficient but the diet lacks sufficient protein, children may develop kwashiorkor. The face and legs will thin, but the abdomen will swell with water.

In Western industrialized countries marasmus and kwashiorkor are rare, but many children experience vitamin and mineral deficiencies. Iron deficiency anemia makes children inattentive and listless, retards their growth rate, and is associated with poor motor and intellectual development. These motor and intellectual deficits are hard to overcome, even when the anemia is corrected through dietary supplements.

Eating disorders are much more common among teenage girls than among teenage boys or among older women. Anorexia nervosa is a potentially fatal eating disorder that may affect up to 5% of adolescent females. Bulimia is another serious eating disorder that is more common than anorexia and may affect up to 3% of young Canadian women. For men, an eating disorder may take the form of perceiving the self to be underdeveloped.

Overnutrition is another nutritional problem that has several long-term consequences. Children who are obese face an increased risk of diabetes, high blood pressure, and heart disease. They may also find it difficult to make friends, and their peer relationships may suffer. There is evidence that the body mass of Canadian children has been increasing steadily over the past two decades. This may be due in part to increases in lifestyle choices that promote sedentary behaviours.

When children receive adequate nourishment, common childhood illnesses have little impact on normal growth and development. However, children who are moderately to severely undernourished may have their growth permanently stunted by common diseases of childhood.

Otherwise healthy children who experience high levels of stress or inadequate affection may show signs of failure-to-thrive syndrome. Nonorganic failure to thrive is a disorder that generally appears in the first 18 months of life. Infants with nonorganic failure to thrive appear to waste away. One factor that may contribute to the onset of this disorder is impatience and hostility in the primary caregivers.

Another growth-related disorder is deprivation dwarfism, which appears between the ages of 2 and 15. Children with this disorder show dramatically reduced rates of growth, even though they do not appear malnourished. These children appear to lack positive involvement with their primary caregivers. This emotional deprivation depresses the production of growth hormone and results in slow physical growth.

Vocabulary Self-Test

Part I: For each of the following definitions provide the appropriate term. (Answers to this portion of the self-test are provided at the end of the chapter.)

1. ________________	The highest brain centre; includes both hemispheres of the brain and the fibres that connect the two hemispheres
2. ________________	A hormone produced by the thyroid gland that is essential for normal growth of the brain and body
3. ________________	Nerve cells that nourish neurons and encase them in insulating sheaths of myelin
4. ________________	A sequence of physical maturation and growth that proceeds from the head to the tail
5. ________________	Sensory information from the muscles, tendons, and joints that helps locate the position of one's body in space
6. ________________	An infant growth disorder, caused by lack of attention and affection, that causes growth to slow dramatically or stop
7. ________________	The connective space between one nerve cell and another
8. ________________	Male sex hormone, produced by the testes, that is responsible for male sexual maturation
9. ________________	The point at which a person reaches sexual maturity and is physically capable of fathering or conceiving a child
10. ________________	Formation of connections among neurons
11. ________________	A growth-retarding disease affecting children who receive enough calories, but little if any protein
12. ________________	A grasp in which the thumb is used in opposition to the fingers, enabling an infant to become more dexterous at lifting objects
13. ________________	The specialization of brain functions in the left and the right cerebral hemispheres
14. ________________	A theory that views motor skills as active reorganizations of previously mastered capabilities, undertaken to find more effective ways of exploring the environment or satisfying other objectives
15. ________________	A trend in industrialized societies toward earlier maturation and greater body size, when compared to the past generations

Part II: For each of the following terms provide the definition.

Adolescent Growth Spurt: ______________________________

____

Corpus Callosum: ______________________________

____

Estrogen: ______________________________

____

Menarche: ______________________________

____

Proximodistal Development: ______________________________

____

Deprivation Dwarfism: ______________________________

____

Cerebral Cortex: ______________________________

____

Pituitary: ______________________________

____

Plasticity: ______________________________

____

Obese: ______________________________

____

Ulnar Grasp: ______________________________

____

Myelinization: ______________________________

____

Rites of Passage: ______________________________

____

Marasmus: ______________________________

____

Skeletal Age: ______________________________

____

Short-Answer Study Questions

AN OVERVIEW OF MATURATION AND GROWTH

1. Explain what is meant by the cephalocaudal trend in physical development and provide an example that illustrates this trend.

2. Explain what is meant by the proximodistal trend in physical development and provide an example that illustrates this trend.

3. Describe the sex differences in skeletal ossification that are present at birth, and compare these to sex differences that are present at age 12.

4. For both sexes, compare the composition of muscle fibres at birth with the composition of muscle fibres in the mid-20s.

DEVELOPMENT OF THE BRAIN

5. Identify two processes that contribute to the increase in brain weight during the brain growth spurt.

   a.

   b.

6. Explain what is meant by the term "synaptic pruning" and discuss what this process implies about brain plasticity.

7. Outline the basic pattern of myelinization and explain how the pattern of myelinization is reflected in motor skill development and coordination.

8. Explain what is meant by cerebral lateralization, and outline some basic developmental trends in lateralization.

MOTOR DEVELOPMENT

9. List three possible explanations for the sequencing and timing of early motor development and briefly summarize each of these views.

   a.

   b.

   c.

10. Outline the typical developmental sequence of voluntary reaching and identify the cues that are used to guide early reaching.

11. Outline the typical developmental sequence of manipulatory skills.

12. Compare and contrast typical motor development in 3-year-olds, 4-year-olds, and 5-year-olds.

    3-year-olds:

    4-year-olds:

    5-year-olds:

13. Discuss possible reasons why there has been a trend over the last century for infants to master certain motor skills at earlier ages (e.g., walking at an earlier age than documented as a norm a century ago).

PUBERTY: THE PHYSICAL TRANSITION FROM CHILD TO ADULT

14. Outline the physical changes that occur at puberty for males and females, and note the typical timing of these changes.

    Males:

    Females:

THE PSYCHOLOGICAL EFFECTS OF PUBERTY

15. Describe the typical impact of maturing "off schedule" for early-maturing males, late-maturing males, and early-maturing females.

    Early-maturing males:

    Late-maturing males:

    Early-maturing females:

CAUSES AND CORRELATES OF PHYSICAL DEVELOPMENT

16. Identify which glands produce each of the following hormones, and describe how each hormone affects growth and development.

    Thyroxine:

    Growth Hormone:

    Estrogen:

    Testosterone:

    Androgen:

17. What is the typical developmental outcome for children who experience short-term or mild undernutrition?

18. Contrast marasmus and kwashiorkor in terms of their causes and their outward physical symptoms.

Marasmus:

Kwashiorkor:

19. What is the typical developmental outcome for children who experience prolonged iron deficiency?

20. Describe two eating disorders that often emerge during adolescence. How prevalent is each of these disorders?

a.

b.

21. Identify two ways in which parents may contribute to the development of obesity in their children.

a.

b.

22. Contrast nonorganic failure to thrive and deprivation dwarfism in terms of their causes and their outward physical symptoms.

Nonorganic failure to thrive:

Deprivation Dwarfism:

Multiple-Choice Self-Test

For each of the following questions select the best alternative. (Answers and explanations for this self-test are provided at the end of the chapter.) Once you have selected your answer, provide a brief explanation for why the answer you selected is the best choice and why the remaining answers would not be correct.

1. Of the following, the one that would be most consistent with the cephalocaudal trend of physical development would be earlier development of:

   a. the feet than the hands
   b. the trunk than the arms
   c. the head than the legs
   d. the arms than the trunk

   Rationale: ____________________

   ____

2. Nerve cells that nourish neurons and encase them in insulating sheets of myelin are called:

   a. synapses
   b. neurotransmitters
   c. corpus callosum
   d. glia cells

   Rationale: ____________________

   ____

3. Current thinking (e.g., William Greenough) on the "plasticity" of the young child's brain attributes its plasticity to:

   a. the rapid increase in the number of neurons during infancy
   b. incomplete myelinization early in life
   c. an excess of neurons and synapses early in life
   d. maturation of the neurons in the corpus callosum

   Rationale: ____________________

   ____

4. Cerebral lateralization refers to:

   a. the fact that the two halves of the brain control different functions
   b. the encasement of neural connections in a waxy insulation
   c. an impairment in the ability to read
   d. the fibres that connect the two halves of the brain

   Rationale: ____________________

   ____

5. Infants and children show earlier motor and muscle control of activities involving the neck and upper extremities than the legs. This sequence of maturation is an example of:

   a. the role of plasticity in early development
   b. the role of lateralization in development
   c. the proximodistal trend in development
   d. the cephalocaudal trend in development

   Rationale: ____

   ____

6. Late maturation is often initially:

   a. a social advantage for boys and a social disadvantage for girls
   b. a social advantage for both boys and girls
   c. a social disadvantage for boys and a social advantage for girls
   d. a social disadvantage for both boys and girls

   Rationale: ____

   ____

7. The greater muscle and bone development that occurs in males than in females has been attributed to:

   a. thyroxine
   b. growth hormone
   c. testosterone
   d. adrenal androgens

   Rationale: ____

   ____

8. The illness that is the result of a diet that supplies insufficient calories and protein is:

   a. anemia
   b. marasmus
   c. kwashiorkor
   d. anorexia nervosa

   Rationale: ____

   ____

Activities and Projects Related to this Chapter

ACTIVITY 5-1a

MY LOOKS AND MY PHYSICAL CAPABILITIES

INTRODUCTION: This activity relates to the material in Chapter 5 on the psychological implications of maturation. "Ho-hum, boring" is the reaction of most people when they open up a text to a chapter on physical development. "So kids grow and they get stronger and they lose and gain teeth and they spurt at adolescence ... so?" The "so" is that what is going on physically does matter a great deal to the person undergoing the development. The first couple of loose teeth are very significant events to the child losing those teeth. The child may talk about little else for days, may be very concerned about losing a piece of herself and may not want to give up the tooth for the tooth fairy, may be very excited about reaching this milestone that indicates "I'm getting pretty grownup," etc. Similarly, not being able to make it across the monkey bars is very significant to the child who cannot do it. Being able to do the best or worst cartwheel in the class is very salient/significant to the child doing it. Being the first or last in your grade to wear a bra is very significant to the girls who are first or last. These are just a few examples of changes and abilities that can affect how others react to a child and how that child feels about himself or herself.

The purpose of this activity is to bring up feelings—not just the descriptions—associated with your appearance and physical capabilities as a child and now. Reading Chapter 5 will be anything but "ho-hum" when you can look at the topic from the perspective of how physical growth and development affect the individual doing the growing and developing.

INSTRUCTIONS: Write a narrative about how you perceived yourself and felt about your LOOKS and your PHYSICAL CAPABILITIES at each of the following times in your life:

a) elementary school years

b) middle school/junior high school years

c) high school years

d) now

REFERENCES OF INTEREST

Eaton, W.O., McKeen, N.A., & Campbell, D.W. (2001). The waxing and waning of movement: Implications for psychological development. *Developmental Review, 21*, 205–223.

Lee, K., & Chen, L. (1996). The development of metacognitive knowledge of basic motor skill: Walking. *Journal of Genetic Psychology, 157(3),* 361–375.

Poudevigne, M.S., O'Connor, P.J., & Laing, E.M. (2003). Body images of 4 to 8-year-old girls at the outset of their first artistic gymnastics class. *International Journal of Eating Disorders, 34(2),* 244–250.

Soubhi, H., Raina, P., & Kohen, D. (2004). Social and behavioral predictors of childhood injury in Canada. *American Journal of Health Behavior, 28(5)*, 397–409.

ACTIVITY 5-1b

MY LOOKS AND MY SELF-ESTEEM

INTRODUCTION: This activity relates to the material in Chapter 5 and in Chapter 12 on the development of self-esteem. Discuss the recent findings that boys and girls are becoming more and more concerned about their body image at earlier ages. In fact, preteens are now called "tweens" due to their apparent increased sophistication. You could discuss the impact of the secular trend on development, but try and think of some socialization factors that might be at play. How has the media played a role? Have tweens been the target of consumer marketing? If so, how would that affect their body images? Do you think this trend in concern for body image will continue?

RELATED REFERENCES

Murnen, S.K., Smolak, L., Mills, J.A., & Good, L. (2003). Thin, sexy women and strong, muscular men: Grade-school children's responses to objectified images of women and men. *Sex Roles, 49 (9/10)*, 427–437.

Thelen, M.H., Powell, A.L., Lawrence, C., & Kuhnert, M.E. (1992). Eating and body image concerns among children. *Journal of Clinical Child Psychology, 21 (1)*, 41–46.

REFERENCES OF INTEREST

Krahnstoever Davison, K., Markey, C.N., & Birch, L.L. (2003). A longitudinal examination of patterns of girls' weight concerns and body dissatisfaction from ages 5 to 9 years. *International Journal of Eating Disorders, 33(3)*, 320–332.

Mendelson, M.J., Mendelson, B.K., & Andrews, J. (2000). Self-esteem, body esteem, and body-mass in late adolescence: Is a competence x importance model needed? *Journal of Applied Developmental Psychology, 21 (3)*, 249–266.

Walker, L.L.M., Gately, P.J., & Bewick, B.M. (2003). Children's weight-loss camps: Psychological benefit or jeopardy? *International Journal of Obesity and Related Metabolic Disorders, 27(6)*, 748–754.

Wardle, J., Watters, R., & Wardle, J. (2004). Sociocultural influences on attitudes to weight and eating: Results of a natural experiment. *International Journal of Eating Disorders, 35(4)*, 589–596.

ACTIVITY 5-2

PUBERTY: ITS TIMING, HOW IT IS EXPERIENCED, AND ITS RELATION TO BODY IMAGE, DIETING, AND BODY BUILDING

INTRODUCTION: This activity relates to the material on puberty and is designed to illustrate the collection and use of data to provide information about variations in (a) the age of onset of puberty, (b) the experience of adolescence, and (c) the impact of puberty on body image and decisions about dieting and body building. Your name will not be used. The data will be used only in summary form (i.e., summarized across your classmates).

Answer the following questions and record the code numbers that correspond to your answers on the Scantron sheet provided by your instructor. Use of Scantron sheets allows for machine scoring. Histograms can then be generated for each item. The Scantron line to be used for each item is indicated in italics.

Gender:

	Female	Male
On Scantron mark line 1:	*(A)*	*(B)*

How old were you when you went through your growth spurt during adolescence?

	9	10	11	12	13
On Scantron mark line 2:	*(A)*	*(B)*	*(C)*	*(D)*	*(E)*
	14	15	16	17	18
On Scantron mark line 3:	*(A)*	*(B)*	*(C)*	*(D)*	*(E)*
	19	20	don't know		
On Scantron mark line 4:	*(A)*	*(B)*	*(C)*		

What do you think is the normal age for girls to go through puberty?

	9	10	11	12	13
On Scantron mark line 5:	*(A)*	*(B)*	*(C)*	*(D)*	*(E)*
	14	15	16	17	18
On Scantron mark line 6:	*(A)*	*(B)*	*(C)*	*(D)*	*(E)*
	19	20	don't know		
On Scantron mark line 7:	*(A)*	*(B)*	*(C)*		

What do you think is the normal age for boys to go through puberty?

	9	10	11	12	13
On Scantron mark line 8:	*(A)*	*(B)*	*(C)*	*(D)*	*(E)*
	14	15	16	17	18
On Scantron mark line 9:	*(A)*	*(B)*	*(C)*	*(D)*	*(E)*
	19	20	don't know		
On Scantron mark line 10:	*(A)*	*(B)*	*(C)*		

Was your own puberty:

On Scantron mark line 11:

A a lot earlier than your peers
B somewhat earlier than your peers
C about average
D somewhat later than your peers
E a lot later than your peers

Do you remember your adolescence as:

On Scantron mark line 12:

A a very painful time psychologically
B having some difficult times, but not too bad
C some difficult times and some very good times
D mostly pretty positive
E a very happy time

Questions about dieting:

Have you ever been "on a diet?"

On Scantron mark line 13: *(A) yes (B) no*

If yes, how many times have you dieted in the past 5 years?

On Scantron mark line 14:

A not in the past 5 years
B once or twice
C two to five times
D six to ten times
E ten times or more

What was the youngest age at which you ever consciously dieted?

On Scantron mark line 15:

A younger than age 8
B age 8 or 9
C age 10 to 12
D age 13 to 15
E age 16 to 18

Questions about body building:

Have you ever lifted weights or exercised to build muscles?

On Scantron mark line 16: *(A) yes (B) no*

If yes, how many times have you undertaken body-building programs in the past 5 years?

On Scantron mark line 17:

A not in the past 5 years
B once or twice
C two to five times
D six to ten times
E ten times or more

What was the youngest age at which you lifted weights or exercised to build muscles?

On Scantron mark line 18:

A younger than age 8
B age 8 or 9
C age 10 to 12
D age 13 to 15
E age 16 to 18

ANSWERS TO SELF-TESTS

VOCABULARY SELF-TEST (The answers may be found on the pages in parentheses.)

1. cerebrum (p. 156)
2. thyroxine (p. 174)
3. glia (p. 154)
4. cephalocaudal development (pp. 150–151)
5. proprioceptive information (p. 163)
6. nonorganic failure to thrive (p. 179)
7. synapse (p. 154)
8. testosterone (p. 174)
9. puberty (p. 166)
10. synaptogenesis (p. 154)
11. kwashiorkor (p. 176)
12. pincer grasp (p. 163)
13. cerebral lateralization (p. 156)
14. dynamical systems theory (p. 159)
15. secular trend (p. 169)

MULTIPLE-CHOICE SELF-TEST (The answers may be found on the pages in parentheses.)

1. **c** (pp. 150–151) The head developing before the legs would illustrate cephalocaudal development (top-down). The feet developing before the hands (a) would illustrate bottom-up development, the opposite of cephalocaudal. Proximodistal is "near-to-far" and the trunk is closer to the centre line than the arms are (b). The arms developing before the trunk (d) would illustrate "far-to-near" development.

2. **d** (p. 154) Glia cells are the cells that provide nourishment for neurons and form myelin sheaths around axons. Synapses (a) are gaps between adjacent neurons. Neurotransmitters (b) are chemicals that transmit messages between adjacent neurons, or between neurons and muscles. The corpus callosum (c) is the band of fibres that links the two hemispheres in the brain.

3. **c** (pp. 154–155) Initially there are excess neurons and synapses in the brain; neurons that do not receive sufficient stimulation lose their synapses and become available to compensate for brain injuries. Infants are born with all the neurons already present (a). Myelinization (b) increases neural efficiency; it does not account for brain plasticity. The corpus callosum (d) allows the two hemispheres of the brain to communicate; it does not play a role in neural plasticity.

4. **a** (pp. 156–157) The two hemispheres each show some evidence of specialized functioning, although they work together. The growth of waxy insulation around axons (b) is called myelinization. An impairment in the ability to read (c) is called dyslexia. The fibres that connect the two halves of the brain (d) are called the corpus callosum.

5. **d** (pp. 150–151) Development from the head down is termed cephalocaudal development (neck before legs). Plasticity (a) refers to the brain's ability to compensate for some early injuries. Lateralization (b) refers to the specialized functioning of each hemisphere of the brain. Proximodistal development (c) would be development from the centre of the body to the extremities (e.g., the upper arms before the hands).

6. **c** (pp. 169–170) Girls who mature late are often at a social advantage, whereas boys who mature late are often at a social disadvantage. Boys usually benefit socially from being among the first in their class to mature, but girls who mature early may be shunned by their peers initially (a). Therefore late maturation is not a social advantage for boys (b), and it does not disadvantage girls (d).

7. **c** (p. 174) Testosterone occurs in higher concentrations in males than females and helps to promote muscle growth and bone development. Thyroxine (a) is most important for brain and nervous system development. Growth hormone (b) is responsible for the general growth of body tissues and the adolescent growth spurt. Adrenal androgens (d) promote muscle growth and bone growth in both males and females.

8. **b** (p. 176) Marasmus results from insufficient calories and insufficient protein. Anemia (a) results from iron deficiency. Kwashiorkor is the illness that results from insufficient protein but sufficient calories (c). Marasmus results from insufficient calories and insufficient protein. Anorexia nervosa (d) is an eating disorder in which the individual consumes insufficient calories.

Chapter Six

Early Cognitive Foundations: Sensation, Perception, and Learning

Learning Objectives

By the time you have finished this chapter you should be able to:

1. Compare and contrast enrichment theory and differentiation theory.
2. Describe how the preference method, the habituation method, evoked potentials, and high-amplitude sucking can be used to assess sensory and perceptual capabilities in infants.
3. Describe a newborn's visual capabilities and outline how vision develops in the first year.
4. Describe a newborn's auditory capabilities and outline how hearing develops in the first year.
5. Discuss what research studies have concluded about the consequences of hearing loss during infancy and early childhood.
6. Outline a newborn's sensory capabilities in the areas of taste, smell, touch, temperature, and pain.
7. Describe how an infant's perception of pattern and form develops during the first year.
8. Discuss how an infant's perception of three-dimensional space develops during the first year.
9. Describe how depth perception changes during the first year and explain how a visual cliff can be used to assess an infant's ability to perceive depth.
10. Explain what is meant by intermodal perception and outline the developmental course of this ability in infants.
11. Explain how culture and cultural influences can influence perception.
12. Identify three key components in the definition of learning.
13. Describe how the rate of habituation changes with age and explain what individual differences in habituation rates may indicate about information-processing capabilities.
14. Define the four key elements in classical conditioning.
15. Describe how classical conditioning might explain the acquisition of fears, phobias, and general attitudes, and explain the process of counterconditioning.
16. Distinguish between positive and negative reinforcement, and positive and negative punishment.
17. Describe the potential side effects associated with the use of punishment and discuss some guidelines for using punishment more effectively.
18. Describe observational learning and outline basic developmental trends in observational learning.

Chapter Outline and Summary

1. Early controversies about sensory and perceptual development

Sensation is the process by which sensory receptor neurons detect information and transmit that information to the brain. Perception is the process of interpreting the sensory input.

Empiricist philosophers believed that infants have to learn to interpret their sensory experiences; nativist philosophers argued that many basic perceptual abilities are innate. Today most developmentalists recognize that a newborn's perception of the world is limited, and that both maturation and learning contribute to the growth of perceptual awareness.

Enrichment theory claims that sensory stimulation is often fragmented or confusing, and that we use our available cognitive schemes to add to that sensory stimulation. In other words, cognition enriches sensory experience. Differentiation theory argues that our task as perceivers is to detect distinctive features that enable us to discriminate one form of experience from others. In other words, the information needed to make fine distinctions is always present, but as perceptual capabilities increase individuals learn to detect distinctive features.

2. "Making sense" of the infant's sensory and perceptual experiences

Researchers rely on behavioural and physiological responses to study sensory and perceptual abilities in infants. There are four methods that can be used by researchers.

With the preference method two stimuli are presented simultaneously and researchers note which stimulus, if either, the infant attends to the most.

Habituation occurs when a stimulus becomes so familiar that responses to the stimulus decline. Once an infant has habituated to one stimulus, a different stimulus is presented. If the infant shows renewed responding to this second stimulus (dishabituates), it can be inferred that the infant can detect some difference between the two stimuli.

Evoked potentials, or brain wave patterns, can also be used to assess sensory and perceptual capabilities in infants. Stimuli that are not detected will not produce a change in brain wave patterns, and stimuli that are perceived as being different will each produce unique patterns of brain wave activity.

Finally, the high-amplitude sucking method can be used to assess preferences in infants. A baseline sucking rate is established; any increase in the rate of sucking will cause an electrical circuit to be tripped. When this happens a sensory stimulus is introduced. If an infant finds this stimulus "interesting," sucking should continue at a high rate; when interest decreases the rate of sucking should also decline, and the stimulus will disappear. This method can also be used to assess infant preferences.

3. Infant sensory capabilities

Newborns are sensitive to brightness and can detect movement in the visual field. They will track a slowly moving stimulus that crosses their visual field. Newborns can also see colours, although for the first two months they have difficulty distinguishing blues, greens, and yellows from whites. Research evidence suggests that infants probably have general immaturities of visual and neural mechanisms that limit their colour vision. By 2 to 3 months, infants can discriminate all the basic colours, and by 4 months they group colours into categories. The visual acuity in newborns is poor, equivalent to approximately 20/600. However, by 6 months of age their acuity has improved to 20/100, and by their first birthday visual acuity is similar to that found in adults.

Newborns can detect differences in the loudness, duration, direction, and pitch of sounds. They are particularly attentive to voices. Infants can also distinguish between basic speech sounds very early in life. Infants less than 1 week old can distinguish between "a" and "i," and by the age of 2 or 3 months they can distinguish between consonant sounds such as "ba" and "pa." By 4 ½ months an infant will turn his or her head to hear their own name, and distinguish it from other names. Otitis media is a common bacterial infection of the middle ear.

Children who develop recurring ear infections early in life show delays in language development and poorer academic performance during the early school years.

Newborns have definite taste preferences and prefer sweet tastes to all other tastes. Different tastes also elicit unique facial expressions in newborns. Sweet tastes produce smiles, sour tastes produce a grimace, and bitter tastes can produce spitting. Newborns will also turn away from unpleasant odours; they prefer the odour of milk, and breast-fed infants less than 2 weeks old can already recognize the unique scent of their own mother.

Newborns are sensitive to touch, and preterm infants show better developmental progress when they are stroked and massaged. Newborns are also quite sensitive to warmth, cold, and changes in temperature. Finally, newborns experience pain and react to painful stimuli with tears and loud crying.

4. Visual perception in infancy

a. Perception of patterns and forms

Young infants prefer to look at high-contrast patterns with sharp boundaries between areas of light and dark. They also prefer moderately complex patterns with curvilinear features, and their attention is attracted by stimuli that move across their visual field.

Recent research suggests that visual input right after birth may be necessary for the development of visual mechanisms in the brain. Newborns do not have good form perception, but by 2 months of age infants can use object movement to perceive form, and by 3 to 4 months of age infants can perceive form in some stationary scenes. By 2 to 3 months, infants show signs that they are responding to faces as if they were meaningful configurations. Indeed, by the age of 3 months infants prefer images of faces to images of scrambled faces, and they show a preference for pictures of their own mothers over pictures of other women who have similar features. By 8 to 10 months of age infants are beginning to interpret emotional expressions in their mother's face and respond to those emotional cues. Some research suggests that certain aspects of face recognition are not developed until middle adolescence.

b. Perception of three-dimensional space

Prior to the age of 2 to 3 months infants do not exhibit stereopsis; stereopsis is the process that combines the separate visual images from each eye into a single, nonoverlapping image that has depth. By 3 to 4 weeks of age infants will blink in response to objects that move closer to them, and this reaction becomes stronger over the next three months. This means that young infants can utilize kinetic cues to perceive depth and distance relations. Newborns also show some evidence of size constancy, but size constancy improves steadily throughout the first year, and the ability is not fully mature until the child is 10 or 11 years of age. The ability to use monocular cues in the perception of depth appears to emerge around 6 or 7 months of age.

An infant's depth perception can also be evaluated using a visual cliff, an apparatus that creates the illusion of a sharp drop-off. Research by Campos suggests that infants can detect differences in depth as early as 2 months of age, but they don't develop a fear of drop-offs until they begin to crawl.

5. Intermodal perception

Intermodal perception is the ability to recognize an object that is familiar through one sensory modality when it is presented via a different sensory modality. Research suggests, and this is supported by differentiation theorists, that intermodal perception is present very early in life. Very young infants are often upset by sensory incongruities, and 1-month-old infants show some evidence of cross-modal oral-to-visual perception. Intermodal perception between vision and hearing emerges at about 4 months of age, and the ability to match tactile sensations with visual sensations emerges at approximately 4 to 6 months of age.

6. Infant perception in perspective—and a look ahead

a. *Perceptual learning in childhood: Gibson's differentiation theory*

Although basic perceptual competencies emerge during infancy, perceptual learning continues as children interact with their environments and detect distinctive features associated with objects they encounter. These finer perceptual discriminations may be necessary for a number of skills, including the ability to read. Gibson found that preschool children often have difficulty differentiating between letters that share similar perceptual characteristics. The phonics approach is supported by the differentiation perspective. The whole-language approach, however, is supported by the enrichment theory.

b. *Cultural influences on perception*

Culture also influences perceptual development. As our perceptual processes mature we lose the ability to detect sensory information that has little cultural relevance, such as sounds that are not part of our native language. So, the way we perceive the world depends not only on the detection of sensory inputs, but also on cultural experiences that provide a framework for interpreting those inputs.

7. Basic learning processes

Learning involves a relatively permanent change in behaviour (or behaviour potential) that results from experience. The fact that learning is relatively permanent means that behaviours that are quickly forgotten, or temporary changes that result from fatigue, do not qualify as learning. A change in behaviour means that the individual thinks, perceives, or reacts in a way that is new or different. Finally, learning results from experience and does not include changes that are a result of maturation or physiological change.

a. *Habituation: Early evidence of information processing and memory*

Habituation occurs when an individual stops attending to or responding to a stimulus that has been presented repeatedly. Dishabituation is an increase in attention or responding when a novel stimulus is presented. Habituation improves dramatically over the first year. Older infants habituate to stimuli more quickly, and they can remain habituated to a stimulus for several days (possibly weeks). Infants who habituate rapidly are quicker to understand and use language during the second year and typically score higher on standardized intelligence tests later in childhood.

b. *Classical conditioning*

Classical conditioning occurs when a neutral stimulus comes to elicit a response because it has been paired with a second stimulus that already elicits a response. There are four key elements in classical conditioning: the unconditioned stimulus (UCS), the unconditioned response (UCR), the conditioned stimulus (CS), and the conditioned response (CR). The UCS is a stimulus that elicits a response without any prior learning; it does not need to be conditioned. The UCR is the unlearned response that the unconditioned stimulus elicits. The CS is a stimulus that is originally neutral, but that comes to elicit a response after it has been paired with the unconditioned stimulus. The CR is the learned response that the conditioned stimulus elicits. If the association between the CS and UCS is broken then the conditioned response will diminish in strength and eventually disappear. This process is called extinction.

Classical conditioning may explain how people develop some of their fears, phobias, and general attitudes. When neutral stimuli are paired with unpleasant events we may learn to fear them, and when neutral stimuli are paired with pleasant events we can learn to like them. Counterconditioning involves pairing an existing conditioned stimulus with a new unconditioned stimulus to produce a different conditioned response. This procedure can be used to treat existing fears or phobias.

c. *Operant (or instrumental) conditioning*

Operant conditioning deals with voluntary behaviours. The basic principle that underlies operant conditioning is that people will tend to repeat behaviours that produce favourable consequences, and they will tend to suppress or reduce behaviours that produce unfavourable consequences.

In operant conditioning, there are four possible consequences that can follow a behaviour. Any consequence that strengthens the behaviour that it follows is called a reinforcer. Positive reinforcers strengthen behaviours because something pleasant or desirable is added as a consequence of the behaviour. Negative reinforcers strengthen behaviours because something unpleasant or undesirable is removed as a consequence of the behaviour. Any consequence that inhibits or suppresses the behaviour that it follows is called a punisher. Positive punishers weaken behaviours because something unpleasant or undesirable is added as a consequence of the behaviour. Negative punishers weaken behaviours because something pleasant or desirable is removed as a consequence of the behaviour.

These terms can sometimes be confusing, but reinforcers always strengthen behaviour, and punishers always weaken behaviour. And if you think of "positive" as a plus sign and "negative" as a minus sign, it may make it easier to remember how each process works. With positive reinforcement and positive punishment, something is added to the situation as a direct consequence of the behaviour; with negative reinforcement and negative punishment, something is removed from the situation as a direct consequence of the behaviour.

Using physical punishment as a form of behavioural control may prove counterproductive or even harmful in the long run. However, when punishment is used properly it can be an effective means of controlling undesirable behaviours. Punishment is most effective when the person administering the punishment follows some basic guidelines, including the following: (1) punish as soon as possible after the misbehaviour; (2) punish firmly, but not with too much intensity; (3) punish consistently; (4) be otherwise warm and accepting; (5) try to use alternatives to physical punishment, such as negative punishment involving the removal of privileges; (6) reinforce desirable behaviours; (7) explain the reasons for the punishment.

d. *Observational learning*

Observational learning is learning that results from watching the behaviour of others. An infant's capacity to reliably imitate novel responses that are not part of his or her behavioural repertoire increases significantly after the age of 8 months. Elementary-school children are even better at learning from social models because they are able to use verbal codes to store and retrieve information.

8. Reflections on perception and learning

It is important to understand the growth of perceptual skills and the ways in which people change in response to their environment because perception and learning are fundamental cognitive processes that are central to all human development.

Vocabulary Self-Test

Part I: For each of the following definitions provide the appropriate term. (Answers to this portion of the self-test are provided at the end of the chapter.)

1. ________________ Decrease in responsiveness to a stimulus that has become familiar through repetition

2. ________________ The ability to use one sensory modality to identify a stimulus or pattern of stimuli that is already familiar through another modality

3. ________________ A learned response to a stimulus that was not originally capable of producing the response

4. ________________ A method used to gain information about infants' perceptual abilities by presenting two (or more) stimuli and observing which stimulus the infant attends to more

5. ________________ Cues created by movements of objects or movements of the body that provide important information for the perception of forms and spatial relations

6. ________________ Punishing consequence that involves the removal of something pleasant following a behaviour

7. ________________ Detection of stimuli by the sensory receptors and transmission of this information to the brain

8. ________________ A stimulus that elicits a particular response without any prior learning

9. ________________ The process by which external stimulation is converted to a mental representation

10. ________________ The tendency to perceive an object as the same size from different distances despite changes in the size of its retinal image

11. ________________ A treatment based on classical conditioning in which the goal is to extinguish an undesirable response and replace it with a new and more adaptive response

12. ________________ A theory specifying that perception involves detecting distinctive features or cues that are contained in the sensory stimulation we receive

13. ________________ Skills, knowledge, and attitudes that precede and seem to promote conventional forms of reading and writing

14. ________________ A type of learning in which freely emitted acts (or operants) become either more or less probable depending on the consequences they produce

15. ________________ A common bacterial infection of the middle ear that produces mild to moderate hearing loss

Part II: For each of the following terms provide the definition.

High-Amplitude Sucking Method: ____________________

____

Learning: ____________________

____

Extinction: ____________________

____

Classical Conditioning: ____________________

____

Perception: ____________________

____

Unconditioned Response: ____________________

____

Visual Contrast: ____________________

____

Positive Punishment: ____________________

____

Deferred Imitation: ____________________

____

Enrichment Theory: ____________________

____

Visual Looming: ____________________

____

Positive Reinforcer: ____________________

____

Dishabituation: ____________________

____

Conditioned Stimulus: ____________________

____

Size Constancy: ____________________

____

Short-Answer Study Questions

EARLY CONTROVERSIES ABOUT SENSORY AND PERCEPTUAL DEVELOPMENT

1. Define sensation and perception.

   Sensation:

   Perception:

2. Outline the basics of enrichment theory and differentiation theory.

   Enrichment theory:

   Differentiation theory:

"MAKING SENSE" OF THE INFANT'S SENSORY AND PERCEPTUAL EXPERIENCES

3. Describe four techniques that can be used to assess sensory and perceptual capabilities in infants.

   a.

   b.

   c.

   d.

INFANT SENSORY CAPABILITIES

4. Describe a newborn's visual capabilities.

5. Describe a newborn's auditory capabilities.

6. Identify one common ear infection among infants and preschool children, and discuss the long-term consequences of recurring ear infections.

7. Describe a newborn's gustatory (taste) and olfactory (smell) capabilities.

   Taste:

   Smell:

8. Describe what is known about touch, temperature, and pain perception in newborns.

9. Identify three characteristics of visual stimuli that young infants prefer.

   a.

   b.

   c.

VISUAL PERCEPTION IN INFANCY

10. Outline how form perception develops over the first year.

11. Outline how face perception develops over the first year.

12. The ability to perceive three-dimensional space improves over the first year. Indicate the cues infants are capable of using at each of the following ages.

    1–3 months:

    3–5 months:

    6–7 months:

13. Describe a visual cliff and summarize key research findings from studies that used this device to test depth perception in infants.

    Visual cliff:

    Research findings:

INTERMODAL PERCEPTION

14. Explain what is meant by intermodal perception.

15. Trace the development of intermodal perception over the first year.

16. Which theory (enrichment or differentiation) best explains the development of intermodal perception? Why?

INFANT PERCEPTION IN PERSPECTIVE—AND A LOOK AHEAD

17. List the three phases in learning to read identified by Gibson and Lewin.

    a.

    b.

    c.

18. Identify two areas where culture can influence perceptual development. For each area present the results from a research study to support the conclusion that culture can influence the ability to make perceptual discriminations.

    a.

    b.

BASIC LEARNING PROCESSES

19. Identify three key components in the definition of learning.

    a.

    b.

    c.

20. Some infants show more rapid habituation, compared to their age-mates. Describe the long-term correlates of rapid habituation during early infancy.

21. Identify four elements in classical conditioning and provide an illustrative example of each component.

a.

b.

c.

d.

22. Explain what counterconditioning is and describe how this process can be used to treat phobias.

23. Explain how operant conditioning differs from classical conditioning.

24. Identify four possible consequences that can follow an operant response and provide an example to illustrate each type of consequence.

a.

b.

c.

d.

25. Identify three potentially harmful side effects of using physical punishment to control behaviour.

a.

b.

c.

26. List seven guidelines that can make the use of punishment more effective.

a.

b.

c.

d.

e.

f.

g.

27. Explain what is meant by deferred imitation and outline how this ability develops between 9 and 24 months of age.

28. Why might elementary-school children learn more than preschoolers from the observation of social models?

Multiple-Choice Self-Test

For each of the following questions select the best alternative. (Answers and explanations for this self-test are provided at the end of the chapter.) Once you have selected your answer, provide a brief explanation for why the answer you selected is the best choice and why the remaining answers would not be correct.

1. Suppose you allow an infant several minutes to "study" a drawing of a human face. Then, you present a second face and assess whether the infant's heart rate changes when the second face appears. The research method you are using is the:

   a. preference method
   b. habituation method
   c. method of evoked potentials
   d. high-amplitude sucking procedure

   Rationale: ______________________________

   ____

2. In newborns, the sense that is the least developed and least similar to adult senses is:

   a. taste
   b. hearing
   c. vision
   d. smell

   Rationale: ______________________________

   ____

3. Of the following, the stimulus that would be least likely to attract a neonate's visual attention would be:

   a. a highly detailed pattern
   b. an object that moved across the visual field
   c. a stimulus display with sharp contrasts between light and dark areas
   d. a human face

   Rationale: ______________________________

   ____

4. Suppose that you studied very hard for a test and you score 100%. However, a few days later you are unable to answer questions about the same material. According to the criteria for learning:

   a. learning clearly took place because initially performance was error-free
   b. learning took place, but it was only temporary
   c. your later performance declined because you habituated to the test material
   d. learning never occurred because the behaviour change was only temporary

   Rationale: ______________________________

   ____

5. The type of learning that is characterized by a new response emerging after seeing others perform that same response is:

   a. habituation
   b. classical conditioning
   c. negative reinforcement
   d. observational learning

   Rationale: ____

   ____

6. Pavlov trained a dog to salivate at the sound of a bell that rang just before food was delivered. In this example, the sound of the bell is:

   a. an unconditioned stimulus
   b. a conditioned stimulus
   c. a conditioned response
   d. an unconditioned response

   Rationale: ____

   ____

7. Of the following, the one that illustrates negative reinforcement would be:

   a. parents withholding a child's allowance following the child's misbehaviour
   b. parents requiring a child to complete his or her homework before watching TV
   c. a child being given "time-out" following misbehaviour
   d. a child who avoids being grounded or scolded by coming home on time

   Rationale: ____

   ____

8. Bandura maintained that observational learning has two advantages over other forms of learning. One is that a new response may be added through imitation of a model. A second advantage is that:

   a. observational learning is possible at any age while other forms of learning are not
   b. the child need not be reinforced to learn the behaviour
   c. only positive behaviours are acquired through observational learning
   d. it eliminates the need for punishment

   Rationale: ____

   ____

Activities and Projects Related to this Chapter

ACTIVITY 6-1

VERBAL COMMENTS AS CONSEQUENCES AFFECTING BEHAVIOUR

INTRODUCTION: Chapter 6 introduces operant learning as an important contributor to development. Through learning, children add new responses to their repertoire and either increase or decrease the frequency of existing behaviours depending on the consequences of those behaviours. As discussed in the text, a response is strengthened and is more likely to occur in the future if it is followed by pleasant consequences (or results in the removal of aversive consequences). Similarly, a response will be weakened and will be less likely to occur if it is followed by unpleasant consequences. We often think of reinforcers and punishers as something concrete such as food, money, a spanking, etc. Not all reinforcers and punishers are concrete, however. A smile, a pat, a kind word as responses to our behaviour may increase the likelihood of those responses being repeated. Likewise, a frown, a slap, an unkind word may decrease the likelihood that the responses they follow will be repeated. One of the implications for us as adults is that what we say to children can affect them markedly by encouraging or discouraging behaviours. The purpose of this activity is to increase your awareness of the impact that one type of consequences, verbal comments, can have on behaviour and attitudes. Part A asks you to recall some of your own reactions to the comments of others. Part B asks you to systematically increase positive verbal comments to someone you know.

INSTRUCTIONS:

Part A

Write down as many examples as you can recall of comments people close to you have made that

a. made you feel good
b. made you want to try even harder
c. made you angry or made you feel down on yourself
d. made you not want to try at all

It would be optimal to do this activity over a few days because it may take some time for various previous experiences and the comments made to you to come to mind. For each comment indicate who made it, how it made you feel, and how it affected your behaviour. Think of how your parents, siblings, teachers, and others responded to you verbally when you shared, when you were helpful, when you were successful, when you were mean, when you were forgetful, when you were unsuccessful, etc.

Part B

Over a two- to five-day period, make a special effort to provide positive verbal statements to someone you know. Keep daily records describing the context, your positive verbal statement, and both the immediate and longer-term effect on the other person's behaviour and emotional reaction.

Before beginning Part B, it would be useful to spend some time "brainstorming" so as to generate possible positive statements to use. Brainstorm with a classmate or small group of students.

ACTIVITY 6-2

EVIDENCE FOR OPERANT CONDITIONING AND MEMORY IN YOUNG INFANTS: PIAGET'S SECONDARY CIRCULAR REACTIONS

INTRODUCTION: The purpose of this activity is to allow you to watch first-hand an infant's fascination with the discovery that she can make interesting things happen to external objects—a cognitive advance that undoubtedly plays a role in the development of competence and sense of self. This activity will also provide you with an example of a special case of operant conditioning, a type of learning described in Chapter 6. It is a special case because not only is the reinforcement (movement of an external stimulus) contingent upon the infant's responses, but the intensity of the reinforcing stimulus is directly in the infant's control. This activity also relates to material on infant memory discussed in Chapter 8. Rovee-Collier and colleagues have shown that a 2-month-old infant will show retention of the kicking response to a mobile for as long as 18 days if given a brief "reminder" exposure to the mobile moving 24 hours before the retention test. These ingenious experiments have shown that infant memory is not as fleeting as once believed. (Note—Rovee-Collier has also shown that secondary circular reactions occur in infants long before the 4 months that Piaget observed.)

This activity focuses on one substage of the sensorimotor stage: the secondary circular reaction substage. During this substage infants begin to repeat actions that lead to interesting external stimulation. According to Piaget this substage represents an important advance over the primary circular reactions—reactions occurring only in response to consequences centring around the infant's own body (e.g., actions such as sucking, cooing, blowing bubbles, etc.). Piaget also viewed secondary circular reactions as a forerunner of intentionality in problem solving (see Chapter 7).

This adaptation of the Rovee-Collier task provides an opportunity to observe the responses Piaget called secondary circular reactions, a special case of operant conditioning.

INSTRUCTIONS:

Children. Ask the parents of an infant 2 to 6 months of age if they can help you with your homework for a class project. Tell the parents that you would like to see how a baby reacts when the baby's own movement controls the duration and intensity of a mobile's movement (rather than it being controlled by an adult or a motor).

Materials. Use a mobile the parents already have for the infant or create your own. If you construct your own, be sure to think about how you will suspend it. Consider including a small bell on your homemade mobile or adding one to the infant's for some auditory stimulation.

Procedure. Attach one end of a ribbon, piece of yarn, or string to the mobile. Place the child in an infant seat facing the mobile and tie the second end to the infant's wrist or foot. Sit back and watch the infant discover that he or she is in control of the movement of the mobile. Take notes on the infant's facial expressions and vocalizations, indicating the end of each 5-minute block of time. (Be prepared to stay a while; some 4-month-olds can keep the mobile going for 40 minutes the first time they are attached.)

If you can arrange for it, return a day or two later. Set the child in the infant seat in front of the same mobile. Observe carefully the infant's facial expressions and movement of the arm or leg that was attached during original learning. Make notes. Then attach the infant again and record the infant's behaviour, again indicating the end of each 5-minute block of time. You should observe evidence of memory for the kicking response when the infant sees the mobile. If the infant shows no evidence of remembering, set it in motion for a moment. You should see good evidence of recognition then, followed by energetic kicking or hand movements. Because the infant does recognize the mobile, habituation will occur more rapidly the second day, i.e., the mobile will lose its reinforcing power sooner—meaning you probably will not have to wait 40 minutes for the infant to get bored!

Note—Many students wonder whether the infant's arm or leg movements are simply reactions to the movement of the mobile. Check this out if you wish. Before starting the project, move the mobile by pulling on the ribbon. Observe and write down the infant's reaction. Compare the infant's behaviour when your movement versus her own movement produced the consequences. Her behaviour should differ markedly in both quality and quantity.

WRITE-UP:
Prepare a write-up that includes:

a. the infant's age in months
b. the number of minutes the infant moved the mobile
c. a description of the infant's reaction when she first discovered the link between her own movements and the mobile's movement, and then how the reaction changed each 5 minutes (both in intensity and frequency)
d. the infant's facial expressions and vocalizations during each 5-minute period of being attached to the mobile
e. a description of how the infant acted as interest waned

If you were able to do the memory test a day or two later, also describe the infant's reactions and behaviour during that session.

RELATED REFERENCES

Bojczyk, K.E., & Corbetta, D. (2004). Object retrieval in the 1st year of life: Learning effects of task exposure and box transparency. *Developmental Psychology, 40(1),* 54–66.

Davis, J. M., & Rovee-Collier, C. K. (1983). Alleviated forgetting of a learned contingency in 8-week-old infants. *Developmental Psychology, 19*, 353–365.

Hayne, H., Rovee-Collier, C., & Perris, E. E. (1987). Categorization and memory retrieval by three-month-olds. *Child Development, 58*, 750–767.

Rovee-Collier, C. (1987). Learning and memory in infancy. In J. D. Osofsky (Ed.), *Handbook of child psychology: Vol. 4 Socialization, personality and social development.* New York: Wiley.

Rovee-Collier, C., & Barr, R. (2001). Infant learning and memory. In G. Bremner & A. Fogel (Eds.), *Blackwell handbook of infant development* (p. 139–168). Malden, MA: Blackwell Publishers.

Shields, P. J., & Rovee-Collier, C. (1992). Long-term memory for context-specific category information at six months. *Child Development, 63*, 245–259.

Whiteley, J.H. (1981). Canadian research on infant development: 1970–1980. *Canadian Psychology, 22(1),* 55–68.

REFERENCES OF INTEREST

Mennella, J.A., & Beauchamp, G.K. (1996). The early development of human flavor preferences. In E.D. Capaldi (Ed.), *Why we eat what we eat: The psychology of eating* (p. 83–112). Washington, DC: American Psychological Association.

Rochat, P., & Striano, T. (2000). Perceived self in infancy. *Infant Behavior and Development, 23(3–4),* 513–530.

Thomas, H., & Gilmore, R.O. (2004). Habituation assessment in infancy. *Psychological Methods, 9(1),* 70–92.

WEBSITES OF INTEREST

For more information on Canadian research on the development of vision, read about the research by Dr. Terri Lewis: www.science.mcmaster.ca/Psychology/terri.html

ACTIVITY 6-3

TO CIRCUMCISE OR NOT TO CIRCUMCISE?

INTRODUCTION: This activity addresses the issue of whether or not very young infants detect and/or experience pain. In your text, you read that newborns are capable of feeling pain. This is evident in their mannerisms, cries, and physiological reactions to certain medical procedures. One such medical procedure is circumcision of infant boys. Currently there is debate in Canada on whether or not circumcision is advisable. Tradition and religion are reasons why many parents decide to circumcise their sons, and hygiene is another reason. Talk with parents who decided to circumcise their son, and talk with parents who decided against circumcising their son. What were their reasons for and against? Given what you've learned from your text, would you advise circumcision? What does the Canadian Pediatric Society recommend? Currently, the procedure is not covered under the general health care program. What are some of the potential implications for policy?

RELATED REFERENCES

Craig, K.D., & Badali, M.A. (1999). On knowing an infant's pain. *Pain Forum, 8,* 74–77.

Craig, K.D., & Grunau, R.V.E. (1993). Neonatal pain perception and behavioral measurement. In K.J.S. Anand & P.J. McGrath (Eds.), *Pain in neonates* (p. 67–105). Amsterdam: Elsevier Science Publishers.

Craig, K.D., McMahon, R.J., Morison, J.D., & Zaskow, C. (1984). Developmental changes in infant pain expression during immunization injections. *Social Science and Medicine, 19,* 1331–1337.

ANSWERS TO SELF-TESTS

VOCABULARY SELF-TEST (The answers may be found on the pages in parentheses.)

1. habituation (pp. 185-186)
2. intermodal perception (pp. 200-201)
3. conditioned response (p. 209)
4. preference method (p. 185)
5. kinetic cues (p. 197)
6. negative punishment (p. 210)
7. sensation (pp. 183-184)
8. unconditioned stimulus (p. 208)
9. encoding (p. 215)
10. size constancy (p. 197)
11. counterconditioning (p. 209)
12. differentiation theory (p. 184-185)
13. emergent literacy (pp. 204-205)
14. operant conditioning (p. 210)
15. otitis media (p. 189)

MULTIPLE-CHOICE SELF-TEST (The answers may be found on the pages in parentheses.)

1. **b** (pp. 185–186) Habituation involves the sequential presentation of two stimuli and measuring whether there is a change in response to the second stimulus. The preference method (a) presents two stimuli simultaneously to determine which stimulus the infant attends to more. With evoked potentials (c) brain wave patterns are recorded. With high-amplitude sucking (d) the infant controls which stimulus appears; this method can be used to assess infant preferences.

2. **c** (pp. 187–188) At birth infants have poor visual acuity and difficulty accommodating. They can already distinguish between different tastes (a) and show taste preferences. Their hearing (b) is equivalent to that of an adult with a head cold. They react vigorously to odours (d), especially unpleasant odours.

3. **a** (p. 192) Prior to the age of 2 months, highly detailed, complex patterns would appear as "blobs" to infants. Newborns will reliably track objects that move slowly across their visual field (b). Young infants attend to patterns that have high contrast (c). Infants as young as 2 days old show a preference for human faces (d).

4. **d** (p. 207) The definition for learning includes a relatively permanent change in behaviour; therefore, in this example learning did not occur because the change was only temporary. Initial performance (a) is not relevant, as it is the long-term change in behaviour that needs to be considered. The change was only temporary (b), and thus it does not meet the criteria of being relatively permanent. Habituation (c) refers to a decrease in responding following repeated exposure to an unchanging stimulus.

5. **d** (p. 215) With observational learning, a new response emerges after seeing others perform that same response. Habituation is a decrease in responding following repeated exposure to a stimulus (a). With classical conditioning (b), a new response develops to a previously neutral stimulus. With negative reinforcement (c), operant responses increase in frequency because they lead to the removal of an aversive stimulus.

6. **b** (pp. 208–209) The conditioned stimulus (b) would be the sound of the bell. The unconditioned stimulus (a) would be the food. Salivation at the sound of the bell is the new response that emerges because the sound of the bell has been paired with the presentation of food (c). The salivation is an unconditioned response (d) to the food.

7. **d** (p. 210) Negative reinforcement occurs when a behaviour increases in frequency because it prevents or terminates an unpleasant consequence. Withholding allowance (a) and time-out (c) are both intended to decrease the misbehaviour; therefore, these would be examples of punishment. Being allowed to watch TV after completing homework (b) is the addition of a privilege (positive reinforcement).

8. **b** (p. 215) With observational learning Bandura distinguished between acquisition and performance, and reinforcers are not necessary for a behaviour to be acquired. Observational learning does not occur any earlier than other forms of learning (a). Children can acquire a wide range of behaviours through observational learning (c), not just positive behaviours. Observational learning can teach which behaviours are inappropriate (d), but those behaviours may emerge in different situations.

Chapter Seven

Cognitive Development: Piaget's Theory, Case's Neo-Piagetian Theory, and Vygotsky's Sociocultural Viewpoint

Learning Objectives

By the time you have finished this chapter you should be able to:

1. Describe Piaget's view of intelligence and intellectual growth.
2. Distinguish between behavioural schemes, symbolic schemes, and operational schemes.
3. Differentiate between assimilation and accommodation and explain the role of each process in cognitive growth.
4. List the major characteristics of, and achievements in, each of Piaget's six substages of sensorimotor development.
5. Trace the emergence of object permanence outlined by Piaget and discuss what Baillargeon's research suggests about Piaget's conclusions.
6. Discuss what neo-nativists and "theory" theorists suggest about Piaget's conclusions about infants.
7. Describe Piaget's two substages of preoperational thought and identify the major developments and limitations found during each substage.
8. Describe the research evidence that suggests that Piaget may have underestimated the cognitive abilities of the preoperational child.
9. List the main characteristics of Piaget's concrete-operational stage and contrast this stage with the preoperational stage.
10. Identify the cognitive skills and abilities that emerge during the concrete-operational stage.
11. Explain what is meant by the term "horizontal décalage."
12. Describe formal-operational thought, focusing on the features that distinguish it from concrete-operational thought.
13. Identify Piaget's main contributions and outline the major challenges to his theory of cognitive development.
14. Describe Pascual-Leon's and Case's neo-Piagetian theories of cognitive development.
15. Contrast Vygotsky's and Piaget's views on general cognitive development.
16. Explain what Vygotsky meant by "zone of proximal development" and "scaffolding."
17. Identify the potential benefits of using cooperative learning exercises in the classroom.
18. Contrast Vygotsky's and Piaget's views on the role of language in cognitive development and use research evidence to evaluate each of these views.

Chapter Outline and Summary

1. Piaget's theory of cognitive development

a. *What is intelligence?*

Piaget defined intelligence as a basic life function that helps organisms adapt to their environments. He believed that all intellectual activity was undertaken to produce cognitive equilibrium among thought processes and the environment. People achieve this state of equilibrium through a process that Piaget termed "equilibration." When environmental events produce a state of cognitive disequilibrium the individual makes mental adjustments designed to restore cognitive equilibrium.

b. *Cognitive schemes: The structure of intelligence*

Piaget used the term "schemes" to identify the mental structures that individuals create. There are behavioural schemes, which are organized patterns of behaviour used to represent and respond to objects and experiences. There are symbolic schemes, which allow the individual to solve problems and think about objects and events without the need to act on them. Finally, there are operational schemes, which involve internal mental activities that an individual performs on his or her objects of thought and which lead to a logical conclusion.

c. *How we gain knowledge: Piaget's cognitive processes*

Schemes are created and modified through the intellectual processes of organization and adaptation. Organization combines existing schemes into new and more complex structures. Adaptation is the process of adjusting to the demands of the environment and occurs through the complementary activities of assimilation and accommodation.

When individuals try to interpret the world in terms of the schemes they already possess, they are using the process of assimilation; in other words, they attempt to fit new experiences into their existing mental structures. When new experiences cannot be understood using existing mental structures, individuals must adapt to these new experiences using the process of accommodation. When accommodation occurs, existing structures are modified or new structures are created to account for the new experiences.

2. Piaget's stages of cognitive development

a. *The sensorimotor stage (birth to 2 years)*

From birth to the age of 2 children are in the sensorimotor stage of cognitive development, and for most of this period they are using behavioural schemes to understand the world around them. There are six substages to the sensorimotor stage.

During the reflex activity substage (0 to 1 month), the newborn is assimilating new objects into reflexive behavioural schemes and showing evidence of modifying reflexive responses to accommodate novel objects. During the substage of primary circular reactions (1 to 4 months), infants repeat actions that they can voluntarily control. At this stage the actions are centred on the infant's own body. During the secondary circular reactions substage (4 to 8 months), infants are repeating interesting voluntary actions that involve external objects. Infants begin to intentionally combine or coordinate actions in order to achieve simple objectives (the beginning of true problem solving) during the next substage (coordination of secondary schemes), which lasts from 8 to 12 months of age. During the substage of tertiary circular reactions (12 to 18 months), infants show evidence of active experimentation and they begin to use familiar objects in novel ways. During the final substage (invention of new means through mental combinations), which lasts from 18 to 24 months, the capacity of mental representation is evident. Toddlers may now show evidence of "insight" as they solve problems and interact with their environment.

Deferred imitation is the ability to reproduce a behaviour when the model is no longer present. Piaget suggested this ability emerges during the last substage of the sensorimotor period, when the capacity for mental representations first develops. Other researchers suggest that the capacity for simple deferred imitation may be present as early as 8 months of age.

One of the major developments that occurs during the sensorimotor stage is the emergence of object permanence, the understanding that objects continue to exist when they are no longer visible or detectable by the senses. Piaget suggested this concept emerges in a slow, invariant sequence. He found that infants under the age of 4 months would not search for objects that were hidden from their view. Between 4 and 8 months infants would search for objects that were partially visible, but not for objects that were completely concealed. Between the ages of 8 and 12 months he found that infants would make A-not-B errors in searching for hidden objects; this means they searched for hidden objects where the objects had previously been found, not where they were last seen. After 12 months of age A-not-B errors were no longer made, but before the age of 18 months infants still did not understand invisible displacements. Piaget suggested that only in the last substage of the sensorimotor period was object permanence completely developed.

Other researchers have questioned Piaget's conclusions, claiming that the use of active search to assess knowledge of object permanence is inappropriate in young infants. A number of researchers who have used techniques that don't involve active search have concluded that (1) object permanence is present much sooner than Piaget suggested, and (2) Piaget had misinterpreted the reason why infants make A-not-B errors.

Neo-nativists believe that babies enter the world with substantial knowledge and are innately prepared to make sense of certain aspects of their physical world. Some research suggests that babies may have much more symbolic knowledge than Piaget proposed. Neo-nativism theory, however, has been criticized by others who offer more simple explanations of the research results. "Theory" theorists combine neo-nativism and Piaget's constructivism and maintain that cognitive development progresses by children generating, testing, and modifying theories about the physical and social world. Both approaches assume, counter to Piaget, that infants possess innate knowledge that guides their development.

b. *The preoperational stage (2 to 7 years)*

During the preoperational stage (2 to 7 years), children are able to use mental symbols to represent objects, events, and situations. Piaget divided this stage into the preconceptual period (2 to 4 years) and the intuitive period (4 to 7 years).

During the preconceptual period, the capacity for symbolic thought emerges. The clearest evidence of this capacity is seen in a child's developing language skills, and it is also evident in the blossoming of symbolic (or pretend) play. DeLoache suggests that dual representation, the ability to recognize the relationship between a symbol and its referent, improves during the preconceptual period and continues to improve dramatically during the preschool years.

Some of the deficits in reasoning that Piaget identified in preconceptual children include animism (a willingness to attribute motives and intentions to inanimate objects), transductive reasoning (a belief that whenever two events occur together, one of the events causes the other to occur), egocentrism (difficulty recognizing how things would appear from the point of view of other people), and difficulty distinguishing between appearance and reality.

During the intuitive period Piaget suggested that children are somewhat less egocentric, but that their understanding of objects and events still centres on their single most salient feature. Piaget found that children at this age have difficulty solving class-inclusion problems and they also fail to display conservation. Conservation is an understanding that certain properties of objects remain unchanged when the appearance of the object is superficially altered. Piaget attributed children's failure at solving conservation problems to a lack of reversibility and the inability to decentre their thinking.

Other researchers have found that children in the preoperational stage are less egocentric than Piaget concluded, and that children display less animistic thinking than Piaget had suggested. Animism is most likely to appear when children are describing unfamiliar objects that appear to move on their own. Also, preschool children do not always display transductive reasoning, and they show some understanding of causal relationships. Finally, children as young as 4 years of age who are exposed to identity training can accurately solve conservation problems.

c. *The concrete-operational stage (7 to 11 years)*

During the concrete-operational stage (7 to 11 years), children acquire two operations that help them solve conservation problems. They are now able to decentre, which means they can focus simultaneously on two dimensions of problems; they also show reversibility, which means they can mentally undo processes. They are able to solve class-inclusion problems because they have acquired the operations of addition and subtraction. They also show evidence of mental seriation (the ability to mentally arrange items along a quantifiable dimension) and transitivity (understanding of the relationships among elements in a series).

Piaget found some developmental inconsistencies in the emergence of these mental operations. For example, he found that most children showed conservation of mass before they showed conservation of volume. Piaget used the term "horizontal décalage" to describe this uneven developmental progression. Horizontal décalage is evident when a child understands a basic concept or operation but is not able to apply that concept to all relevant situations.

d. *The formal-operational stage (11 to 12 years and beyond)*

As preadolescents (age 11 or 12), children enter the last stage of cognitive development that Piaget described, the stage of formal-operational thought. During this stage the ability to apply relational logic to abstract concepts and ideas emerges. Two types of reasoning that are evident during the formal-operational stage are hypothetico-deductive reasoning and inductive reasoning. Hypothetico-deductive reasoning includes the ability to generate hypotheses and the ability to solve hypothetical, abstract reasoning problems. Inductive reasoning includes the ability to systematically test hypotheses and the ability to use specific observations to infer broad generalizations.

Piaget didn't identify any stages of cognitive development beyond formal operations, and he believed that most people show some signs of hypothetico-deductive and inductive reasoning skills by middle to late adolescence. Other investigators have suggested that not everyone reaches the stage of formal operations. However, suboptimal performance on problems in one area should not be taken as an indication that an individual is incapable of formal-operational thought. It appears that formal-operational performance is inconsistent and that this level of reasoning will most likely be displayed in areas in which an individual has a high level of interest or experience. Indeed, recent research suggests that today's adolescents are acquiring formal operations faster or earlier than adolescents from previous generations.

3. An evaluation of Piaget's theory

a. *Piaget's contributions*

Piaget founded the discipline known today as cognitive development, and he was the first researcher to suggest that children actively construct their own knowledge. His theory was one of the first that tried to explain, rather than simply describe, the process of development, and the general sequence of development he proposed is reasonably accurate. Piaget's ideas have had wide applicability in a variety of settings, and his theory has generated considerable research and new insights into the development of children's thought processes.

b. *Challenges to Piaget*

There are five major criticisms that have been raised with respect to Piaget's theory. First, he routinely underestimated children's cognitive abilities, especially the abilities of infants and young children. Second, in his research he failed to distinguish between competence and performance. He assumed that children who failed to perform lacked the underlying ability to complete the task. Third; cognitive development may be far less stage-like than Piaget suggested. There is little evidence for consistencies in cognitive development across domains that would support broad, holistic stages of the type suggested by Piaget. Fourth, his theory is an elaborate description of cognitive development, but the descriptions of the processes that actually produce cognitive change are vague. Fifth, Piaget's descriptions emphasize the self-directed aspects of cognitive growth and may underestimate the impact of social and cultural influences on cognitive development.

4. Case's neo-Piagetian theory

Case's neo-Piagetian theory expands and develops Piaget's theory of cognitive development. For example, Case refined the general concepts of accommodation and assimilation to explain how the processes occur. According to Case, accommodation occurs through exploration and problem solving, and assimilation occurs through consolidation and automatization. According to this view, related skills (such as conservation of volume and mass) may be acquired at different times. Case also emphasized the influences of processing capacity, biological factors, experience, and cultural factors on the growth of cognition. Pascual-Leone, another prominent neo-Piagetian, explains cognitive development in terms of information-processing capacity (or M-space).

5. Vygotsky's sociocultural perspective

a. The role of culture in intellectual development

Vygotsky proposed that we should evaluate human development from the perspective of four interrelated levels in interaction with children's environments: ontogenetic, microgenetic, phylogenetic, and sociohistorical. Vygotsky claimed that infants are born with a few elementary mental functions that are eventually transformed into higher mental functions by the culture they experience. In Vygotsky's view, human cognition is affected by the beliefs, values, and tools of intellectual adaptation passed to individuals by their culture. Research on individual differences in mathematical ability and guidance of children's play activities support Vygotsky's views on cultural influence.

b. The social origins of early cognitive competencies

Vygotsky placed less emphasis than Piaget on the role of self-initiated discovery; instead, he stressed the role of collaborative dialogues between skillful tutors and novice pupils. Two key aspects in his theory are the zone of proximal development and scaffolding. The zone of proximal development represents tasks that a learner is not able to complete independently, but that he or she can complete with the guidance of a more skilled partner. Scaffolding is the tendency of expert participants to tailor their support so that the novice cannot only complete the problem, but can also increase his or her understanding of the problem.

Like Piaget, Vygotsky stressed active rather than passive learning. However, in a Piagetian classroom children would be involved in independent, discovery-based activities; in a classroom designed by Vygotsky, children would experience more guided participation and take part in cooperative learning exercises. In using guided participation, the teachers would engage each child in his or her own zone of proximal development and use scaffolding to build and expand competencies. The use of cooperative learning exercises would allow less competent students to learn from more skillful peers.

There are three reasons why cooperative learning may be effective. First, motivation is often higher when children work with others on problems; second, the need to explain and clarify ideas leads children to examine their ideas more closely; third, children who work with others on a problem are more likely to utilize high-quality cognitive strategies.

c. The role of language in cognitive development

Vygotsky and Piaget had sharply differing views regarding the role of language in cognitive development. Piaget called self-directed utterances "egocentric speech," and he believed that this speech was simply a reflection of the child's ongoing mental processes. In contrast, Vygotsky called these same types of dialogues "private speech," and he believed that this speech helped young children plan strategies and regulate their behaviour. This view suggests that private speech aids cognitive development and makes children more organized and more efficient problem solvers. Vygotsky believed that private speech never completely disappears; instead, it simply becomes less overt and changes to "inner speech" in older children and adults.

Consistent with Vygotsky's view are findings that (1) private speech often reflects social speech that was part of guided learning episodes; (2) children utilize private speech more when facing difficult tasks or when deciding how to correct errors; (3) children who display higher levels of cognitive competence are more likely to use private speech; and (4) private speech does change in form, from overt speech to whispers, to inner speech.

d. Vygotsky in perspective: Summary and evaluation

Vygotsky's sociocultural theory stresses the importance of social and cultural processes that Piaget largely overlooked. Therefore, unlike the universal cognitive progression outlined by Piaget, Vygotsky's theory leads to the expectation that there will be wide variations in cognitive development across different cultures. These differences in cognitive capabilities reflect alternative forms of reasoning that enable children to adapt successfully to their own particular culture.

Vocabulary Self-Test

Part I: For each of the following definitions provide the appropriate term. (Answers to this portion of the self-test are provided at the end of the chapter.)

1. ________________	Piaget's second stage of cognitive development, lasting from about age 2 to age 7, when children think at a symbolic level but do not yet use cognitive operations
2. ________________	Piaget's term for the subset of a young child's utterances that are nonsocial—that is, neither directed to others nor expressed in ways that listeners might understand
3. ________________	The tendency to view the world from one's own perspective while failing to recognize that others may have different points of view
4. ________________	Piaget's stage of cognitive development when children are acquiring cognitive operations and thinking more logically about real objects and experiences
5. ________________	The process of modifying existing schemes in order to incorporate or adapt to new experiences
6. ________________	The range of tasks that are too complex to be mastered alone but that can be accomplished with guidance from a more skillful partner
7. ________________	The ability to compare a class of objects with its subclasses without confusing the two
8. ________________	The ability to reproduce a modelled activity that has been witnessed at some point in the past
9. ________________	The ability to recognize relations among elements in a serial order
10. ________________	The tendency to attend to one aspect of a situation to the exclusion of others
11. ________________	An inborn tendency to combine and integrate available schemes into coherent systems or bodies of knowledge
12. ________________	Play in which one object or action symbolizes or stands for another
13. ________________	The tendency to search for a hidden object where it has previously been found, even after witnessing the object being moved to a new location
14. ________________	The recognition that the properties of an object or substance do not change when its appearance is altered in some superficial way
15. ________________	An organized pattern of thought or action that an individual constructs to interpret some aspect of his or her experience

Part II: For each of the following terms provide the definition.

Object Permanence: ______________________________

____

Intuitive Period: ______________________________

____

Sociocultural Theory: ______________________________

____

Mental Seriation: ______________________________

____

Genetic Epistemology: ______________________________

____

Scaffolding: ______________________________

____

Cognitive Development: ______________________________

____

Sensorimotor Stage: ______________________________

____

Horizontal Décalage: ______________________________

____

Private Speech: ______________________________

____

Cognitive Equilibrium: ______________________________

____

Dual Representation: ______________________________

____

Formal Operations: ______________________________

____

Decentration: ______________________________

____

Assimilation: ______________________________

____

Short-Answer Study Questions

PIAGET'S THEORY OF COGNITIVE DEVELOPMENT

1. Give Piaget's definition of intelligence, and identify his view of the goal of intellectual activity.

   Intelligence is:

   The goal of intellectual activity is:

2. List three types of schemes identified by Piaget and provide examples that illustrate each type of scheme.

   a.

   b.

   c.

3. Differentiate between organization and adaptation.

   Organization involves:

   Adaptation involves:

4. Identify the two processes involved in adaptation and provide examples that illustrate each process.

   a.

   b.

PIAGET'S STAGES OF COGNITIVE DEVELOPMENT

5. List the six substages of the sensorimotor stage, the ages associated with each substage, and the types of cognitive activities that are dominant during each substage.

	Substage	Age	Dominant Form of Activity
a.			
b.			
c.			
d.			
e.			
f.			

6. Trace the development of object permanence originally outlined by Piaget.

   1–4 months:

   4–8 months:

   8–12 months:

   12–18 months:

   18–24 months:

7. Discuss what the results from research by Baillargeon (and colleagues) suggest about Piaget's conclusions regarding object permanence. Is Baillargeon measuring what Piaget claimed to measure and, if not, then what is being measured?

8. Discuss neo-nativism and "theory" theories of cognitive development. How do they compliment and how do they differ from Piaget's theory?

9. List the two substages of the preoperational stage and the ages associated with each stage.

	Substage	Age
a.		
b.		

10. DeLoache (and colleagues) conducted several research studies designed to map the development of preschool children's symbolic abilities. Describe the basic findings from these studies.

11. List four deficits that are evident in preconceptual reasoning and provide examples that illustrate each of these deficits.

    a.

    b.

    c.

    d.

12. Use class-inclusion and conservation problems to illustrate Piaget's assertion that during the intuitive period children's understanding of objects and events is "centred" on a single, salient feature.

    Class inclusion:

    Conservation:

13. Summarize the results from studies that have provided new evidence on egocentrism, causal reasoning, and conservation during the preoperational stage of cognitive development.

    Egocentrism:

    Causal reasoning:

    Conservation:

14. During the concrete-operational stage children show the ability to solve conservation problems. Explain what a conservation problem is, and identify two cognitive operations that aid in solving this type of problem.

    Conservation:

    Mental operations:

15. An important development during the concrete-operational stage is a better understanding of relational logic. Identify two mental operations necessary to successfully answer problems involving relational logic.

    a.

    b.

16. Explain what is meant by the term "horizontal décalage."

17. List three key aspects that would be found in a Piagetian-based curriculum.

    a.

    b.

    c.

18. Identify two types of logical reasoning that emerge during the formal-operational stage that distinguish formal-operational thought from concrete-operational thought.

a.

b.

AN EVALUATION OF PIAGET'S THEORY

19. List six major contributions that Piaget has made in the field of human development.

a.

b.

c.

d.

e.

f.

20. List five criticisms that have been raised concerning Piaget's theory of cognitive development.

a.

b.

c.

d.

e.

CASE'S NEO-PIAGETIAN THEORY

21. How does Case explain the Piagetian processes of assimilation and accommodation? How has his perspective expanded our understanding of Piaget's model of development?

VYGOTSKY'S SOCIOCULTURAL PERSPECTIVE

22. Compare and contrast Vygotsky's and Piaget's views on general cognitive growth.

The theories are similar because:

The theories are different because:

23. Explain what Vygotsky meant by "zone of proximal development" and use an example to illustrate this concept.

24. List three reasons why cooperative learning may be an effective classroom technique.

a.

b.

c.

25. Contrast Piaget's and Vygotsky's views on the role of language in cognitive development.

Piaget:

Vygotsky:

26. Outline four research findings that lend support to Vygotsky's views regarding private speech.

a.

b.

c.

d.

Multiple-Choice Self-Test

For each of the following questions select the best alternative. (Answers and explanations for this self-test are provided at the end of the chapter.) Once you have selected your answer, provide a brief explanation for why the answer you selected is the best choice and why the remaining answers would not be correct.

1. Behavioural or sensorimotor schemes refer to those objects and events that can be represented through:

   a. abstract ideas
   b. mental representations
   c. overt actions
   d. internal mental activities

   Rationale: ____

   ____

2. According to Piaget, the end of the sensorimotor period is marked by a good understanding that objects continue to exist even when they cannot be seen. Piaget labeled this understanding:

   a. object permanence
   b. accommodation
   c. assimilation
   d. conservation

   Rationale: ____

   ____

3. Rene sees a cow (an animal he has not seen before) and calls out, "Doggie!" Rene's reaction demonstrates the process that Piaget referred to as:

   a. egocentrism
   b. assimilation
   c. accommodation
   d. organization

   Rationale: ____

   ____

4. Regarding problem solving, the fifth stage of the sensorimotor period (tertiary circular reactions) is marked by the child's ability to:

   a. reach a solution to a problem internally by using symbolic mental combinations
   b. repeat behaviours that result in interesting consequences
   c. engage in overt trial-and-error behaviours to explore the properties of objects
   d. show reversibility of thought operations

   Rationale: ____

   ____

5. Hala and Chandler (1996) found that $2^{1}/_{2}$- to 5-year-olds delight in "deceiving" a second player in a treasure-search game by destroying evidence of the location of the treasure or laying down false trails. These results:

   a. contradict Piaget's claim that preschoolers are incapable of perspective taking
   b. support Piaget's claim that preschoolers are incapable of perspective taking
   c. are not relevant to the issue of preschool perspective-taking capability
   d. support Piaget's view that perspective taking first emerges during the sensorimotor period

   Rationale: ____

   ____

6. Michael is an 8-year-old who shows an understanding of seriation, class inclusion, and conservation of number and amount. However, he fails to understand other types of conservation problems. This pattern of development:

   a. indicates that Michael is advanced for his age
   b. is common, and it is termed "horizontal décalage"
   c. indicates that Michael is delayed for his age
   d. is uncommon, and likely indicates Michael will show cognitive deficits later

   Rationale: ____

   ____

7. Suppose we asked children to make drawings of all the life forms that might occur on another planet. According to Piaget, the most novel, creative ideas of life forms are likely to come from children at the:

   a. sensorimotor stage of cognitive development
   b. preoperational stage of cognitive development
   c. concrete-operational stage of cognitive development
   d. formal-operational stage of cognitive development

   Rationale: ____

   ____

8. Two of the obvious forms of symbolism that flourish during the preoperational period are language and:

   a. symbolic (pretend) play
   b. secondary circular reactions
   c. conservation
   d. propositional thinking

   Rationale: ____

   ____

Activities and Projects Related to this Chapter

ACTIVITY 7-1

CONSERVATION OF NUMBER

INTRODUCTION: The purpose of this activity is to gain first-hand observations of how children of different ages respond to Piagetian tasks. This experience can demonstrate quite graphically how children at different developmental levels approach the same situation. It also makes very clear that we cannot always assume that a child will get the same information or use the information from a situation in the same way we do.

Read the author's coverage of conservation and also look at the Piagetian conservation tasks illustrated in the text. Note that common to all of the tasks is a transformation in shape, location, container, etc., a transformation that changes the appearance of one of the initially identical materials. In all cases, except number conservation, there is no way to know that the transformed substance is still the same amount (or area or volume) unless you actually observed the transformation and used that as your basis for making a judgment regarding sameness, rather than using how the transformed substance looked. It is a tendency to rely on how things look that is believed to lie behind the nonconservation responses of young children.

Mastery of the **conservation of number task** is believed by some educators and developmental psychologists to be a prerequisite to understanding arithmetic since it requires the ability to establish a 1:1 correspondence between two sets of objects and to understand that those sets do not change in number unless something is added or taken away. It would be difficult to truly understand addition and subtraction if you believed sets could lose their equality just by rearranging positions of the objects within a set.

There is considerable controversy in the literature about what constitutes a conservation response, leading to inconsistencies in conclusions about children's capabilities. For the purposes of this project a child will be considered a "conserver" if he: (a) asserts that there are still the same number of candies even when they have been rearranged, **and** (b) gives an explanation that falls in at least one of the following categories:

1. <u>reversibility</u>, e.g., "could just put the candies back the way they were, and there would still be the same number"
2. <u>compensation</u>, e.g., "this row has gotten longer/shorter, but there's more/less space between the candies"
3. <u>addition/subtraction</u>, e.g., "haven't added any candies or taken any away so must still be the same number"
4. <u>identity</u>, e.g., "they are still the same candies, so must still be the same number"

A child will be considered "transitional" if he is inconsistent across subtasks or answers "yes, there are the same number" but does not give a convincing reason such as one of the four above. A child will be considered to be a "nonconserver" if he gives a "no, they are not the same any more" answer and/or gives a perceptually based reason or an idiosyncratic response (e.g., "I just know" or "my mom told me").

INSTRUCTIONS:

<u>Children.</u> Locate two children, one 3 to 5 years of age and the second 6 to 9 years. Ask parental permission to do some tasks with their child as homework for your developmental class.

<u>Materials.</u> Small bag of M & Ms or other small, uniformly sized candies.

<u>Procedure.</u> Before actually working with a child, go through the procedure by yourself or with a friend playing the child. Practise placing the candies and going through the procedure. When you feel comfortable with the task presentation, then you are ready to meet with your first child.

1. Lay out a row of 5 candies, e.g., **0 0 0 0 0**

Say: **"I'm going to make a second row that has just the same number of candies."**

2. Lay out a second row of 5 candies **0 0 0 0 0**

Ask: **"Do both rows have the same number of candies? How do you know that?"**

Response: (younger child)

Response: (older child)

Say: **"Now I'm going to move this row of candies close together like this."**

3. Move the candies in the second row close together so there is no space between them, e.g., **00000**

Ask: **"Are there still the same number of candies in both rows? How do you know that?"** (Write down child's verbatim response)

Response: (younger child)

Response: (older child)

Ask: **"What if we were going to eat the candies and I took this row (longer) and you took this one (shorter). Would it be fair? Would we both have the same amount of candy to eat?"**

Response: (younger child)

Response: (older child)

4. Space the short row out now so that it is much longer than the first row, e.g.,
0 0 0 0 0

Ask: **"Are there still the same number of candies in each row? How do you know that?"**

Response: (younger child)

Response: (older child)

5. Try any variations you want in (a) the presentation of the materials, or (b) the way the questions are asked. Be sure to write down exactly what you did and said and exactly how each child responded. Also write about what effect you thought your variation might have and why, and then indicate whether your expectation was confirmed or disconfirmed.

6. Thank the child for participating and allow the child to eat one row of the candies. Note which row the child actually chooses, the longer row or the shorter, and what the child says.

Questions for you to answer.

1. Based on your limited sample of children, what tentative conclusions would you draw about conservation of number for the two ages you assessed?

2. Do your findings support Piaget's view that preschoolers have no understanding of conservation of number, or do they support the view that even preschool children show some evidence of understanding of conservation?

3. What factors do you think might affect whether or not a young child shows conservation of number (or substance, weight, or liquid, etc.)?

RELATED REFERENCES

Desrochers, S., Ricard, M., & Decarie, T.G. (1995). Understanding causality in infancy: A reassessment of Piaget's theory. *Cahiers de Psychologie Cognitive/Current Psychology of Cognition, 14(3),* 255–268.

Gelman, R., & Baillargeon, R. (1983). A review of some Piagetian concepts, p. 181–184. In P. H. Mussen (Ed.), *Handbook of Child Development, Vol. III.* New York: John Wiley & Sons.

Gelman, R., & Gallistel, C. R. (1986). *The child's understanding of number.* Harvard University Press.

Rothenberg, B. B. (1969). Conservation of number among four- and five-year-old children: Some methodological considerations. *Child Development*, *40*, 383–406.

Sophian, C. (1988). Early developments in children's understanding of number: Inferences about numerosity and one-to-one correspondence. *Child Development*, *59*, 1397–1414.

Winer, G. A., Hemphill, J., & Craig, R. K. (1988). The effect of misleading questions in promoting nonconservation responses in children and adults. *Developmental Psychology*, *24*, 197–202.

Xu, F. (2002). The role of language in acquiring object kind concepts in infancy. *Cognition, 85,* 223–250.

Xu, F. (2003). The development of object individuation in infancy. In H. Hayne & J. Fagen (Eds.), *Progress in Infancy Research, vol. 3* (p. 159–192). Mahwah, NJ: Lawrence Erlbaum.

Xu, F. (2003). Numerosity discrimination in infants: Evidence for two systems of representations. *Cognition, 89,* B15–B25.

Xu, F., Spelke, E.S., & Goddard, S. (in press). Number sense in human infants. *Developmental Science.*

ACTIVITY 7-2

ANIMISM AND ANTHROPOMORPHISM

INTRODUCTION: In a discussion of causal thinking, your text noted that Piaget's research had led him to conclude that preoperational children are animistic thinkers, i.e., they tend to attribute life and, sometimes, human qualities to inanimate objects. Although there is little question that animistic responses are produced by children (and by adults in some cultures), there is considerable controversy about whether it is appropriate to characterize preschoolers' thought as pervasively animistic. It is possible that animistic responses simply reflect ignorance about qualities of a particular object. Some have suggested that the age-related decrease in animistic responses to various objects reflects an increase in familiarity with and knowledge of the defining properties of objects, rather than a decline in the pervasiveness of animistic thought.

Whether because of a pervasive animistic quality of thought or because of uncertainty of attributes or some other reason, children seem to be particularly fascinated by stories about trucks that have personalities and can talk, about animals with human qualities, about stuffed animals that come to life (such as the timid, weak Piglet or the pessimistic Eeyore in *Winnie the Poo*), with cartoons that feature animals with human characteristics, with dolls or stuffed animals that have built-in tapes, animal puppets, etc. There is little question that younger children are particularly fascinated with such toys, books, and cartoons. The question is, why? Does their fascination reflect a pervasive tendency to attribute life to everything, as Piaget maintained, or does their fascination perhaps reflect that they are less certain than adults about the boundaries between alive and not-alive, human and not-human? Could the young child's fascination with talking animals also reflect a lack of constancy regarding identity?

The purpose of this activity is to provide you with an opportunity to gain first-hand interaction with children and to explore ways of assessing their understanding of the distinctions between alive/not-alive and human/not-human.

INSTRUCTIONS:

Part A

Visit the children's department of your local public library. Ask where the books for preschoolers are located. Sample several books. Briefly describe those books that feature animals with human qualities (talk, have feelings, engage in human activities, etc.) or feature inanimate objects as characters with personalities and other human qualities.

Part B

Children. Locate two children, one 3 to 5 years old and another 6 to 9 years old. Get parental permission to ask the child some questions about how she knows something is living or human (or neither). Tell the child that you need help on your homework for one of your classes (children love the idea of helping a big person with homework!).

Materials. Cut out pictures of several objects from magazines and catalogues to use for this project. Possible pictures to include are real animals, stuffed toy animals, dolls, real children, wind-up toys, real cars, toy cars, a mountain, a rock, a waterfall, a swing, etc. The pictures should include some things that are:

1. human and alive
2. human, but not alive (for example, dolls or animated characters)
3. nonhuman and alive (for example, animals or trees)
4. nonhuman and not alive (for example, trucks or swings)

Include a maximum of three examples of each of those four categories.

Develop a set of questions to ask the child about each picture. The questions will concern attributes that distinguish living from nonliving and human from nonhuman, e.g.,

1. Do ______ eat?
2. Do ______ ever get sick or die?
3. Do ______ grow from babies to adults?
4. Do ______ talk like we do or just make sounds or nothing at all?
5. Do ______ have happy feelings and sad feelings and angry feelings like we do?
6. Do ______ think about things the way we do?
7. Are ______ alive/living? (choice of word "alive" or "living" may elicit somewhat different responses)

Be sure that you prepare a response-recording sheet ahead of time that includes the age of the child at the top and the name of each object presented. Under each object record the number of each question and the child's response.

Procedure. Present the pictures one by one in random order. Each time a picture is presented ask the child each of the questions that you developed. Record the child's responses. Also record any questions the child asks you.

The literature on animism has produced very inconsistent results, in part because there are apparently many factors that affect how a child will respond. The particular objects presented or wording of the questions can affect the child's response. You may want to see whether you get a different response by changing the wording. (Be sure to record exactly what you asked as well as the child's response.)

WRITE-UP: Write a summary of your children's books survey and a summary of the data collected from the two children you questioned. Be sure to include a copy of the questions that you asked and a list of the pictures you presented. Note whether the children showed inconsistency in response over objects of the same type. Indicate what factors you think might affect how a child responds and why. If you made systematic variations in wording when questioning children, include the results. What conclusion would you draw based on the material presented in the text and your limited questioning of two children regarding the pervasiveness of animism and anthropomorphism in the thinking of young children?

RELATED REFERENCES

Behrend, K. G., & Dolgrin, D. A. (1984). Children's knowledge about animates and inanimates. *Child Development*, *55*, 1646–1650.

Blanchet, N., Dunham, P. J., & Dunham, F. (2001). Differences in preschool children's conceptual strategies when thinking about animate entities and artifacts. *Developmental Psychology, 37,* 791–800.

Bullock, M. (1985). Animism in childhood thinking: A new look at an old question. *Developmental Psychology*, *21*, 217–225.

Loft, W. R., & Bartz, W. H. (1969). Animism revisited. *Psychological Bulletin*, *71*, 1–19.

ACTIVITY 7-3

CHILDREN'S USE OF IMAGINED SPATIAL COORDINATES IN DRAWING CHIMNEYS, TREES, AND WATER LEVEL

INTRODUCTION: This activity relates to material presented in Chapter 7 and Chapter 8, specifically children's concept development and the nature of memory. It involves the administration of a Piagetian task not discussed in the text and the collection of two types of drawings from children. It is recommended because these tasks are a good catalyst for interaction with children as well as a means of obtaining interesting data. The three tasks are drawing a house with a chimney, drawing a hill with trees, and performing a Piagetian water-level task.

Although children get many exposures to what a house with a chimney looks like or what trees look like growing out of the side of a hill, many preschool and early elementary-school children err in the orientation of chimneys on pitched roofs and trees on hillsides. They draw them perpendicular to the roofline or hillside rather than perpendicular to the less salient (but imaginable) "ground line." What is striking is that the nature of the error made is common across children of about the same age and developmental level—it is not random, suggesting that the error may reflect some incorrect, oversimplified assumption about reality. Also striking is the fact that many children will persist with the error in their drawing even when a correct drawing is in view and even when they can distinguish between a correctly drawn chimney and one drawn perpendicular to the roofline. Errors in placement of trees and chimneys is also quite independent of drawing ability. Some children will draw beautifully detailed pictures with the chimney at a cockeyed angle. It strikes older children and adults as odd, just the way it strikes adults as odd when children misconstrue an explanation that we have given them (perhaps about conception, electricity, the tides, etc.).

Even once their drawings of chimneys and trees are more in keeping with reality, many children still exhibit difficulty on another task that also involves using imagined coordinates: the Piagetian water-level task. The water-level task involves the child indicating the water level in jars that are tipped in various orientations. Even by 11 years of age only about 50% of children respond correctly. Some individuals have difficulty into adulthood (even some university students!) despite the fact that they have undoubtedly seen liquid in tipped containers hundreds of times.

Some researchers have suggested that these errors reflect the fact that human memory is constructive. They further suggest that a similar type of error may occur across individuals if these individuals have all arrived at an oversimplified, erroneous notion. In the case of the chimney and tree drawing tasks, that oversimplified notion may be one about spatial relations. Young children may equate "on a surface" with perpendicular. In the case of the tipped bottles, erroneous responders may be assuming that the contents of a container move with the container or that the contents are always at the bottom.

INSTRUCTIONS:

Children. Locate two (or more) children between ages 4 and 12. Ask parental permission for the children to do some drawings for you as part of your homework for a class project. (Children will typically beam and be eager to cooperate if you also tell them that they are helping you with your homework.)

Materials. You will need paper, coloured pens or crayons, and the water-level task (provided in this manual), and, for some children, prepared pictures of houses and hills for follow-up assessment (also provided in this manual). You may need a protractor to measure the deviation from correct orientation.

Part A (Drawing Tasks): After you have become acquainted with the child, ask the child to draw a house with a chimney. Tell the child you would like the kind with a steep roof (show what you mean using your index fingers to make an upside-down V). Then ask for a mountain with trees on it. Praise the child's work and thank the child for making pictures for you. Explain that you would like to take the pictures to show your teacher.

Possible complications that you may run into include a child drawing a flat roof, putting the tree between two mountains, or drawing the chimney or trees on the face of the roof or hillside. Encourage the child to draw a sloped roof or draw one for the child if the child is young. If you are unable to obtain a sloped roof, let it go but recognize that the drawing is "unscoreable" for this assignment.

Part A-1 (Memory Task): If a child's chimney or trees were not drawn correctly, i.e., not drawn perpendicular to the imaginary ground line, show the child a picture of a house/mountain and say: **"Here is a picture of a house/mountain. Notice that it has a chimney/tree."** Now show the child the half of the page that has the chimney/tree missing and say: **"Here is another house/mountain. The chimney/tree is missing. Would you put it on, please?"** Be sure to have the child draw from memory, without being able to see the correct drawing (fold the half of the page with the correct drawing underneath).

Part A-2 (Copying Task): If a child's drawing of the chimney or tree still is not correct even after being shown the correct drawing (Part A-1), then leave the correct models in view and ask the child to add the chimney/tree to the pictures missing a chimney and tree.

Part A-3 (Recognition Task): If a child fails to "match" the model chimney and tree orientations, then show the child the pair of drawings, one with the correct chimney/tree orientation and one incorrect. Ask the child to choose the drawing that shows how chimneys on houses really look and the one that shows how trees on mountains really look. Record the child's choice.

Part B (Water-Level Task): Inform the child that you have one more thing you would like help with. Put out the sheet that has jars tipped in various orientations. Explain that the bottles all have caps so that no juice can run out no matter how they are tipped. Then ask the child to pretend that each bottle is about half-full and to colour in the juice to show where it would be. You may demonstrate what you mean by colouring in the untipped jar. (Make a distinct line showing the level of the juice and then fill in the juice.)

WRITE-UP: Prepare a summary of your project that includes:

1. Age of each child.

2. Description of each child's drawings, particularly the orientation of the chimney and tree (correct, perpendicular to roof or hill, or number of degrees of deviation from true vertical).

3. Whether accuracy was the same or different for the two drawings (accuracy on the chimney orientation often precedes correct orientation for trees).

4. Comparison of the two children's drawings (note if accuracy was related to age as is typical or if not).

5. For the children who erred in their chimney/tree orientations, note whether there was improvement when drawing from memory (Part A-1), when drawing with a visible model (Part A-2), or not until the recognition task (Part A-3) (most children can recognize the correct orientation irrespective of how deviant the orientation is in their own drawings).

6. Description of the water-level results indicating the number of jars in which the "top" of the juice was parallel with the bottom of the paper, i.e., correct; description of the nature of incorrect responses, e.g., level parallel with side of jar, level parallel with bottom of jar no matter what the orientation, water in correct end of the bottle but level not parallel with the bottom of the paper (or imagined horizontal coordinate), etc. (Place a letter beside each jar to refer to in your write-up of the description of each child's task performance if it varied from jar to jar.)

7. Comparison of the water-level results for the two children.

8. The children's actual drawings and water-level sheets, attached.

9. Analysis of errors using the notions of assimilation, accommodation, and schema.

COMPARISONS WITH CLASSMATES' RESULTS: It is useful to be able to look over drawings brought in by classmates. You will see a clear developmental trend in the maturity of the chimney/tree orientations and water-level results, but you will also see considerable individual variability. An occasional 10-year-old will draw a chimney or tree at quite a deviant angle. Some 6-year-olds' orientations of chimneys and trees will be very deviant from the vertical, whereas others' will be perfectly vertical. You will see a lack of relationship between "artistic ability" and accuracy of orientation. You will see some surprising errors in children's representations of water level, and you will find most children are not accurate. You will find yourself generating hypotheses about why children may have erred on the water-level task and have interesting ideas about alternative ways of tapping their understanding of water level.

RELATED REFERENCES

Beilin, H., Kagan, J., & Rabinowitz, R. (1966). Effects of verbal and perceptual training on water-level representations. *Child Development, 37*, 317–328.

Bjorklund, D. (1989). *Children's thinking: Developmental function and individual differences*. Pacific Grove, CA.: Brooks/Cole Publishing Co., pp. 158–160.

Cowan, P. A. (1978). *Piaget: With feeling.* New York. Holt, Rinehart and Winston, pp. 156–157. (See Fig. 10 for drawings of the stages in the development of chimney, tree, and water-level orientation.)

Liben, L. S. (1981). Copying and reproducing pictures in relation to subjects' operative levels. *Developmental Psychology, 17*, 357–365.

Madden, J. (1986). The effects of schemes on children's drawings of the results of transformations. *Child Development, 57*, 924–933.

Pascual-Leone, J., & Morra, S. (1991). Horizontality of water level: A neoPiagetian developmental review. *Advances in Child Development and Behaviour*, 23, 231–276.

Perner, J., Kohlmann, R., & Wimmer, H. (1984). Young children's recognition and use of the vertical and horizontal in drawings. *Child Development, 55*, 1637–1645. (Good discussion of possible interpretations.)

Vasta, R., Belongia, C., & Ribble, C. (1994). Investigating the orientation effect on the water-level task: Who? When? and Why? *Developmental Psychology, 30*, 893–904.

Memory
A-1

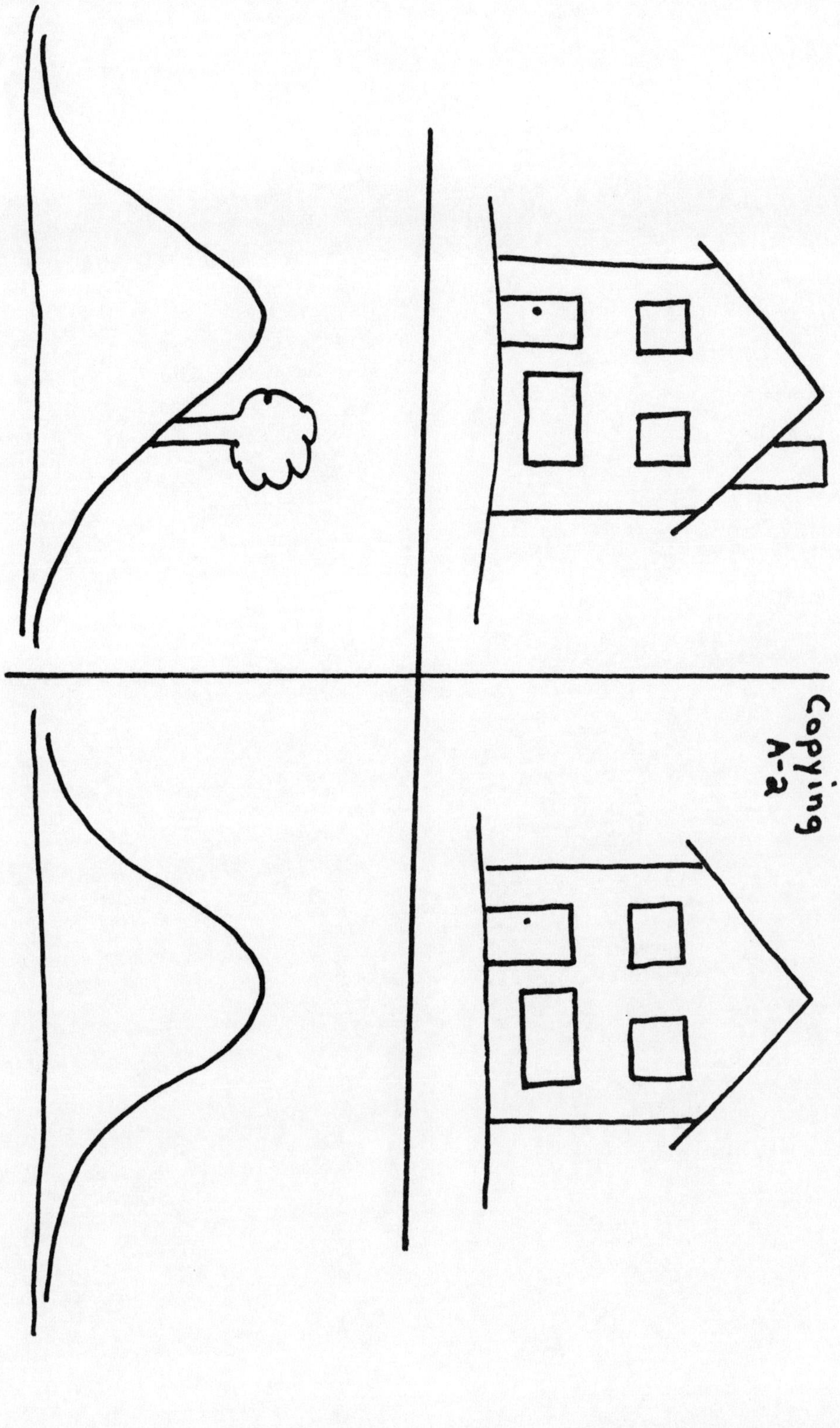
Copying
A-a

Recognition A-3

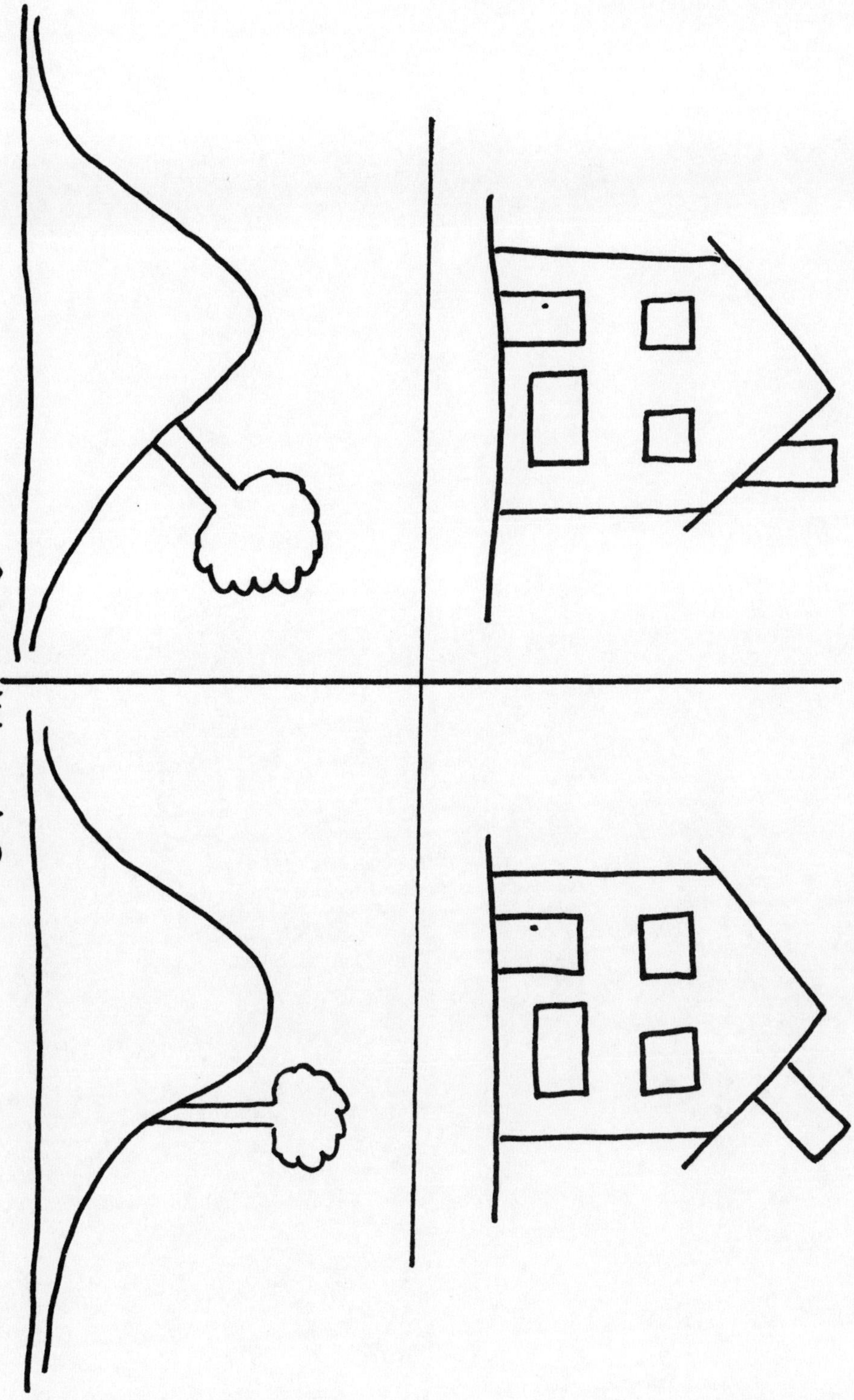

TOP
age ___

TOP
age ___

ACTIVITY 7-4

EXAMPLES OF THREE FORMAL-OPERATIONAL ACQUISITIONS

INTRODUCTION: This activity focuses on the formal-operational stage of Piaget's theory of cognitive development. Piaget maintained that adolescents develop formal thought operations that finally give them the tools to think logically, systematically, and hypothetically. There are more than a dozen different thought operations that Piaget identified as emerging during adolescence. Based on his original work, Piaget assumed that nearly everyone of normal intelligence would develop formal thought operations. Piaget subsequently modified that assumption as he and others found that by the end of adolescence (or even in adulthood) not everyone acquires facility with all of the formal thought operations that Piaget had identified, nor is everyone adept at utilizing the ones they do acquire with unfamiliar content. Education, experience, and utility for daily living are factors influencing whether an individual will develop a particular thought operation.

INSTRUCTIONS: Try all three problems. Do the best you can and realize that some may be easier than others for you, depending, in part, on your major, interests, and previous education. Show your work. This activity is intended to serve as the basis for discussion of formal thought or as an accompaniment to your reading in the text. Getting the answer "right" is incidental to the activity, although it is important to understand the steps involved in determining the answer so that you can better appreciate the particular thought operation utilized in the solution.

Problem 1: Proportional Reasoning

What weight child sitting at a distance of 2.5 m (9 ft) from the fulcrum of a teeter-totter would balance a 68-kg (150-lb) man sitting at a distance of 1 m (3 ft)?

Answer: ______-kg child

(Show the "formula" for computing the answer; note that the "formula" provides a content-free strategy for arriving at a solution, i.e., it is an example of what Piaget meant by a thought operation.)

Problem 2: Combinatorial Logic

If your art teacher gave you four jars of paints and told you to combine the colours in all the possible ways, what would be all the logical possibilities (whether or not it would be a good resulting colour is not important)? The four colours were:
(W) white (R) red (B) blue (Y) yellow

Problem 3: Separation of Variables

The coaches of a basketball team are in disagreement about the best diet for their players before games. One read that a high-carbohydrate diet is best and the other read that a high-protein diet is preferable. Let's assume that you have worked out a good way of measuring endurance and plan to assess each player after each quarter of the next two games. How could you set up a "fair" (unconfounded) test of the effects of diet on endurance? What factors would you have to control?

ACTIVITY 7-5

CONSTRUCTING CLASSROOM SETTINGS

INTRODUCTION: This activity incorporates material from Chapters 1, 7, and 8 and is meant to be applied in nature. Imagine that you are asked by three teachers to help set up three different styles of classroom and curriculum in order to evaluate the effectiveness of each. You decide to give one teacher instructions on how to construct a Piagetian classroom, a second teacher instructions on how to set up a Vygotskian classroom, and you give the third teacher instructions on how to construct a classroom based on neo-Piagetian theory (see also Chapter 8 for more information on classroom activities). Describe the activities you would design and suggest for each style of classroom. For example, talk about the degree of and nature of teacher–student interaction, the interactions amongst students needed for particular projects, and the nature of each project (e.g., hands-on activities, problem-solving activities and/or literature-based activities, etc.). Include discussion and suggestions for children's play activities and discuss potential effects on social and cognitive development. How would each classroom differ? What would be the advantages and disadvantages of each? How could you test the effectiveness of each classroom style? Think about a research design (e.g., longitudinal over the school year) that could test your hypotheses.

WEBSITES OF INTEREST

For more information on Canadian research, visit the Centre for Research in Children's Cognition web page: www.carleton.ca/cricc

ANSWERS TO SELF-TESTS

VOCABULARY SELF-TEST (The answers may be found on the pages in parentheses.)

1. preoperational stage (p. 233)
2. egocentric speech (p. 259)
3. egocentrism (p. 236)
4. concrete operations (p. 241)
5. accommodation (p. 225)
6. zone of proximal development (p. 254)
7. class inclusion (p. 237)
8. deferred imitation (p. 228)
9. transitivity (p. 242)
10. centration (p. 238)
11. organization (p. 224)
12. symbolic (or pretend) play (p. 234)
13. A-not-B error (p. 229)
14. conservation (p. 238)
15. scheme (p. 223)

MULTIPLE-CHOICE SELF-TEST (The answers may be found on the pages in parentheses.)

1. **c** (p. 223) Behavioural schemes are organized patterns of behaviour. Abstract ideas (a) are represented through operational schemes. Mental representations (b) would be examples of symbolic schemes. Internal mental activities (d) that act on other schemes would be operational schemes.

2. **a** (p. 228) Object permanence reflects an understanding that objects continue to exist, even when they cannot be seen. Accommodation (b) is creating new schemes for new information. Assimilation (c) is fitting new information into existing schemes. A recognition that change in appearance does not change physical properties reflects an understanding of conservation (d).

3. **b** (p. 224) Rene is fitting this new animal into his scheme for "doggie," showing assimilation. Egocentrism (a) is the failure to understand the world through the perspective of others. Accommodation (c) would occur if Rene had not referred to the animal as doggie, but instead had created a new scheme. Organization (d) is the process of combining existing schemes into new and more complex structures.

4. **c** (p. 227) Overt trial and error emerges during the fifth stage (tertiary circular reactions). Use of symbolic schemes and mental representations first emerges in the final stage of the sensorimotor period (a). Repeating actions (b) is evident early on, during the stage of primary circular reactions. Reversibility (d) doesn't emerge until children reach the stage of concrete-operational thought.

5. **a** (p. 236) In this research children showed evidence of understanding the perspective of others. So, this did not support Piaget's claim that children are incapable of perspective taking (b). The results are relevant to perspective taking (c) because the children understood what other children were likely to think. Piaget claimed perspective taking would not emerge until the concrete-operational stage (d).

6. **b** (p. 242) Children typically show an uneven understanding of some concepts (such as conservation); Piaget referred to this as horizontal décalage. Michael is neither advanced (a) nor delayed (c) for an 8-year-old. Uneven development is often seen as children acquire complex concepts (d).

7. **d** (p. 243) The formal-operational stage is the first stage where abstract reasoning skills emerge. Based on Piaget's theory, during the sensorimotor stage (a) and the preoperational stage (b), children are not likely to understand what they are being asked to do in this situation. In the concrete-operational stage (c) their answers would be bound by their previous experiences and would therefore be less creative.

8. **a** (p. 234) Symbolic (pretend) play—in which one object, action, or actor symbolizes or stands for another—and language blossom in the preoperational stage. Secondary circular reactions are seen in the third substage of the sensorimotor period (b). Conservation is accomplished in the concrete operations stage (c). Propositional thinking is characteristic of the formal operations stage (d).

Chapter Eight

Cognitive Development: Information-Processing Perspectives and Connectionism

Learning Objectives

By the time you have finished this chapter you should be able to:

1. Discuss how the human mind can be compared to a digital computer, focusing on the concepts of hardware and software.
2. Describe each of the storage systems in human memory.
3. Describe the role of executive control processes in the processing of information.
4. Contrast the information-processing view of cognitive development with Piaget's view.
5. Outline the developmental changes that typically occur in short-term memory.
6. Identify maturational and social influences that will affect a child's speed of processing.
7. Differentiate between production deficiencies and utilization deficiencies.
8. Discuss what children know about thinking. Distinguish between implicit and explicit cognition and identify any age-related changes.
9. Describe the fuzzy-trace theory of problem representation.
10. Describe basic developmental trends in attentional processes.
11. Distinguish between event memory and strategic memory.
12. Identify four different memory strategies and outline the typical developmental progression in the use of each strategy.
13. Describe typical age-related changes in metamemory.
14. Discuss the correlation between knowledge base and memory.
15. Trace the developmental progression of event memory.
16. Discuss the evidence from research studies that have investigated the accuracy of children's eyewitness testimony.
17. Describe developmental differences in the ability to problem solve and reason. Discuss age differences in understanding the use of rules, analogical reasoning, and learning to learn.
18. Define what the relational primacy hypothesis is.
19. Outline the typical developmental sequence in numerical reasoning and in arithmetic skills.
20. Identify some cultural influences that may affect mathematical performance.
21. Outline the strengths and weaknesses of the information-processing approach.
22. Compare the information-processing approach to the connectionism perspective.

Chapter Outline and Summary

1. Basic assumptions of information-processing theories

The information-processing approach employs a mind/computer analogy or, rather, metaphor. The mind's hardware includes the brain, the sensory receptors, and their neural interconnections—in other words, our nervous system. The mind's software includes rules and strategies that specify how information is registered, interpreted, stored, retrieved, and analyzed.

a. The limited-capacity assumption

The limited-capacity assumption implies that there are constraints on how much information we can think about at one time, how long we can hold information, and how quickly we can process information. With practice, processing becomes more efficient and may become automatic; automatic processing uses fewer of our limited cognitive resources than effortful, conscious processing of information.

b. Information flow and the multistore model

Information enters the information-processing system through the sensory registers. There are separate sensory registers for each of our senses, and these registers hold large amounts of information for very brief periods of time. If the information that enters the sensory registers is not attended to, it is typically gone in less than a second. If the information is attended to it passes into the short-term store, which has an extremely limited capacity. On average the short-term store holds between five and nine pieces of information. The short-term store is also called working memory, and it can hold information for a brief period of time while the information is processed.

New information that is operated on while in the short-term store passes into the long-term store. This is a vast and relatively permanent storehouse that includes a general knowledge base, memories of past experiences, and strategies that can be used to process information.

c. Metacognition: How humans control cognitive processes

For information to pass between the various stores it must be actively channelled or processed. Executive control processes is the general name used to refer to the processes involved in planning and monitoring attention and information processing. The term "metacognition" refers to an individual's knowledge of his or her own cognitive abilities and cognitive processes. So, unlike computers, humans are active in initiating, organizing, and monitoring cognitive strategies, and even in choosing what problems to solve.

2. Developmental differences in information processing capacity

a. Development of the short-term store

Children's memory span for digits shows regular increases with age. A 3-year-old can typically recall approximately 3 digits in this type of task; there is an increase of approximately 1 digit with each additional 2 years of age until the span levels out at approximately 7 digits. Reliable age differences are also found in working memory; working-memory span is usually one or two items lower than short-term memory span.

One suggestion is that the observed age-related increases in memory span partially reflect an increase in processing efficiency. Another contributor may be the increased use of memory strategies, as well as the development of more sophisticated and more efficient memory strategies, rather than simply age differences in the capacity of short-term store. However, recent research on age differences in span of apprehension suggests that there are developmental changes in capacity of short-term store. Nonetheless, differences observed in memory span are also influenced by children's prior knowledge of the material to be remembered as they can more rapidly process information in that domain. However, despite the domain-specific processing efficiency observed, older children still tend to process most types of information faster than younger children, which contributes to larger memory spans.

b. *Changes in processing speed*

Young children require more time to execute cognitive operations than older children do. Increased myelinization of neurons in the associative areas of the brain and the pruning of unnecessary neural synapses that could interfere with efficient information processing are two maturational processes that may underlie an increase in processing speed.

Another important contributor to individual differences in processing capacity is speed of articulation. The speed-of-articulation hypothesis suggests that the faster children can articulate the items they are processing, the larger their memory span will be. With age, children are able to read and speak more quickly, and this increase in articulation speed may produce a corresponding increase in short-term memory capacity. This suggestion is supported by cross-cultural studies that have compared children who speak different languages. Individuals who speak languages that have relatively short names for numbers, for example, typically have longer digit spans than individuals who speak languages that have relatively long names for numbers.

The operating efficiency hypothesis assumes that as children mature, many mental operations become automatized and therefore require less time and less cognitive effort. Therefore, age-related increases in memory span may partially result from the fact that older children encode information and execute mental operations faster and more efficiently than younger children.

3. Developmental differences in "software": Strategies and knowledge of thinking

There are clear age-related differences in the use of cognitive operations to assist in the processing of information. Strategies are deliberately implemented, goal-directed operations; age differences in strategy use account for a substantial portion of the age-related differences in overall cognitive performance. In general, younger children use strategies less effectively than older children, and they utilize fewer strategies in the processing of information.

a. *Production and utilization deficiencies*

Even preschool children show some evidence of strategy use, although the strategies that they devise tend to be simple. Some researchers have found that children who do not spontaneously use complex strategies can be taught more elaborate strategies and will often benefit from the use of these strategies. This suggests that younger children may be experiencing production deficiencies. Rather than lacking the cognitive capacity to use advanced strategies, they simply fail to produce or devise strategies that are more complex.

However, when children first acquire a more sophisticated strategy they may actually appear to be less efficient than when they were using a simpler strategy that had been well practised. This represents a utilization deficiency, rather than a production deficiency. The child is generating (producing) the strategy but using it inefficiently. There are three reasons why utilization deficiencies might occur.

First, executing novel strategies may require a large portion of the child's limited cognitive capacity; consequently, working memory may have few cognitive resources remaining to select and store the information needed to solve the problem effectively. When this occurs the child may actually abandon the new strategy and utilize a simpler fall-back strategy that requires fewer cognitive resources. However, with continued practice the new strategy should also become "automatized" and thus require fewer cognitive resources. Second, new strategies can be intrinsically interesting, and children may become caught up in the "fun" of the mechanics of the strategy and may not effectively monitor the accuracy of the information they are processing. Third, metacognition is less developed in younger children, and they may not be aware that they are failing to benefit from using a new strategy.

b. *Multiple- and variable-strategy use*

The development of strategy use is not stage-like. Instead, individuals generally have a variety of strategies to draw from in processing information, and they select from among those strategies in trying to solve problems; older children typically have a larger number of strategies from which to select. Siegler and his colleagues have formulated a strategy choice model to capture this concept of multiple-strategy use and to describe how strategies change over time. In this model, when children first encounter novel problems, simple or well-practised strategies will be selected most of the time; but with practice and maturation, more effortful strategies that are more efficient will be selected with increasing frequency. According to this adaptive strategy choice model, children choose amongst suitable strategies for different problems such that strategy use may change with time and with changing problems.

4. What children know about thinking

While a lot of our thinking is implicit, or unconscious, much of our thinking or cognition is explicit, or conscious. In order to regulate our thinking, we need to understand what thinking is. Preschool children often confuse remembering, knowing and guessing, and young children also think they have greater control over their thoughts than they really do. Research has shown that children's awareness of their own thoughts and their ability to distinguish between consciousness and unconsciousness develop during childhood.

Implicit cognition, or thought without awareness

Most of infants' and young children's knowledge or cognition is implicit, that is, without awareness. Implicit learning is an early-developing ability. For example, recent research has shown that 6- and 10-year-old children learn serial sequences of responses as well as adults do, despite having no explicit knowledge of what they have learned. Similarly, research has demonstrated that implicit memory is an early-developing ability. Further, although age differences are found on tests of explicit learning and memorization and on children's understanding of what it means to think, few age differences are found on tests of implicit learning or memory. Together, these results suggest that although both implicit and explicit cognition can be explained in terms of information-processing mechanisms, they may follow very different developmental patterns.

Fuzzy-trace theory: An alternative viewpoint

Fuzzy-trace theory proposes that there are important developmental differences in the way in which children represent problem information. Information can be represented along a continuum that ranges from literal verbatim representations to vague, fuzzy representations (gists). Gists preserve essential content, but not precise details. Fuzzy traces are accessed more easily than verbatim traces; fuzzy traces also generally require fewer of our limited cognitive resources when they are utilized to solve problems. Gist information is less susceptible to interference and less likely to be forgotten than verbatim information. Prior to age 5 or 7, children seem to encode and remember verbatim traces more than gist information. Older children are more likely to encode and remember information in the form of fuzzy traces.

Recently, researchers have proposed that age-related changes in children's abilities to inhibit preferred responses may play an important role in cognitive development. Research findings imply that maturation of the frontal lobes plays a major role in permitting individuals to inhibit a variety of thoughts and behaviours.

5. The development of attention

a. Changes in attention span

The capacity for sustained attention gradually improves throughout childhood and early adolescence. Part of the reason for this increase in attention span may be maturational changes within the reticular formation of the brain. This is the area of the brain that is responsible for the regulation of attention, and it is not fully myelinated until a child reaches puberty.

b. Development of planful attentional strategies

As they mature, children also become increasingly planful and systematic in the gathering of information. Across the late preschool and early school years (from ages 3 through 7), children are able to formulate more systematic plans for directing their attention.

c. *Selective attention: Ignoring information that is clearly irrelevant*

Selective attention is the ability to concentrate on task-relevant stimuli while ignoring distracting stimuli that are not relevant to the task at hand. Across middle childhood (from ages 7 through 13), children become increasingly capable of concentrating on relevant information and filtering out extraneous information that can interfere with task performance.

d. *What do children know about attention?*

Young children are often aware that distractions can be a problem and that distractions can make it difficult to process information effectively; they usually understand that they "should" pay attention to the relevant aspects of a problem situation. However, they seem to have difficulty in executing attentional strategies. Some researchers suggest that children experience utilization deficiencies when they first acquire attentional strategies; it takes so much cognitive effort to execute the strategy that they fall back on less efficient strategies that take less effort to execute. Although the development of attention is a lengthy process, with practice, the effort required for strategy execution declines and children experience fewer utilization deficiencies. However, some children who have attention deficit-hyperactivity disorder find sustaining attention and use of attentional strategies almost impossible.

6. Memory: Retaining and retrieving information

Memory consists of the processes people use to store and retrieve information. This information may be part of event memory, which includes autobiographical memories of experiences we have had, or it may be part of strategic memory, which includes the processes used for conscious retention and retrieval of information. Event memory rarely requires the use of any strategies; strategic memory can be aided by the use of memory strategies, or mnemonics.

a. *The development of memory strategies*

Researchers have found that the number and effectiveness of memory strategies used increases with age. Mnemonics include memory strategies such as rehearsal, organization, elaboration, and retrieval. Rehearsal involves repetition of the to-be-remembered material. Children who are 3 or 4 years old rarely rehearse. Past this point there is a steady increase in the use of rehearsal. Approximately 10% of 5-year-old children utilize rehearsal; over 50% of 7-year-old children use this strategy; and by the age of 10, 85% of children use rehearsal to aid their memory. Older children also rehearse more efficiently, using cluster rehearsal rather than single-item rehearsal.

Organization involves grouping the to-be-remembered material into meaningful clusters of information in which the items within a cluster share common characteristics. Prior to the age of 9 or 10, children appear to make few attempts to organize information in a way that might aid later recall. Another mnemonic is elaboration. With elaboration the individual adds to, or elaborates, the to-be-remembered material in some way. Elaboration rarely emerges as a common memory strategy prior to adolescence, perhaps because adolescents have a relatively large knowledge base and are better able to imagine relations amongst to-be-remembered stimuli.

Once information has been transferred into the long-term store, it needs to be retrieved if it is to be used later. Under conditions of free recall, individuals are expected to recall information on their own, with no cues to assist in retrieval. Under conditions of cued recall, individuals are provided with focused cues that prompt them to retrieve specific information. For all age groups memory is the poorest when tested under conditions of free recall.

b. *Metamemory and memory performance*

Metamemory refers to an individual's knowledge of memory and memory processes. Knowledge about memory increases dramatically between the ages of 4 and 12. Children who are 3 or 4 years old typically overestimate how much they will remember, and they know very little about forgetting. Yet many 5-year-old children already know that if items such as phone numbers are not written down they will be forgotten.

However, knowledge about memory strategies develops very gradually. Literature reviews have found only low to moderate positive correlations between metamemory and actual memory performance. The aspect of metamemory that appears to be most closely associated with memory performance is knowledge about *how* or *why* a strategy works, rather than knowledge about the mechanics of executing a given strategy.

c. Knowledge base and memory development

Age differences in recall memory may be due in part to age-related increases in a child's knowledge base. Having a more extensive knowledge base in a particular subject area allows an individual to process information more quickly because he or she already has a scheme for organizing and elaborating information in that subject area. Retaining information about an unfamiliar topic requires more effort. Because older children typically know more than younger children about most subjects, they are able to organize and elaborate general information (for example, through elaborative interrogation) with less effort and as a result their recall memory is better.

d. Culture and memory strategies

Western industrialized societies, whose school activities involve much rote memorization and list learning, support and encourage such memory strategies as rehearsal, organization, and elaboration. Nonindustrialized societies, however, promote memory strategies for the recall of the location of objects in a natural setting or remembering instructions passed along in the context of proverbs or stories. These findings support Vygotsky's sociocultural theory that cognitive development takes place within and is influenced by certain cultural contexts.

e. Summing up

Older children have greater information-processing capacity than younger children do. Older children also use more effective memory strategies for encoding, storing, and retrieving information. Older children know more about memory processes and this allows them to select more appropriate memory strategies. Finally, older children have larger general knowledge bases, and this enhances their overall ability to learn and remember new material.

7. The development of event and autobiographical memory

a. Origins of event memory

At 8 to 12 months of age infants begin to illustrate recall memory when they search for and find hidden toys in object permanence tests. Most 9-month-old infants show some evidence of deferred imitation, which also demonstrates recall memory; infants less than 2 years old are capable of reconstructing sequences of actions that were observed several months earlier. And yet, as adolescents and adults, most of us display infantile amnesia, or an inability to recall events that happened during the first few years of life.

One possible reason for the phenomenon of infantile amnesia may be that early memories are stored in a nonverbal code that cannot be retrieved once people become proficient language users. Another possibility is that during infancy we lack a sense of "self" and therefore lack a meaningful way to organize our experiences. Recent research, however, suggests that even very early memories for some significant event can be recalled.

b. Development of scripted memory

Toddlers and preschoolers show the best memory when they recall recurring events that happen in familiar contexts. They often organize these familiar routines into scripts that preserve the ordering and causal relations among the events in a familiar sequence. However, young children's use of scripts to organize memories has a cost; children tend to show poorer memory for events that are novel or atypical.

c. The social construction of autobiographical memories

Parents play an important role in the growth of a child's autobiographical memory. When parents talk to their children about events that the child has experienced, children learn what components of their experiences they should focus on. Parents also help children to organize their experiences into story-like narratives, which can make the events easier to recall later. Parental co-constructions of events become increasingly detailed as children develop more competent language skills. Recent research suggests that the development of narrative skills reflects change in the way children think.

d. Children as eyewitnesses

Increasingly, children are being called on to testify in court cases that affect their welfare. Typical developmental differences are found when children are asked to recall witnessed events. Older children typically remember far more than younger children do. However, even though younger children recall few precise details, what they do remember is generally accurate and central to the event in question. Unfortunately, when children are prompted or cued in recalling events they have witnessed, although they remember more correct facts, they also tend to relate some incorrect events, or false memories. These false memories often persist and can be resistant to forgetting.

People of all ages report more inaccurate information if asked leading questions, but most of the available evidence suggests that children younger than 8 or 9 years of age are more susceptible to this type of memory distortion than are older children, adolescents, or adults. So, false memories can be induced in people of all ages, but it is easier to create them in preschool and young elementary-school children. However, on average, children's memories of events that actually happened to them tend to be clearer than their recollections of false memories.

If legal practitioners want to preserve the accuracy of testimony provided by child witnesses, they should ask nonleading questions, limit the number of times children are interviewed, and tell children that it is better to say "I don't know" than to guess or go along with the interviewer. Being friendly and patient also seems to reduce the probability that children will report inaccurate details.

8. Problem solving and reasoning

Problem solving is defined as dealing with a situation where there is a specific goal in mind but it cannot be attained immediately due to the presence of one or more obstacles. Learning to problem solve may involve learning to use rules and/or analogical reasoning. Research illustrates that 2- to 3-year-olds are able to induce and follow a simple rule, especially when given verbal instructions. Yet, when a rule of a task is changed, young children have difficulty following the new rule, even if they can verbalize the new rule. These perseverative errors are thought to stem from poor inhibitory control and lack of developed explicit cognition.

Reasoning is problem solving that involves making inferences, that is, going beyond the information provided in order to arrive at a new conclusion. Analogical reasoning, based on similarity relations, involves using something you already know to help you understand some new information. According to the relational primacy hypothesis, analogical reasoning is available early in infancy, at least in a simple implicit form. Research suggests that 1-year-olds are able to use analogical reasoning to solve simple perceptual problems. Relational problems, in contrast, require more complex analogical reasoning skills. Children tend to use relational similarity more effectively if they are familiar with the underlying relations used to make the analogy. Piaget claimed that children cannot make transitive inferences until age 6 to 7, yet research suggests that 3- and 4-year-olds are capable of transitivity by analogy as long as the relation is familiar to them. Further, preschool children can be trained successfully in analogical reasoning if they receive explicit instruction that helps them understand the base relations from which inferences might be drawn.

9. Development of number and arithmetic skills

Arithmetic reasoning is another type of reasoning important for children to understand and use in today's society. Arithmetic skills may be innate. Research indicates that very young infants can discriminate visual displays containing different numbers of objects, and by age 16 to 18 months, toddlers have even acquired a rudimentary sense of ordinal relationships. These early understandings are fostered by language skills and use of words such as big, lots, small, and little. So, children are prepared from a very early age to learn to count and to think about quantities.

a. *Development of number and arithmetic skills*

Counting normally begins shortly after children begin to talk, and by age 3 to 4, most children can count "accurately." By age $4^1/_2$ to 5, most children have acquired the principle of cardinality, which means they understand that the last word in a counting sequence represents the number of items in the set they counted.

b. *Development of mental arithmetic*

Children's earliest addition strategies are based on counting and include the *sum* and *min* strategies. At some point during the early elementary-school years, children's solutions to simple arithmetic problems become more covert, and once children begin to perform computations "in their heads" it is more difficult to know precisely what strategy they are using. However, strategies can be inferred by timing how long it takes for the child to arrive at the correct answer. Using this research method, researchers have found that children's mental arithmetic strategies become more complex with age. They may start to use a decomposition strategy and may eventually utilize fact retrieval to solve simple arithmetic problems.

c. *Cultural influences on mathematics performance*

Testing conducted in 1993 showed that U.S. children performed much worse than their age-mates in both Japan and Taiwan. The differences were evident as early as the first grade, and the cultural differences became more pronounced with age. One reason for this difference may be linguistic. Number words in Asian languages can be articulated more quickly than number words in English. This means that Asian children may be able to hold more number words in short-term memory, and they may also be able to retrieve math facts more quickly from long-term memory.

In addition, the structure of East Asian languages differs from English in another fundamental way. In Asian language systems the structure of number names reflects the properties of the base 10 number system; in contrast, the irregular form of many English multidigit numbers makes the meaning of larger numbers less intuitive. Recent research suggests that language may also influence children's understanding of more complicated arithmetic such as the concept of fractions. These results and others lend support for Vygotsky's ideas about the importance of a culture's tools of intellectual adaptation for cognitive development.

10. Evaluating the information-processing perspective

Information-processing researchers have provided a reasonably detailed description of how cognitive processes change with age. Also, detailed investigations into specific academic skills have led to important instructional changes designed to enhance scholastic performance. However, despite its strengths, the information-processing perspective has been criticized for largely ignoring neurological, evolutionary, and sociocultural influences on cognitive growth.

Most information-processing theories view cognitive development as gradual (rather than stage-like), with changes being quantitative (rather than qualitative). Some neo-Piagetian models suggest age-related changes in cognitive processing, but thinking at a given age level is less consistent across problems and situations than suggested by Piaget. However, both the information-processing view and Piaget's view of cognitive development focus on the child as an active agent in his or her own cognitive development.

11. Connectionist approaches to cognitive development

a. *The origins of connectionism*

The connectionist approach to cognitive development attempts to map the neural activity that occurs in the brain by using sophisticated computer simulations of neural networks. Whereas the information-processing model uses the computer as a metaphor for understanding how the brain manages information, the human brain is seen as a single processing unit and cognitive processes are seen as the product of many simple processing units that are interconnected and form a network.

Research in connectionism was pioneered by Canadian scientist D. O. Hebb in the 1940s. In an attempt to understand how the brain learned complex mathematical functions, Hebb, using a computer simulation, discovered that complex mathematical functions could be learned and computed by small groups of simple neurons. This result was exciting since it suggested to scientists that all types of learning and knowledge could be understood at the level of neurons. Today, more sophisticated approaches such as the Parallel Distributed Processing approach are being used.

b. *How are networks created?*

As in the human brain, networks created to perform tasks vary in number of processing units (neurons) and in the strength of the connections among the units. The number and strength of the connections among units varies with the task being performed. Computer simulations are created based on the theoretically expected number and strength of the connections among units, and the output that is generated is analyzed as to its usefulness in explaining how human processing occurs.

c. *How connectionist networks work*

Computer simulations have been created to explain how people learn to read words aloud. Past models of reading had suggested that two separate pathways—one for reading regular words and one for reading irregular words—were required. Recent research suggests that only one pathway is required, namely, one that reads all types of English words by encoding spelling-to-sound regularities.

d. *Connectionism and development*

Computer simulations have been created that model interesting developmental patterns of language acquisition. Just like children, the connectionist model displayed the appearance, disappearance, and then re-appearance of the correct use of the past tense for irregular verbs in English. Similar to children, the network attempted first to memorize each past tense form, to then adopt a rule to derive past tenses—a rule that was overgeneralized to irregular past tenses—and lastly to learn about and allow for exceptions to the rule for correct performance. Computer simulations have also been used to investigate the development of cognitive skills, including traditional Piagetian tasks, how knowledge is represented in children, and how developmental change in knowledge occurs.

Vocabulary Self-Test

Part I: For each of the following definitions provide the appropriate term. (Answers to this portion of the self-test are provided at the end of the chapter.)

1. ________________ Reasoning that involves using something one knows already to help reason about something not known yet

2. ________________ A general representation of the typical sequencing of events in some familiar context

3. ________________ Information-processing model that depicts information as flowing through three processing units (or stores): the sensory store, the short-term store, and the long-term store

4. ________________ Memory for important experiences or events that have happened to us

5. ________________ Goal-directed and deliberately implemented mental operations used to facilitate task performance

6. ________________ A recollection that is prompted by a cue associated with the setting in which the recalled event originally occurred

7. ________________ Improvements in performance on novel problems as a result of acquiring a new rule or strategy from the earlier solution of similar problems

8. ________________ Area of the brain that activates the organism and is thought to be important in regulating attention

9. ________________ The number of items that people can keep in mind at any one time, or the amount of information that people can attend to at a single time without operating mentally to store this information

10. ________________ A strategy for remembering that involves grouping or classifying stimuli into meaningful clusters that are easier to retain

11. ________________ The processes involved in regulating attention and in determining what to do with information just gathered or retrieved from long-term memory

12. ________________ Effortful techniques used to improve memory that include rehearsal, organization, and elaboration

13. ________________ A failure to spontaneously generate and use known strategies that could improve learning and memory

14. ________________ Siegler's model to describe how strategies change over time; the view that multiple strategies exist within a child's cognitive repertoire at any one time, with these strategies competing with one another for use

15. ________________ The ability to prevent ourselves from executing some cognitive or behavioural response

Part II: For each of the following terms provide the definition.

Selective Attention: ______________________________

____

Fuzzy-Trace Theory: ______________________________

____

Relational Primacy Hypothesis: ______________________________

____

Implicit Cognition: ______________________________

____

Attention Deficit-Hyperactivity Disorder: ______________________________

____

Gist: ______________________________

____

Elaboration: ______________________________

____

Metacognition: ______________________________

____

Adaptive Strategy Choice Model: ______________________________

____

Cardinality: ______________________________

____

Operating Efficiency Hypothesis: ______________________________

____

Strategic Memory: ______________________________

____

Metamemory: ______________________________

____

Long-term Store: ______________________________

____

Utilization Deficiency: ______________________________

____

Short-Answer Study Questions

BASIC ASSUMPTIONS OF INFORMATION-PROCESSING THEORIES

1. Explain what information-processing theorists mean when they refer to the mind's hardware and software.

   The mind's hardware refers to:

   The mind's software refers to:

2. Identify each of the three memory stores in Atkinson and Shiffrin's model of the human information-processing system and note the capacity and duration of each store.

   a.

   b.

   c.

3. Explain what is meant by metacognition.

4. Explain what is meant by inhibition and identify the portion of the brain that appears to be related to inhibitory control.

DEVELOPMENTAL DIFFERENCES IN INFORMATION-PROCESSING CAPACITY

5. Explain what memory span refers to, and provide the typical memory span found in preschool children and in elementary-school children.

   Memory span refers to:

   Memory span for preschool children is approximately:

   Memory span for elementary-school children is approximately:

6. Identify two maturational developments that may partially account for age-related increases in speed of processing.

   a.

   b.

7. Explain how speed of articulation can affect processing capacity (memory span).

DEVELOPMENTAL DIFFERENCES IN "SOFTWARE": STRATEGIES AND KNOWLEDGE OF THINKING

8. Explain what production deficiencies and utilization deficiencies are.

   Production deficiencies:

   Utilization deficiencies:

9. List three reasons why children might display utilization deficiencies when they first acquire a new and more sophisticated strategy.

   a.

   b.

   c.

WHAT CHILDREN KNOW ABOUT THINKING

10. Define and distinguish between implicit cognition and explicit cognition. Identify any age-related changes suggested by research. What does the research imply about the developmental patterns each follows; in other words, does implicit and explicit cognition follow similar or different developmental patterns, and what is the evidence?

11. List three ways in which fuzzy traces differ from verbatim traces.

    a.

    b.

    c.

THE DEVELOPMENT OF ATTENTION

12. Identify the area of the brain that is responsible for the regulation of attention.

13. Assume you are watching children as they compare two pictures to determine if the pictures are identical. Describe the strategies that would most likely be used by a 4-year-old child and a 7-year-old child on this type of task.

    A 4-year-old child would most likely:

    A 7-year-old child would most likely:

MEMORY: RETAINING AND RETRIEVING INFORMATION

14. Describe what is meant by event memory and strategic memory, and provide an example of each type of memory.

    Event memory:

    Strategic memory:

15. List and describe three memory strategies.

    a.

    b.

    c.

16. Outline how the use of rehearsal and elaboration changes across childhood and adolescence.

17. Distinguish between free recall and cued recall.

    Free recall:

    Cued recall:

18. Outline how metamemory typically changes between the ages of 4 and 12.

19. List four general conclusions about the development of strategic memory that are supported by evidence from a variety of research studies.

    a.

    b.

    c.

    d.

20. Discuss how culture influences the memory strategies we learn and employ. Does the evidence support Vygotsky's sociocultural theory?

THE DEVELOPMENT OF EVENT AND AUTOBIOGRAPHICAL MEMORY

21. Explain what is meant by infantile amnesia and discuss two contemporary cognitive explanations for this phenomenon.

    Infantile amnesia is:

    a.

    b.

22. Describe what scripted memories are and discuss how scripts may interfere with memories of novel events.

    Scripts are:

    They may interfere with memories for novel events because:

23. Discuss research evidence that relates to the suggestibility of child witnesses.

24. Identify five procedures that can help to preserve the accuracy of children's eyewitness testimony.

    a.

    b.

    c.

    d.

    e.

PROBLEM SOLVING AND REASONING

25. Discuss how learning to use rules and analogical reasoning is important to problem solving. Next, discuss any developmental, age-related changes identified in your text.

DEVELOPMENT OF NUMBER AND ARITHMETIC SKILLS

26. Identify five strategies that children might use to solve addition problems, and illustrate each strategy using the problem 12 + 8.

    a.

    b.

    c.

    d.

    e.

27. Identify two differences between East Asian languages and English that may partially explain observed differences in mathematical skills.

    a.

    b.

EVALUATING THE INFORMATION-PROCESSING PERSPECTIVE

27. Discuss the strengths and weaknesses of the information-processing approach to understanding cognitive development. Compare the approach with Piaget's theory.

28. Identify two ways in which information-processing theories of cognitive development differ from Piaget's theory.

    a.

    b.

CONNECTIONIST APPROACHES TO COGNITIVE DEVELOPMENT

29. Compare the information-processing approach to the connectionist approach.

Multiple-Choice Self-Test

For each of the following questions select the best alternative. (Answers and explanations for this self-test are provided at the end of the chapter.) Once you have selected your answer, provide a brief explanation for why the answer you selected is the best choice and why the remaining answers would not be correct.

1. One fundamental difference between the information-processing model and Piaget's model of cognition is that:

   a. the information-processing model emphasizes that a variety of processing deficiencies may result in a failure to solve problems
   b. the information-processing model places less emphasis on the development of long-term memory
   c. the information-processing model suggests that immaturity of cognitive structures is the key reason children are unable to solve certain types of problems
   d. the information-processing model suggests that a child's inability to assimilate new experiences is the main reason that problem-solving failures occur

   Rationale: ____

   ____

2. Research comparing the amount of information different-age children (preschool or older) hold in their "sensory register" has shown that:

   a. sensory memory increases dramatically with age
   b. sensory memory span decreases as short-term memory span increases
   c. there is no evidence of age-related differences in sensory memory
   d. sensory memory decreases throughout the preschool years and then begins to increase during the elementary school years

   Rationale: ____

   ____

3. Miller and Weiss asked 7-, 10-, and 13-year-olds to remember the locations of animals hidden behind flaps. Telling the children to pay attention to the animals and ignore other objects behind each flap:

   a. was equally helpful to all three age groups
   b. was helpful only for the youngest age group; the 10- and 13-year-olds did well whether told what to ignore or not told
   c. was not helpful for any of the age groups; even at 13 years of age children have difficulty ignoring irrelevant information
   d. was most helpful for the 13-year-olds; younger children tended to have difficulty ignoring irrelevant information, even when instructed to

   Rationale: ____

   ____

4. The treatment that has been found to be least effective in helping children with attention deficit-hyperactivity disorder (ADHD) is:

   a. the use of stimulant medication
   b. cognitive-behavioural training
   c. a combination of medication and cognitive-behavioural training
   d. dietary modification that focuses on the elimination of sugar

   Rationale: ____

   ____

5. The most accurate statement regarding recognition and recall memory in children would be:

   a. recall memory exceeds recognition memory
   b. recognition memory typically exceeds recall memory
   c. recognition memory and recall memory are equivalent
   d. recall is superior for strategic memory, but recognition is superior for event memory

   Rationale: ____

   ____

6. The memory strategy that typically develops first in children is:

   a. elaboration
   b. semantic organization
   c. rehearsal
   d. labelling objects

   Rationale: ____

   ____

7. Of the following educational strategies, the strategy that would most likely be supported by an information-processing theorist would be:

   a. increasing the short-term memory demands of tasks to promote the development of short-term memory
   b. emphasizing rote learning of factual knowledge to increase a child's general knowledge base
   c. focusing on whether or not final answers are correct, rather than focusing on the processes used to obtain the answers
   d. encouraging children to participate in strategic memory games that are fun

   Rationale: ____

   ____

Activities and Projects Related to this Chapter

ACTIVITY 8-1

DEVELOPMENT OF SYSTEMATIC ATTENTIONAL/SEARCH STRATEGIES

INTRODUCTION: This activity relates to material in Chapters 6 and 8 on the development of the ability to carry out systematic visual searches. Young children characteristically do not gather information needed for making judgments in a systematic way. We can see the effects of unsystematic visual search in the errors young children make on word match tests, in finding a needed puzzle piece from an assortment of a dozen possibilities, in finding a lost sock, etc. The following task will provide an opportunity to observe individual and/or age-related differences in efficiency of visual search—and the consequences for task performance. The stimuli are adapted from Vurpillot's classic study and the response mode from P. Miller's 1986 study.

INSTRUCTIONS:

Children. Locate two children between 3 and 8 years of age. Ask parental permission for the children to help you with your homework for a developmental psychology class.

Materials. Two identical apartment houses are pre-printed for you at the end of this activity description. Cover each window with a piece of index card cut to fit. Put a loop of tape on top of each cover so each can be picked up with the touch of an index finger.

Procedure.

1. Place the two apartment house pages side by side on a table or on the floor. All windows should be individually covered when the child first sees the apartment houses.

2. Introduce the task to the child by saying, **"There are two apartment houses in front of us. The windows are all covered up. I would like you to find out if the windows are all just the same on this apartment building (point) and on this other apartment building (point)—or if some windows are different. Uncover the windows one at a time and leave them uncovered once you look at them. Tell me when you know for sure that the apartment houses are just the same or are different."**

   (Note: There is no way to know for sure that the windows are all the same without first looking at all 16 windows. The number of windows the child opens and the order will provide you with a "measure" of the strategy the child used, if any.)

3. Record each child's sequence of lifting the covers by recording the order (1, 2, 3 ...) in the blanks provided. Also indicate the child's verbalizations, record the number of windows opened before making a conclusion, and record the child's conclusion.

CHILD 1 **age** ________ **CHILD 2** **age** ________

CHILD 1				CHILD 2			
_____	_____	_____	_____	_____	_____	_____	_____
_____	_____	_____	_____	_____	_____	_____	_____
_____	_____	_____	_____	_____	_____	_____	_____
_____	_____	_____	_____	_____	_____	_____	_____

Number of windows opened before concluding that the houses are the same:

CHILD 1 ________ **CHILD 2** ________

Verbalizations of interest:
<u>**Child 1**</u>

<u>**Child 2**</u>

<u>**Question.**</u> How did the two children differ in their approach to the task and in the accuracy of their conclusions?

RELATED REFERENCES

Jacques, S., & Zelazo, P.D. (2001). The flexible item selection task (FIST): A measure of executive function in preschoolers. *Developmental Neuropsychology, 20(3)*, 573–591.

Jacques, S., Zelazo, P.D., Kirkhman, N.Z., & Semcesen, T.K. (1999). Rule selection versus rule execution in preschoolers: An error-detection approach. *Developmental Psychology, 35(3)*, 770–780.

Miller, P. H., Haynes, V. F., DeMarie-Drelow, D., & Woody-Ramsey, J. (1986). Children's strategies for gathering information in three tasks. *Child Development*, *57*, 1429–1439.

Vliestra, A. G. (1982). Children's responses to task instructions: Age changes and training effects. *Child Development*, *53*, 534–542.

Vurpillot, E. (1968). The development of scanning strategies and their relation to visual differentiation. *Journal of Experimental Child Psychology*, *6*, 632–650.

REFERENCES OF INTEREST

Klein, J., & Bisanz, J. (2000). Preschoolers doing arithmetic: The concepts are willing but the working memory is weak. *Canadian Journal of Experimental Psychology, 54,* 105–115.

Johnson, J., Im-Bolter, N., & Pascual-Leone, J. (2003). Development of mental attention in gifted and mainstream children: The role of mental capacity, inhibition, and speed of processing. *Child Development, 74(6),* 1594–1614.

Niaz, M. (2001). Are neo-Piagetian and neo-Vygotskian interpretation of potential for learning complementary? *Perceptual and Motor Skills, 93(2),* 416–418.

Niaz, M., & Caraucan, E. (1998). "Learning-to-learn": A neo-Piagetian interpretation of the potential for learning. *Perceptual and Motor Skills, 86(3, Pt2),* 1291–1298.

Pascual-Leone, J. (1995). Learning and development as dialectical factors in cognitive growth. *Human Development, 38,* 338–348.

Pascual-Leone, J. (1987). Organismic processes for neo-Piagetian theories: A dialectical causal account of cognitive development. *International Journal of Psychology, 22,* 531–570.

Pascual-Leone, J., & Johnson, J. (1991). The psychological unit and its role in task analysis. A reinterpretation of object permanence. In M. Chandler & M. Chapman (Eds.), *Criteria for competence: Controversies in the assessment of children's abilities* (pp. 153–187). Hillsdale, NJ: Erlbaum.

Pascual-Leone, J., & Johnson, J. (1999). A dialectical constructivist view of representation: Role of mental attention, executives, and symbols. In I. E. Sigel (Ed.), *Development of mental representation: Theories and applications* (pp. 169–200). Mahwah, NJ: Erlbaum.

Pascual-Leone, J., Johnson, J., Baskind, D., Dworsky, S., & Severtston, E. (2000). Culture-fair assessment and the processes of mental attention. In A. Kozulin, Y. Rand, & R. Feuerstein (Eds.), *Experience of mediated learning: An impact of Feuerstein's theory in education and psychology* (pp. 191–214). New York: Pergamon Press.

Peterson, C. (2002). Children's long-term memory for autobiographical events. *Developmental Review, 22,* 370–402.

Robertson, E.M., Theoret, H., & Pascual-Leone, A. (2003). Studies in cognition: The problems solved and created by Transcranial Magnetic Stimulation. *Journal of Cognitive Neuroscience, 15(7),* 948–960.

ANSWERS TO SELF-TESTS

VOCABULARY SELF-TEST (The answers may be found on the pages in parentheses.)

1. analogical reasoning (p. 294)
2. script (p. 286)
3. multistore model (p. 265)
4. autobiographical memory (p. 277)
5. strategies (p. 268)
6. cued recall (p. 280)
7. learning to learn (p. 297)
8. reticular formation (p. 275)
9. span of apprehension (p. 266)
10. semantic organization (p. 280)
11. executive control processes (p. 266)
12. mnemonics (p. 277)
13. production deficiency (p. 269)
14. adaptive strategy choice model (p. 270)
15. inhibition (p. 274)

MULTIPLE-CHOICE SELF-TEST (The answers may be found on the pages in parentheses.)

1. **a** (p. 264) The information-processing model suggests problem solving may fail for a number of reasons related to deficiencies in the processing of information. This approach emphasizes the development of long-term memory (b) more than Piaget. Piaget focused more heavily on the maturation of cognitive structures (c). The information-processing approach doesn't refer to assimilation (d) (or accommodation) as the key to cognitive growth and development.

2. **c** (pp. 265–266) Sensory memory capacity does not change with age. It neither increases (a) nor decreases (b or d). Sensory memory registers environmental stimuli; the memory system that shows the most evidence of age-related changes is short-term memory.

3. **d** (pp. 276–277) The older children benefited the most from being told to ignore the irrelevant information. The younger children were less able to selectively attend to the relevant information, even when told to ignore the irrelevant features (eliminating alternatives a and b). The 13-year-olds were able to ignore the irrelevant information (c).

4. **d** (p. 276) Dietary modification has not been shown to effectively reduce the symptoms of ADHD. When medication is combined with cognitive-behavioural training, treatment is most effective (c). Either treatment on its own (a and b) is more effective than simple dietary modification.

5. **b** (p. 280) Children are often able to recognize information that they cannot spontaneously recall from memory, making recognition better than recall memory. This means that recall memory does not exceed recognition memory (a), nor are the two types of memory equivalent (c). It doesn't matter which memory system is being tested (d); in general recognition memory is superior to free recall.

6. **d** (p. 279) Labelling information to be recalled is evident in children as early as 3 years of age. Elaboration is rarely seen before adolescence (a). Semantic organization (b) is evident in 9-year-old children. Rehearsal (c) is evident in 50% of 7-year-olds and 85% of 10-year-olds.

7. **d** (pp. 280, 304) When children participate in memory games that are "fun," children develop an appreciation for why it is important to be able to recall information at a later time. Information-processing theorists would suggest that short-term memory demands be minimized (a). They would also suggest that it is more important to teach strategies for solving problems (b) and to focus on the processes a child uses (c), rather than focusing on the correctness of the final answer.

Chapter Nine

Intelligence: Measuring Mental Performance

Learning Objectives

By the time you have finished this chapter you should be able to:

1. Describe the testing procedure developed by Alfred Binet and discuss how his procedure could be used to determine a child's mental age.
2. Compare and contrast the factor-analytic models of intelligence developed by Spearman, Thurstone, Guilford, and Carroll.
3. Distinguish between fluid and crystallized intelligence.
4. Outline the key components in Sternberg's triarchic theory of intelligence.
5. Describe Gardner's theory of multiple intelligences.
6. Describe a variety of methods that have been used to assess intelligence in preschool and school-aged children.
7. Describe and evaluate the Bayley scales of infant development.
8. Identify three measures of early information-processing ability that correlate with later IQ scores.
9. Discuss the stability of IQ scores during childhood and adolescence.
10. Discuss how well IQ can predict scholastic achievement, vocational outcomes, and general adjustment and life satisfaction.
11. Summarize the evidence concerning genetic and environmental influences on IQ.
12. Describe how a child's home environment can be assessed, and identify the aspects of the home environment that appear to exert the greatest influence on intellectual development.
13. Summarize the findings that relate to social class, racial, and ethnic differences in IQ, and discuss three potential reasons for these differences.
14. Identify two levels of intellectual ability proposed by Jensen.
15. Evaluate the overall effectiveness of compensatory interventions such as Head Start and Learning to Learn, and identify some factors that can influence the effectiveness of these types of programs.
16. Differentiate between convergent and divergent thinking.
17. Describe the key aspects of the investment theory of creativity and discuss the results from research studies designed to test this theory.
18. Discuss some methods for promoting creativity in classroom settings.

Chapter Outline and Summary

1. What is intelligence?

When behavioural scientists are asked to provide a "one-sentence" definition of intelligence, virtually all definitions centre on the ability to think abstractly or solve problems effectively. However, different theorists have very different ideas about the attributes that are at the core of intelligence.

a. Psychometric views of intelligence

In all psychometric theories, intelligence is conceptualized as a trait or set of traits that characterize some people to a greater extent than others. The goal for psychometric theorists is to identify those traits and to measure them so that intellectual differences among individuals can be described. Alfred Binet produced the first modern test of intelligence. The test items were age-graded for ages 3 through 13. A child's performance on the Binet-Simon test allowed the tester to estimate a child's mental age, based on the items that the child was able to successfully answer.

Other theorists challenged the notion that a single score, such as mental age, could adequately represent human intellectual performance. They suggested that intelligence was made up of several distinct mental abilities, and these abilities could be identified using a statistical procedure known as factor analysis. Over the years a number of different factor-analytic models of intelligence have been proposed. Spearman proposed that intellectual performance has two basic aspects: a *g*-factor, or general intellectual ability, and *s*-factors, or special abilities that are specific to particular types of tests. In his view the general mental factor (*g*) affects an individual's performance on most cognitive tasks. Thurstone disagreed with Spearman's theory and suggested there were seven primary mental abilities, including spatial ability, perceptual speed, numerical reasoning, verbal meaning, word fluency, memory, and inductive reasoning.

Guilford took a different approach to analyzing intellectual ability and suggested that there are five types of intellectual content (areas that a person can think about), six types of mental operations (the type of thinking required by a task), and six types of intellectual products (the type of answer that is required for a given problem). When these three dimensions are crossed with each other, there are 180 possible basic mental abilities. However, the scores that people obtain on tests designed to measure these intellectual factors are often correlated; this suggests that the abilities are not as independent as Guilford has presumed.

Cattell and Horn suggested that Spearman's *g*-factor and Thurstone's seven primary mental abilities can actually be reduced to two major dimensions of intellect. They propose that overall intelligence is composed of fluid intelligence (one's ability to solve novel and abstract problems that are relatively free of cultural influences) and crystallized intelligence (one's ability to solve problems that depend on knowledge acquired as a result of intentional learning and life experiences).

Many of today's psychometric models of intelligence are hierarchical models. One model of this type is Carroll's three-stratum theory of intelligence. In this model Spearman's *g*-factor is at the first level; but the model implies that each of us may have particular intellectual strengths or weaknesses that depend on the patterns of second-stratum intellectual abilities we display. At the third stratum are narrow, domain-specific skills.

b. A modern information-processing viewpoint

One criticism of psychometric views of intelligence is that they have a narrow focus; they do not consider the ways in which knowledge is acquired and used to solve problems. They also do not measure common sense, interpersonal skills, and creativity. Sternberg proposed a triarchic theory of intelligence that emphasizes three components of intelligent behaviour: context, experience, and information-processing skills.

The contextual component implies that the context in which a behaviour occurs will partially determine whether or not the behaviour is "intelligent." In everyday language this component is practical intelligence or "street smarts." The experiential aspect of Sternberg's theory suggests that individuals may take a long time to solve novel problems, but that they should show some automatization of cognitive processing on familiar tasks. It is important that test items be equally familiar to all test takers in order to reduce any biases, particularly in terms of culture.

Finally, the componential aspect of Sternberg's model encompasses actual information processing. He argues that traditional psychometric measures of intelligence focus on the correctness of the final answer that is produced, without considering the processes that an individual used to produce the response. He suggests that some people process information faster and more efficiently than others, and our cognitive tests would be improved if they were able to measure these differences.

c. Gardner's theory of multiple intelligences

Gardner has also criticized psychometric views of intelligence, suggesting that people display at least seven distinct types of intelligence. The intelligences that Gardner has identified include linguistic intelligence, spatial intelligence, logical-mathematical intelligence, musical intelligence, body-kinesthetic intelligence, interpersonal intelligence and intrapersonal intelligence, naturalist intelligence, and spiritual/existential intelligence. Gardner claims that each of these abilities is distinct, is linked to a specific area of the brain, and follows a different developmental course. Two major criticisms that have been raised with respect to Gardner's theory are that the different intelligences he has identified may not be as independent as he claims, and that some of the characteristics are not the same kind of mentalistic activities most people define as core to intelligence.

2. How is intelligence measured?

a. The Stanford-Binet intelligence scale

In 1916 Terman translated and published a revised version of the Binet scale which came to be known as the Stanford-Binet Intelligence Scale. Originally the Stanford-Binet was scored using a ratio measure of intelligence developed by Stern. The child's mental age was divided by his or her chronological age, and the result was multiplied by 100. This ratio was termed an intelligence quotient, or IQ. When a child's mental age and chronological age were the same, the resulting intelligence quotient would be 100. A score greater than 100 indicated that the child was performing at a level equivalent to that seen in older children; a score less than 100 indicated that the child was performing at a level equivalent to that seen in younger children. IQs are no longer calculated using the actual ratio of mental age to chronological age, although the interpretation of the score still reflects a child's performance relative to that of typical age-mates.

b. The Wechsler scales

Wechsler has constructed two intelligence tests for children (the WISC-III and the WPPSI-R) that contain nonverbal, or performance, subtests in addition to verbal subtests. Three scores are provided following the administration of a Wechsler test: a verbal IQ, a performance IQ, and a full-scale IQ. Because the Wechsler tests have separate verbal and performance components, they are sensitive to inconsistencies in mental skills that may be early signs of neurological problems or learning disorders. Major cultural differences between the United States and Canada make devising a Canadian version of the IQ tests important and a challenge.

c. Distribution of IQ scores

On all modern IQ tests, people's scores are normally distributed with a mean of 100 points and a standard deviation of 15 points. Fewer than 3% of all test takers will obtain scores greater than 130 points, and fewer than 3% will obtain scores less than 70 points. The cutoff that is commonly used today to define mental retardation is a score of less than 70 points on a standardized intelligence test.

d. Group tests of mental performance

The Stanford-Binet and Wechsler scales are individual tests that can take more than an hour to complete. Today, much more intelligence testing is conducted using group tests. Some of the more widely used group tests are the Canadian Cognitive Abilities Test, the Canadian Achievement Test—2, the Lorge-Thorndike Test, and the Graduate Record Examination (GRE). These tests typically measure only crystallized intelligence and are designed to predict future academic success.

e. Newer approaches to intelligence testing

The Kaufman Assessment Battery for Children (K-ABC) is based on modern information-processing theory. This test primarily measures fluid intelligence and is largely nonverbal in content. Another new approach to assessing intelligence is dynamic assessment, which attempts to evaluate how well children actually learn new material when an examiner provides them with competent instruction.

f. Assessing infant intelligence

Because traditional intelligence tests rely heavily on verbal skills, they are unsuitable for use with infants. Attempts have been made to measure intelligence in infants by assessing the rate at which infants achieve important developmental milestones. The best known and most widely used test of infant development is the Bayley Scales of Infant Development. It can be used with infants ranging in age from 2 to 30 months, and it has three components: the motor scale, the mental scale, and the infant behavioural record. Scores from the first two scales are used to determine the infant's developmental quotient (DQ).

Developmental quotients are useful for charting developmental progress, and also for diagnosing neurological disorders and other signs of mental retardation. However, DQs generally fail to predict a child's later IQ; in fact, DQs from early in infancy may not even predict a child's DQ later in infancy.

Three information-processing skills in infancy do appear to be correlated with later IQ scores. These measures are visual reaction time, rate of habituation, and preference for novelty. Measures of these skills obtained between the ages of 4 and 8 months show an average correlation of .45 with IQ scores in childhood. Visual reaction time is best at predicting performance IQ; the other two measures are better at predicting verbal IQ.

g. Stability of IQ in childhood and adolescence

Starting at about age 4, there is a meaningful relationship between early and later IQ scores, and the relationship grows even stronger during the elementary-school years. However, these findings are based on group averages and do not chart the stability of IQ scores in individual children. It turns out that IQ is more stable for some children than for others. McCall and his colleagues found that for almost half the children they tested, IQ scores fluctuated an average of 20 points between the ages of $2^1/_2$ and 17.

Children who show gains in IQ across childhood and adolescence typically come from homes in which parents are interested in their children's intellectual accomplishments and in which the parenting style is neither too strict nor too relaxed. Children who show declines in IQ across childhood and adolescence typically live in poverty and have parents who are low in intellectual functioning. Klineberg proposed a cumulative-deficit hypothesis to explain these declines in IQ. He suggested that impoverished environments dampen intellectual growth, and these inhibiting effects accumulate over time. Support for Klineberg's hypothesis comes from research on the effects of early deprivation on the intellectual (and social) development of Romanian children adopted into middle-class English and Canadian homes.

3. What do intelligence tests predict?

a. IQ as a predictor of scholastic achievement

The average correlation between children's IQ scores and their grades in school is about .50. Not only do children with high IQs tend to do better in school, but they also stay in school longer. However, even though IQ and aptitude tests predict academic achievement better than other types of tests, judgments about a student's prospects for academic success should never be based solely on a test score. Actual academic performance also depends on a student's work habits, interests, and motivation.

b. IQ as a predictor of vocational outcomes

There is a clear relationship between IQ and occupational status. Generally the average IQ for an occupation increases as the prestige of the occupation increases. Still, IQs vary considerably in every occupational group, and many people in low-status jobs have high IQs. The correlation between mental test scores and job performance ratings from supervisors is approximately .50, but interpersonal scores and motivation to succeed may be equally important in predicting actual job performance.

c. *IQ as a predictor of health, adjustment, and life satisfaction*

A high IQ, by itself, does not guarantee health, happiness, or success. When children with superior IQs are followed across the lifespan, researchers have found that the quality of the home environment and social expectations contribute substantially to future outcomes and accomplishments.

In a recent Canadian study, the prevalence of mental retardation in adolescents was estimated at 7.18 per 1000, and as much as 3% of school-age children. In general, mentally retarded adults are more likely to hold semiskilled or unskilled jobs than are individuals with higher IQs. They tend to have lower incomes, less adequate housing, and poorer social skills. However, Ross (and colleagues) found that the vast majority of the mildly retarded individuals they studied were generally satisfied with their accomplishments.

4. Factors that influence IQ scores

a. *The evidence for heredity*

The intellectual resemblance between pairs of individuals living in the same home increases as a function of their genetic similarity. Also, the IQs of adopted children are more highly correlated with the IQs of their biological parents than with those of their adoptive parents.

b. *The evidence for the environment*

There is a small to moderate intellectual resemblance between pairs of genetically unrelated children who live in the same household. Also, children from impoverished backgrounds show a progressive decline in IQ as they grow older. These findings, along with the findings from a variety of "natural experiments," suggest that the phenotype a person displays for a genetically influenced attribute, like intelligence, is clearly influenced by the environment.

Evidence is also accruing that indicates that people are getting smarter with each generation. This secular trend, call the Flynn effect, cannot be explained in terms of evolution, but rather in terms of changes in the environment. For example, improvements in education, nutrition, and health care may have contributed to improved intellectual performance by fostering positive physiological and brain development.

5. Social and cultural correlates of intellectual performance

a. *Home environment and IQ*

Sameroff and his colleagues have identified 10 environmental factors that place children at risk for displaying low IQ scores. The HOME inventory is designed to assess how intellectually stimulating a child's home environment is. There are three steps to completing the inventory. First, one of the parents is asked to describe the household's daily routines and child-rearing practices. Next, the parent is carefully observed while interacting with the child. Finally, the researcher notes the kinds of play materials that are available for the child. The information is then grouped into six subscales, with higher scores indicating the home environment is more intellectually stimulating.

Research has consistently shown that scores from the HOME inventory are able to predict the intellectual performance of children from toddlerhood through the elementary-school years. In an intellectually stimulating home, parents are warm and involved with their children. They stimulate their children's language skills, and they provide a variety of challenges that are appropriate for their child's level of development.

b. *Birth order, family size, and IQ*

Children who score higher in IQ tend to come from smaller families, and intellectual performance tends to decline for later-born children. However, these effects are small (perhaps 3–4 IQ points) and they are found only when large numbers of families are compared. This means that these trends cannot be applied to children within any particular family.

c. *Social class, racial, and ethnic differences in IQ*

One of the most reliable findings in the intelligence literature is a social class effect. Children from lower-class and working-class homes average 10–15 points below their middle-class age-mates on standardized IQ tests. There are also racial and ethnic differences in intellectual performance. On average, individuals of Asian ancestry typically outperform Whites, who typically outperform Blacks and First Nations groups on IQ tests. However, it is important to realize that these differences are group differences, and they cannot be used to predict IQ or intellectual performance for individuals. As well, different subcultural groups display different patterns of performance on the different subtests.

d. *Why do groups differ in intellectual performance?*

Three general hypotheses have been proposed to account for racial, ethnic, and social class differences in IQ. Those who favour the cultural test bias hypothesis suggest that group differences in IQ are an artifact of IQ testing procedures. It may be that the content of tests is biased against certain groups of test takers, although when "culture-fair" tests have been used the same types of ethnic and racial differences often emerge. However, some argue that the actual testing procedures may cause minority children to do less well on formal intelligence tests. When minority children interact with a "friendly" examiner who is patient and supportive, their scores are often higher than scores obtained when traditional testing procedures are used. However, individuals' performances may still be hindered by the impact of negative stereotypes.

Those who favour the genetic hypothesis suggest that group differences in IQ are hereditary. Jensen claims that intellectual abilities can be separated into Level I abilities and Level II abilities. Level I abilities are important for rote learning; Level II abilities underlie abstract reasoning skills. Jensen found that there were few racial, ethnic, or social class differences in Level I abilities, but he did find performance differences related to racial, ethnic, or social class when measuring Level II abilities. However, to date, there is no evidence to conclusively demonstrate that group differences in IQ are genetically determined.

Those who favour the environmental hypothesis suggest that groups that score lower in IQ come from intellectually impoverished backgrounds. There are three ways in which living in an impoverished environment might affect intellectual performance. First, children from low-income families are often undernourished, which may inhibit early brain growth. Second, economic hardship may make parents irritable and cause them to be less supportive and less involved in their child's learning activities. Finally, low-income parents are often poorly educated and may lack both the knowledge and the economic resources to provide age-appropriate books and toys for their children. Further research into racial and ethnic differences in IQ test performance suggests that almost all of these differences may reflect differences in the economic environments in which these children are raised.

6. Improving cognitive performance through compensatory education

The best-known compensatory intervention program is Project Head Start. This program was designed to provide disadvantaged children with the types of educational experiences middle-class children were presumably getting in their homes and in nursery-school classrooms. The earliest reports showed that program participants were posting an average gain of about 10 points on IQ tests, compared to nonparticipants from similar social backgrounds. Unfortunately, later testing found few, if any, lasting gains in IQ scores. However, supporters have argued that the goal of compensatory education is to improve overall academic performance, not simply to "boost" IQ scores.

a. *Long-term follow-ups*

Results from longitudinal studies suggest that participants in programs such as Head Start score higher in IQ than nonparticipants for 2 to 3 years after the interventions have ended, but that their IQ scores eventually decline. However, children who participated in compensatory intervention programs were much more likely to meet their school's basic requirements, were less likely to be assigned to special education classes, and were more likely to complete high school. They also had more positive attitudes about school than nonparticipants, and their mothers held higher occupational aspirations for them.

b. *The importance of parental involvement*

Comparisons of various early intervention programs suggest that the most effective programs are the ones that involve parents in one way or another.

c. *The importance of intervening early*

The Carolina Abecedarian Project (CAP) identified a group of "high-risk" children and began working with them when the children were only 6 to 12 weeks old. CAP was a full-time program that ran 10 hours a day, 5 days a week, 50 weeks each year, until the children entered school. The children who took part in the program began to outperform their counterparts by 18 months of age, and they maintained their intellectual advantage throughout high school.

Programs such as the Abecedarian Project are expensive, but if we consider the long-term economic benefits that could result when gainfully employed adult "graduates" pay more taxes, need less welfare, and are less likely to be maintained at public expense, the net return on the initial investment may well justify the costs involved in setting up and administering programs of this type.

7. Creativity and special talents

Recent definitions of giftedness have been broadened to include not only a high IQ, but also special talents in areas such as music, art, literature, or science. In other words, gifted individuals are not only bright, but are also creative.

a. *What is creativity?*

Creativity represents the ability to generate novel ideas and innovative solutions. Creative solutions or ideas are not only new or unusual, but they are also appropriate for the context and are valued by others.

b. *The psychometric perspective*

Convergent thinking requires individuals to generate the one best solution for a problem. Divergent thinking requires individuals to generate a variety of potential solutions for a given problem. Guilford suggested that creativity requires divergent, rather than convergent, thinking. However, scores obtained during childhood and adolescence on tests of divergent thinking are only modestly correlated with later creative accomplishments.

c. *The multicomponent (or confluence) perspective*

Sternberg and Lubart believe that creativity depends on the convergence, or confluence, of six interrelated sets of resources. First, in terms of intellect, creative individuals are able to find new problems, evaluate their ideas for solving the problems they have identified, and convince others of the value of these novel solutions. Second, an individual must be knowledgeable about the area in which the creative ideas will apply. Third, thinking in novel or divergent ways is important; Sternberg and Lubart referred to this as a legislative cognitive style. Fourth, creative individuals have self-confidence, are willing to take sensible risks, and persevere in the face of uncertainty. Fifth, creative people tend to have high levels of intrinsic motivation. Finally, there has to be an environment that supports and encourages creative endeavours. Results from tests designed to evaluate investment theory indicate that the first five components are moderately to highly correlated with overall levels of creativity.

Investment theory suggests several ways in which creative potential might be enhanced in classroom settings. Allowing students more freedom to explore unusual interests in depth will nurture curiosity, risk taking, perseverance, and intrinsic interest. Less emphasis on memorizing facts, and more emphasis on discussing complex problems with multiple possible solutions, may help in the development of divergent thinking skills.

Vocabulary Self-Test

Part I: For each of the following definitions provide the appropriate term. (Answers to this portion of the self-test are provided at the end of the chapter.)

1. ________________ Standards of typical performance on psychometric instruments that are based on the average scores and the range of scores obtained by a large, representative sample of test takers

2. ________________ Statistical procedure for identifying clusters of tests or test items (called factors) that are highly correlated with one another and unrelated to other test items

3. ________________ Theoretical perspective that portrays intelligence as a trait (or set of traits) on which individuals differ

4. ________________ The ability to size up everyday problems and solve them

5. ________________ Gardner's theory that humans display at least seven distinct kinds of intelligence, each linked to a particular area of the brain

6. ________________ The possession of unusually high intellectual potential or other special talents

7. ________________ Spearman's abbreviation for neogenesis, which means one's ability to understand relations

8. ________________ A symmetrical, bell-shaped curve that describes the variability of certain characteristics within a population

9. ________________ The notion that impoverished environments inhibit intellectual growth and that these inhibiting effects accumulate over time

10. ________________ A numerical measure of a person's performance on an intelligence test relative to the performance of other examinees

11. ________________ Guilford's factor-analytic model of intelligence, which proposes that there are 180 distinct mental abilities

12. ________________ Jensen's term for higher-level cognitive skills that are involved in abstract reasoning and problem solving

13. ________________ Thinking that requires one to come up with a single correct answer to a problem; what IQ tests measure

14. ________________ An approach to assessing intelligence that evaluates how well individuals learn new material when an examiner provides them with competent instruction

15. ________________ The ability to understand relations or solve problems that depend on knowledge acquired from schooling and other cultural influences

Part II: For each of the following terms provide the definition.

Wechsler Intelligence Scale for Children—III (WISC-III): ______________________________

____

Primary Mental Abilities: ____

____

Triarchic Theory: ____

____

Divergent Thinking: ____

____

Mental Age (MA): ____

____

Level I Abilities: ____

____

Fluid Intelligence: ____

____

Creativity: ____

____

Factor Analysis: ____

____

Stanford-Binet Intelligence Scale: ____

____

HOME Inventory: ____

____

Three-Stratum Theory of Intelligence: ______________________________________

____

Spearman's *s*: ____

____

Compensatory Interventions: ____

____

Kaufman Assessment Battery for Children (K-ABC): ____________________________

____

Short-Answer Study Questions

WHAT IS INTELLIGENCE?

1. Explain how a child's mental age would be determined using Binet's testing procedure.

2. Identify the two aspects of intellectual performance that were proposed by Charles Spearman.

   a.

   b.

3. List the seven primary mental abilities identified by Thurstone.

   a.

   b.

   c.

   d.

   e.

   f.

   g.

4. List the three dimensions Guilford proposed for classifying cognitive tasks and indicate what each dimension includes.

   a.

   b.

   c.

5. Identify the two major dimensions of intellect proposed by Cattell and Horn, and describe the abilities included in each of these dimensions.

   a.

   b.

6. List the eight second-stratum abilities proposed in Carroll's three-stratum theory of intelligence and identify one third-stratum ability that is associated with each of the second-stratum abilities.

   a.

   b.

   c.

   d.

   e.

   f.

   g.

   h.

7. List the three components of intelligent behaviour in Sternberg's triarchic theory of intelligence and briefly describe each component.

   a.

   b.

   c.

8. List the seven kinds of intelligence Gardner proposed in his theory of multiple intelligences and identify vocations in which each type of intelligence would be a valuable asset.

   a.

   b.

   c.

   d.

   e.

   f.

   g.

9. Explain what is meant by savant syndrome and provide an illustrative example of this syndrome.

HOW IS INTELLIGENCE MEASURED?

10. When Lewis Terman translated Binet's intelligence scale he originally calculated IQ using the formula (MA/CA) x 100. Based on this formula, what would it mean if a 10-year-old child had an IQ score of:

    80 points:

    100 points:

    120 points:

11. Wechsler developed his own intelligence tests because he was dissatisfied with the Stanford-Binet. What did he feel was the major problem with the Stanford-Binet? What is one advantage to having separate verbal and performance scales?

    Problem with Stanford-Binet:

    Advantage of separate scales:

12. Researchers have "Canadianized" the Wechsler tests. What were some of the issues they were concerned about in using the American tests on Canadian populations? What did their results suggest?

13. Assume that Dana, Jesse, and Chris have recently completed a standardized IQ test. Dana's IQ score is 135, Jesse's IQ score is 100, and Chris's IQ score is 80. Explain the meaning of each of these scores.

    Dana:

    Jesse:

    Chris:

14. Explain how dynamic assessment of intelligence differs from more traditional psychometric assessment methods.

15. List the scales that make up the Bayley Scales of Infant Development. Discuss when these scales can be useful, as well as their limitations.

    Scales are:

    i)
    ii)
    iii)

    Useful for:

    Limitations:

16. Three measures that can be obtained in the first four to eight months of infancy show a moderate correlation with later IQ scores in three ways. Identify these three attributes.

    a.

    b.

    c.

17. Describe the general stability of IQ scores across childhood and adolescence within groups, and within individuals.

    Within groups:

    Within individuals:

18. Discuss research evidence that relates to the "cumulative-deficit" hypothesis.

WHAT DO INTELLIGENCE TESTS PREDICT?

19. Describe how well IQ scores predict scholastic achievement, vocational success, and health and adjustment.

    Scholastic achievement:

    Vocational success:

    Health and adjustment:

20. Differentiate between organic retardation and cultural-familial retardation.

    Organic retardation:

    Cultural-familial retardation:

FACTORS THAT INFLUENCE IQ SCORES

21. Discuss the impact of environmental enrichment on IQ scores using the evidence from natural experiments involving social change.

SOCIAL AND CULTURAL CORRELATES OF INTELLECTUAL PERFORMANCE

22. List ten environmental factors that place children at risk for displaying low IQ scores.

    a.

    b.

    c.

    d.

    e.

    f.

    g.

    h.

    i.

    j.

23. Identify the six subscales of the HOME inventory and provide an illustrative example of items from each subscale.

    a.

    b.

    c.

    d.

    e.

    f.

24. List three general hypotheses that have been proposed to account for group differences in intellectual performance and briefly describe the basic premise of each of these hypotheses.

    a.

    b.

    c.

25. Describe the two types of intellectual abilities proposed by Jensen.

    a.

    b.

IMPROVING COGNITIVE PERFORMANCE THROUGH COMPENSATORY EDUCATION

26. Discuss the research evidence that relates to the long-term impact of early compensatory intervention programs.

CREATIVITY AND SPECIAL TALENTS

27. Explain what creativity is and contrast divergent and convergent thinking.

    Creativity is:

    Divergent thinking involves:

    Convergent thinking involves:

28. Identify six key components of creativity.

    a.

    b.

    c.

    d.

    e.

    f.

Multiple-Choice Self-Test

For each of the following questions select the best alternative. (Answers and explanations for this self-test are provided at the end of the chapter.) Once you have selected your answer, provide a brief explanation for why the answer you selected is the best choice and why the remaining answers would not be correct.

1. Factor-analytic studies of intelligence have been instrumental in demonstrating that intelligence:

   a. is a single attribute
   b. is made up of three components
   c. consists of several attributes
   d. has two distinct components

   Rationale: ______________________________

   ____

2. One major criticism of traditional psychometric definitions of intelligence is that they:

   a. are too focused on intellectual content, i.e., what an individual knows
   b. are too broad in their focus and encompass too many abilities
   c. are too focused on processes, i.e., information-processing skills
   d. fail to include problem-solving ability

   Rationale: ______________________________

   ____

3. Gardner's theory of multiple intelligences includes the following four types of intelligence:

   a. fluid, crystallized, naturalist, and contextual
   b. word fluency, numerical reasoning, spatial ability, and inductive reasoning
   c. musical, spiritual/existential, linguistic, and intrapersonal
   d. general memory, visual perspective, spiritual/existential, and processing speed

   Rationale: ______________________________

   ____

4. Brennan never did well in school, but he was always considered "street smart." Sternberg would label this component of intelligence:

   a. body-kinesthetic
   b. contextual
   c. experiential
   d. componential

   Rationale: ______________________________

   ____

5. Infant developmental scales such as the Bayley have been found to be:

   a. poor predictors of later IQ, probably because IQ performance is such an unstable attribute
   b. good predictors of later IQ, probably because intelligence is so highly canalized
   c. good predictors of later IQ, probably because intelligence is such a stable attribute
   d. poor predictors of later IQ, probably because infant tests and later IQ tests tap different abilities

   Rationale: ____

   ____

6. The higher correlation of IQ for identical than fraternal twins is typically interpreted as evidence for the influence of:

   a. heredity in intellectual performance
   b. environment in intellectual performance
   c. both heredity and environment in intellectual performance
   d. neither heredity nor environment in intellectual performance

   Rationale: ____

   ____

7. According to the cumulative-deficit hypothesis:

   a. impoverished environments inhibit intellectual growth, but the effects do not accumulate over time
   b. impoverished environments do not inhibit or foster intellectual growth
   c. impoverished environments inhibit intellectual growth and these inhibiting effects accumulate over time
   d. impoverished environments foster intellectual growth because of the many challenges

   Rationale: ____

   ____

8. Guilford suggests that creativity requires a different type of thinking than that normally measured by standardized IQ tests. He suggests that IQ tests typically measure:

   a. divergent thinking, while creativity requires convergent thinking
   b. convergent thinking, while creativity requires divergent thinking
   c. concrete thinking, while creativity requires abstract thinking
   d. fluid intelligence, while creativity requires crystallized intelligence

   Rationale: ____

   ____

Activities and Projects Related to this Chapter

ACTIVITY 9-1

WAYS IN WHICH HOME ENVIRONMENT SUPPORTS INTELLECTUAL DEVELOPMENT

INTRODUCTION: This activity relates to material on the relationship between home environment and intellectual performance. Bradley, Caldwell, and Rock (1988) and Gottfried (1984) found that of six home environment variables assessed, the three that best predicted children's later IQ were parental involvement with the child, provision of age-appropriate play materials, and opportunities for variety in daily stimulation. Other researchers (Crockenberg, 1983; Estrada, et al., 1987) added that the warmth and responsiveness of the parents is as important as the amount of involvement and stimulation.

INSTRUCTIONS:

Part A. For this activity give specific examples of ways adults can promote the intellectual development of children (both preschool and school-aged children) in each of the major categories listed below. (If you have children, you could give examples of ways you are supporting the intellectual development of your children and examples of additional ways that you might do so.) See the text for examples of some specific parent behaviours as a starting point in generating ideas for activities that might help to optimize intellectual development.

1. Adult involvement with the child
2. Age-appropriate play materials
3. Opportunities for variety in daily stimulation
4. Warm, responsive interaction

Part B. Explain/hypothesize why each of the four categories of environment is likely to make a difference in children's intellectual development. Then look in Chapters 7, 8, 9, and 10 for evidence that supports your hypothesis/explanation.

RELATED REFERENCES

Kohen, D. E., Hertzman, C., & Brooks-Gunn, J. (2000). Affluent neighborhoods and school readiness. *Education Quarterly Review, 6,* 44–52.

Kohen, D. E., Hertzman, C., & Brooks-Gunn, J. (1998). Neighborhood influences on children's school readiness. *Applied Research Branch*, HRDC, W-98-15E.

ACTIVITY 9-2

WHO IS INTELLIGENT?

INTRODUCTION: This activity relates to the material discussed in your text on the issue of defining intelligence. In particular, what defines an intelligent person? We all seem to understand what someone means when they say "Oh, he is very intelligent," or "She acted very intelligently." But, what does it really mean? Are these two people comparable? For this activity, think of a few people that you personally know whom you deem intelligent. Next, make a list of characteristics describing each person. Compare the lists. Are there some shared traits? Is one person intelligent because of one particular trait, and another intelligent because of a different trait? Are the traits the sort of traits you might find on a traditional IQ test? Have a friend or fellow student read your lists. Would they agree with your assessment?

REFERENCES OF INTEREST

Beal, A.L., Dumont, R., & Branche, A.H. (1996). Practical implications of differences between the American and Canadian norms for WISC-III and a short form for children with learning disabilities. *Canadian Journal of School Psychology, 12(1),* 7–14.

Beiser, M., Sack, W., & Manson, S.M. (1998). Mental health and the academic performance of first nations and majority-culture children. *American Journal of Orthopsychiatry, 68(3),* 455–467.

Bickersteth, P., & Das, J.P. (1981). Syllogistic reasoning among school children from Canada and Sierra Leone. *International Journal of Psychology, 16(1),* 1–11.

Colom, R., & Garcia-Lopez, O. (2003). Secular gains in fluid intelligence: Evidence from the Culture-Fair Intelligence Test. *Journal of Biosocial Science, 35(1),* 33–39.

Reiter, B.A. (2002). A comparison of WISC-III short forms for screening gifted elementary students in Canada. *Canadian Journal of School Psychology, 17(2),* 31–44.

Saklofske, D.H., Caravan, G., & Schwartz, C. (2000). Concurrent validity of the Wechsler Abbreviated Scale of Intelligence (WASI) with a sample of Canadian children. *Canadian Journal of School Psychology, 16(1),* 87–94.

ANSWERS TO SELF-TESTS

VOCABULARY SELF-TEST (The answers may be found on the pages in parentheses.)

1. test norms (p. 320)
2. factor analysis (p. 313)
3. psychometric approach (p. 312)
4. tacit (practical) intelligence (p. 327)
5. theory of multiple intelligences (p. 318)
6. giftedness (p. 344)
7. *g* (p. 313)
8. normal distribution (p. 322)
9. cumulative-deficit hypothesis (p. 326)
10. intelligence quotient (IQ) (p. 320)
11. structure-of-intellect model (p. 314)
12. Level II abilities (p. 337)
13. convergent thinking (p. 344)
14. dynamic assessment (p. 323)
15. crystallized intelligence (p. 315)

MULTIPLE-CHOICE SELF-TEST (The answers may be found on the pages in parentheses.)

1. **c** (p. 313) Factor-analytic studies have suggested that intelligence consists of a number of distinct attributes. It is not a single global attribute (a). However, there is disagreement about the exact number of components (b and d). Some researchers suggest there are as few as 3 components, and others have suggested there are as many as 180 components.

2. **a** (p. 312) Psychometric theories tend to measure accumulated knowledge or knowledge base and exclude other aspects of intelligence. Some are very focused (b) and include only a few abilities. These theories tend to ignore intellectual processes (c). However, some psychometric theories include a component that reflects problem-solving ability (d); one example is fluid intelligence as defined in Horn and Cattell's theory.

3. **c** (pp. 318–319) The intelligences identified by Gardner are linguistic, spatial, logical-mathematical, musical, body-kinesthetic, interpersonal and intrapersonal, naturalist, and spiritual/existential. Fluid and crystallized (a) were identified by Horn and Cattell; experiential and contextual (also a) were identified by Sternberg. The abilities in (b) were identified by Thurstone. The abilities in (d) were identified by Carroll.

4. **b** (pp. 316–317) Contextual or practical intelligence, also known as "street smarts," implies that the context in which a behaviour occurs will partially determine whether or not the behaviour is intelligent. Body-kinesthetic (a) is not a component of Sternberg's triarchic theory of intelligence. Gardner, however, included this aspect of intelligence in his theory of multiple intelligences. The experiential aspect of Sternberg's theory (c) suggests that how well individuals perform on certain tasks is partially determined by their familiarity and experience with those tasks. The componential aspect of Sternberg's theory (d) encompasses information processing.

5. **d** (pp. 324–325) The Bayley Scales of Infant Development are poor predictors of later IQ (eliminates alternatives b and c). However, past the age of 4, intelligence is relatively stable (eliminating alternative a). It appears that the Bayley Scales tap into different abilities than those that are later measured with standardized IQ tests.

6. **a** (p. 330) When individuals who share the same genetic makeup show greater similarity on some attribute than individuals who are less genetically similar, it is taken as an indication that heredity influences the attribute in question. Environment would be a contributor (b) if both correlations were the same. To determine the effects of both heredity and the environment (c) you need to also compare individuals reared apart with individuals reared together. For any attribute, either heredity, the environment, or both will have an influence (d).

7. **c** (p. 326) The cumulative-deficit hypothesis states that impoverished environments inhibit intellectual growth and that these inhibiting effects accumulate over time. So, the answer is not (a), (b), or (d).

8. **b** (p. 344) Guilford suggested that creativity represents divergent thinking, but that standardized IQ tests measure convergent thinking. Alternative (a) is the opposite of Guilford's assertion. Standardized IQ tests do measure both abstract reasoning skills (c) and crystallized intelligence (d).

Chapter Ten

Development of Language and Communication Skills

Learning Objectives

By the time you have finished this chapter you should be able to:

1. Differentiate between the language components of phonology, morphology, semantics, syntax, and pragmatics.
2. Discuss and evaluate the basic features of the empiricist (learning) view of language acquisition.
3. Discuss and evaluate the basic features of the nativist view of language acquisition.
4. Summarize the interactionist view of language acquisition and identify biological, cognitive, and environmental contributors to language development.
5. Describe how infant reactions to speech change over the first year.
6. Describe the development of prelinguistic vocalizations.
7. Describe the language cues infants use to infer meaning, and distinguish between receptive and productive vocabulary.
8. Describe early vocabulary development.
9. Explain what is meant by "fast-mapping" and contrast overextensions and underextensions in early word usage.
10. Outline some strategies children may use to infer the meaning of words.
11. Explain what holophrases are and identify the communicative function they serve.
12. Explain what telegraphic speech is, and provide examples of the most common semantic relations that emerge in telegraphic speech.
13. Explain what overregularization is, and discuss what it suggests about children's understanding of language.
14. Describe the developmental course of questions and the use of negatives in conversation.
15. Discuss the main developments in semantics during the preschool years.
16. Describe the types of pragmatic and communicative knowledge that young children show.
17. Describe some of the continuing advances that are made in communication skills during middle childhood and adolescence.
18. Explain what metalinguistic awareness is and how it contributes to a growth in communication skills.
19. Discuss the role of siblings and peers in the growth of early communication skills.
20. Outline the main findings from studies designed to investigate the advantages and disadvantages associated with a bilingual education.

Chapter Outline and Summary

1. Five components of language

There are five components to spoken language: phonology, morphology, semantics, syntax, and pragmatics. Phonology refers to the basic sounds that make up a language and the rules for combining those sounds into units of speech that convey meaning. Each distinct unit of sound within a spoken language is called a phoneme. Morphological rules specify how words are formed from speech sounds.

The expression of meaning, either in words or sentences, is called semantics. Individual phonemes are combined to create either free morphemes or bound morphemes, both of which represent the smallest units of a language to convey meaning. Morphemes include root words, prefixes (such as *un-*), and suffixes (such as *-ing*). Prefixes and suffixes are morphemes because their use can alter the meaning of root words.

The rules that specify how words are combined to form meaningful phrases or sentences make up the syntax of a language. Pragmatics involves sociolinguistic knowledge, or rules about the use of language in a social context. This component of language includes the ability to adapt speech patterns to different audiences or different settings, and also the ability to use and interpret nonverbal cues that frequently accompany speech.

2. Theories of language development

a. The learning (or empiricist) perspective

Learning theorists emphasize the processes of imitation and reinforcement in their theories of language learning, and both processes play a role in early language development. The fact that children learn to speak the same language, dialect, and accent as those around them shows the influence of imitation. When parents pay attention to their children's early vocalizations, the number and frequency of vocalizations increase; this indicates that reinforcement has an impact on early language learning. Parents who frequently converse with their children and who use a diverse vocabulary tend to have children who are relatively more advanced in their language development.

However, learning theorists have difficulty accounting for the development of syntax (grammar). Analyses of conversations show that parents are more likely to pay attention to (and therefore reinforce) the truth value of a child's statements, rather than the grammatical correctness of those same statements. This suggests that reinforcement may not play a significant role in "shaping" children's grammatical skills. There is also not much evidence to suggest that imitation can account for the development of syntax. During the preschool years children's speech often includes creative, ungrammatical terms (such as "broked" and "wented") that are clearly nonimitative.

b. The nativist perspective

Nativist theories are based on the assumption that humans are biologically programmed to acquire language. Noam Chomsky proposed that humans come equipped with a language acquisition device (LAD), which contains a universal grammar. Other nativists do not assume that the knowledge of language is innate, but rather that there are inborn cognitive and perceptual abilities that are specialized for language acquisition. Slobin referred to these abilities as a language-making capacity (LMC). Regardless of the internal mechanism, nativists see language acquisition as natural and relatively automatic, as long as children are exposed to language.

Several observations support the nativist perspective. First, there are a number of linguistic milestones that appear to be universal in terms of both the timing and the sequencing of acquisition. Second, specific areas of the brain have been identified that are linked to language. Broca's area is involved in the production of speech, and Wernicke's area is involved in the comprehension of speech. Third, nativist theorists have suggested that there may be a sensitive period when language is most easily acquired, and the results from a number of studies support this view; it appears that language is most easily acquired before puberty. In fact, there are differences in brain organization between early and late second language learners. Fourth, only humans use an abstract, rule-bound linguistic system. Finally, children who lack formal linguistic models appear to "invent" language to communicate with their companions.

Some developmentalists have challenged the research findings that nativists use to support their theories, and others have argued that attributing language development to a built-in LAD doesn't explain *how* language develops. Still other critics suggest that nativists overlook the ways in which the environment promotes language development.

c. *The interactionist perspective*

Theorists who take an interactionist view of language development suggest that language development involves an interaction among biological maturation, cognitive development, and the linguistic environment a child experiences. The fact that there are some clearly identified linguistic universals implies that physiological maturation contributes to language acquisition. However, interactionist theorists suggest language universals emerge, in part, owing to the fact that the brain is not fully mature at birth. During the first two years of life children around the world experience the same pattern of brain maturation, and this universal pattern of brain development may account for the presence of universals in language development.

Interactionist theorists also stress that the environment can support or enhance language development. Joint activities teach the give-and-take of conversation, and infants are more likely to attend to child-directed speech (motherese), which is higher in pitch, slower, and more repetitive than typical adult speech patterns. Parents also foster the development of syntax when they utilize expansions and recasts. Expansions are grammatically correct, enriched versions of ungrammatical utterances by the child; recasts involve transformations of sentences generated by children into new grammatical forms. It is the dynamic interaction of conversations that appears to be essential for language development; children who passively listen to language, without engaging in conversational interactions, show slower language development. According to Bates, grammatical speech arises out of social necessity.

3. Before language: The prelinguistic period

a. *Early reactions to speech*

Newborn infants can already discriminate speech from other sound patterns, and they pay particular attention to speech sounds. Within the first few days after birth, infants already show a preference for the sound pattern of the language that their mother speaks, over foreign language patterns. Both of these findings suggest that the ability to discriminate speech from nonspeech sounds and the ability to differentiate among a variety of speech sounds is either innate or is acquired during the first days or weeks of life.

Parents typically use rising intonations to capture the attention of their infant, and they use falling intonations to comfort or to elicit a positive response from their infant. Between the ages of 2 and 6 months infants frequently produce vocalizations that match the intonation of speech sounds they have just heard. By 7 months of age infants prefer to listen to speech that has natural breaks, rather than speech that has pauses inserted in the middle of phrases. By 9 months of age infants are beginning to lose the ability to discriminate phonemes that are not part of the language they hear spoken around them.

b. *Producing sounds: The infant's prelinguistic vocalizations*

Cooing is the first linguistic milestone, and it typically emerges around the age of 2 months. Cooing consists of repetitive vowel sounds, and cooing is most frequent when the infant is alert and contented. Between 4 and 6 months of age babbling emerges. Babbling consists of repetitive consonant-vowel combinations. Babies around the world sound very similar during the first 6 months, and, what's more, deaf infants exposed to sign language will babble manually, suggesting that early, prelinguistic vocalizations are heavily influenced by maturation. However, after this point the effects of the environment become evident. Deaf infants begin to fall behind hearing infants in their ability to produce well-formed phonemes, and soon non-native phonemes begin to disappear from the sounds made by hearing infants.

As babbling progresses vocables may emerge. Vocables are babbling sounds that are used in specific situations. The emergence of vocables indicates the infant is now aware that certain sounds have consistent meanings.

c. *What do prelinguistic infants know about language and communication?*

Evidence of pragmatic understanding also emerges during the first year. Early cooing and babbling often occurs while parents are speaking, and infants appear to try to harmonize the sounds they make with the sounds they hear. By 4 months of age, infants show signs of positive responding to organized versus disorganized social games. By 7 to 8 months of age, this pattern shifts, and infants are often quiet while the parent is speaking; they begin to vocalize only when the parent stops speaking. This vocal turn-taking is the first evidence of language as "conversation."

By 8 to 10 months of age infants are also using gestures and facial expressions to communicate. Two types of preverbal gestures that are commonly used are declarative gestures (which are used to direct the attention of other people) and imperative gestures (which are used to try to convince others to grant a request). When children begin to speak they often use the same types of gestures to help clarify the meaning of their early utterances. The use of gestures increases as speech becomes more complex.

By the age of 12 months infants are beginning to demonstrate that they understand the meaning of many words that they do not yet use spontaneously. This indicates that after the first year receptive vocabulary (words that children understand) is somewhat ahead of productive vocabulary (words that children spontaneously generate and use in communicating with others).

4. One word at a time: The holophrastic period

Holophrases are single words that are used to represent the meaning of an entire sentence. Early words are often limited by production constraints. In other words, at first children have difficulty forming some phonetic combinations. Often unstressed syllables are omitted from words, and ending consonant sounds are often replaced by vowel sounds. As the vocal tract matures during the preschool period, pronunciation errors become less frequent.

a. Early semantics: Building a vocabulary

When infants first begin to speak, vocabulary acquisition is slow. It may take three to four months for a 10-word vocabulary to be acquired. However, between 18 and 24 months of age, when there is much development in cognitive skills such as attention, infants experience a vocabulary spurt, sometimes called a naming explosion. During this time 10 to 20 new words can be added to a child's productive vocabulary each week. The first 50 words that children acquire typically fall into five categories. Nearly two-thirds of the words refer to objects that can be manipulated, or objects that move; just over 10% are action words; and approximately 10% are modifier words. This early vocabulary also includes some social words, such as "please" and "thank you," and some words that have grammatical functions, such as "what." Infants exposed to multimodal motherese are especially likely to understand and use more words.

There also appear to be two styles of expression in early language: a referential style and an expressive style. Most infants have a referential style, which consists mainly of words that refer to people or objects. These children seem to use language as a means of naming or describing things and events in their environment. A smaller number of infants utilize an expressive style, which contains a larger number of personal or social words. These children are more likely to use language to call attention to their feelings and the feelings of others, or to regulate social interactions.

First-born infants are more likely to adopt a referential style; later-born infants are more likely to adopt an expressive style. There are also cross-cultural differences in early language styles. American parents often treat interactions with their children as opportunities to teach their children about objects, and this may encourage a referential style of speech. In Asian cultures parents are more likely to emphasize social routines and consideration of others, and this may encourage an expressive style of speech.

b. Attaching meaning to words

Toddlers seem to use a process known as fast-mapping to figure out the meaning of words. Fast-mapping occurs when the meaning of a word is acquired after hearing the word applied to its referent only one or two times. By 13 to 15 months of age, infants begin to fast-map names of objects, and by 18 to 20 months, infants can fast-map the meaning of more words, especially when the infant and speaker are jointly attending to the object being labeled. By 24 to 30 months, toddlers can fast-map a novel word to its referent even if they are not jointly attending to the object or referent being labeled. However, fast-mapping can produce some errors in understanding the meaning of words. One phenomenon that is seen is overextension; this occurs when a word is used too broadly. The opposite type of error is underextension, when a word is used too narrowly.

In some instances social and contextual cues can be used to help determine the meaning of novel words. In other instances, toddlers can use cognitive strategies, known as processing constraints, to help them infer the meaning of words. Some processing constraints that have been identified are the object scope constraint, the taxonomic constraint, the lexical contrast constraint, and the mutual exclusivity constraint.

The object scope constraint is the assumption that words refer to whole objects rather than to object attributes. The taxonomic constraint is the assumption that words label categories of objects that share common properties. The lexical contrast constraint is the assumption that each word has a unique meaning. The mutual exclusivity constraint is the assumption that different words refer to separate, nonoverlapping categories.

Finally, children may use syntactical bootstrapping to infer the meaning of some words. Children pay attention to the way a word is used in a sentence, and by using sentence structure they can often determine whether novel words refer to objects (nouns), actions (verbs), or attributes of objects (adjectives). By the age of 3, children become proficient at using syntactical cues to infer the meaning of words.

c. *When a word is more than a word*

The one-word utterances of infants are sometimes referred to as "holophrases." Holophrases are single words that are attempts to convey the meaning of an entire sentence. Often, holophrases are accompanied by gestures that can clarify the meaning of the single-word sentences.

5. From holophrases to simple sentences: The telegraphic period

Sometime between the ages of 18 and 24 months, children begin to combine single words into simple two-word sentences, known as telegraphic speech. These sentences typically contain only critical content words; noncritical parts of speech are omitted. These sentences often serve one of the following six functions: they locate or name objects, they demand things, they are used to signify negation, they are used to indicate possession, they can modify or assign attributes to objects, and they can ask questions. Researchers suggest that telegraphic speech results from production constraints.

a. *A semantic analysis of telegraphic speech*

Children's early two-word sentences follow some grammatical rules. However, young children often use the same two-word sentences to convey different meanings, depending on the context. To properly interpret telegraphic speech, one must determine the child's intent by considering both the words that are used and the context in which the statement is made.

b. *The pragmatics of early speech*

By the age of 2 children are typically proficient at turn-taking, and soon after this they begin to understand that when a listener is standing farther away, the speaker must move closer or raise his or her voice to communicate accurately. Also, by the age of 2 or $2^1/_2$ children consider the knowledge that another person has during their conversations. They prefer to talk about events that the other person doesn't already know about. They are also able to monitor comprehension in others and clarify their meaning if it appears that something they say has been misunderstood.

6. Language learning during the preschool period

a. *Grammatical development*

Grammatical morphemes are prefixes and suffixes that give more precise meaning to sentences. The use of grammatical morphemes typically emerges sometime during the third year. Children vary considerably with respect to the age at which they begin to use grammatical morphemes and the length of time it takes them to master a variety of syntactical rules. However, the sequence in which syntactical rules are mastered appears to be consistent. Brown discovered that the morphemes that are acquired early are less semantically and syntactically complex than the morphemes that emerge later.

Occasionally, once a child has acquired a new grammatical morpheme, the morpheme will be overextended and applied to nouns or verbs that have irregular forms. This phenomenon is called overregularization.

Overregularizations seem to occur when children fail to retrieve the correct form of a noun or a verb from memory, and instead construct a regular form using their newly acquired grammatical morpheme.

Each language also has syntactic rules for transforming declarative sentences into questions, negations, imperatives, relative clauses, and compound sentences. Creating these variations requires the use of transformational grammar rules, and transformational rules are acquired in a step-by-step fashion. This can be illustrated by looking at the phases children progress through in learning to ask questions.

At first questions may consist of a simple declarative sentence that has a rising intonation at the end; *wh-* questions are formed by placing a *wh-* word at the beginning of a declarative sentence that ends with a rising intonation. During the next phase of asking questions, children use the correct auxiliary verbs, but the auxiliary verb is placed after the subject of the sentence, rather than before the subject. Finally, children learn to move the auxiliary verb ahead of the subject when asking *wh-* questions.

Negative sentences also develop in a step-like manner. Initially a negative word is placed at the beginning of the sentence. In the next phase the negative word is embedded in the sentence, but auxiliary verbs are still omitted. Finally, negative markers are combined with proper auxiliary verbs to convey either nonexistence ("There is no..."), rejection ("I will not..."), or denial ("That is not..."). By the age of 3 or 4, children are forming correct *wh-* questions, correct negative sentences, and complex sentences. By the age of 5 or 6, children are using most of the grammatical rules that adults use.

b. Semantic development

During the preschool years, children also begin to understand words that express relational contrasts. Spatial contrasts are typically acquired in predictable order. Children learn overall comparative size (big/little) before they learn comparative length (tall/short or long/short). Next, they learn comparative placement (high/low), followed by comparative width (wide/narrow or thick/thin). The final relational contrast to emerge is deep/shallow.

Preschoolers often misinterpret sentences that are stated in the passive voice. When the passive voice is used, the subject of the sentence comes after the object. However, children younger than 5 or 6 typically assume that the first noun in the sentence is the subject and the last noun is the object of the sentence. It is not that preschoolers lack the cognitive capacity to understand the more syntactically complex passive sentences; rather, it is likely that they are simply not exposed often to the sentences. Indeed, 3-year-olds can correctly interpret such sentences when taught to focus on the relevant aspects.

c. Development of pragmatics and communication skills

One of the pragmatic skills that emerges during the preschool period is an understanding of illocutionary intent (recognition that the literal meaning of the words may differ from the speaker's intended meaning). Referential communication skills also improve during the preschool years. In laboratory tasks designed to assess these skills preschoolers often fail to appreciate that certain messages are uninformative or ambiguous; however, in natural environments they often display better referential communication skills.

7. Language learning during middle childhood and adolescence

a. Later syntactic development

During middle childhood children become more proficient at utilizing personal pronouns, and they can understand and produce complex passive sentences and conditional statements. Still, syntactic elaboration is slow, and the development of syntactical skills often continues into adolescence or young adulthood.

b. Semantics and metalinguistic awareness

During middle childhood children are also gaining morphological knowledge. As they begin to understand the meaning of morphemes that are used to create words, they can often infer the meaning of unfamiliar words. During this time children are also becoming more proficient at semantic integrations (drawing inferences that enable them to understand more than is actually said). An appreciation of sarcasm is evident at age 6 years, but a true appreciation of the humour of sarcastic remarks appears later. One reason they are able to draw these types of inferences is that their metalinguistic awareness is increasing. In addition, this increasing awareness may have educational implications. For example, 4- to 6-year-olds who have relatively high phonological awareness, learn to read earlier and faster.

c. *Further development of communication skills*

During middle childhood there are also significant increases in referential communications owing, in part, to a growth in sociolinguistic understanding. In addition to promoting the use of pronouns, siblings can promote the development of effective communication skills; when siblings fail to understand a message children learn to restate ambiguous messages and clarify their meaning for the listener.

8. Learning more than one language: Bilingualism

Children exposed to two languages before the age of 3 have little difficulty becoming proficient in both languages. When preschool children are exposed to a second language after the age of 3, it often takes no more than a year to reach near-native fluency in the second language. Bilingual children often score as high, or higher, than their monolingual peers on tests of language proficiency, Piagetian conservation problems, and nonverbal intelligence, and they also tend to outperform monolingual children on measures of metalinguistic awareness and at nonlinguistic tasks that require selective attention. Indeed, bilingual children may use their knowledge of language in order to enhance communication.

Results from research studies that have investigated the efficacy of two-way bilingual educational programs, such as core language or immersion programs, indicate that these programs can be beneficial to both English-speaking students and English-as-a-second-language (ESL) students. English-speaking students perform just as well (or better) than comparable students taught in English-only classrooms, and they often achieve near-native proficiency in the second language. Also, both English-speaking and ESL students in these programs are more optimistic about their academic and personal competencies than are students who receive English-only instruction.

Vocabulary Self-Test

Part I: For each of the following definitions provide the appropriate term. (Answers to this portion of the self-test are provided at the end of the chapter.)

1. ________________	A grammatically correct and enriched version of a child's ungrammatical statement
2. ________________	The expressed meaning of words and sentences
3. ________________	A young child's tendency to use general words to refer to a smaller set of objects, actions, or events than adults do
4. ________________	A single-word utterance that represents an entire sentence's worth of meaning
5. ________________	Knowledge of language and its properties and an understanding that language can be used for purposes other than communication
6. ________________	Chomsky's term for the innate knowledge of grammar that humans were said to possess
7. ________________	The notion that young children make inferences about the meaning of words by analyzing the way words are used in sentences and inferring whether they refer to objects, actions, or attributes
8. ________________	The smallest meaningful language units
9. ________________	Early linguistic style in which toddlers use language mainly to call attention to their own and others' feelings and to regulate social interactions
10. ________________	Older companion's use of information that is exaggerated and synchronized across two or more senses to call an infant's attention to the referent of a spoken word
11. ________________	The notion that young children will assume that each object has only one label and that different words refer to separate and nonoverlapping categories
12. ________________	Words and ideas that an individual comprehends when listening to the speech of others
13. ________________	Structure located in the temporal lobe of the left hemisphere of the cerebral cortex that is responsible for interpreting speech
14. ________________	Principles that underlie the effective and appropriate use of language in social contexts
15. ________________	Process of linking a word with its referent underlying concept after hearing the word only once or twice

Part II: For each of the following terms provide the definition.

Syntax: ____

____

Referential Style: ____

____

Overregularization: ____

____

Broca's Area: ____

____

Babbles: ____

____

Overextension: ____

____

Psycholinguists: ____

____

Interactionist Theory: ____

____

Morphology: ____

____

Object Scope Constraint: ____

____

Productive Language: ____

____

Phonemes: ____

____

Transformational Grammar: ____

____

Telegraphic Speech: ____

____

Recasts: ____

____

Short-Answer Study Questions

FIVE COMPONENTS OF LANGUAGE

1. List the five components of language and briefly describe each component.

   a.

   b.

   c.

   d.

   e.

THEORIES OF LANGUAGE DEVELOPMENT

2. Outline the empiricist (learning) perspective of language development and evaluate evidence that relates to the role of learning in the development of semantics (vocabulary) and syntax (grammar).

   Learning perspective:

   Evidence that relates to learning and vocabulary development:

   Evidence that relates to learning and the development of syntax:

3. Outline the nativist perspective of language development.

4. List three research findings that support the nativist view of language development.

   a.

   b.

   c.

5. Outline some of the key criticisms that have been raised with respect to the nativist approach to language development.

6. Outline the interactionist perspective of language development.

7. List three characteristics that are typical in child-directed speech (motherese).

   a.

   b.

   c.

8. Identify two types of responses that might be made to a child's ungrammatical speech, and provide an example to illustrate each type of response.

   a.

   b.

BEFORE LANGUAGE: THE PRELINGUISTIC PERIOD

9. Describe the different responses parents can elicit from preverbal infants by using rising or falling intonations.

   Rising intonation can be used to:

   Falling intonation can be used to:

10. Outline the typical developmental course of prelinguistic vocalizations during the first year.

11. Contrast declarative and imperative gestures, and use examples to illustrate each type of gesture.

    Declarative gestures:

    Imperative gestures:

12. Distinguish between receptive language and productive language.

    Receptive language is:

    Productive language is:

ONE WORD AT A TIME: THE HOLOPHRASTIC PERIOD

13. List and describe the five categories that typically characterize a toddler's first 50 words, and provide examples of words that would belong in each category.

	Category	Description	Examples
a.			
b.			
c.			
d.			
e.			

14. Describe Werker's research on infant language acquisition. Discuss what she and her colleagues suggest may account for the dramatic development in word-learning ability between 18 and 24 months.

15. Contrast a referential style with an expressive style of early language use.

    Referential style:

    Expressive style:

16. Explain what is meant by overextension and underextension and provide examples to illustrate each type of linguistic error.

    Overextension:

    Underextension:

17. List and describe four processing constraints that may guide children's inferences about the meaning of new words.

    a.

    b.

    c.

    d.

18. Explain what is meant by syntactical bootstrapping.

19. Explain what holophrases are, and how children use them in early communication.

FROM HOLOPHRASES TO SIMPLE SENTENCES: THE TELEGRAPHIC PERIOD

20. List six functions of children's two-word sentences and provide an example that illustrates each type of sentence.

    a.

    b.

    c.

    d.

    e.

    f.

21. List 10 common semantic relations found in telegraphic speech.

    a.

    b.

    c.

    d.

    e.

    f.

    g.

    h.

    i.

    j.

LANGUAGE LEARNING DURING THE PRESCHOOL PERIOD

22. Five grammatical morphemes that children acquire during the preschool period are (1) standard plurals (formed by adding *-s*); (2) regular past tense (formed by adding *-ed*); (3) progressive tense (formed by adding *-ing*); (4) possession (formed by adding *-'s*); (5) definite and indefinite articles (use of *the/an/a*). Various research studies suggest these grammatical morphemes tend to emerge in an invariant order. List the five morphemes above in their typical order of emergence.

    a.

    b.

    c.

    d.

    e.

23. Outline the typical developmental progression in children's use of questions in conversation.

24. Outline the typical pattern of acquisition for relational and spatial contrasts.

    a.

    b.

    c.

    d.

    e.

LANGUAGE LEARNING DURING MIDDLE CHILDHOOD AND ADOLESCENCE

25. Describe what morphological knowledge is, and explain how morphological knowledge might allow children to figure out the meaning of novel words.

26. Explain what is meant by metalinguistic awareness.

27. Outline two ways in which siblings may help to promote the growth of communication skills.

    a.

    b.

LEARNING MORE THAN ONE LANGUAGE: BILINGUALISM

28. Identify two potential benefits for English-speaking students enrolled in core language or immersion programs.

    a.

    b.

29. Discuss the potential benefits for minority children (e.g., First Nations children in Canada) enrolled in heritage language programs.

Multiple-Choice Self-Test

For each of the following questions select the best alternative. (Answers and explanations for this self-test are provided at the end of the chapter.) Once you have selected your answer, provide a brief explanation for why the answer you selected is the best choice and why the remaining answers would not be correct.

1. When a child shows a preference for the nonsense word "blek" over "bkel," the child is showing evidence of having acquired:

   a. knowledge about the phonology of language
   b. semantic knowledge
   c. syntactic knowledge
   d. knowledge about pragmatics

   Rationale: ______________________________

   ____

2. A child must acquire five types of knowledge about language. One kind is called the morphology of language, which refers to:

   a. the basic units of sound
   b. the rules governing the formation of meaningful words from sounds
   c. the basic meaningful units, i.e., words, past-tense markers, plural markers, etc.
   d. the meaning of words and sentences

   Rationale: ______________________________

   ____

3. Ebony's parents are articulate, provide an environment that is rich in verbal stimuli, and spend a great deal of time talking with Ebony. They state that when Ebony was only 4 months old she started to talk "sentences" that were three or four words long. A developmentalist would be most likely to:

   a. accept this as true if he or she supported the nativist view of language development
   b. accept this as true if he or she supported the learning view of language development
   c. reject this as being untrue, regardless of his or her view of language development
   d. accept this as true if he or she supported the interactionist view of language development

   Rationale: ______________________________

   ____

4. You are in an airport and hear three 11-month-old babies babbling, each from a different racial/ethnic background (Oriental, Hispanic, and European-American). The babbling of each of these infants:

   a. will sound very similar, because maturation is the major determinant of language acquisition during the first year
   b. will consist mainly of vowel sounds, because consonant sounds don't usually emerge until 12 months of age
   c. will consist mainly of two-word phrases (telegraphic speech)
   d. will sound very different, with each child's babbles sounding quite similar to the language that is heard in the child's home

   Rationale: ______________________________

   ____

5. When comparing language production and language comprehension:

   a. there is no general pattern; the development depends on the particular item or syntactic structure being considered
   b. production and comprehension generally proceed at about the same rate
   c. production typically is ahead of comprehension
   d. comprehension typically is ahead of production

   Rationale: ____

   ____

6. At the holophrastic stage of language acquisition, the one-word terms the child uses are:

   a. simply labels for common objects or actions that occur frequently
   b. typically imitations of adult words that have little meaning for the child
   c. believed to be attempts to express complex or elaborate ideas with only a single word
   d. the first evidence that the child's speech is rule-governed, rather than imitative

   Rationale: ____

   ____

7. When a child learns that saying "please" to grandma with a smile will get him a cookie, the child has learned what aspect of language?

   a. phonology
   b. syntax
   c. semantics
   d. pragmatics

   Rationale: ____

   ____

8. Of the following, the passive-voice sentence that children younger than 9 or 10 would typically have the most difficulty understanding would be:

   a. The yellow car was hit by the green car.
   b. The tiny kitten was hit by the green car.
   c. The yellow car was washed by the two boys.
   d. The red-haired boy chased the brown horse.

   Rationale: ____

   ____

Activities and Projects Related to this Chapter

ACTIVITY 10-1

CHILDREN'S UNDERSTANDING OF NONLITERAL LANGUAGE

INTRODUCTION: As your text author made clear in Chapter 10, children make tremendous gains in language during the preschool years. They are very sophisticated language producers and comprehenders by the time they go to school—so much so that parents, older siblings, and teachers sometimes wish children came with "off" buttons for both their mouths and their ears. Language acquisition is not totally complete by the time a child begins school, however. Children still make gains in understanding of concepts such as kinship terms, comprehension and production of passives, metalinguistic awareness, pragmatics, comprehension of nonliteral language, etc. Much of the language arts curriculum during the elementary grades attempts to increase a child's knowledge about language in all of these areas and more. Language arts workbooks contain lessons in using idioms; using language to create headlines and subtitles; using descriptive words; placing phrases close to the word being described, etc. All these activities provide practice with the subtleties of language and increase children's awareness of the characteristics of language, i.e., their metalinguistic awareness.

The purpose of this activity is to give you a chance to explore the extent of children's understanding of some types of nonliteral language. Because comprehension of metaphors, similes, idioms, and other forms of nonliteral language is so automatic for adults, we sometimes fail to appreciate how confusing these forms can be for children and adolescents, or for non-native speakers. The research literature on children's understanding of similes, metaphors, proverbs, and other types of nonliteral language indicates that there are many factors that influence children's accuracy of interpretation. Some of these factors are mode of response (verbal explanation, choosing from alternatives, enacting meaning with toy), abstractness of the expression, availability of contextual cues, and familiarity with underlying concepts.

It was once believed that young children simply were not capable of comprehending metaphoric language, but more recent studies have found that even 2- and 3-year-olds spontaneously produce some metaphor-like expressions and understand some perceptually based metaphors by age 4 (Vosniadous, 1987). This suggests that even though we may find that preschool and elementary-school children have difficulty with some of the examples of nonliteral language presented to them, we need to be cautious about assuming total lack of competence if a child fails to comprehend the particular metaphoric examples we present.

INSTRUCTIONS:

Children. Locate three children, one 4–7, another 8–11, and another 12–14 years of age. Ask parental permission to have each child help you with your homework for a class project. Tell the parents you are studying children's language development.

Procedure. Spend a few minutes getting acquainted with the child. Then tell the child you have some sentences you would like to read, and you would like his or her ideas about what they might mean. Read each saying to the child and ask him or her to tell you what the person who said it probably meant. Write down the child's reaction (laughs, looks puzzled, etc.) and the child's interpretation.

1. Tree bark is like skin.
2. A cloud is like a marshmallow.
3. Anger ate him up.
4. He had a pickle for a nose.
5. The grass is always greener on the other side of the fence.
6. He "beat around the bush."
7. He "got wind" of it.
8. (a saying, idiom, or metaphor of your choice; specify)

Questions. Include the following in your write-up:

1. Describe each child's performance on the sayings, noting the following information: the child's reaction (laughter, confusion, etc.); the number of metaphors that were correctly interpreted; and a qualitative description of the nature of the child's errors (e.g., did the child only think of the concrete, literal interpretation of the words?).

2. How did children of different ages differ in the number of metaphors they interpreted correctly and in the nature of the errors they made?

RELATED REFERENCES

Billow, R. M. (1975). A cognitive developmental study of metaphor comprehension. *Developmental Psychology, 11*, 415–423.

Evans, M. A., & Gamble, D. (1988). Attribute saliency and metaphor interpretation in school-age children. *Journal of Child Language, 15,* 435–449.

Evans, M. A., Shaw, D., & Bell, M. (2000). Home literacy activities and their influence on early literacy skills. *Canadian Journal of Experimental Psychology, 2,* 65–75.

Gentner, D. (1988). Metaphor as structure mapping: The relational shift. *Child Development, 59*, 47–59.

Hancock, J. T., Dunham, P. J., & Purdy, K. (2000). Children's comprehension of critical and complimentary forms of verbal irony. *Journal of Cognition and Development, 1,* 227–248.

Johnson, J. (1991). Developmental versus language-based factors in metaphor interpretation. *Journal of Educational Psychology, 83,* 470–483.

Johnson, J. (1989). Factors related to cross-language transfer and metaphor interpretation in bilingual children. *Applied Psycholinguistics, 10,* 157–177.

Johnson, J. (1996). Metaphor interpretations by second language learners: Children and adults. *Canadian Modern Language Review, 53,* 217–239.

Johnson, J., & Pascual-Leone, J. (1989). Developmental levels of processing in metaphor interpretation. *Journal of Experimental Child Psychology, 48,* 1–31.

Marks, L., Hammeal, R., & Bornstein, M. (1987). Perceiving similarity and metaphor comprehension. *Monographs of the Society for Research in Child Development, Serial No. 215.*

Vosniadous, S. (1987). Children and metaphors. *Child Development, 58*, 870–885.

ACTIVITY 10-2

"WHERE BALL?," "NO WET," "GHETTI," AND OTHER EARLY UTTERANCES

INTRODUCTION: Chapter 10 of the text reviews the course of language acquisition from cooing and babbling to the production of sophisticated passives and questions. This activity focuses on the periods of acquisition between single-word utterances and simple three- and four-word negatives and questions. The purpose is to provide you with a chance to listen to examples of the early forms of language discussed in Chapter 10, specifically, holophrastic language, telegraphic language, overregularizations of plurals and past tense, and early negative sentences and questions.

INSTRUCTIONS:

Children. Obtain permission to visit a daycare facility that has children 18 months to 3 years of age, or obtain permission from parents you know who have children in that age range to spend some time at their home. Explain that you are studying children's language development and want an opportunity to listen to young children as they play. Obtain language examples from at least two children.

Procedure. You may be an unobtrusive observer or interact with the child.

1. Write down (or tape record for later transcription) examples of the children's language that fit the categories below. (Be sure to include each child's age in months on your record sheet.)

    a. Holophrastic language

    b. Telegraphic language

    c. Overgeneralization of rules for plurals and past-tense verbs

    d. Preposing of negative or question, such as: "No" + "he go" or "Who" + "he is?"

2. For the holophrastic and telegraphic examples include a brief description of the most likely meaning of the utterance (base your inference of meaning on both the words and the contextual cues).

ACTIVITY 10-3

BILINGUALISM AND EDUCATION

INTRODUCTION: This activity relates to the discussion in your text on bilingualism and education. Imagine that you are asked to give advice to parents on whether or not to enroll their children in an immersion program or in a core language program. What would your advice be given the research discussed in your text? Would your advice be different for French-speaking families versus English-speaking families? If so, why? What about for immigrant (non-English/non-French) families? What implications could you imagine for policy?

RELATED REFERENCES

Bain, B., Panarin, A.I., & Panarin, I.A. (1995). Rearing children bilingually (with yet again reference to Vygotsky and Luria). *Journal of Russian and East European Psychiatry, 33(3),* 35–56.

Bialystok, E. (1988). Levels of bilingualism and levels of linguistic awareness. *Developmental Psychology, 24(4),* 560–567.

Bialystok, E., Majumder, S., & Martin, M.M. (2003). Developing phonological awareness: Is there a bilingual advantage? *Applied Psycholinguistics, 24(1),* 27–44.

Caldas, S.J., & Caron-Caldas, S. (1999). Language immersion and cultural identity: Conflicting influences and values. *Language, Culture, and Curriculum, 12(1),* 42–58.

Capirci, O., Iverson, J.M., & Montanari, S. (2002). Gestural, signed and spoken modalities in early language development: The role of linguistic input. *Bilingualism: Language and Cognition, 5(1),* 25–37.

Chen, X., Anderson, R.C., & Li, W. (2004). Phonological awareness of bilingual and monolingual Chinese children. *Journal of Educational Psychology, 96(1),* 142–151.

Furtado, J.C., & Webster, W.G. (1991). Concurrent language and motor performance in bilinguals: A test of the age of acquisition hypothesis. *Canadian Journal of Psychology, 45(4),* 448–461.

Nicoladis, E. (2002). Some gestures develop in conjunction with spoken language development and others don't: Evidence from bilingual preschoolers. *Journal of Nonverbal Behavior, 26(4),* 241–266.

Nicoladis, E. (2002). What's the difference between 'toilet paper' and 'paper toilet'? French-English bilingual children's crosslinguistic transfer in compound nouns. *Journal of Child Language, 29(4),* 843–863.

Patterson, J.L. (2002). Relationships of expressive vocabulary to frequency of reading and television experience among bilingual toddlers. *Applied Psycholinguistics, 23(4),* 493–508.

Safty, A. (1988). French immersion and the making of a bilingual society: A critical review and discussion. *Canadian Journal of Education, 13(2),* 243–262.

WEBSITES OF INTEREST

For more information on Canadian research, visit the Canadian Language and Literacy Research Network web page: www.cllrnet.ca

For more information on Canadian research on the development of psycholinguistic skills in children in French Immersion, read about the research by Pierre Cormier: www.umoncton.ca/cormiep

REFERENCES OF INTEREST

Fennell, C.T., & Werker, J.F. (2003). Early word learners' ability to access phonetic detail in well-known words. *Language and Speech, 46(2),* 245–264.

Frijters, J., Barron, R.W., & Brunello, M. (2000). Child interest and home literacy as sources of literacy experience: Direct and mediated influences on letter-name and -sound knowledge and oral vocabulary. *Journal of Educational Psychology*, 92 (3), 466–477.

Girolametto, L., Bonafacio, S., & Visini, C. (2002). Mother-child interactions in Canada and Italy: Linguistic responsiveness to late-talking toddlers. *International Journal of Language and Communication Disorders, 37(2),* 151–171.

Lovett, M.W., Lacerenza, L., Borden, S.L., Frijters, J.C., Steinbach, K.A., & De Palma, M. (2000). Components of effective remediation for developmental reading disabilities: Combining phonological and strategy-based instruction to improve outcomes. *Journal of Educational Psychology*, 92 (2), 263–283.

Moore, C., & Davidge, J. (1989). The development of mental terms: Pragmatics or semantics? *Journal of Child Language, 16(3),* 633–641.

Patterson, M.L., & Werker, J.F. (2003). Two-month-old infants match phonetic information in lips and voice. *Developmental Science, 6(2),* 191–196.

Peterson, C., & McCabe, A. (2004). Echoing our parents: Parental influence on children's narration. In M.W. Pratt & B.E. Fiese (Eds.), *Family stories and the lifecourse: Across time and generations.* Erlbaum.

Rome-Flanders, T., & Cronk, C. (1995). A longitudinal study of infant vocalizations during mother-infant games. *Journal of Child Language, 22(2),* 259–274.

Senechal, M., & LeFevre, J. (2002). Parental involvement in the development of children's reading skill: A five-year longitudinal study. *Child Development, 73(2),* 445–460.

Shi, R., & Werker, J.F. (2003). The basis of preference for lexical words in six-month-old infants. *Developmental Science, 6(5),* 484–488.

Werker, J.F., Fennell, C., Corcoran, K., & Stager, C.E. (2002). Infants' ability to learn phonetically similar words: Effects of age and vocabulary size. *Infancy, 3,* 1–30.

ANSWERS TO SELF-TESTS

VOCABULARY SELF-TEST (The answers may be found on the pages in parentheses.)

1. expansions (p. 360)
2. semantics (p. 352)
3. underextension (p. 368)
4. holophrase (p. 365)
5. metalinguistic awareness (p. 380)
6. language acquisition device (LAD) (p. 354)
7. syntactical bootstrapping (p. 369)
8. morphemes (p. 352)
9. expressive style (p. 367)
10. multimodal motherese (p. 367)
11. mutual exclusivity constraint (p. 369)
12. receptive language (p. 364)
13. Wernicke's area (p. 355)
14. pragmatics (p. 352)
15. fast-mapping (p. 367)

MULTIPLE-CHOICE SELF-TEST (The answers may be found on the pages in parentheses.)

1. **a** (p. 351) Phonology is knowledge about the basic sounds and sound combinations in a language. Semantics (b) would be knowledge about the meaning of words (and this is a nonsense word with no meaning). Syntactic knowledge (c) is knowledge about combinations of words and word orderings in sentences. Pragmatics (d) refers to the use of language in a social context.

2. **b** (p. 352) Morphology refers to the rules governing the formation of meaningful words from sounds. Units of sounds (a) are the phonology of language. Grammatical markers (c) in a language are part of syntax. The meaning of words and sentences (d) is the semantics of a language.

3. **c** (p. 353, 361) Infants are preverbal for the first 10 to 13 months of life, and by 4 months of age babbling would just be emerging. Therefore, a developmentalist would likely reject the claims made by Ebony's parents, regardless of whether he or she took a nativist (a), learning (b), or interactionist (d) view of language development.

4. **d** (p. 363) By 11 months of age non-native phonemes are disappearing from infant babbles and babies are acquiring a "babbling accent." At 8 months the babbles would have sounded very similar for all three infants (a). Consonant sounds emerge between 4 and 6 months of age (b). Telegraphic speech doesn't normally emerge until children are between 18 and 24 months of age (c).

5. **d** (p. 364) Children typically comprehend more words than they spontaneously produce. This pattern is universal and continues across childhood (a). This means that production and comprehension do not proceed at the same rate (b) and that production is typically behind comprehension (c).

6. **c** (p. 365) Because the same word may be used by a child in different contexts to convey different messages, holophrases seem to be attempts to convey complex ideas with single words. They are not simply labels (a) because they are used in different ways. They are not imitations (b) because they can be creative forms the child doesn't hear adults say. They don't show evidence of rule-governed speech (d) because that would require the correct syntactic ordering of two or more words.

7. **d** (p. 352) The pragmatics of language encompass the principles of when to say what, and how to say it. A gain in pragmatics would be if the child used different word combinations for different audiences. A gain in phonology (a) would be illustrated by an increased understanding of word sounds. A gain in syntax (b) would be illustrated by an increased understanding of the ordering of words within a sentence (b). A gain in semantics (c) would be an increased understanding of word meaning.

8. **a** (p. 378) The first sentence can "make sense" in either direction, so it would be difficult for young children to understand which car was hit and which car did the hitting. The second sentence (b) and the third sentence (c) only "make sense" in one direction, and therefore are less likely to be misunderstood. The fourth sentence (d) is in the active voice, not the passive voice, and it shouldn't be misunderstood.

Chapter Eleven

Emotional Development and the Establishment of Intimate Relationships

Learning Objectives

By the time you have finished this chapter you should be able to:

1. Describe the developmental sequence of discrete emotions during infancy and distinguish between primary and secondary emotions.
2. Describe developments in the ability to control emotions and to comply with cultural rules regarding the display of emotions.
3. Explain what is meant by social referencing and describe changes in children's ability to interpret the emotions of others.
4. Identify five components of temperament and evaluate the evidence regarding genetic and environmental influences on temperament.
5. Discuss the stability of temperament across childhood and adolescence.
6. Contrast the three temperamental profiles outlined by Thomas and Chess.
7. Describe the main characteristics of emotional attachments.
8. Describe the role of synchrony between the infant and the caregiver in establishing attachment.
9. Identify and describe the major characteristics in each of the four phases of attachment.
10. Compare and contrast the psychoanalytic, learning, cognitive-developmental, and ethological theories of attachment.
11. Distinguish between stranger anxiety and separation anxiety and compare the ethological and cognitive explanations for why these anxieties develop.
12. Describe Ainsworth's "strange situation" test of attachment.
13. Compare and contrast the four patterns of attachment that have been identified in infants and children.
14. Describe some caregiver characteristics and some ecological considerations that may hinder the development of a secure attachment.
15. Describe some characteristics of infants that may promote attachment and some that may interfere with attachment.
16. Discuss some long-term correlates of both secure and insecure attachments.
17. Outline the key components in the "working models" theory and relate the different dimensions of the model to different patterns of attachment.
18. Describe the effects of early social deprivation on children.
19. Discuss the factors that have been found to influence the extent of recovery from the effects of early deprivation.
20. Discuss the key findings from research investigating the effects of maternal employment and alternative care on children's emotional development.

Chapter Outline and Summary

1. An overview of emotional development

a. *Displaying emotions: The development (and control) of emotional expressions*

Newborns show interest, distress, disgust, and contentment. Between the ages of $2^1/_2$ months and 7 months the primary emotions of anger, sadness, joy, surprise, and fear emerge. Primary emotions appear to be biologically programmed because they emerge in all normal infants at approximately the same time, and they are displayed and interpreted in the same ways in different cultures.

After the age of 1 secondary emotions begin to be displayed. These complex emotions include embarrassment, shame, guilt, envy, and pride. However, toddlers and young preschool children often only display self-evaluative emotions (such as pride or shame) when adult observers are present. It is typically not until middle childhood that children display self-evaluative emotions in the absence of an external observer.

Emotional display rules specify the circumstances under which various emotions should or should not be expressed; these display rules differ between cultures. To comply with emotional display rules, children must first develop strategies to help them regulate their emotional responses. Young infant boys have a more difficult time at regulating unpleasant arousal than young infant girls. Toddlers have an exceptionally difficult time regulating fear. As children move through infancy, toddlerhood, and the preschool years they develop more effective ways of regulating their emotional responses. Effective regulation of emotions involves the ability to suppress, maintain, or intensify emotional arousal.

However, regulating emotional reactions is only the first step in complying with social emotional display rules. Often "unacceptable" emotional responses must be suppressed and "acceptable" emotional responses must be exhibited. During the preschool years children are not very skilled at disguising their true emotions; throughout the elementary-school years children become much more skilled at following social emotional display rules. Girls are more motivated and more skilled in complying with social emotional display rules than boys are. The strength and timing of compliance with social emotional display rules are influenced by culture; however, across cultures, children who tend to comply also tend to be viewed as more likable and more competent by both their teachers and their peers.

b. *Recognizing and interpreting emotions*

Social referencing (the ability to monitor the emotional reactions of others and use that information to regulate one's own behaviour) is first evident in infants between the ages of 7 and 10 months. During the second year toddlers often look to companions after they have already appraised a new object or situation; this suggests that they are now using the reactions of others to assess the accuracy of their own judgments.

Understanding and interpreting emotions in others is enhanced when preschoolers discuss emotional experiences. By the age of 4 or 5 children can use expressive body movements to recognize emotional states in others, and they are better at understanding that a person's emotional state may stem from current or past events. During elementary school children improve in their ability to interpret emotional reactions and are more likely to consider internal factors, as well as external factors, in their interpretation. By age 6, children begin to recognize that they can experience multiple emotions of varying intensity, and by age 8, children begin to understand that they can experience multiple emotions of varying intensity and valence.

c. *Emotions and early social development*

Emotional displays in infants are adaptive because they help to promote social contact with caregivers, and they also help caregivers to adjust their behaviour to the infant's needs. Also, social referencing helps children better understand the positive and negative aspects of the world around them. The reactions of others can be used as guides about which events and objects are enjoyable (and should therefore be approached) and which are dangerous or unenjoyable (and should therefore be avoided).

2. Temperament and development

Temperament refers to an individual's tendency to respond to environmental events in predictable ways. It includes activity level (typical pace of activities), irritability (how easily a person becomes upset, or the intensity of distress that an individual experiences), soothability (how easily a person is calmed down after being upset), fearfulness (wariness of new or intense stimuli), and sociability (receptiveness to social stimulation).

a. Hereditary and environmental influences on temperament

From very early in infancy, identical twins are more similar than fraternal twins on most dimensions of temperament. The heritability coefficients for most temperamental attributes are modest, but it does appear that many components of temperament are influenced by genetics. The strongest environmental contributors to temperament appear to be nonshared environmental influences (NSE).

b. Stability of temperament

In general, activity level, irritability, and sociability are moderately stable through infancy and childhood, and sometimes these characteristics remain stable into the early adult years. Behavioural inhibition is another trait that shows stability across infancy and early childhood, but only for children who fall at the extremes of the continuum. Children who do not fall at the extremes show more fluctuation in their level of behaviour inhibition over time.

c. Early temperamental profiles and later development

Thomas and Chess identified three temperamental profiles: easy, difficult, and slow-to-warm-up. Children with an easy temperament are open and adaptable to new experiences; their habits are regular and predictable. Children with a difficult temperament react vigorously to new experiences and are slow to adapt to new situations; their habits are irregular and unpredictable. Children with a slow-to-warm-up temperament respond to new experiences in mildly resistant ways and are slow to adapt to new situations; they tend to be somewhat moody and inactive. Thomas and Chess found that approximately 40% of the children they studied had easy temperaments, 10% had difficult temperaments, and 15% had slow-to-warm-up temperaments; the temperaments of the remaining 35% of the children did not fit any of the three temperamental profiles.

Children who have a difficult temperament are more likely to have problems adjusting to school activities. Approximately half the children who have a slow-to-warm-up temperament have difficulties in peer relations, and they often end up being ignored or neglected by peers. The stability of a child's temperamental profile over time is influenced to a large degree by the "goodness of fit" between the child's temperament and the parents' style of child rearing.

3. What are emotional attachments?

Emotional attachments are the strong affectionate ties we feel for special people in our lives. The attachment relationships that form between infants and parents are reciprocal; infants become attached to their parents, and parents also become attached to their infants. One important contributor to the establishment and growth of an attachment relationship is the presence of synchronized routines.

4. How do infants become attached?

a. The growth of primary attachments

In developing an attachment to their caregivers infants pass through four phases. For the first six weeks infants are in the asocial phase, which means that there are many kinds of social and nonsocial stimuli that will produce favourable reactions in the infant, and there are few social stimuli or situations that evoke signs of protest. The next phase (indiscriminate attachments) lasts until the infant is approximately 6 or 7 months of age. During this stage infants show a clear preference for social stimuli over nonsocial stimuli. They may show differential responding to familiar and unfamiliar people, but they seem to enjoy attention from anyone, including strangers.

Between 7 and 9 months of age infants typically begin to show evidence of specific attachments. They protest being separated from people they have formed an attachment for, and they may be wary of strangers or people who are unfamiliar. Shortly after an infant shows a specific, primary attachment, other attachment relationships become evident. By the age of 18 months most infants are attached to a number of people.

b. *Theories of attachment*

There are four different types of theories that might explain why an infant develops an attachment relationship with his or her parents. Psychoanalytic theory suggests that during the first year of life oral activities are a source of pleasure, and therefore infants will develop loving feelings for people who feed them. Learning theories also suggest that infants become attached to people who feed them. However, learning theories suggest that the attachment relationship develops because the caregivers become associated with all the pleasurable sensations that accompany feeding. Harry Harlow's work with infant monkeys showed that monkeys developed stronger attachments to surrogate "mothers" who provided comfort contact than to surrogate "mothers" who provided nourishment.

Cognitive-developmental theories suggest that between 7 and 9 months of age infants begin to show evidence of attachment to a primary caregiver because object permanence is developing. Theorists who take this view argue that until an infant understands that objects continue to exist, he or she will not protest when separated from primary caregivers.

Ethological theories suggest that human infants and their caregivers have evolved in ways that predispose them to respond favourably to each other and to form close attachments. In this view, the formation of a strong attachment relationship promotes the survival of the infant, and ultimately the survival of the species. However, the ethological view also recognizes the influence of environmental factors. The suggestion is that humans are biologically prepared to form close attachments, but that parents and infants have to learn how to respond appropriately to innate cues and signalling behaviours.

c. *Two attachment-related fears of infancy*

Stranger anxiety is a negative reaction to an unfamiliar person. Stranger anxiety peaks at about 8 to 10 months of age and then gradually declines. Not all children show evidence of stranger anxiety, and not all strangers provoke the same level of anxiety in infants. Separation anxiety is evident when an infant protests at being separated from someone to whom he or she is attached. This type of reaction normally emerges between 6 and 8 months of age, peaks at 14 to 18 months of age, and then gradually declines in both intensity and frequency.

The ethological viewpoint suggests that both these fears originate from an infant's general apprehension of the unfamiliar. This view suggests that unfamiliar situations qualify as natural cues to danger. In contrast, the cognitive-developmental viewpoint suggests that these same fears stem from an infant's inability to explain who a stranger is or what has become of a familiar companion.

5. Individual differences in attachment quality

a. *Assessing attachment security*

Mary Ainsworth's strange situation procedure is the most widely used technique for assessing the quality of the attachment between an infant and his or her caregivers. During the procedure the child is exposed to (1) a novel environment that can be explored; (2) the presence of strangers; (3) brief separations from the primary caregiver; and (4) reunions with the caregiver following the separations. The infant's reactions to each of these elements is recorded. In assessing attachment between mothers and their infants, different patterns of attachment have emerged.

A securely attached infant will actively explore the novel setting while the mother is present. He or she may become visibly upset when the mother leaves, but typically greets the mother warmly when she returns. Often the child is outgoing with strangers as long as the mother is present. This pattern of attachment is seen in approximately 65% of North American infants.

An infant with a resistant attachment will stay close to his or her mother and be reluctant to explore the novel setting. He or she will become very distressed when the mother leaves. When she returns the infant will again remain close but will resist the mother's efforts to cuddle or comfort the infant. These infants are typically wary of strangers, even when the mother is present. This pattern of attachment is seen in approximately 10% of North American infants.

An infant with an avoidant attachment shows little distress when the mother leaves, and when the mother returns, the infant may turn away from her and ignore her attempts at "reconciliation." Some infants who show an avoidant pattern of attachment are sociable with strangers; others avoid strangers or ignore them. This pattern of attachment is seen in approximately 20% of North American infants.

The most recently defined pattern of attachment is a disorganized or disoriented attachment. Infants who display this attachment pattern show a mixed reaction when their mother returns following a brief separation. They may act dazed, or they may move toward their mother, only to abruptly move away as the mother approaches. This pattern of attachment is seen in approximately 5 to 10% of North American infants.

The strange situation procedure is less useful for assessing attachment patterns in children past the age of 2. By this age children are more accustomed to brief separations from their mothers, and both stranger anxiety and separation anxiety are declining. With toddlers and preschool children (up to the age of 5) the Attachment Q-set (AQS) can be used to assess the quality of attachment in the child's natural environment.

b. Cultural variations in attachment classifications

Cross-cultural studies show that most infants develop a secure attachment with their caregivers. However, the percentages of infants and toddlers who fall into the different categories vary across different cultures. In cultures where parents encourage independence in their infants, while discouraging clingy, close contact, a higher proportion of infants show avoidant attachments (compared to North American norms). In cultures where caregivers rarely leave their infants with others, and in communal cultures where parents are less accessible to their infants, a higher proportion of infants show resistant attachments (compared to North American norms). Besides differences in rearing practices, it may also be true that what qualifies or defines secure or insecure attachment varies from culture to culture.

6. Factors that influence attachment security

a. Quality of caregiving

Infants tend to form secure attachments with their primary caregivers when those caregivers respond promptly and appropriately to the infant's signals; express affection toward the infant; have smooth, reciprocal interactions with the infant; attend to the same things as the infant during interactions; provide emotional support for the infant; and frequently direct actions toward the infant.

Parents who are inconsistent in their caregiving are more likely to have infants who show a resistant pattern of attachment. Infants are more likely to develop an avoidant pattern of attachment if their parents are self-centred and rigid, or if their parents are overzealous and provide too much stimulation. Infants who are neglected or physically abused are more likely to develop a disorganized or disoriented pattern of attachment.

Caregivers who are clinically depressed and parents who were neglected or abused when they were children are more likely to be insensitive caregivers. This type of parenting increases the likelihood of an infant developing an insecure (resistant or avoidant) attachment. Also, caregivers whose pregnancies were unplanned and whose babies are "unwanted" often show insensitive caregiving, which can lead to an insecure attachment bond with the infant. Finally, insensitive caregiving is more likely when caregivers face health-related, legal, or financial problems, or when the relationship between the infant's parents is strained or unhappy.

Intervention studies have shown that at-risk parents can be taught to be sensitive caregivers; when caregiving becomes more sensitive the likelihood that a secure attachment will form is increased.

b. *Infant characteristics*

Low-birth-weight babies are more likely than full-term babies to establish an insecure primary attachment, but most infants can form secure attachments if the caregiving they receive is sensitive and responsive. In terms of infant temperament, secure attachments are found when there is a "good fit" between an infant's temperament and the caregiving that he or she receives. Insecure attachments are more likely when caregivers are unable to accommodate their caregiving to their infant's particular temperament.

7. Attachment and later development

a. *Long-term correlates of secure and insecure attachments*

Infants who form secure attachments with their caregivers become toddlers who are better problem solvers, more creative in their symbolic play, and show more positive and fewer negative emotions. As preschoolers these same children initiate more play activities, are more popular, and are more curious. By the time they are young adolescents they show better social skills and are more likely to have close friends; as young adults they are likely to have secure attachment relationships with their romantic partners.

In contrast, infants whose primary attachments are disorganized or disoriented are often hostile and aggressive, and this puts them at a higher risk for being rejected by peers when they are preschoolers and when they reach elementary school. Children who form resistant or avoidant primary attachments are more likely to be socially and emotionally withdrawn and less curious. As young adults these individuals are more likely to have resistant or avoidant attachment relationships with their romantic partners. Finally, youngsters whose attachments to parents were insecure are more likely than those with secure attachments to display deviant behaviours and other psychopathological symptoms throughout childhood and adolescence.

b. *Why might attachment quality forecast later outcomes?*

Some ethological theorists suggest that infants develop internal working models as they interact with their primary caregivers. Responsive caregiving should lead to the conclusion that people are dependable, while insensitive, neglectful, or abusive caregiving may lead to the conclusion that people cannot be trusted. At the same time, when caregivers are responsive to an infant's bids for attention, the infant is likely to develop a positive working model of himself or herself; when caregivers are nonresponsive, a negative working model of self is more likely to develop.

The working-models hypothesis leads to four predictions. Infants who have positive models of both themselves and others should display secure attachments. Infants who develop positive models of themselves but negative models of others should display avoidant attachments. Infants who develop positive models of others but negative models of themselves should display resistant attachments. Finally, infants who develop negative models of both themselves and others should display disorganized or disoriented attachments.

So far the available evidence is consistent with the idea that the working models established at home may influence our reactions to cognitive challenges, the nature of our interpersonal relationships, our memories of positive and negative experiences, our self-confidence, and our success at school. Research also suggests that a parent's working models of attachment relationships can accurately predict the type of attachment relationship that will eventually form between the parent and his or her infant.

However, working models are dynamic and they can change based on later experiences with caregivers, close friends, or romantic partners. In other words, secure attachments during infancy do not guarantee positive outcomes later in life, and insecure attachments during infancy do not mean that negative outcomes are inevitable.

8. The unattached infant

a. Effects of social deprivation in infancy and childhood

Infants raised under conditions of extreme social deprivation may fail to develop any form of attachment. Many children raised under these adverse conditions display reactive attachment disorder, which is an inability to become securely attached to adoptive or foster parents, even when the new caregivers are loving and responsive.

b. Why is early deprivation harmful?

Two hypotheses have been put forward to explain why early social deprivation has such profound and lasting effects. The maternal deprivation hypothesis suggests that the lack of a single attentive caregiver is the primary reason for the developmental outcomes that have been observed. However, results from research studies of children who had multiple responsive caregivers found that social development in these children was quite normal. This suggests that it is not the lack of an exclusive attachment that disrupts development.

The social stimulation hypothesis suggests that infants need sustained interactions with responsive companions in order to develop normally. A lack of responsiveness can foster a sense of learned helplessness and result in a child who simply stops trying to elicit responses from others. This seems to be a plausible reason for why socially deprived infants are often passive, withdrawn, and apathetic.

c. Can children recover from early deprivation effects?

Infants who have experienced severe social and emotional deprivation over the first two years often show a strong capacity for recovery if they are placed into high-quality, stimulating home environments where they receive a great deal of individualized attention. However, it is more difficult for children to recover from the effects of early deprivation when the deprivation extends over a longer period of time. Attachment therapy has been beneficial in helping children form strong attachments with adoptive or foster caregivers, although the success rate is much lower among teenagers who display reactive attachment disorder.

9. Maternal employment, child care, and early emotional development

a. Quality of alternative care

Children who receive high quality daycare do not show an increased risk for developing insecure attachment relationships, regardless of the age of the child at the time daycare is initiated. Indeed, early entry into high quality daycare is associated with positive social, emotional, and intellectual outcomes. The quality of a daycare facility can be assessed by considering five factors: the physical setting; the child/caregiver ratio; the caregiver characteristics and qualifications; the quality of the toys and activities; and the links to the families of the children at the facility. In addition, the daycare facility should be licensed by the province.

b. Parenting and parents' attitudes about work

Research has shown that parental attitudes toward parenting, and the quality of care that parents provide at home, has far more to do with an infant's development than the type of alternative care the infant receives. As well, a mother's attitude about working and child care may be as important to her child's well-being as her employment status. Positive child outcomes are most likely when a working mother has positive attitudes both about working and about being a mother, and especially when combined with approval and support from her spouse.

Vocabulary Self-Test

Part I: For each of the following definitions provide the appropriate term. (Answers to this portion of the self-test are provided at the end of the chapter.)

1. ________________ A person's characteristic modes of emotional and behavioural responding to environmental events

2. ________________ An infant–caregiver bond characterized by little separation protest and a tendency of the child to avoid or ignore the caregiver

3. ________________ Self-conscious or self-evaluative emotions that emerge in the second year and are partially dependent on cognitive development

4. ________________ Inability to form secure attachment bonds with other people

5. ________________ Generally harmonious interactions between two persons in which participants adjust their behaviour in response to the partner's actions

6. ________________ Cognitive representations of self, others, and relationships that infants construct from their interactions with caregivers

7. ________________ Strategies for managing emotions or adjusting emotional arousal to a comfortable level of intensity

8. ________________ Wary or fretful reaction that infants and toddlers often display when approached by an unfamiliar person

9. ________________ Temperamental profile in which the child is irregular in daily routines and adapts slowly to new experiences, often responding negatively and intensely

10. ________________ Alternative method of assessing attachment security that is based on observations of the child's attachment-related behaviours at home

11. ________________ Period in which infants prefer social to nonsocial stimulation and are likely to protest whenever any adults put them down or leave them alone

12. ________________ The use of the emotional expressions of others to infer the meaning of otherwise ambiguous situations

13. ________________ An insecure infant–caregiver bond characterized by the infant's dazed appearance on reunion, or a tendency to first seek and then abruptly avoid the caregiver

14. ________________ An innate or instinctual form of learning in which the young of certain species will follow and become attached to moving objects

15. ________________ The ability to understand and to experience the emotions others display

Part II: For each of the following terms provide the definition.

Asocial Phase of Attachment: ______________________________

____

Easy Temperament: ______________________________

____

Resistant Attachment: ______________________________

____

Preadapted Characteristic: ______________________________

____

Maternal Deprivation Hypothesis: ______________________________

____

Behavioural Inhibition: ______________________________

____

Attachment: ______________________________

____

Caregiving Hypothesis: ______________________________

____

Secure Base: ______________________________

____

Emotional Display Rules: ______________________________

____

Strange Situation: ______________________________

____

Goodness-of-Fit Model: ______________________________

____

Secure Attachment: ______________________________

____

Primary Emotions: ______________________________

____

Learned Helplessness: ______________________________

____

Short-Answer Study Questions

AN OVERVIEW OF EMOTIONAL DEVELOPMENT

1. Identify four primary emotions that newborns display and five additional primary emotions that emerge by 7 months of age.

   At birth infants display:

   By 7 months of age infants also display:

2. Identify five secondary emotions that emerge during the second year.

   a.

   b.

   c.

   d.

   e.

3. Explain what emotional display rules are, and identify two skills children must acquire in order to comply with emotional display rules.

   Emotional display rules are:

   To comply with emotional display rules children must be able to:

   a.

   b.

4. Explain what social referencing is, and describe how social referencing changes over the first two years.

5. Contrast the typical explanation a preschooler would provide for a playmate's emotional display with the type of explanation an elementary-school child would provide.

TEMPERAMENT AND DEVELOPMENT

6. Identify and describe five components of temperament.

   a.

   b.

   c.

   d.

   e.

7. Describe the environmental influences that appear to have the largest effect on temperament.

8. Explain what is meant by "behavioural inhibition" and discuss how stable this characteristic is across early childhood.

9. Describe the three temperamental profiles identified by Thomas and Chess and indicate the proportion of children who fit each of these profiles.

   a.

   b.

   c.

10. Provide an example that illustrates a "good fit" between a child's temperament and the pattern of child-rearing used by his or her parents, and contrast this with a "poor fit."

    Example of a "good fit":

    Example of a "poor fit":

WHAT ARE EMOTIONAL ATTACHMENTS?

11. Explain what emotional attachments are, and identify one important contributor to the growth of an emotional attachment between an infant and his or her parents.

    Emotional attachments are:

    One important contributor is:

HOW DO INFANTS BECOME ATTACHED?

12. Identify and describe four phases that infants pass through as they develop an attachment to their parents.

    a.

    b.

    c.

    d.

13. Briefly outline the psychoanalytic theory of attachment formation.

14. Briefly outline the learning theory of attachment formation.

15. Describe the study Harlow designed to test the importance of feeding in the formation of attachment, and summarize the main conclusions from his research.

16. The cognitive-developmental viewpoint suggests that there is an important cognitive milestone that infants must reach before an attachment relationship can form. Identify the milestone these theorists believe is necessary before primary attachments can develop.

17. Briefly outline the ethological theory of attachment formation.

18. Identify and describe two fears that are related to the formation of an attachment relationship.

a.

b.

INDIVIDUAL DIFFERENCES IN ATTACHMENT QUALITY

19. Describe how the "strange situation" procedure is used to assess the security of an attachment relationship.

20. Describe four patterns of attachment and indicate the proportion of children who fit each pattern.

    a.

    b.

    c.

    d.

FACTORS THAT INFLUENCE ATTACHMENT SECURITY

21. Identify and describe six aspects of caregiving that promote secure attachment relationships between an infant and his or her caregivers.

    a.

    b.

    c.

    d.

    e.

    f.

22. Identify the types of parenting that are most likely to promote resistant, avoidant, or disorganized/ disoriented attachments in infants.

    Resistant attachments are associated with:

    Avoidant attachments are associated with:

    Disorganized/disoriented attachments are associated with:

23. Identify three characteristics that place parents at risk for displaying insensitive patterns of parenting.

    a.

    b.

    c.

24. Discuss Kochanska's integrative theory of infant–caregiver attachments. What do her findings suggest with regard to caregiving, temperament, and attachment style?

ATTACHMENT AND LATER DEVELOPMENT

25. Describe some of the characteristics that are seen in later childhood when a child has formed a secure attachment with his or her caregivers during infancy.

26. Describe some of the characteristics that are seen in later childhood when a child has formed a resistant, avoidant, or disorganized/disoriented attachment with his or her caregivers during infancy.

    Childhood characteristics associated with a resistant attachment:

    Childhood characteristics associated with an avoidant attachment:

    Childhood characteristics associated with a disorganized/disoriented attachment:

27. Briefly describe the "working-models" theory outlined by ethological researchers, and describe the type of events that would promote positive or negative working models of self and of others.

28. Identify the types of working models that ethologists suggest might be present in securely attached individuals and in individuals with resistant, avoidant, or disorganized/disoriented attachments.

    Working models present in a secure attachment:

    Working models present in a resistant attachment:

    Working models present in an avoidant attachment:

    Working models present in a disorganized/disoriented attachment:

THE UNATTACHED INFANT

29. Explain what reactive attachment disorder is, and discuss the types of situations that are likely to produce this disorder.

30. Two hypotheses have been suggested to explain why early social deprivation can have long-lasting effects. Briefly evaluate the research evidence that relates to each of these hypotheses.

    Maternal deprivation hypothesis:

    Social stimulation hypothesis:

31. Discuss the Romanian orphan research project. What do the results suggest about the effects of early deprivation on children and their later development? What advice would you give to parents interested in adopting children who experienced early deprivation?

MATERNAL EMPLOYMENT, CHILD CARE, AND EARLY EMOTIONAL DEVELOPMENT

32. Identify and describe six characteristics parents should consider in evaluating the overall quality of a daycare facility for their children.

    a.

    b.

    c.

    d.

    e.

    f.

33. Compare the parental-leave policy in Canada with those in other countries. How does Canada stand up? What would you recommend to policymakers?

Multiple-Choice Self-Test

For each of the following questions select the best alternative. (Answers and explanations for this self-test are provided at the end of the chapter.) Once you have selected your answer, provide a brief explanation for why the answer you selected is the best choice and why the remaining answers would not be correct.

1. Of the following, the statement that best describes the emergence of emotions would be:

   a. the full range of emotions is evident at birth
   b. all of the types of emotions emerge during the first year
   c. distinct emotions are not reliably observed until the second year of life when children's cognitive capabilities are more mature
   d. the various emotions appear at roughly the same times in all normal infants over the first two years

   Rationale: ______________________________

   ____

2. The set of emotions that has been found to be closely tied to cognitive development, particularly self-recognition and an understanding of acceptable and unacceptable behaviour, is:

   a. interest, distress, disgust, and contentment
   b. anger, surprise, fear, and sadness
   c. embarrassment, shame, guilt, and pride
   d. joy, happiness, frustration, and boredom

   Rationale: ______________________________

   ____

3. At about 7 to 9 months of age there is a change in an infant's social responses. In particular, infants:

   a. begin to show distinct preference for social interactions over nonsocial stimuli
   b. begin to show differential responses to individuals and a clear preference for one particular companion
   c. change from multiple attachments to one or two specific attachments
   d. start to become less anxious around strangers

   Rationale: ______________________________

   ____

4. The ethological perspective suggests that the basis for the development of attachment is/are:

   a. pleasure derived from oral activities such as sucking and feeding
   b. the mother acting as a conditioned stimulus for positive outcomes
   c. the maturing of the infant's concept of "object" permanence
   d. preprogrammed responses (such as smiling, crawling, and vocalizing) that help to initiate or maintain contact

   Rationale: ______________________________

   ____

5. Belinda is 8 months old. She turns away and starts crying when a stranger approaches her at the grocery store. This reaction:

   a. would be unusual in a child of that age
   b. would be evidence that Belinda was insecurely attached
   c. would be considered a typical response to a stranger for a child that age (but not necessarily a universal response)
   d. would simply indicate Belinda is tired or hungry

   Rationale: ______________________________

   ____

6. Five-month-old Trevor and twelve-month-old Sondra are left in the care of a babysitter. According to the research on separation anxiety, it is most likely that:

   a. Trevor will cry much more than Sondra when he realizes that his mother is gone
   b. Sondra will show more distress than Trevor when she realizes that her mother has left
   c. all other things being equal, both Trevor and Sondra should show about the same degree of separation anxiety
   d. neither child is likely to show separation anxiety, as long as the babysitter is warm and responsive

   Rationale: ______________________________

   ____

7. The most common form of attachment to the primary caregiver is the attachment pattern described as:

   a. a secure attachment
   b. a resistant attachment
   c. an avoidant attachment
   d. a disorganized or disoriented attachment

   Rationale: ______________________________

   ____

8. In a study using the strange situation, 1-year-old Carl displays little distress when his mother leaves and seemingly ignores her when she returns. This is the type of behaviour you might observe with a child and a parent who share an attachment relationship that Ainsworth labelled as:

   a. resistant
   b. secure
   c. avoidant
   d. disorganized or disoriented

   Rationale: ______________________________

   ____

Activities and Projects Related to this Chapter

ACTIVITY 11-1

SYNCHRONOUS INTERACTION BETWEEN BABY AND ADULT

INTRODUCTION: This activity relates to material in Chapter 11 on interactional synchrony between infants and caregivers. These synchronous routines are exchanges that involve taking turns in social interactions: baby coos—caregiver vocalizes back; baby clicks tongue—caregiver clicks tongue back or vocalizes; caregiver smiles—infant smiles and vocalizes, etc. Such moments of seemingly inconsequential interaction are believed by Stern and others to be important building blocks for successful social attachment and later relationships.

Truly synchronous interactions reflect a sensitivity of the caregiver to the infant's needs at that moment. The caregiver takes cues from the infant regarding what kind and how much stimulation to provide. The caregiver "reads" the infant's need for an occasional time-out from the interaction and the infant signals that she is ready to engage again. For the interaction to be synchronous, it is important that the caregiver be sensitive to the child's needs and feelings at that moment.

This activity will provide an opportunity for you to observe synchronous interactions and to see an example of what is meant by a caregiver responding "sensitively" to a child—an important aspect of parenting that is mentioned at several points throughout the text as being critical to effective parenting.

INSTRUCTIONS:

Accessing an Infant. Contact parents you know who have an infant between 1 and 12 months (3 to 9 months is optimal). Ask if you can spend some time observing their infant for a class project. Tell them you would like to take notes on the infant's behaviour for this project. Arrange to visit during a time when the infant is likely to be awake, fed, and in the mood for play (although you can also see many instances of synchronous interaction during routine caregiving if necessary). (Note: you will probably observe a higher level of infant–parent interaction if only one parent is present.)

Gathering Your Data. Keep a running record of behaviours that the parent and child direct toward each other. Connect with a line (in the left margin) those pairs of behaviours that reflect a response of one to the other that would qualify as synchronous. Do not connect any behaviours initiated by one that are ignored by the other. Place an **X** beside any interactions that you judge to be nonsynchronous, i.e., the interaction is uncomfortable or conflictive (e.g., the parent is intrusive and pushes the infant to interact when the infant is signalling the need for a time-out, or the parent remains neutral in expression and does not return a vocalization).

Write-up. Summarize the interactions you observed. Give the percentage of interactions that were synchronous and the percentage that were clearly nonsynchronous. Briefly describe your impressions of the affective quality of the interaction.

RELATED REFERENCES

Bornstein, M.H., & Arterberry, M.E. (2003). Recognition, discrimination and categorization of smiling by 5-month-old infants. *Developmental Science, 6(5),* 585–599.

Dixon, W.E., Jr., & Smith, P.H. (2003). Who's controlling whom? Infant contributions to maternal play behaviour. *Infant and Child Development, 12(2),* 177–195.

Drotar, D., Woychik, J., Mantz-Clumpner, B., Negray, J., Wallace, M., & Malone, C. (1985). The family context of failure to thrive. In D. Drotar (Ed.), *Failure to thrive: Implications for research and practice.* New York: Plenum Press.

Martini, T.S., Root, C.A., & Jenkins, J.M. (in press). Low and middle income mothers' regulation of negative emotion: Effects of children's temperament and situational emotional responses. *Social Development.*

Moss, E., Cyr, C., St-Laurent, D., & Humber, N. (2000). Attachment at preschool and school-age and its relation to patterns of caregiver-child interaction. In G. M. Tarabulsy, S. Larose, D. R. Pederson, & G. Moran (Eds.), *Attachement et developpement I: Petite et jeune enfance* (pp. 155–177). Sainte-Foy, Quebec: Les Presses de l'Université du Québec.

Moss, E., Rousseau, D., Parent, S., St-Laurent, D., & Saintonge, J. (1998). Correlates of attachment at school-age: Maternal-reported stress, mother-child interaction and behavior problems. *Child Development, 69,* 1390–1405.

Stern, D. (1985). *The interpersonal world of the infant.* New York: Basic Books.

Symons, D. K. (2001). A dyad-oriented approach to distress and mother-child relationship outcomes in the first 24 months. *Parenting: Science and Practice, 1,* 101–122.

Symons, D. K., & Clark, S. E. (2000). A longitudinal study of mother-child relationships and theory of mind during the preschool period. *Social Development,* 1–23.

Thoman, E., & Browder, S. (1988). *Born dancing: How intuitive parents understand their baby's unspoken language and natural rhythms.* New York: Harper & Row.

van Ijzendoorn, M.H., Moran, G., & Belsky, J. (2000). The similarity of siblings' attachments to their mother. *Child Development, 71(4),* 1086–1098.

Waters, E., Merrick, S., & Treboux, D. (2000). Attachment security in infancy and early adulthood: A twenty-year longitudinal study. *Child Development, 71(3),* 684–689.

Weinfield, N.S., Ogawa, J.R., & Egeland, B. (2002). Predictability of observed mother-child interaction from preschool to middle childhood in a high-risk sample. *Child Development, 73,* 528–543.

ACTIVITY 11-2

WORKING MOTHERS AND DAYCARE

INTRODUCTION: Today the majority of mothers work, even those with preschool children. Daycare of some sort is a fact of life for their children. Most parents worry about leaving their children. They worry about the child becoming more attached to the alternative caregiver than to the parents, they worry about whether the child will be insecure, etc. In the chapter the author includes a review of research on the relationship between maternal employment/daycare and attachment. This activity asks you to make use of the material presented in the text to build an "advice column" to parents on the impact of daycare on children. Some references are provided should you want/need additional resources.

INSTRUCTIONS: Assume that you were contacted by Ann Landers because you are knowledgeable about the research on the relationship between maternal employment/daycare and emotional attachments in young children. You were asked to give a response to a question raised by a column reader:

> "I have to go back to work a few weeks after my twins are born. I'm worried that my babies will not know who their mother really is if I have to leave them every day with someone else. Can you tell me if daycare is always bad for infants and young children?"

Using the information presented in the text, construct a reply to the mother that will calm her fears but will also alert her to the factors that place an infant's attachment at risk. Provide information that will help her evaluate daycare settings.

(Keep in mind that the research in this area uses the quasi/natural method, i.e., existing groups. Causal statements must be made with caution because there may be differences between the daycare and non-daycare children and families in addition to maternal employment and daycare that could be contributing to the outcomes. See Chapter 1 to review the limitations of quasi/natural research designs.)

RELATED REFERENCES

Andersson, B. (1992). Effects of day-care on cognitive and socioemotional competence of thirteen-year-old Swedish schoolchildren. *Child Development*, *63*, 20–36.

Belsky, J. (1988). The "effects" of infant day care reconsidered. *Early Childhood Research Quarterly*, *3*, 235–272.

Booth, A. (Ed.). (1992). *Child care in the 1990s: Trends and consequences*. Hillsdale, NJ: Erlbaum.

Fox, N., & Fein, G. G. (1990). *Infant day care: The current debate*. Norwood, NJ: Ablex.

Hoffman, L. (1989). Effects of maternal employment in the two-parent family. *American Psychologist*, *44*, 283–292.

Kohen, D. E., Brehaut, J., Pence, A., & Hunter, M. (2002). After-school care and adolescent competencies. *Canadian Journal of Infancy and Early Childhood, 9(1).*

Kohen, D. E., Forer, B., & Hertzman, C. (2002). National data sets: Valuable sources of information for Canadian Child Care Data. Final report prepared for Child Care Visions, Human Resources Development Canada.

Kohen, D. E., & Hertzman, C. (2002). The importance of quality child care. In Doug Willms (Ed.), *Vulnerable Children* (p. 261–276). University of Alberta Press, Edmonton, Alberta.

Kohen, D. E., Hunter, T., Pence, A., & Goelman, H. (2000). The Victoria day care research project: Overview of a longitudinal study of child care and human development in Canada. *Canadian Journal of Research in Early Childhood Education, 8,* 49–54.

Kohen, D. E., Lauzon, D., & Hertzman, C. (2002). Participation and patterns of care arrangements for Canadian school-aged children. Final report prepared for Child Care Visions, Human Resources Development Canada.

Symons, D. K. (1998). Post-partum employment patterns, family-based care arrangements, and the mother-infant relationship at age two. *Canadian Journal of Behavioural Science, 30,* 121–131.

ANSWERS TO SELF-TESTS

VOCABULARY SELF-TEST (The answers may be found on the pages in parentheses.)

1. temperament (p. 398)
2. avoidant attachment (p. 413)
3. secondary (or complex) emotions (p. 393)
4. reactive attachment disorder (p. 425)
5. synchronized routines (p. 403)
6. internal working models (p. 422)
7. emotional self-regulation (p. 394)
8. stranger anxiety (p. 409)
9. difficult temperament (p. 400)
10. Attachment Q-set (p. 413)
11. phase of indiscriminate attachments (p. 405)
12. social referencing (p. 396)
13. disorganized/disoriented attachment (p. 413)
14. imprinting (p. 408)
15. empathy (p. 397)

MULTIPLE-CHOICE SELF-TEST (The answers may be found on the pages in parentheses.)

1. **d** (p. 393) The sequence for displaying the various emotions seems to be fairly consistent across cultures, with most emotions emerging in the first two years. At birth (a) only a few primary emotions are apparent. During the first year (b) other primary emotions emerge, but secondary emotions don't appear until the second year. In newborns primary emotions such as interest and distress are present (c).

2. **c** (p. 393) These emotions are all secondary (or complex) emotions that relate to our sense of self-esteem; therefore, they may require self-recognition and self-evaluation. The set of emotions in (a) are primary emotions that are evident at birth. The set of emotions in (b) are primary emotions that emerge between the ages of $2^1/_2$ and 7 months. The four emotions listed in (d) are not a recognized "set" of emotions.

3. **b** (p. 405) At this age specific attachments begin to emerge and infants will protest when separated from the person they have formed an attachment with. Preference for social stimuli (a) appears as early as 6 weeks. Infants move from specific attachments to multiple attachments (c) a few weeks after their first initial attachment forms. As children become attached, they are more likely to become wary around strangers (d).

4. **d** (pp. 407–408) Reference to preprogrammed responses reflects the ethological perspective. Certain behaviours emitted by the infant, such as smiling or crying, work to draw the caregiver closer and, therefore, foster the attachment relationship. Freud suggested that attachments developed because the mother is a source of oral pleasure during the oral stage of development (a). Viewing the mother as a conditioned stimulus (b) is consistent with learning views of attachment. Referring to the maturity of the object permanence concept (c) reflects a cognitive-developmental view of attachment formation.

5. **c** (pp. 409, 411) Many infants (but not all infants) begin to show separation anxiety at the same time that they first show evidence of a primary attachment. Stranger anxiety is not unusual for infants of this age (a), and it is not an indication of an insecure attachment (b). Children's responses to strangers typically depend more on what the stranger does than on the infant's current state (d).

6. **b** (pp. 409, 411) Sondra will show more distress because she will already have formed an attachment to her mother, whereas Trevor has not yet reached the age at which specific attachments are formed. This means that Trevor is less likely to be upset (a), and the reactions in the two children are likely to differ (c). Separation anxiety is a universal response (d), and the initial level of anxiety would not be affected by the actions of the babysitter.

7. **a** (p. 413) Secure attachments are found in approximately 65% of 1-year-old North American infants. Resistant attachments (b) are evident in about 10% of children, and avoidant attachments (c) are evident in about 20% of children. Disorganized or disoriented attachments occur only 5 to 10% of the time (d).

8. **c** (p. 413) An avoidantly attached infant would not show a high level of separation anxiety. Unwillingness to explore and high distress at separation are typical of a resistant attachment (a). A securely attached infant (b) would actively explore the room while the mother was present. Ainsworth did not see disorganized or disoriented attachments (d) in the children she tested.

Chapter Twelve

Development of the Self and Social Cognition

Learning Objectives

By the time you have finished this chapter you should be able to:

1. Trace the development of self-recognition during infancy and toddlerhood.
2. Explain what is meant by a belief-desire theory of mind and outline how children's theory of mind changes over the preschool years.
3. Outline the continuing changes in self-concept that occur during middle childhood and adolescence.
4. Discuss how attachment may influence early self-esteem, and identify some of the factors that can contribute to high or low self-esteem in adolescents.
5. Discuss the relationship between self-esteem and parenting style.
6. Discuss how social comparisons to peers can influence self-esteem.
7. Explain what is meant by achievement motivation and trace the development of achievement self-evaluation during infancy and toddlerhood.
8. Discuss how attachment quality, home environment, child-rearing practices, and peers can influence motivation.
9. Outline the key aspects in Weiner's model for achievement attributions.
10. Contrast an incremental view with an entity view of ability, and discuss typical changes in how children view their ability as they move from preschool through the elementary-school years.
11. Differentiate between a mastery orientation and a learned-helplessness orientation, and describe some ways to minimize or prevent learned helplessness.
12. Describe Marcia's four identity statuses and discuss some factors that can influence identity formation.
13. Trace the developmental course of person perception.
14. Outline Seligman's stages of role taking and relate these stages to changing conceptions of friendship.
15. Discuss how social experience can affect both role-taking skills and person perception.

Chapter Outline and Summary

1. Development of the self-concept

a. The emerging self: Differentiation and self-recognition

Two-month-old infants may have some limited sense of personal agency; to some extent they understand that they are able to produce or cause external events. However, they will not show evidence of self-recognition (and consequently self-awareness) for at least another 12 to 18 months.

The development of self-recognition can be tested using a "rouge test." When children under the age of 15 months are given this test they show no evidence of self-recognition. By the age of 15 to 17 months a few children will show self-recognition, but it is not until the last part of the sensorimotor stage (18 to 24 months) that the majority of infants show evidence of self-recognition on this test. By this age many toddlers can also recognize themselves in current photographs. Once self-recognition is evident, children begin to categorize themselves along a variety of dimensions. This represents the emergence of the "categorical self." However, children at this age are still not fully aware that the self is stable over time.

A certain level of cognitive development appears to be necessary for the development of self-recognition, but social experiences are also important. On tests of self-knowledge securely attached toddlers outperform their insecurely attached age-mates, and the differences in self-knowledge between these two groups increase over time.

b. Who am I? Responses of preschool children

When preschool children describe themselves they tend to talk about physical attributes, possessions, or actions that they feel proud of; they rarely use psychological descriptors. However, research by Rebecca Eder suggests that preschool children have the rudiments of psychological self-awareness; they just lack the ability to express this knowledge using trait-like terminology.

c. Children's theory of mind and emergence of the private self

As adults, people understand they are cognitive beings who have mental states that are not always shared or accessible to others. In other words, adults have a *theory of mind.* This theory of mind emerges slowly as the developing ability of infants and toddlers to use other people to find out about the world increases. The first steps toward acquiring a theory of mind are apparent as early as 2 months of age. At 18 months, toddlers can already reason accurately about other people's desires. By the time children are 2 to 3 years old they may show some understanding of connections between different mental states. They also are aware that they may know something that other people don't know and that other people cannot observe their thoughts. Theory of mind may be fostered by the development of causal reasoning skills and by experience with social interactions, such as pretend play. Humans may be biologically predisposed to develop a theory of mind.

Between the ages of 3 and 4, children develop a belief-desire theory of mind. This means they recognize that beliefs and desires are different and that behaviour can be influenced by either beliefs or desires (or both). Although 3-year-old children understand the distinction between beliefs and desires, they don't yet understand that beliefs may be inaccurate or that different people can hold different beliefs. In contrast, 4- to 5-year-old children understand that beliefs can be inaccurate and that people may act on false beliefs. When this understanding emerges, children may begin to use deception in an attempt to purposely mislead other children or adults.

d. Conceptions of self in middle childhood and adolescence

In middle childhood, children's self-descriptions begin to shift from listing their physical or behavioural attributes to listing their inner qualities. In adolescence these self-descriptions begin to include more abstract qualities. By adolescence children are also beginning to recognize that they are sometimes "different" people in different situations; early adolescents may be troubled by these perceived inconsistencies in their behaviour.

For older adolescents inconsistencies in personal traits across different situations, or in the presence of different groups of people, are less troublesome and are more likely to be integrated into a coherent self-concept.

An important contributor to the development of self-concept is culture. Research shows that individualistic societies foster self-concepts that are based on individualistic attributes, such as independence, whereas collectivistic cultures foster self-concepts that emphasize social connections.

2. Self-esteem: The evaluative component of self

a. *Origins and development of self-esteem*

By the age of 4 or 5 children are already showing evidence of self-evaluation. Compared to children who have insecure attachments with their parents, children with secure attachments, especially to both parents, are much more likely to view themselves favourably. Children with secure attachments are also rated by others as being more competent and more socially skilled.

Before the age of 7 children can provide an assessment of their social acceptance and their general competence, and research shows that they tend to rate themselves positively. Although it is possible that the positive self-ratings may reflect a desire to be liked or to be competent, the ratings nonetheless are moderately correlated with ratings that teachers give them. By age 8 children can accurately assess their physical and academic competence and their social acceptance; their ratings in these areas match the ratings that others provide. During adolescence new dimensions (romantic appeal and quality of close friendships) are incorporated into an individual's view of self-esteem. According to Harter, adolescents begin to perceive their self-worth somewhat differently in different relational contexts.

Generally, self-esteem is lower in males who feel they lack romantic competence and higher in males who feel they have the ability to influence others. In contrast, self-esteem in females is lower if they feel they lack the approval of their friends; self-esteem is higher in females who have supportive relationships with their friends. In general, girls' satisfaction with their bodies and physical appearance declines in early adolescence. Although some adolescents, particularly girls, experience declines in self-esteem as they leave elementary school and enter junior high, by the time they emerge from adolescence, their self-esteem is at approximately the same level they displayed in late childhood.

b. *Social contributors to self-esteem*

Research has consistently shown a correlation between self-esteem and parenting style. Children are more likely to have high self-esteem when they have parents with a nurturing, democratic style of parenting. This correlation shows up across a number of different cultures. In competitive, Western cultures social comparisons with peers also have a strong influence on a child's self-esteem. The influence of peers becomes increasingly stronger during adolescence. In cooperative, communally based cultures peer influences on self-esteem appear to be much less pronounced.

3. Development of achievement motivation and academic self-concept

Achievement motivation is a willingness to strive for success when faced with challenging tasks and a desire to meet high standards of accomplishment. The mastery motive emerges very early in life, and even young infants seek out challenges they can master and show pleasure when they succeed.

a. *Early origins of achievement motivation*

Stipek and her associates have identified three phases in the way children evaluate their performance in achievement situations. Before the age of 2, infants show pleasure when they master challenges, but they do not seek recognition from others when they succeed at meeting challenges. They also show little distress at failure. This suggests that during this phase (joy in mastery) infants are not yet evaluating their outcomes in relation to external standards of performance.

Approval-seeking emerges as children reach their second birthday. When toddlers at this age succeed at a task they often call attention to their success and show visible pleasure in their accomplishment. At this age their behaviour when they are unsuccessful also suggests that they expect others will disapprove or criticize their unsuccessful efforts.

The next phase emerges around the age of 3; from this point on children are less dependent on others to tell them whether they have done well or done poorly. They are capable of self-evaluation and show pride in their achievements and shame when they fail.

b. *Achievement motivation during middle childhood and adolescence*

Three home influences that appear to have a strong influence on a child's overall achievement motivation are the quality of the child's attachment relationships, the child's home environment, and the parenting style that the child experiences. Children who have secure attachments with their parents typically feel more comfortable about taking risks and seeking new challenges, and consequently show a higher level of achievement motivation in the preschool years and throughout middle childhood and adolescence. Achievement motivation also seems to be fostered in home environments that are intellectually stimulating. The quality of a child's home environment during infancy can be used to predict the child's academic performance during elementary school. Stimulating home environments promote intrinsic orientations to achievement. Finally, parents who have a warm, firm, democratic style of parenting (authoritative), and who scaffold tasks for young children to allow them to succeed on their own, tend to foster high levels of achievement motivation in their children.

In addition to home influences, achievement motivation can be affected by peer influences. Sometimes peers can help to support parental efforts to encourage a strong sense of achievement motivation; in other cases peer groups can undermine these efforts. Achievement motivation will be highest among children and adolescents who have a supportive home environment and who also have peers who endorse academic success and achievement.

c. *Beyond achievement motivation: Development of achievement-related attributions*

To accurately predict behaviour in achievement settings it is also necessary to understand how the individual interprets personal success and failure (his or her achievement attributions).

Weiner suggested that there are two dimensions in achievement (or failure) attributions. Outcomes can be perceived as being the result of stable or unstable factors, and they can also be perceived as resulting from internal or external causes. When an individual makes a stable, internal attribution the outcome is seen as the result of individual ability; when an individual makes a stable, external attribution the outcome is seen as the result of task difficulty. In contrast, when an individual makes an unstable, internal attribution the outcome is seen as the result of individual effort; when an individual makes an unstable, external attribution the outcome is seen as the result of luck.

The stable/unstable dimension affects future achievement expectancies. When attributions are made to stable causes (ability or task difficulty), it is less likely that performance will change in the future; when attributions are made to unstable causes (effort or luck), it is more likely that performance will vary from situation to situation. The internal/external dimension affects the value that individuals place on accomplishments. When attributions are made to internal causes (ability or effort), success is more likely to be valued; when attributions are made to external causes (task difficulty or luck), success is less likely to be highly valued.

There are age-related changes in the type of achievement attributions that individuals make. Children under the age of 7 often believe that they have the ability to succeed on almost any task, even when they have failed repeatedly on similar tasks in the past. This reflects their incremental view of ability; they believe that ability is not stable, and that it can increase through effort or practice. Experiences at school may foster a shift in how children view ability. By the mid- to late elementary-school years children typically begin to show an entity view of ability; they now believe that ability is a stable trait that is not influenced by effort.

Dweck and her colleagues found that by the time children are in middle school there are clear individual differences in the types of achievement attributions that children make. Some children display a mastery orientation; they attribute success to ability (internal, stable cause) while attributing failures to external or unstable causes. Other children display a learned-helplessness orientation; they attribute successes to external or unstable factors while attributing failures to a lack of ability (internal, stable cause).

A helpless orientation may be fostered by evaluators who praise effort when a child succeeds, but who criticize a lack of ability when a child fails. A helpless orientation is even evident in preschool children who are often punished or criticized when they fail. In contrast, a mastery orientation can be promoted by evaluators who praise a child's efforts at devising effective problem-seeking strategies when he or she succeeds, while encouraging a greater effort following a failure. A helpless orientation can be overcome in children if they are exposed to attribution retraining and are encouraged to try harder after experiencing a failure. Process-oriented rather than person-oriented praise for success promotes a mastery orientation and prevents learned helplessness.

4. Who am I to be? Forging an identity

Forming an identity involves exploring alternatives and making a firm commitment to an occupation, a religious ideology, a sexual orientation, and a set of political values. In each of these areas individuals can be classified into one of four identity statuses that reflect the degree to which an individual has considered or explored options and has made a commitment to a particular alternative.

Individuals in a state of identify diffusion have not really contemplated any alternatives and consequently have not yet made a commitment to any particular alternative; they are individuals who lack direction in one or more areas that make up a personal identity. Individuals in a state of foreclosure have made firm commitments, but they have done so without exploring alternatives or options; often these individuals "borrow" or "adopt" an identity based on choices made by family members or role models.

Individuals in a state of moratorium are currently in the midst of exploring their options; they have not yet made a commitment but are in the process of actively seeking answers to their questions. Finally, individuals in a state of identity achievement have made a commitment to a set of goals, beliefs, or values after actively questioning and exploring a number of options and alternatives.

a. Developmental trends in identity formation

Erikson assumed that, during the adolescent years (the stage of identity versus role confusion), identity issues were dealt with and resolved. However, subsequent research, utilizing the categories identified by James Marcia, has indicated that the majority of individuals do not begin to actively question different aspects of their identity until the early adult years. This pattern applies to both males and females; however, women appear to attach greater importance to the aspects of identity that focus on sexuality, gender roles, and the issue of how to balance career and family goals.

Even when identity issues are successfully resolved during late adolescence or the early adult years, in middle or late adulthood people may find themselves once again questioning some aspects of their identity. Also, identity statuses can vary across different aspects of identity. When Sally Archer assessed identity statuses in terms of occupation, gender-role attitudes, religious beliefs, and political ideologies, she found that 95% of those she tested were in different phases of identity achievement across the four areas.

b. How painful is identity formation?

It doesn't appear that the formation of an identity is a time of "crisis." As a matter of fact, adolescents in the moratorium phase of identity formation feel better about themselves than do peers who are still in diffusion or peers who are in foreclosure. The most negative aspects of identity seeking are seen in individuals who remain in a state of identity diffusion. These individuals often have low self-esteem and express a sense of hopelessness about the future.

c. Influences on identity formation

The four factors that have the greatest influence on identity formation are the individual's level of cognitive development, the type of parenting the individual experiences, the level of education the individual attains, and the broader social-cultural context that the individual experiences.

Individuals who achieve a solid mastery of formal-operational thought are more likely to resolve identity issues. Also, adolescents who experience a democratic style of parenting, which allows them the freedom to disagree with their parents, are more likely to reach identity achievement. Attending university can help push an individual toward a firm occupational commitment. However, the new ideas and questioning that a person experiences in university settings can sometimes push individuals back into moratorium or diffusion with respect to their religious or political identities. Finally, identity formation is strongly influenced by the broader social-cultural context that an individual experiences as he or she is growing up. The number of new and different occupations that are emerging mean that today's adolescents and young adults have more options from which to choose, and the changes in the nature of some occupations may make it difficult for adolescents who had been planning to follow in their parents' "footsteps."

5. The other side of social cognition: Knowing about others

a. *Age trends in person perception*

Although children between the ages of 3 and 4 develop a belief-desire theory of mind that allows them to understand the beliefs, motives, and intentions that underlie others' behaviour, their knowledge about other people becomes more accurate with age. Children 6 or younger often describe others in much the same way they describe themselves. They focus on observable characteristics, and any psychological descriptors tend to be general, broad descriptors that reflect the individual's recent behaviour more than enduring personality characteristics. Although 4- to 6-year-olds are capable of thinking about traits in psychologically meaningful ways, and 5- to 6-year-olds are becoming more aware of behavioural consistencies in their companions, they are less likely than older children to view traits as stable over time and, thus, less likely to use trait words to describe their companions. Between the ages of 6 and 8 the use of behavioural comparisons to describe others increases; these types of comparative descriptions decline rapidly after the age of 9. The behavioural comparisons are now replaced by trait descriptors that reflect stable psychological constructs.

By the time they are adolescents (between the ages of 12 and 16) individuals are describing others using psychological comparisons. In mid- to late adolescence individuals are not only able to characterize other people in terms of their dispositional qualities, they are also aware that situational influences can affect a person's behaviour, and they recognize that people may act "out of character" under some circumstances.

b. *Theories of social-cognitive development*

Piaget's cognitive-developmental approach and Robert Selman's role-taking analysis have both been used to explain the developmental trends in social cognition. Piaget's cognitive-developmental theory would suggest that during the preoperational stage (3 to 6 years), children centre on the most salient perceptual aspects of stimuli and events in their environment. Therefore, they would likely focus on concrete, observable characteristics when they describe other people.

During the concrete-operational stage, children are decentring and are recognizing that some properties of objects remain unchanged, even when the object changes in superficial ways. At this time their descriptions of others show the same characteristics. There is an understanding that people have certain ways of responding that are stable across different situations, and they describe these qualities in others as enduring traits.

Finally, when adolescents begin to use formal-operational thought, they are able to reason about abstract concepts. At this point they are able to make comparisons among people with respect to psychological traits and describe individuals using psychological comparisons.

Selman believes that one specific aspect of cognitive development underlies social cognition: growth in role-taking skills. Selman suggests that role taking develops in a stage-like manner. Preschool children (through the age of 6) have an undifferentiated or egocentric perspective; they are not able to engage in role taking or see a different point of view.

From approximately age 6 through age 8, children display social-informational role taking. At this point children recognize that another person may have a perspective that differs from the child's own, *if* that person has different information. From approximately age 8 through age 10, children show evidence of self-reflective role taking. At this stage children recognize that another person may have a different point of view, even if that person has the same information as the child. However, at this stage children cannot consider two conflicting perspectives at the same time. The ability to simultaneously consider conflicting perspectives, as well as the ability to assume the perspective of a disinterested third party, is seen in the stage of mutual role taking (10 to 12 years). Finally, as children reach adolescence (12 to 15 years of age and older), they begin to use societal role taking to understand the perspective of others.

As children acquire role-taking skills their understanding of friendship also changes. Preschoolers who are operating at the egocentric stage think of any playmate they enjoy playing with as a "friend." During the stage of social-informational role taking, children begin to view people as friends if they "do nice things"; the child usually does not feel an obligation to reciprocate kind acts.

By the time children reach the stage of self-reflective role taking, friendships are seen as reciprocal relationships that are based on mutual trust. At this age children prefer friends who are psychologically similar to themselves. By early adolescence (stage 3 or 4), friendship also involves loyalty and emotional support.

The growth of interpersonal understanding is also enhanced by equal-status contacts among peers. One specific type of peer contact that seems to foster the development of interpersonal understanding is the occurrence of conflicts or disagreements among friends. Friends who disagree with each other often show an increase in their overall social understanding once the disagreement has been resolved.

Vocabulary Self-Test

Part I: For each of the following definitions provide the appropriate term. (Answers to this portion of the self-test are provided at the end of the chapter.)

1. ________________ An inborn motive to explore, understand, and control one's environment

2. ________________ Tendency to form impressions of others by comparing and contrasting these individuals on abstract psychological dimensions

3. ________________ A person's evaluation of his or her worth as a person, based on an assessment of the qualities that make up the self-concept

4. ________________ Identity status characterizing individuals who have carefully considered identity issues and have made firm commitments to an occupation and ideologies

5. ________________ Feelings of self-esteem within a particular relationship context (e.g., with parents, with male classmates); may differ across relationship contexts

6. ________________ The ability to assume another person's perspective and understand his or her thoughts, feelings, and behaviours

7. ________________ Those aspects of self that others can see or infer

8. ________________ Erikson's term for the uncertainty and discomfort that adolescents experience when they become confused about their present and future roles in life

9. ________________ Society that values cooperative interdependence, social harmony, and adherence to group norms. These societies generally hold that the group's well-being is more important than that of the individual.

10. ________________ A tendency to give up or to stop trying after failing because these failures have been attributed to a lack of ability that one can do little about

11. ________________ A person's classification of the self along socially significant dimensions such as age and sex

12. ________________ Identity status that characterizes individuals who are currently experiencing an identity crisis and who are actively exploring occupational and ideological positions

13. ________________ A desire to achieve in order to satisfy one's personal needs for competence or mastery (as opposed to achieving for external incentives such as grades)

14. ________________ The belief that ability can be improved through increased effort and practice

15. ________________ The combination of physical and psychological attributes that is unique to each individual

Part II: For each of the following terms provide the definition.

Social Comparisons: ______________________________

____

Entity View of Ability: ______________________________

____

Identity Diffusion: ______________________________

____

Looking-Glass Self: ______________________________

____

Attribution Retraining: ______________________________

____

Person Praise: ______________________________

____

Psychological Constructs Phase: ______________________________

____

Self-Concept: ______________________________

____

Identity: ______________________________

____

Achievement Motivation: ______________________________

____

Foreclosure: ______________________________

____

Private Self: ______________________________

____

Mastery Orientation: ______________________________

____

Achievement Expectancy: ______________________________

____

Performance Goal: ______________________________

____

Short-Answer Study Questions

DEVELOPMENT OF THE SELF-CONCEPT

1. Describe the "rouge test" of self-recognition, and discuss the typical responses that are seen in 9-month-old, 16-month-old, and 21-month-old infants.

   Rouge test:

   9-month-old infants will:

   16-month-old infants will:

   21-month-old infants will:

2. Identify three of the first dimensions that toddlers typically incorporate into their categorical self.

   a.

   b.

   c.

3. Explain what a belief-desire theory of mind is, and discuss how children's understanding of beliefs and desires changes from toddlerhood through preschool (2 through 5 years).

   Belief-desire theory of mind:

   2-year-old children typically believe:

   3-year-old children typically believe:

   4- to 5-year-old children typically believe:

4. Outline how children's responses to the question "Who am I?" change during middle childhood and adolescence.

5. How does culture affect the development of self-esteem? Describe the results of research investigating self-concept and the differences between individualistic and collectivistic societies.

SELF-ESTEEM: THE EVALUATIVE COMPONENT OF SELF

6. Describe the correlation between the nature of a child's attachment relationships and his or her overall level of self-esteem.

7. During adolescence new dimensions become important contributors to global self-esteem, and these dimensions affect the self-appraisals of males and females in different ways. Identify factors associated with high and low self-esteem in both adolescent males and females.

   In adolescent males high self-esteem is associated with:
   In adolescent females high self-esteem is associated with:

   In adolescent males low self-esteem is associated with:
   In adolescent females low self-esteem is associated with:

8. Discuss the general stability or instability of self-esteem during the adolescent years, and identify some of the factors that can cause a drop in self-esteem during adolescence.

9. Describe how parents and peers can influence self-esteem in children and adolescents.

   Parents:

   Peers:

DEVELOPMENT OF ACHIEVEMENT MOTIVATION AND ACADEMIC SELF-CONCEPT

10. Explain what is meant by achievement motivation.

11. Identify and describe the three phases that children progress through in learning to evaluate their own performance in achievement situations.

    a.

    b.

    c.

12. Identify and discuss three home influences that can have a strong impact on a child's mastery/achievement motivation, and also on his or her actual achievement behaviour.

    a.

b.

c.

13. Discuss how peer influences can enhance or undermine parental efforts to encourage academic achievement. What implications are seen for different cultural peer groups?

14. Describe four different types of achievement attributions that might be made for success or failure, and indicate whether each involves a stable or unstable factor and an internal or external cause for the outcome.

a.

b.

c.

d.

15. Contrast an incremental view of ability with an entity view of ability, and describe how achievement-related attributions change from the preschool years through the end of the elementary-school years.

Incremental view of ability:

Entity view of ability:

Age-related changes in attributions for achievement during early and middle childhood:

16. Contrast a mastery orientation with a learned-helplessness orientation.

Children with a mastery orientation:

Children with a learned-helplessness orientation:

17. Explain what attribution retraining is, and discuss the impact of this technique on learned helplessness. Discuss the results of research on the effects of person-oriented praise versus process-oriented praise on performance goals and learning goals.

WHO AM I TO BE? FORGING AN IDENTITY

18. Identify and describe the four identity statuses originally described by James Marcia.

a.

b.

c.

d.

19. Identify four factors that influence an adolescent's progress toward achieving an identity and discuss how these factors affect identity achievement.

a.

b.

c.

d.

THE OTHER SIDE OF SOCIAL COGNITION: KNOWING ABOUT OTHERS

20. Outline how children's descriptions of other people typically change from the preschool years through to the end of adolescence.

21. Describe each of Selman's five stages of social perspective taking (including Stage 0).

a.

b.

c.

d.

e.

22. Outline how children's views of friendships change from the preschool years through to early adolescence. What potential sex differences can you identify?

Multiple-Choice Self-Test

For each of the following questions select the best alternative. (Answers and explanations for this self-test are provided at the end of the chapter.) Once you have selected your answer, provide a brief explanation for why the answer you selected is the best choice and why the remaining answers would not be correct.

1. Damon & Hart, and Keller et al., have found that the self-descriptions of 3- to 5-year-old children typically focus on:

   a. physical characteristics, possessions, and actions, e.g., "I can ride a bicycle."
   b. physical characteristics and psychological descriptions, e.g., "I'm happy a lot" or "I like people."
   c. possessions and comparisons to others, e.g., "I'm the tallest in my preschool."
   d. names of friends, and likes or dislikes, e.g., "I love pizza."

   Rationale: ______________________________

   ____

2. Studies of self-esteem among adolescents found that adolescent girls who have the highest self-esteem are:

   a. those who can successfully exert social influence over their friends
   b. those who have successful romantic relationships
   c. those who have supportive relationships with friends
   d. those who feel they have high academic and physical competence

   Rationale: ______________________________

   ____

3. A child who has an intrinsic orientation to achievement would be most likely to say:

   a. "I do my work at school so I can get good grades"
   b. "I like challenging tasks/problems"
   c. "I try hard because it's important to my parents"
   d. "My dad gives me ten dollars for every 'A' I get on my report card"

   Rationale: ______________________________

   ____

4. According to Weiner's attribution theory, a stable, external cause for an achievement outcome would be:

   task

   a. effort
   b. ability
   c. task difficulty
   d. luck

   Rationale: ______________________________

   ____

5. Locus of control is only one factor influencing achievement behaviour. Stability also influences achievement outcomes because, in a given achievement situation, stability determines:

a. an individual's overall effort
b. an individual's expectations for success or failure
c. how much the individual will value the outcome
d. the probability of success

Rationale: ______________________________

____

6. Abdul is a 23-year-old university student who has changed majors several times and cannot decide what he wants to be "when he grows up." It appears that Abdul is currently in the state that Marcia named:

a. foreclosure
b. identity diffusion
c. moratorium
d. identity avoidance

Rationale: ______________________________

____

7. In contrast to individuals who grow up in individualistic societies, individuals who grow up in collectivistic societies tend to have self-concepts centred around:

a. relationships with others
b. personal preferences
c. personal attributes
d. self achievements

Rationale: ______________________________

____

8. When young children under the age of 6 describe other people, they tend to:

a. focus on psychological comparisons, e.g., "Mary is less confident than Jane."
b. focus on behavioural comparisons, e.g., "Jason runs faster than Billy."
c. use mostly physical comparisons, e.g., "Adam has bluer eyes than Sara."
d. use the same type of concrete, non-psychological descriptors as they use to describe themselves

Rationale: ______________________________

____

Activities and Projects Related to this Chapter

ACTIVITY 12-1

WHO AM I?

INTRODUCTION: This activity relates to Chapter 12's material on children's conceptions of themselves. Developing a sense of who we are is one of the major tasks of development. It is a long, gradual process complicated by the fact that abilities and characteristics change with development, sometimes slowly, sometimes rapidly. The self-definition must evolve with development. It is based on the feedback an individual gets from interacting with his or her physical and social environment. In turn, self-definition can influence all areas of our functioning—social, emotional, and cognitive.

One of the ways researchers have attempted to trace the development of children's self-concept has been to ask them to complete sentences beginning, "I am a __________" or "I am a boy/girl who __________." Another strategy has been to ask individuals to give 10 to 20 responses to the question "Who Am I?" Below you are asked to write down 20 self-descriptors to (a) make you more aware of the many dimensions by which individuals define themselves, (b) help put you in touch with the personal importance of your self-concept, and (c) acquaint you with one methodology used to study development of self-concept. Some things you write down will seem mundane, others will make you smile and have a good feeling, and others may make you frown and feel sad or anxious. The feelings evoked reflect our self-evaluation or self-esteem and whether we consider that trait to be a "good" one, a "bad" one, or a neutral one. Take stock of yourself in the assignment below. Just who are you and how do you feel about that person? Why do you think you feel the way you do about yourself?

After completing the activity as instructed, note which self-statements match the types of self-descriptors discussed in the text.

INSTRUCTIONS:

1. Write down 20 answers to the question "Who am I?" on the following page.

2. Beside each number, use the following symbols to indicate how you feel about yourself with respect to that characteristic:
   + = I feel good about this characteristic
   X = I have negative feelings about this characteristic
   N = I feel neutral about this characteristic

3. For those marked by a plus or an X, briefly indicate any person or incident that you think might have contributed to how you feel about yourself with regard to that trait. The purpose of this component is to raise your awareness of the roles peers, parents, and other significant adults play in the formation of how individuals feel about themselves.

4. As a follow-up to this activity, ask a peer to describe you using the same procedure. Next, compare your evaluation with your friend's. Are they similar/different? Why or why not? Were you surprised by your friend's evaluation? This should make you think about how you deem yourself, how others see you, the difference between public and private self, how others influence how we think about ourselves, and the impressions we make (or try to make) on others. Did your friend's evaluation change in any way how you see yourself?

______ 1. ______________________________

______ 2. ______________________________

______ 3. ______________________________

______ 4. ______________________________

______ 5. ______________________________

______ 6. ______________________________

______ 7. ______________________________

______ 8. ______________________________

______ 9. ______________________________

______ 10. ______________________________

______ 11. ______________________________

______ 12. ______________________________

______ 13. ______________________________

______ 14. ______________________________

______ 15. ______________________________

______ 16. ______________________________

______ 17. ______________________________

______ 18. ______________________________

______ 19. ______________________________

______ 20. ______________________________

ACTIVITY 12-2

WHO AM I TO BE?

INTRODUCTION: This activity relates to material presented in Chapter 12 on the development of a mature identity. Adolescence and young adulthood are often times of search for a vocational, political, and religious identity. According to Erik Erikson and James Marcia, the crisis/search process can sometimes go on for several years before the individual commits to a particular career or to particular beliefs. Not all individuals go through an active search process; rather, they commit to a career or belief system recommended by parents or others. A few never go through an active search nor do they make a commitment, but instead remain directionless. Sometimes an individual may have settled into a career and set of beliefs, but a change in life circumstances precipitates a renewed search. Some of you may be students now as a result of a search process that led to a decision to change careers. This activity asks that you review your own history with regard to career, political, and religious identity using the identity status descriptions below.

INSTRUCTIONS: Study the descriptions of each of the four identity statuses. Then proceed with Parts A and B of this activity.

IDENTITY STATUSES

Identity Diffusion: The individual identified as diffuse either has not yet experienced an identity search or has abandoned the search prematurely. No commitment has been made to career, values, and beliefs, or to plan for the future. Rather, the individual lives for the moment. These individuals seem directionless and in a state of suspension from life.

Identity Foreclosure: The foreclosed individual has made a commitment without having gone through an identity search process. The foreclosed individual has avoided the uncertainty of the identity search/crisis by accepting whatever role parents or influential friends have prescribed with little questioning of whether it really fits the individual or is what the individual wants.

Moratorium: Diffusion and moratorium often look similar because both statuses are characterized by a lack of commitment to a particular career, political ideology, or religious beliefs. The individual in moratorium differs, however, in that the individual is engaged in an active search process, not simply existing from day to day. A moratorium period during which an individual explores alternatives is viewed by Marcia and by Erikson as an essential step to reaching the "identity-achieved" status. The early university years are a period of moratorium for many individuals.

Identity Achieved: The identity-achieved individual has undergone a crisis/search phase (moratorium) and has made a commitment. This individual differs from the foreclosed one in that he has a personal identity that is not borrowed from parents or friends. The individual is self-directed and has strong personal reasons for the choices made for a career, for political orientation, or for religious beliefs. The identity-achieved individual's choice and commitment typically are accompanied by a strong investment in the career or beliefs adopted, making the individual especially effective in carrying through on those self-chosen goals or beliefs.

Part A

Indicate below which status would best describe your career, political, and religious identity status at each of the following times in your life. (NOTE—You may be on the same line at more than one time period.)

five years ago (use a 5)
one year ago (use a 1)
now (write NOW)

	CAREER CHOICE	POLITICAL IDEOLOGY	RELIGIOUS BELIEFS
IDENTITY DIFFUSION	_____	_____	_____
IDENTITY FORECLOSURE	_____	_____	_____
MORATORIUM	_____	_____	_____
IDENTITY ACHIEVEMENT	_____	_____	_____

Part B

Write a personal history about "where you have been" and how you got to "where you are now" in each of the three areas: career choice, political ideology, and religious beliefs. Mention factors that influenced your decisions along the way. Also include how you felt (frustrated, depressed, satisfied, apprehensive, confused, relieved, etc.) at various points along the path to where you are today in your commitment (or lack of commitment) to a career, a political orientation, and religious beliefs.

REFERENCES OF INTEREST

Cheah, C.S.L., & Nelson, L.J. (in press). The role of acculturation in the emerging adulthood of Aboriginal college students. *International Journal of Behavioral Development.*

Jenkins, J.M., Turrell, S.L., Kogushi, Y., Lollis, S., & Ross, H. (2003). A longitudinal investigation of the dynamics of mental state talk in families. *Child Development, 74(3),* 905–920.

ANSWERS TO SELF-TESTS

VOCABULARY SELF-TEST (The answers may be found on the pages in parentheses.)

1. mastery motivation (p. 451)
2. psychological comparisons (p. 465)
3. self-esteem (p. 446)
4. identity achievement (p. 460)
5. relational self-worth (p. 448)
6. role taking (p. 466)
7. public self (p. 439)
8. identity crisis (p. 459)
9. collectivistic (or communal) society (p. 444)
10. learned-helplessness orientation (p. 457)
11. categorical self (p. 438)
12. moratorium (p. 460)
13. intrinsic achievement motivation (p. 453)
14. incremental view of ability (p. 456)
15. self (p. 434)

MULTIPLE-CHOICE SELF-TEST (The answers may be found on the pages in parentheses.)

1. **a** (p. 439) In describing themselves preschool children talk mostly about physical attributes, possessions, or actions. Psychological descriptors (b) usually don't emerge until preadolescence or adolescence. Comparisons to others (c) emerge in the early to middle elementary-school years. Likes and dislikes (d) are apparent from early elementary school on.

2. **c** (p. 448) Social influence over friends (a) is associated with high self-esteem in adolescent boys. Success in romantic relationships (b) is most important in adolescent boys; when this is lacking the boys can experience low self-esteem. High academic and physical competence (d) are more important in preadolescent views of self-esteem.

3. **b** (p. 453) Intrinsic motivation means doing a task because it is interesting and enjoyable. Working for good grades (a), working for social approval (c), or working for money (d) would all be examples of extrinsic motivation.

4. **c** (pp. 455–456) Task difficulty is a stable, external factor. Effort is an internal attribute that can change, depending on the situation (a). Ability (b) is a stable, internal attribute. Luck (d) is an unstable, external factor.

5. **b** (pp. 455–456) The stable/unstable dimension of attributions affects achievement expectancies; stable factors are unlikely to change, whereas unstable factors may change in the future. Effort (a) is jointly determined by expectations for success and the value that is placed on success. Value of success or failure (c) is determined by the internal/external dimension of attributions. The probability of success (d) depends on the interactions of both dimensions: the effort and ability of the individual, as well as the task difficulty and "luck."

6. **c** (p. 460) Abdul is currently exploring options and trying to decide on a career; this is consistent with moratorium. An individual in foreclosure (a) would have decided on a career without exploring any other options. An individual in identity diffusion (b) wouldn't see the need to make a decision at this point in time. Identity avoidance (d) is not one of the identity statuses identified by Marcia.

7. **a** (pp. 444–445) Children who grow up in societies, or even families, that emphasize relationships, harmony with others, and respect for others, tend to have self-concepts centred around these collectivistic ideals. Whereas children who grow up in individualistic societies, or families, tend to have self-concepts centred around personal preferences (b), personal attributes (c), and/or self achievements (d).

8. **d** (p. 463) Before the age of 6, children tend to describe others in the same ways that they describe themselves: using physical characteristics, possessions, and actions. Psychological comparisons (a) emerge during adolescence. Behavioural comparisons (b) emerge in the early elementary-school years, and then decrease. Physical comparisons (c) do not dominate the descriptions children provide of others at any age.

Chapter Thirteen

Sex Differences and Similarities, Gender-Role Development, and Sexual Behaviour

Learning Objectives

By the time you have finished this chapter you should be able to:

1. Explain what a gender-role standard is and contrast expressive and instrumental roles.
2. Identify psychological and behavioural differences between the sexes that have been supported by research evidence.
3. Identify some common beliefs about psychological and behavioural sex differences that have not been supported by research.
4. Discuss how influences in the home and in the school may contribute to the emergence of sex differences in different areas of academics.
5. Outline how a child's gender concept typically changes across early childhood.
6. Outline basic developmental trends in the development of gender-role stereotypes, and explain what gender intensification is.
7. Outline basic developmental trends in the development of sex-typed behaviour.
8. Identify the critical events in Money and Ehrhardt's biosocial theory of sex typing.
9. Discuss research findings that relate to both the biological and social components of Money and Ehrhardt's theory.
10. Describe Halpern's psychobiosocial model of the development of gender-typed attributes.
11. Describe how Freud's psychoanalytic theory accounts for the sex-typing process and describe research evidence that is problematic for Freud's theory.
12. Describe the ways that parents, peers, family, and the media can influence sex-role development.
13. Describe Kohlberg's cognitive-developmental theory of sex typing and discuss the research evidence relating to this theory.
14. Describe Martin and Halverson's gender schema theory and discuss the research evidence relating to this theory.
15. Describe how an integrative theorist might characterize the process of gender-role development.
16. Contrast androgynous individuals with undifferentiated individuals.
17. Outline some of the advantages associated with androgynous personalities.
18. Identify some ways in which attitudes about gender roles might be changed.
19. Describe what research studies have concluded about current sexual attitudes and behaviours among adolescents.
20. Discuss some of the potential personal and social consequences of sexual activity among adolescents.

Chapter Outline and Summary

1. Categorizing males and females: Gender-role standards

A gender-role standard is a value, motive, or class of behaviours that is considered more appropriate for members of one sex than the other. Two contrasting types of roles are expressive roles and instrumental roles. Sensitivity, caring, and cooperation are components of an expressive role; assertiveness, competitiveness, and independence are components of an instrumental role. Females have typically been encouraged or expected to take on expressive roles; males have typically been encouraged or expected to take on instrumental roles.

2. Some facts and fictions about gender differences

a. Actual psychological differences between the sexes

Girls typically acquire language at an earlier age than boys. Girls also consistently outscore boys on tests of reading comprehension throughout childhood and adolescence, although the differences are small. On the other hand, boys outperform girls on tests of visual/spatial abilities, and once they reach adolescence boys consistently outperform girls on tests of arithmetic reasoning, but again the differences are small. Also, boys are more aggressive (both physically and verbally); the differences in levels of aggression are already evident in early toddlerhood. However, girls are more likely to display covert hostility.

There are also reliable sex differences in activity level (with boys being more active); risk taking (with girls taking fewer risks); developmental vulnerability (with boys being more likely to show evidence of a variety of developmental problems); and emotional expressivity (with girls showing higher levels of emotional expression). Girls tend to be more compliant to authority figures than boys are, and, when trying to persuade others, girls are more likely to make polite requests and boys are more likely to use demanding or controlling strategies of persuasion. However, it is important to remember that these differences represent differences between groups, and they cannot be used to characterize individuals.

b. Cultural myths

In other areas, there are no consistent differences between the two sexes. For example, both sexes are equally interested in social stimuli; neither sex appears to be more "suggestible"; the two sexes are very similar in their overall self-confidence throughout childhood and adolescence; neither sex is better at rote learning or concept formation; males and females do not differ on tests of analytical or logical reasoning; and there are no differences between the sexes in terms of achievement motivation.

c. Do cultural myths contribute to sex differences in ability (and vocational opportunity)?

Women are overrepresented in occupational fields that require verbal ability and underrepresented in the sciences and in technical fields that require a math or science background. These observed sex differences may partially result from self-fulfilling prophecies that originate with differential parental expectations for sons and daughters. Parents who expect their daughters to have trouble with mathematics may get what they expect. If parents attribute their daughters' successes in areas such as math to effort, rather than to ability, daughters may begin to internalize the belief that they lack the ability to succeed in math, and may therefore become less confident in their abilities and less interested in pursuing nonrequired mathematics courses. Similar parental beliefs may contribute to observed sex differences in English and sports. The same types of self-fulfilling prophecies may originate in the classroom, fuelled by differential expectations that teachers have about male and female abilities.

3. Developmental trends in gender typing

a. Development of the gender concept

Recent Canadian research indicates that even at the early age of 18 months, infants show some awareness of gender labels. Sometime between the ages of 2 and 3 most children are able to accurately label themselves as either boys or girls. However, it takes somewhat longer for them to understand that sex cannot be changed; preschool children often think that boys can become "mommies," or girls can become "daddies," if they really want to. Between the ages of 5 and 7 most children come to understand that sex is an unchanging attribute.

b. Development of gender-role stereotypes

Once children develop an understanding of gender labels and can correctly label themselves or other children as boys or girls, they show evidence of gender-role stereotypes. By the age of 2 years, toddlers begin to show signs of knowledge of gender-role stereotypes, especially for feminine activities. During the preschool and early elementary-school years gender-role stereotypes centre on toys, activities, and areas of achievement that are considered appropriate for the different sexes. In the later elementary-school years children show evidence of gender stereotypes with respect to psychological dimensions such as personality traits.

Elementary-school children are less tolerant of boys who pursue cross-sex interests than of girls who violate gender stereotypes. During early adolescence children become more flexible and are more tolerant of individuals who display cross-sex interests. However, by mid-adolescence both males and females are showing a strong intolerance of cross-sex mannerisms when they are displayed by either males or females. Strong adolescent intolerance toward individuals who violate gender stereotypes is part of a larger process known as gender intensification. Parental influence undoubtedly plays some role in the emergence of gender intensification, but peers probably have a stronger influence.

c. Development of gender-typed behaviour

Children's preferences for "gender-appropriate" toys are evident even before they have a clear gender identity. From 14 to 22 months of age boys usually prefer trucks and cars, while girls prefer dolls and other soft toys. Toy preferences are so strong at this age that toddlers will often refuse to play with cross-sex toys, even if no other toys are available.

Gender segregation also appears early, and it is evident in a variety of cultures. In the early preschool years children typically select same-sex play companions, and by the late preschool years they will actively reject play companions of the other sex and even behave more negatively toward opposite-sex peers. In preadolescence, children who violate gender segregation rules tend to be less popular than children who show evidence of strong gender segregation. Gender boundaries and biases against other-sex companions diminish once adolescents reach puberty.

4. Theories of gender typing and gender-role development

a. Money and Ehrhardt's biosocial theory

Biosocial theory focuses on the biological forces that may constrain or channel the development of males and females. However, the theory also acknowledges that biologically based physical differences between males and females affect how others react to children, and these social forces have a strong influence on gender-role development. In Money and Ehrhardt's theory there are a number of critical episodes or events that influence an individual's final gender role.

During the prenatal period, the initial chromosome pairing at site #23 determines whether testes or ovaries will form in the fetus. If testes form (as a result of an XY pairing at site #23), testosterone and mullerian inhibiting substances are released. In the presence of these two hormones a male internal reproductive system forms in the early part of the fetal stage, and 3 to 4 months after conception male external genitalia form. In the absence of these two hormones a female internal reproductive system will form, followed by female external genitalia. Testosterone also alters the development of the brain and nervous system.

Once the infant is born, others label the child based on the appearance of the external genitalia, and they react to the child on that basis. Finally, biological changes at puberty stimulate the development of primary and secondary sex characteristics. This sexual maturation, combined with the individual's self-concept as male or female, provides the basis for adult gender identity.

Several behavioural genetic studies of adolescent twins have investigated genetic influences on gender-role development. Results from these studies suggest that genotype accounts for approximately 50% of the variability in masculine self-concepts, but less than 20% of the variability in feminine self-concepts. There have also been a number of studies that have investigated the impact of prenatal exposure to hormones. Female fetuses that are exposed to high levels of testosterone or androgens often develop masculine external genitalia, despite their XX genotype and their internal female organs.

Money and Ehrhardt followed a number of androgenized females (female infants born with masculine external genitalia) who had undergone corrective surgery. Compared to other girls, these individuals were more likely to pursue traditionally male pursuits and to begin dating at a later age. A high proportion described themselves as bisexual or homosexual. One of the complications in interpreting the results from this research is that the females who had undergone corrective surgery often also received cortisone therapy. Therefore, it is not clear whether the behaviours displayed by these individuals reflect prenatal exposure to male hormones or postnatal medical treatments.

Animal studies have shown that female monkeys who are exposed to testosterone later display behaviours that are more characteristic of male monkeys; as well, castrated male rats tend to be more passive and display sexual behaviours similar to those seen in female rats. In humans, high testosterone levels in men are linked to higher rates of delinquency and violence. (Also, human participants who win at competitive games show increases in testosterone.) However, this research is correlational in nature, and it is not clear whether the high testosterone levels produce the violent behaviour, or whether the violent behaviour leads to an increase in testosterone levels.

One important component in Money and Ehrhardt's theory is the idea that social labelling can modify (and potentially reverse) biological predispositions. Some evidence that relates to this aspect of the biosocial theory comes from studies of individuals with genital abnormalities who spent at least part of their preadolescent years "living" a gender role that conflicted with their genotype. Overall these studies suggest that the first three years of life may be a sensitive period (but not a critical period) in gender-role development. However, the results from these studies also indicate that neither biology nor social labelling fully accounts for gender-role development. Indeed, according to Halpern's psychobiosocial model, the different early experiences that boys and girls have influence the neural pathways in their developing brains, making them more or less receptive to certain activities or skills.

b. Freud's psychoanalytic theory

Freud believed that gender identity and gender-role preferences emerged during the phallic stage, when children identified with the same-sex parent and began to internalize gender-appropriate attributes and behaviours. Although children do show evidence of gender-typed preferences at the ages when the phallic stage would occur, evidence from research studies suggests these behaviours do not emerge for the reasons that Freud suggested. First, Freud would argue that boys who show more fear of their fathers should show stronger identification; however, the research evidence suggests identification is strongest when fathers are warm and nurturant. Also, school-age and adolescent children are not necessarily psychologically similar to either parent, suggesting something other than identification underlies the development of gender-role preferences.

c. Social learning theory

Social learning theory suggests that children acquire their gender identities and gender-role preferences through differential reinforcement and observational learning. Evidence from research studies suggests that, beginning in early infancy, parents do differentially reinforce gender-appropriate behaviours in their children. By the time children reach the preschool years, parents show less direct monitoring of the gender appropriateness of their children's behaviour; however, differential reinforcement of gender-appropriate behaviours by other children in the peer group is evident during the preschool years.

During the preschool years children appear to attend more to the labels attached to toys (or to activities) than to the sex of the individual who serves as a model. However, between the ages of 5 and 7 children start to attend more selectively to same-sex models and are more likely to avoid toys and activities that other-sex models show a preference for.

d. Kohlberg's cognitive-developmental theory

Unlike psychoanalytic theory and social learning theory, Kohlberg's theory suggests that children first establish a stable gender identity and then actively seek out same-sex models. In Kohlberg's view, children pass through three stages as they develop a mature understanding of being male or female. Basic gender identity is evident by the age of 3, when children can accurately label themselves as boys or girls. During the next stage children recognize that gender is stable over time (gender stability), and finally they come to recognize that gender is stable across situations (gender consistency). Children reach this last stage sometime between the ages of 5 and 7; at this point gender self-socialization begins, as children actively seek out same-sex models.

Cross-cultural studies show that the sequencing of Kohlberg's stages accurately reflects children's understanding of gender at various points during the preschool period. Also, once children have reached the stage of gender consistency, they are more likely to attend to same-sex models. However, children show a strong preference for gender stereotypic toys and activities even before they can accurately label themselves either boys or girls. In other words, a mature understanding of gender is not necessary for the process of gender typing to begin.

e. Gender schema theory

Like Kohlberg's theory, Martin and Halverson's gender schema theory suggests that children pursue interests and behaviours that match their self-image (as male or female). However, unlike Kohlberg, Martin and Halverson suggest that self-socialization begins as soon as a basic gender identity is acquired. In their information-processing theory, as soon as a child has acquired a basic gender identity he or she begins to incorporate information about gender-appropriate interests and conduct into gender schemas. At first these are simple "in-group/out-group" schemas that allow children to classify objects and behaviours as being appropriate "for boys" or "for girls." Children also construct an own-sex schema that prompts them to seek out information that is consistent with their gender role, while ignoring information that relates to the gender role for the other sex.

f. An integrative theory

It may be necessary to combine a number of different theories to fully understand sex differences and gender-role development. Biological theories can account for the major biological developments that occur during the prenatal period, events that will induce others to label the child as a boy or a girl and treat the child in accordance with the label that is applied.

During infancy and toddlerhood differential reinforcement may account for the gender-consistent behaviours that young children display. These early social experiences help preschool children acquire a basic gender identity, which may prompt them to form gender schemas. During the preschool years gender schemas can be used to guide activities and interests, and also to focus information processing in such a way that children attend more to information they perceive as being relevant to their own gender. Finally, once gender consistency emerges (approximately age 6 or 7), children begin to attend more to same-sex models as guides for gender-appropriate attitudes and behaviours.

5. Psychological androgyny: A prescription for the future?

a. Do androgynous people really exist?

Psychological androgyny refers to a balancing or blending of "masculine" and "feminine" traits in one individual. In other words, an androgynous person could be assertive, analytical, and independent, while also displaying affection, compassion, and understanding. In personality tests conducted among college students, approximately one-third of those who were evaluated displayed a gender type that matched his or her sex. Roughly the same proportion of individuals were androgynous, and the remainder were either undifferentiated or showed "sex-reversed" gender types.

b. Are there advantages to being androgynous?

Individuals categorized as androgynous are more flexible than more traditionally gender-typed individuals. Androgynous individuals also typically have higher self-esteem and are better adjusted than their traditionally gender-typed peers. Androgynous couples tend to be more satisfied with their relationships, with the feminine aspect of androgyny best predicting their relationship satisfaction. Some research, nonetheless, suggests that children who actively express many of the traits considered more appropriate for the opposite sex are more likely to experience low self-esteem and be rejected by peers.

c. Applications: On changing gender-role attitudes and behaviour

Bem suggests that androgyny may be encouraged in children if parents hold non-traditional attitudes toward gender roles and encourage cross-sex play as well as same-sex play in their children, while teaching their children that sex is a biological attribute that has no bearing on the activities or interests an individual chooses to pursue.

In addition, gender stereotypes can be modified by challenging their accuracy (through rule training) or by promoting cognitive skills (such as classification training) that assist children in seeing the fallacies in their existing gender schemas.

6. Adolescent sexuality

a. Cultural influences on sexuality

Canadian and Western societies are relatively restrictive in their view of sexuality. Cultures differ in the sex education they provide children. Canadian adolescents receive most of their information about sex from peers and teachers. Although parents are a good source for accurate information about sex, North American parents do not provide the level or amount of discussion required by their adolescents. As well, few youth consult their family physician about sexual matters.

b. Sexual attitudes and behaviour

Today's adolescents often believe that premarital sex with affection is acceptable, and that casual or exploitive sex is wrong. Also, Western societies are rapidly moving toward a single standard of sexual behaviour that is applicable for both males and females. Although today's adolescents are often involved in more intimate forms of sexual activity at an early age than were adolescents of earlier generations, it is a myth to assume that they are having sex as early and as often as possible. For Canadian adolescents, peers and teachers serve as their primary sources of information about sex and dating.

c. Personal and social consequences of adolescent sexual activity

Large numbers of sexually active adolescents fail to use contraception. Unprotected sex puts these adolescents at high risk for sexually transmitted diseases and teenage pregnancy. In Canada, the rate of some sexually transmitted diseases (STDs) has been decreasing. The implementation of more effective sex educational programs has increased children's and adolescents' knowledge about STDs and their prevention.

According to Statistics Canada, the rate of teenage pregnancies in Canada has declined over the past few years. However, an average of over 40 000 Canadian teens aged 15 to 19 get pregnant each year. Some of these pregnancies end in miscarriage or abortion, but adolescents who do give birth often face an interruption in education and a loss of social support. Teenage mothers are more likely than older mothers to be at risk for poor nutrition and they are more likely to receive inadequate prenatal care. Consequently they experience more prenatal and birth complications and are more likely to deliver preterm or small-for-date babies. Compared to older mothers, adolescent mothers know less about child development, and this can have long-term consequences for their children. Children born to teens often show evidence of intellectual deficits and emotional disturbances during the preschool years, and poor academic achievement and peer relations later in childhood. Sex education programs that include information about contraception and decision-making skills, in addition to the biological facts of reproduction, may be effective at reducing the incidence of unprotected sex and teenage pregnancies. As well, early and open discussions about sexual matters between parents and their children can be a helpful preventative strategy.

Vocabulary Self-Test

Part I: For each of the following definitions provide the appropriate term. (Answers to this portion of the self-test are provided at the end of the chapter.)

1. ________________ Females who develop male-like external genitalia because of exposure to male sex hormones during the prenatal period

2. ________________ Process by which a child becomes aware of his or her gender and acquires motives, values, and behaviours considered appropriate for members of that sex

3. ________________ Phenomenon whereby people cause others to act in accordance with the expectations they have about those others

4. ________________ The stage of gender identity formation in which the child recognizes that a person's sex is invariant, despite changes in the person's activities or appearance

5. ________________ Freud's term for the child's tendency to emulate another person, usually the same-sex parent

6. ________________ A magnification of sex differences early in adolescence associated with increased pressure to conform to traditional gender roles

7. ________________ Freud's term for the conflict a girl is said to experience when she envies her father for possessing a penis and chooses him as a sex object in the hope that he would share with her this valuable organ that she lacks

8. ________________ A behaviour, value, or motive that members of a society consider more typical or appropriate for members of one sex

9. ________________ The finding that individuals who reach puberty late tend to perform better on visual/spatial tasks compared to those who mature early

10. ________________ Detailed knowledge or plans of action that enable a person to perform gender-consistent activities and to enact his or her gender role

11. ________________ Teaching young children how to behave by reinforcing appropriate behaviours and punishing or otherwise discouraging inappropriate conduct

12. ________________ A social prescription, usually directed toward females, that one should be cooperative, kind, nurturant, and sensitive to the needs of others

13. ________________ A genetic anomaly in which a male fetus is insensitive to the effects of male sex hormones and will develop female-like external genitalia

Part II: For each of the following terms provide the definition.

Phallic Stage: ______________________________

____

Basic Gender Identity: ______________________________

____

Visual/Spatial Abilities: ______________________________

____

Androgyny: ______________________________

____

Gender Segregation: ______________________________

____

Oedipus Complex: ______________________________

____

Instrumental Roles: ______________________________

____

Gender Stability: ______________________________

____

Congenital Adrenal Hyperplasia (CAH): ______________________________

____

In-group/Out-group Schema: ______________________________

____

Gender Schemas: ______________________________

____

Castration Anxiety: ______________________________

____

Gender Identity: ______________________________

____

Short-Answer Study Questions

CATEGORIZING MALES AND FEMALES: GENDER-ROLE STANDARDS

1. Explain what a gender-role standard is, and contrast the qualities associated with expressive and instrumental roles.

   Gender-role standard:

   Expressive roles:

   Instrumental roles:

SOME FACTS AND FICTIONS ABOUT SEX DIFFERENCES

2. List four sex differences originally identified by Maccoby and Jacklin, and describe the nature of the differences that exist in each of these areas.

   a.

   b.

   c.

   d.

3. List five additional sex differences, identified by recent research that has combined the results from several studies, and describe the nature of the differences that exist in each of these areas.

   a.

   b.

   c.

   d.

   e.

4. List six "myths" about sex differences and describe the findings from research studies that have investigated each of these differences.

   a.

   b.

   c.

   d.

   e.

   f.

5. Explain what a self-fulfilling prophecy is, and discuss how cultural myths may actually contribute to sex differences in ability.

   Self-fulfilling prophecy:

   Cultural myths may contribute to sex differences in the following way:

DEVELOPMENTAL TRENDS IN GENDER TYPING

6. Outline the developmental course of the gender concept in young children from infancy through the early elementary-school years.

7. Outline the developmental course of gender-role stereotypes from toddlerhood through early adolescence.

8. Explain what gender intensification is and when it emerges, and discuss some reasons why gender intensification might occur.

9. Outline changes in children's preferences for same-sex or other-sex playmates from toddlerhood through to preadolescence.

10. Describe sex differences in the display of gender-typed behaviour during the preschool and elementary-school years, and discuss some potential reasons as to why these differences might occur.

THEORIES OF GENDER TYPING AND GENDER-ROLE DEVELOPMENT

11. Briefly outline the key aspects of Money and Ehrhardt's biosocial theory of gender typing and gender-role development.

12. Describe what the results from behavioural genetic studies of adolescent twins suggest regarding genetic influences on gender self-concepts.

13. Describe congenital adrenal hyperplasia (CAH), and describe the conclusions from research that has tracked individuals with CAH through adolescence.

14. It has been suggested that high levels of testosterone may produce increases in aggression. Outline the results from animal studies that have manipulated testosterone levels in both male and female subjects. Also, discuss the conclusions that can be drawn regarding the link between testosterone and levels of aggression in humans.

    In animal studies:

    In humans:

15. Briefly outline the key aspects of Freud's psychoanalytic theory of gender typing and gender-role development.

16. Briefly outline the key aspects in social learning theories of gender typing and gender-role development.

17. List and describe the three stages Kohlberg suggested children pass through as they develop a mature understanding of what it means to be male or female.

    a.

    b.

    c.

18. Briefly outline the key aspects of Kohlberg's cognitive-developmental theory of gender typing and gender-role development, and discuss some of the criticisms of his theory.

    Key aspects of Kohlberg's theory:

    Criticisms of the theory:

19. Briefly outline the key aspects of Martin and Halverson's gender schema theory of gender typing and gender-role development.

20. An integrative approach to understanding gender typing and gender-role development would suggest that the key factors that influence these processes can change during early development. Outline the factors that might be most influential during the following developmental periods:

The prenatal period:

The first three years of infancy and toddlerhood:

The preschool and early school years (ages 3–6):

The elementary-school years (age 7 to puberty):

Puberty and beyond:

21. Discuss gender typing and gender role development in terms of cross-cultural (or subcultural) differences. How might culture shape our gender perceptions? As well, our perceptions may change from generation to generation. How might culture interact with changes in gender perception with different generations?

PSYCHOLOGICAL ANDROGYNY: A PRESCRIPTION FOR THE FUTURE?

22. Explain what is meant by the term "psychological androgyny."

23. What proportion of university students display psychological androgyny, and how does psychological androgyny appear to influence an individual's overall adjustment?

24. Identify two things parents can do to promote psychological androgyny in their children.

a.

b.

25. One intervention program exposed kindergarten, fifth-grade, and ninth-grade students to readings and activities designed to teach the children about the problems created by sexism. Evaluate the effectiveness of programs of this type by discussing the outcomes seen in the youngest and the oldest age groups.

Kindergarten children:

Ninth-grade children:

26. Two cognitive interventions that are aimed at reducing children's gender schematic thinking are rule training and classification training. Describe each type of intervention, and evaluate its effectiveness with preschool children.

Rule training:

Classification training:

27. Programs designed to modify children's gender-stereotyped attitudes and behaviours appear to be more effective when the person leading the program is a male. Discuss why this might occur.

ADOLESCENT SEXUALITY

28. Describe what research studies have concluded about current sexual attitudes and behaviours among Canadian adolescents.

29. Identify two potential personal and social consequences of sexual activity among adolescents.

a.

b.

Multiple-Choice Self-Test

For each of the following questions select the best alternative. (Answers and explanations for this self-test are provided at the end of the chapter.) Once you have selected your answer, provide a brief explanation for why the answer you selected is the best choice and why the remaining answers would not be correct.

1. In their classic study of 110 nonindustrialized societies, Barry, Bacon, and Child found that most societies valued the following qualities in males:

   a. achievement and self-reliance
   b. nurturance and obedience
   c. obedience and responsibility
   d. nurturance and achievement

   Rationale: ______________________________

   ____

2. Gender differences have been consistently found in ________, with boys showing higher levels than girls:

   a. activity level
   b. emotional expressivity
   c. social interest
   d. verbal ability

   Rationale: ______________________________

   ____

3. Evidence cited in the text regarding the influence of parents and teachers in promoting sex-stereotyped attitudes indicates that:

   a. only parents have different expectations and/or respond differently to boys and girls
   b. both parents and teachers have different expectations and/or respond differently to boys and girls
   c. only teachers have different expectations and/or respond differently to boys and girls
   d. neither parents nor teachers have different expectations and/or respond differently to boys and girls

   Rationale: ______________________________

   ____

4. Children tend to be most tolerant of cross-sex behaviours during:

   a. infancy and toddlerhood
   b. infancy and early adolescence
   c. the preschool years and late adolescence
   d. the preschool years and early adolescence

   Rationale: ______________________________

   ____

5. Sex differences in play patterns and a preference for same-sex peers:

a. is not clearly evident until the late elementary-school years
b. emerges only after children start attending elementary school
c. is evident in toddlers (18 months to 3 years of age) and increases throughout the elementary-school years
d. is first evident in the play of preschoolers (about 4 to 5 years of age)

Rationale: ____

____

6. According to Kohlberg's cognitive-developmental theory, the stage of sex typing at which a girl first recognizes that she can never become a father is:

a. gender stability
b. basic gender identity
c. gender consistency
d. gender intensification

Rationale: ____

____

7. The theory that emphasizes the role of selective information gathering and recall in the development of sex stereotypes, patterns of gender-appropriate behaviour, and gender-appropriate preferences, is:

a. biosocial theory
b. Kohlberg's cognitive-developmental theory
c. psychoanalytic theory
d. gender schema theory

Rationale: ____

____

8. The integrative theory outlined in your text suggests that children show evidence of intrinsic motivation to seek sex-role information and acquire sex-appropriate behaviours:

a. right from early infancy and toddlerhood (under the age of 3)
b. starting at approximately the age of 3
c. only after they reach 6 or 7 years of age
d. only after they reach adolescence

Rationale: ____

____

Activities and Projects Related to this Chapter

ACTIVITY 13-1

MEDIA (ADS, TELEVISION, FILMS) AS A POTENTIAL INFLUENCE ON SEX TYPING AND SELF-CONCEPT

INTRODUCTION: This activity relates to material in several chapters: Chapter 5 on the psychological importance of physical maturation, Chapter 12 on self-concept, Chapter 13 on sex typing, and Chapter 16 on extrafamilial influences on development. An important task in childhood is learning what gender-appropriate behaviours are and how to interact appropriately with the other sex (i.e., in accordance with cultural norms). In addition, each child develops some feeling about how adequately he or she meets the cultural ideal of maleness or femaleness and the cultural ideal of attractiveness. At adolescence individuals become particularly concerned with how well they meet those cultural ideals.

Children are dependent on external feedback throughout childhood for developing self-concept and self-esteem. Parents, peers, teachers, and other important people in a child's life are all potential sources of input. Children also actively compare themselves to others. How well they perceive that they measure up to what is culturally valued in that comparison will affect how children feel about themselves. A potential source of input about what that cultural ideal is comes from the media—television, films, and advertisements.

Many individuals today are concerned about what kind of messages the media may be giving children about appearance and about sex roles. For example, are ads contributing to a cultural definition of beauty so narrow that no one can possibly meet that ideal? The message seems to be that whatever we look like, it is not good enough—that what we really need is the right make-up, the right diet program, the right exercise machine, the right deodorant, etc., before we can possibly be attractive to the other sex. Are ads telling our young people that they will magically be attractive and popular if they drink the right beer or smoke the right cigarette? Do character portrayals in television programs and in films perpetuate stereotypes about roles by defining them very narrowly? Do they convey the message that sex is the route to intimacy and acceptance, etc.?

The purpose of this activity is to explore the kinds of messages that one source of input, the media, may be giving to our children and to think about (a) how those messages might influence how a teen feels about her or his physical attractiveness and (b) how they might affect a teen's behaviour and attitudes about herself or himself and about others.

INSTRUCTIONS:

1. Using films, television, and/or magazines, "collect" five examples of ad and character portrayals of males and five of females. Describe each example (identify source; attach magazine ads).

2. After you have described each example, comment on what "message" you think a child seeing that particular advertisement or seeing that character portrayal in a film or on TV may be receiving. Discuss what impact that message might have on the child's notion of what is sex appropriate as well as on the child's notion of the basis for close relationships. Finally, comment on how each example might influence the way individuals feel about themselves.

RESEARCH OF INTEREST

For more information on important Canadian research on the effects of media on attitudes toward sexual behaviour, read the research conducted by Dr. Arleigh Reichl at Kwantlen University College, British Columbia. Dr. Reichl has found that latent sexism in print advertisements can negatively affect people's attributions of blame and responsibility when considering rape situations—a finding that suggests nonconscious processing of undetected sexism.

Reichl, A.J. (2004). Evidence for nonconscious effects of undetected sexism in print advertisements. Manuscript submitted for publication.

ACTIVITY 13-2

MEDIA (CHILDREN'S TELEVISION PROGRAMS) AS A POTENTIAL INFLUENCE ON CHILDREN'S GENDER STEREOTYPES

INTRODUCTION: This activity relates to material in Chapter 13 on sex typing and self-concept and to material in Chapter 16 on the media's influence on children's gender stereotypes. The activity asks you to do an analysis of the portrayal of males and females based on a sampling of children's television programs and address the question: What are the explicit and implicit messages about gender roles and characteristics in the programs viewed?

INSTRUCTIONS: Watch at least two hours of children's programming, e.g., cartoons and puppet shows, family comedy programs. Look specifically for the characteristics of female and male characters and the roles played. Take notes as you watch. It will help if you use the material from Chapter 13 to create a list of stereotypic male and female roles and characteristics before beginning to view the programs. Then, for each character in a program, you can simply check off which of the listed characteristics/roles he or she displayed. This will allow you to easily determine whether male characters tend to display only stereotypic masculine characteristics/roles and whether female characters tend to display only stereotypic feminine characteristics/roles.

WRITE-UP:

Organize your observations as follows for your write-up.

1. PROGRAM CLASSIFICATION:

Name of program:

Classification of program (cartoon, adventure show, comedy series, variety entertainment):

2. ROLES AND CHARACTERISTICS DISPLAYED:

Summarize the number (and types) of gender stereotypic and nonstereotypic characteristics displayed by the primary characters, e.g.,

<u>Program 1</u>	number of stereotypic male characteristics	number of stereotypic female characteristics
Male character A:		
Male character B:		
Female character A:		
Female character B:		

3. SUMMARY OF MESSAGES TO CHILDREN REGARDING WHAT IS GENDER APPROPRIATE:

Explicit message:

Implicit message:

ACTIVITY 13-3

GENDER ROLES: PAST AND PRESENT

INTRODUCTION: The purpose of this activity is to help you develop a sense of the extent to which gender roles are a product of a particular social/cultural/historical period and, hence, change over time. To achieve this goal, you are asked to conduct four semi-structured interviews of two senior citizens and two individuals your own age. The results will provide a basis for reflecting on the extent to which gender roles define and sometimes limit who a person is and what a person is allowed to become within a particular culture/time period.

INSTRUCTIONS: Interview one male and one female over age 60. Also interview one male and one female your age (one may be yourself). Contrast and compare the details of the responses across these two generations. What changes in roles have occurred and what effects have these changes had on the lives of individuals (choices open to them, responsibilities, stresses, life satisfaction, etc.)?

SUGGESTIONS FOR QUESTIONS TO ASK:

1. Describe some of the ways boys and girls were treated differently when you were a child regarding (a) chores/responsibilities, (b) toys, (c) clothing, (d) independence given by parents, (e) expectations regarding school, (f) expectations regarding a career, (g) expectations/tolerance regarding expression of emotions, (h) dating, (i) ________.
2. Describe the duties of your mother and father in your home and outside the home.
3. If you could have changed the way you were brought up regarding what was expected of you as a boy/girl and how you were treated, what would you have changed?
4. What do you think were the best and worst things about how boys and girls were raised when you were a child?
5. What do you think is the biggest change in gender roles over the past 30 to 50 years? Do you think it is a good change?
6. What, if any, changes would you like to see in gender roles for the next generation?
7. What do you think will be the single most significant change in men's and women's roles in the future?

REFERENCES OF INTEREST

Lacasse, A., Purdy, K.T., & Mendelson, M.J. (2003). The mixed company they keep: Potentially offensive sexual behaviors among adolescents. *International Journal of Behavioral Development, 27*, 532–540.

Lindsey, E.W., & Mize, J. (2001). Contextual differences in parent–child play: Implications for children's gender role development. *Sex Roles, 44,* 155–176.

Rogers, D., & Dilworth, K. (2002). Reducing the rate of teen pregnancy in Canada: A framework for action. *International Journal of Adolescent Medicine and Health, 14(2),* 97–100.

ANSWERS TO SELF-TESTS

VOCABULARY SELF-TEST (The answers may be found on the pages in parentheses.)

1. androgenized females (p. 491)
2. gender typing (p. 474)
3. self-fulfilling prophecy (p. 481)
4. gender consistency (p. 498)
5. identification (p. 495)
6. gender intensification (p. 485)
7. Electra complex (p. 495)
8. gender-role standard (p. 474)
9. timing-of-puberty effect (p. 490)
10. own-sex schema (p. 499)
11. direct tuition (p. 495)
12. expressive role (p. 474)
13. testicular feminization syndrome (TFS) (p. 490)

MULTIPLE-CHOICE SELF-TEST (The answers may be found on the pages in parentheses.)

1. **a** (p. 475) Over 85% of the countries studied encouraged achievement and self-reliance for males; less than 5% of the countries encouraged these qualities for females. Nurturance and obedience (b) and obedience and responsibility (c) were encouraged in girls more than boys. Achievement is encouraged in boys, but none of the countries encouraged nurturance in boys (d).

2. **a** (pp. 477–478) Activity level is higher in boys than in girls. Girls appear to be more emotionally expressive than boys (b). The two sexes are equally interested in social stimuli and equally responsive to social reinforcement (c). Girls have greater verbal abilities than boys (d).

3. **b** (pp. 481–482) Parents and teachers can both create self-fulfilling prophecies based on their differential expectations regarding the abilities of boys and girls. Parents are not the only ones who exert this influence (a), nor are teachers the only ones (c). Both parents and teachers are likely to respond differently to children based on their own gender expectations (d).

4. **a** (pp. 484–485) In infancy and toddlerhood children understand that there are gender differences, but they are less likely to "judge" the behaviour of other children on this basis. In late adolescence, individuals are more flexible in their thinking about gender. In the preschool and early elementary-school years children are rigid and intolerant of sex-role transgressions, and during early adolescence gender intensification leads to a high intolerance for cross-sex mannerisms and behaviours (b, c, and d).

5. **c** (p. 486) Gender segregation in play is evident in children by the age of 2 (girls) or 3 (boys), and sex differences in toy preferences are evident as early as 14 months of age. Therefore, sex differences in these areas are evident before the late elementary-school years (a); they emerge before children start school (b); and they are present before children reach the preschool years (d).

6. **a** (p. 498) Gender stability is when children recognize that gender is stable over time. Basic gender identity (b) is when children can first label themselves as boys or girls. Gender consistency (c) is when children finally recognize that gender is also stable across situations. Gender intensification (d) is not one of the stages in Kohlberg's theory of gender typing.

7. **d** (pp. 498–499) Martin and Halverson's gender schema theory is an information-processing theory that focuses on selective information gathering. Biosocial theory (a) emphasizes the interaction between biological factors and social factors in gender typing. Kohlberg's theory (b) emphasizes cognitive development as the mechanism underlying gender typing and gender-role development. Psychoanalytic theory (c) emphasizes the Oedipus and Electra conflicts and identification with the same-sex parent.

8. **b** (pp. 500–501) The integrative theory suggests that as soon as children acquire a basic gender identity (age 3), they become active self-socializers who try to acquire the attributes they see as being consistent with their self-image. They will not be internally motivated to seek out this information during infancy and toddlerhood (a); but they will show this internal motivation before the elementary-school years (c) and well before adolescence (d).

Chapter Fourteen

Aggression, Altruism, and Moral Development

Learning Objectives

By the time you have finished this chapter you should be able to:

1. Define aggression and distinguish between hostile and instrumental aggression.
2. Outline basic developmental trends in aggressive behaviour and discuss sex differences in the quantity and the nature of aggressive acts.
3. Discuss general trends in the stability of aggressive behaviour from early childhood through adulthood.
4. Contrast proactive and retroactive aggressors and outline differences in the way each type of aggressor may process social information.
5. Compare and contrast passive and provocative victims.
6. Identify some cultural and subcultural factors that are correlated with overall levels of aggression.
7. Explain what is meant by a coercive home environment, and discuss how this type of environment may promote aggressive interactions and contribute to delinquent behaviour.
8. Identify some methods parents and teachers can use to counter aggression and antisocial behaviour.
9. Define altruism and outline basic developmental trends in altruistic behaviour.
10. Outline the five levels of prosocial moral reasoning identified by Eisenberg and discuss the typical responses that are seen at each of the different levels.
11. Differentiate between sympathetic empathic arousal and self-oriented distress, and explain how parents can help to promote sympathetic empathic arousal.
12. Outline the basic age trends in the link between empathy and altruism.
13. Identify some cultural factors that are correlated with overall levels of altruism.
14. Explain how parents and other adults can promote altruistic behaviour in children.
15. Define morality and distinguish between moral affect, moral reasoning, and moral behaviour.
16. Outline and evaluate Freud's psychoanalytic explanation of moral development.
17. Outline and evaluate Piaget's theory of moral development.
18. Describe each of the six stages of moral reasoning identified by Kohlberg.
19. Discuss the research evidence that supports some of the key aspects of Kohlberg's theory.
20. Evaluate the major criticisms that have been raised concerning Kohlberg's theory.
21. Discuss how individuals acquire moral standards and are motivated to act in accordance with those standards, using concepts from social learning theory.
22. Discuss the relative effectiveness of different disciplinary styles in promoting moral maturity in children.

Chapter Outline and Summary

1. The development of aggression

Aggression is any form of behaviour intended to harm or injure a living being who is motivated to avoid such treatment. This definition focuses on the actor's intention, not the consequences of the behaviour. Therefore, actions that cause harm but are unintentional are not considered to be aggressive acts, and actions that are intended to harm, even if there is no actual harm done, are considered to be aggressive acts.

Aggressive acts can also be classified based on the actor's motivation. If the sole motivation for an act is to inflict harm on the individual who is the victim, the behaviour is considered to be hostile aggression. If the motivation for an act is to obtain some objective, and the harm occurs as a byproduct of reaching the intended objective, the behaviour is considered to be instrumental aggression. Therefore, one child pushing another child off a swing in order to be able to play with the swing would be an example of instrumental aggression. If the child who is pushed from the swing retaliates and physically or verbally attacks the child who took the swing, that child's behaviour would be an example of hostile aggression.

a. Origins of aggression in infancy

By the time infants are 12 months of age, instrumental aggression can be seen in some of their interactions. Frequently, aggressive acts at this age centre on the control of toys. Over the next 12 months toddlers continue to have disputes over toys, but by the time children are 2 the disputes are more likely to be resolved by negotiating or sharing, rather than by fighting.

b. Developmental trends in aggression

During the early preschool years the majority of aggressive interactions among children tend to involve instrumental aggression; however, physical aggression is gradually replaced by verbal aggression. Over the later preschool years and middle childhood, interactions involving instrumental aggression decline as children learn to resolve conflicts in amicable ways; however, hostile aggression continues to increase slightly. As children acquire better perspective-taking skills they are also better able to understand another child's intent, and consequently they are more likely to retaliate when they are harmed. These age trends apply to both males and females, but there are distinct sex differences in the types of aggressive acts that are displayed. In general, males are more likely to show overt physical and verbal aggression; in contrast, females are more likely to display covert relational aggression.

Hostile and overt forms of aggression continue to decline from middle childhood throughout adolescence. However, relational aggression among adolescent females becomes more widespread and more malicious, and adolescent males often express anger and frustration indirectly, through antisocial behaviours. Also, it appears that aggression is a relatively stable attribute. In studies that have tracked individuals from early childhood through to early adulthood, highly aggressive children have a tendency to show high levels of aggression as adults. In fact, recent research suggests that there is little evidence for a late onset of physical aggression. Detection of problems in preschool thus becomes an important component of problem prevention and intervention.

c. Individual differences in aggressive behaviour

Highly aggressive children can generally be classified as proactive or reactive aggressors. Proactive aggressors display high levels of instrumental aggression, intended to achieve personal goals and exert dominance over peers. Reactive aggressors display high levels of hostile aggression, often in retaliation to acts by others. Each type of aggressor shows a distinct bias in social information processing.

According to research by Dodge, reactive aggressors tend to display a hostile attributional bias, overattributing hostile intent to peers. In contrast, Dodge suggests that when proactive aggressors are harmed under ambiguous circumstances they consciously formulate aggressive responses that are likely to help them achieve a specific goal. Habitual bullies have often observed aggression and conflict in their homes, but have rarely been the target of aggression. Bullies are usually proactive aggressors.

Chronic victims of aggression can also be classified in one of two ways: passive victims (who are reluctant to fight back) and provocative victims (who are hot-tempered and who are inclined to fight back). Often, provocative victims have been abused or otherwise victimized at home, and they tend to show the same hostile attributional bias that is seen in reactive aggressors.

d. Cultural and subcultural influences on aggression

Cross-cultural studies consistently indicate that some societies and subcultures are more violent and aggressive than others. On a percentage basis, the incidence of rape, homicide, and assault is higher in the United States than in any other industrialized nation. Other cross-cultural research indicates that there are social class differences in aggression. Children and adolescents from lower socioeconomic groups exhibit higher levels of aggression than their middle-class age-mates.

A number of factors may contribute to social class differences in aggression. Physical punishment is typically more common among lower-income families. In addition, parents in lower-income families may inadvertently foster a hostile attributional bias among their children by encouraging their children to respond forcefully to provocation. Finally, lower-income parents may find that it is more difficult for them to monitor their children's activities; this may lead to an increase in antisocial behaviour, especially when the child's peer group endorses antisocial conduct.

e. Coercive home environments: Breeding grounds for aggression and delinquency

In coercive home environments, family members bicker frequently and are reluctant to initiate conversations. The conversations that do occur often consist of threats or are used to irritate other family members. These coercive interactions are maintained by negative reinforcement: the coercive behaviours increase in frequency because they succeed in temporarily getting the antagonist to stop his or her irritating or hostile behaviour. In these families the parents rarely use social approval as a method of behavioural control. Instead of rewarding prosocial conduct and ignoring misconduct, these parents tend to ignore prosocial conduct when it occurs, and focus their attention on dealing with perceived misconduct.

Coercive parenting during early childhood can contribute to the development of hostile attributional biases and a lack of self-restraint in children. These types of behaviours can cause children to be rejected by their elementary-school peers. These children are also often defiant toward authority figures; general opposition to and negative interactions with teachers may contribute to the academic deficiencies that are often evident in children raised in coercive home environments. By early adolescence these children are often associating with peers who are also hostile and antisocial, and this can promote delinquent or antisocial behaviours. Further, antisocial teens tend to have intimate relationships with other antisocial teens, which, in turn, puts them at risk of experiencing hostile and abusive relationships, teen pregnancy, and, subsequently, puts their children at risk of experiencing negative home environments.

f. Methods of controlling aggression and antisocial conduct

Parents and teachers can utilize a number of different strategies in dealing with aggressive children. Three of these strategies are the creation of nonaggressive environments; elimination of benefits for aggressive acts; and social-cognitive interventions.

Providing sufficient space to allow children to play together without feeling crowded, providing enough play materials so that children do not need to compete for toys, and eliminating the presence of toys that promote aggression (such as toy guns and knives) are some things that parents or teachers can do to create nonaggressive environments.

Proactive aggressors engage in instrumental aggression that produces some benefit. Two techniques that can be combined to reduce proactive aggression are the incompatible-response technique and the use of time-outs. The incompatible-response technique ensures that children do not receive adult attention for their aggressive acts. Minor aggressive acts are ignored, and only prosocial behaviours are attended to. However, more serious aggressive acts must be responded to, and the best technique to use under these circumstances is a time-out. This removes the aggressor from the situation and prevents the child's behaviour from being reinforced.

Reactive aggressors often benefit from social-cognitive interventions. The most effective interventions focus on minimizing the rewards for aggression, teaching aggressive children to regulate their anger and replace aggressive responses with prosocial responses, while at the same time helping the children to develop better perspective-taking skills. Improvements in perspective-taking skills assist reactive aggressors in overcoming their hostile attributional bias. Aggression can also be reduced by promoting empathic concern. Parents should point out the harmful consequences of aggressive acts and encourage children to imagine how the victim feels.

2. Altruism: Development of the prosocial self

Altruism is a genuine selfless concern for the welfare of others and a willingness to act on that concern. Altruistic acts include prosocial behaviours such as sharing, cooperating, and helping.

a. Origins of altruism

Children who are only 1 to $1^1/_2$ years old will occasionally offer toys to their companions, and they may attempt to help with household chores. However, some toddlers who are behaviourally inhibited may become so highly upset by others' distress that they are more likely than uninhibited toddlers to turn away from a distressed acquaintance in order to regulate their arousal.

b. Developmental trends in altruism

Although toddlers show evidence of sympathy toward distressed peers, they rarely show spontaneous self-sacrifice in their attempts to comfort a distressed companion. However, children at this age are aware that helping behaviour is beneficial, and they often perform kind acts during pretend play. As children move through the preschool years altruistic acts during pretend play decrease, but acts of real helping increase. Cross-cultural research has indicated that from the early elementary-school years through adolescence, prosocial behaviour continues to increase. Over this same age range, there are no reliable sex differences in the amount of helping or in help seeking.

c. Social-cognitive and affective contributors to altruism

Children who have well-developed affective and social perspective-taking skills show higher levels of altruism than children who are less able to recognize what others are feeling or intending. Another important contribution to altruistic behaviour is the child's level of prosocial moral reasoning. Eisenberg (and colleagues) have found five levels of prosocial moral reasoning in children; there are age-related changes in children's level of prosocial moral reasoning.

Hedonistic reasoning (concern for one's own needs) is typical during the preschool and early elementary-school years. Needs-oriented reasoning is seldom seen in preschool children. At this level there is little guilt expressed for failures to assist others, but the needs of others are recognized in evaluating helping situations. At the stereotyped, approval-oriented level the reactions of others are considered when deciding whether or not to help. In children who show an empathic orientation in their reasoning there is evidence of sympathetic feelings for the person who is in distress. Finally, by the time adolescents are in high school, an internalized values orientation may be evident. At this level justifications for providing (or not providing) help are based on internalized norms and convictions. Eisenberg argues that one contributor to a child's level of prosocial reasoning is his or her ability to empathize with others who are in distress. According to Eisenberg, children who are relatively mature in their level of prosocial moral reasoning at ages 4 to 5 are more helpful and considerate of others, and reason more complexly about prosocial issues and social responsibility through until young adulthood.

Empathy refers to an individual's ability to experience the emotions of others. When seeing other people in distress, individuals may experience self-oriented distress or sympathetic empathic arousal. Someone who experiences personal distress may turn away, to reduce his or her level of distress. Someone who experiences sympathetic empathic arousal is more likely to offer assistance, because that is the only way to reduce the arousal he or she is experiencing. The link between empathic arousal and altruistic behaviour increases with age as children become better at regulating negative emotionality and suppressing personal distress to others' misfortunes, and while developing their role-taking skills and emotional understanding.

There is only a moderate link between empathy and altruism in preschool children and children in the early elementary-school years. In preadolescents, adolescents, and adults the link is much stronger.

d. Cultural and social influences on altruism

In cross-cultural studies, children living in less industrialized societies show higher levels of altruistic behaviour that their age-mates in industrialized societies. Within industrialized societies, children who take part in family-maintenance activities show higher levels of altruistic behaviour than age-mates whose family responsibilities consist mainly of self-care routines. Another difference that is evident in cross-cultural research studies is the finding that children from individualistic, competitive cultures show lower levels of altruistic behaviour than children raised in collectivist, cooperative cultures, who view acting prosocially as a moral obligation.

Parents can help their children develop altruistic behaviours in a number of ways. Verbal and social reinforcement of altruistic behaviours fosters the growth of altruism. However, tangible, external rewards are less likely to increase prosocial reasoning and concern for others. Modelling altruistic behaviour also has a positive impact on children's levels of altruism, especially when children have a warm, affectionate relationship with the individual who is modelling the altruistic behaviour. Finally, parental reactions to harmdoing by their children can affect the development of altruism. Punitive or forceful reactions by parents are less likely to foster high levels of altruism in children; nonpunitive reactions that encourage children to take responsibility for their actions are more likely to foster altruistic behaviour.

3. What is morality?

a. How developmentalists look at morality

Morality has three basic components: moral affect, moral cognition, and moral behaviour. Moral affect includes the feelings or emotions that motivate moral behaviour (such as compassion or guilt); moral cognition includes conceptualizations of right and wrong as well as moral decision making; moral behaviour reflects the actual actions that occur in situations involving moral reasoning. In "morally mature" individuals principles of morality have been internalized.

4. Psychoanalytic explanations of moral development

a. Freud's theory of Oedipal morality

According to Freud, when preschool children resolve the Oedipus or Electra conflict during the phallic stage of psychosexual development, the superego emerges. The superego is the moral component of an individual's personality and it will cause individuals to feel guilt or shame for moral transgressions and feel pride for virtuous behaviour. In Freud's view, children resist temptation to maintain high self-esteem and avoid experiencing negative emotions, such as guilt or shame.

b. Evaluating Freud's theory and newer psychoanalytic ideas about morality

Freud's theory would lead to the prediction that children who perceive their parents as threatening and punitive will develop stronger superegos, and consequently show higher levels of morality, than children who have warm, nonthreatening relationships with their parents. However, the opposite pattern is a more accurate reflection of children's actual levels of morality. Children who have warm, nurturing parents generally show higher levels of moral reasoning and moral behaviour, compared to children whose parents use harsh forms of discipline. In addition, Freud's theory would lead to the prediction that males will show higher levels of moral reasoning than females; however, there is no evidence of sex differences in moral reasoning. Finally, in Freud's view the superego emerges when a child is approximately 5 or 6 years old, and this personality structure is necessary before a child will show evidence of moral behaviour. However, children show evidence of both pride and shame well before this age. Also, research shows that as early as 13 to 15 months toddlers begin complying with some prohibitions in the absence of external monitoring, and by the age of 2 years toddlers begin to show distress when they violate rules and sometimes try to correct their mishaps without someone present to tell them to.

Modern psychoanalytic theories do not see the resolution of the Oedipus or Electra conflict as the cornerstone of moral development. Instead, theorists who take this approach argue that children may begin to form a conscience much earlier if they have a secure attachment with their parents. Toddlers who have warm, responsive parents are already showing evidence of committed compliance. By contrast, toddlers who have aloof or insensitive parents show evidence of situational compliance. Indeed, research indicates that children who have warm, mutually responsive emotional relationships with their mothers show more signs of having strong internalized consciences.

5. Cognitive-developmental theory: The child as moral philosopher

Cognitive-developmental theories focus on changes in moral reasoning. Theorists who take this approach to understanding moral development suggest that cognitive growth and social interactions help children to better understand the meaning of rules and interpersonal obligations. Two main theories that have a cognitive-developmental perspective are Piaget's theory and Kohlberg's theory. In both these theories moral development is viewed as progressing through an invariant sequence of stages.

a. Piaget's theory of moral development

The first stage in Piaget's theory is a premoral stage. This level of reasoning is evident in preschool children who show little concern or awareness for rules that might govern behaviour.

During the early and middle elementary-school years (ages 5 to 10) Piaget suggested that children show heteronomous morality. At this point children are aware of the existence of rules, but they believe that authority figures make the rules and that rules cannot be changed. At this stage children think of rules as moral absolutes; there are no exceptions to rules. Heteronomous reasoning typically focuses on the consequences of an individual's behaviour, rather than on the individual's intent. Behaviour that has harmful outcomes should be punished, regardless of the actor's intent. Children at this age also believe in immanent justice; this is the idea that violations of social rules will always be punished in one way or another.

By the time children reach preadolescence they show evidence of moral relativism, or autonomous morality. Children now recognize that social rules can be challenged and even changed. They also recognize that some rule violations are not deserving of punishment; they focus more on an individual's intentions, rather than on the consequences that result from a behaviour. Children at this age also usually favour reciprocal punishments; in other words, they think that punishments should reflect the consequences of the actions. During this stage children no longer believe in immanent justice; they recognize that violations of social rules may often be undetected.

b. An evaluation of Piaget's theory

Cross-cultural research has shown that younger children are more likely than older children to emphasize consequences over intentions when judging a behaviour, and they are more likely to show a belief in immanent justice. Research studies have also provided some support for the idea that children who have a greater number of interactions with equal status peers tend to make more mature moral judgments than their age-mates. However, Piaget's theory may underestimate the moral capacity of preschool children and children in the early elementary-school years.

Other researchers have found that preschool children will consider an actor's intentions when making moral judgments; however, younger children do assign more weight to consequences and less weight to intentions than older children do. Even 3- to 5-year-olds discriminate and react more negatively to blatant lies than to honest mistakes. In addition, young children do not treat all rules equally. They are capable of distinguishing between moral rules (rules dealing with the welfare and rights of others) and social-conventional rules. Even during the preschool years children are more likely to consider moral transgressions as being more serious and more deserving of punishment than violations of social-conventional rules. Also, between the ages of 6 and 10 children recognize that authority is sometimes limited by contexts; at this age they have clear ideas about what constitutes legitimate authority. Research by Larry Walker has shown that, contrary to Piaget's theory, parents can foster moral growth if, when they discuss real-life moral issues with their children, they present their own, more sophisticated reasoning in a gentle, supportive manner, rather than in a lecture-like format.

c. Kohlberg's theory of moral development

Kohlberg developed his theory of moral development by asking preadolescent and adolescent boys to respond to a series of problems that required making a choice between (1) obeying a rule or a law and (2) violating a rule or a law with the goal of aiding another person. Kohlberg was less interested in whether the individuals he interviewed chose to obey or to violate the rule; he was more interested in the reasoning for their final decision.

In Kohlberg's theory moral reasoning develops through three levels, with two stages at each level. At the first level of moral reasoning, the preconventional level, conformity to rules is motivated by objective personal gains and losses. At the second level of moral reasoning, the conventional level, conformity to rules is motivated by social gains and losses. At the third level of moral reasoning, the postconventional level, moral principles have been internalized and broad principles of justice underlie moral reasoning.

At each of these levels, Kohlberg identified two distinct stages of moral reasoning. Preconventional moral reasoners may follow rules to avoid punishment (punishment-and-obedience orientation) or to gain rewards (naive hedonism). Conventional moral reasoners may follow rules to gain the approval of others ("good boy/girl" orientation) or to conform to rules of legal authority (social-order-maintaining morality). Finally, postconventional moral reasoners can make the distinction between legally sanctioned but morally wrong behaviour (social-contract orientation) and may define right and wrong on the basis of personal principles of ethical and moral conduct (morality of individual principles of conscience). The final stage of Kohlberg's progression (Stage 6) is viewed as a hypothetical construct that encompasses the ideal in moral reasoning, but is seldom, if ever, attained.

d. Support for Kohlberg's theory

Results from cross-cultural research studies provide evidence that Kohlberg's levels and stages of moral reasoning are universal and that there is a clear age-related progression through the stages. In addition, results from longitudinal research studies provide evidence that Kohlberg's stages of moral development represent an invariant sequence. However, for many individuals Stage 3 or Stage 4 is the highest level of moral reasoning that is attained, even in adulthood.

Results from research studies that have investigated the role of general cognitive capabilities and social cognition in the development of moral reasoning have suggested that role-taking skills are necessary, but not sufficient, for the emergence of conventional moral reasoning. In addition, formal-operational thought appears to be necessary, but not sufficient for the emergence of postconventional moral reasoning.

The finding that growth in cognitive skills is not, in itself, sufficient to advance moral reasoning skills supports Kohlberg's belief that cognitive growth is only one of the prerequisites for moral development. The other prerequisite is relevant social experience. Interactions with parents and peers contribute to an individual's ability to reason about moral issues. In peer interactions, one of the more important contributors to growth of moral-reasoning skills appears to be transactive interactions. Finally, both advanced education and exposure to diverse social contexts promote growth in moral-reasoning skills.

e. Criticisms of Kohlberg's approach

One of the criticisms that has been raised regarding Kohlberg's theory is that it is culturally biased and reflects a Western ideal of justice. Cross-cultural studies have suggested that individuals throughout the world think in more complex ways about issues of morality as they become older; however, individuals in different cultures have different notions about the types of behaviours that are considered personal choices versus moral obligations.

Other critics have suggested that Kohlberg's theory is biased against women, but there is little research evidence to suggest that there are consistent sex differences in moral reasoning. When faced with real-life moral dilemmas, both males and females are likely to adopt a morality of care and interpersonal responsibility. A morality of justice style of reasoning is more evident when people reason about abstract or hypothetical moral issues. Kohlberg has also been criticized as largely ignoring the role of emotions such as pride, shame, guilt, and remorse that influence our moral thoughts and actions.

Kohlberg also assumed that the links between moral reasoning and moral behaviour would become stronger as individuals progressed through the stages he identified, and most of the available data is consistent with this point of view. However, there is only a moderate overall correlation between an individual's stage of moral reasoning and his or her moral behaviour. It seems that personal qualities and situational factors also influence everyday moral conduct. Further, recent research suggests that even the process of moral growth may contribute to inconsistencies between moral reasoning and moral behaviour.

Finally, there is evidence to suggest that Kohlberg underestimated the moral-reasoning abilities of young children. Young elementary-school children often consider the needs of others when considering prosocial actions, and during the later elementary-school years children show an understanding of distributive justice. And yet, when children of this age are assessed using Kohlberg's procedure they usually show evidence of only preconventional moral reasoning.

6. Morality as a product of social learning (and social information processing)

a. How consistent are moral conduct and moral character?

Specific types of moral behaviours (such as sharing or refusing to break rules) are reasonably consistent within individuals, both over time and across situations. However, the three components of morality (affect, reasoning, and behaviour) become more consistent and more interrelated with age. Also, it appears that morality may never become a unitary attribute (that one either does or does not possess). An individual's willingness to violate moral norms appears to depend, at least to some extent, on contextual factors. Therefore, moral character is unlikely to ever be perfectly consistent across all situations.

b. Learning to resist temptation

An individual who resists the temptation to violate moral norms, even when the possibility of detection and punishment is remote, has internalized moral standards of conduct. Moral behaviour increases when moral actions are reinforced by warm, caring adults; standards for conduct are especially likely to be internalized when social reinforcers (such as praise) are used, rather than tangible, external reinforcers.

Punishment and fear of detection are often not sufficient to persuade children to resist temptation in the absence of external surveillance. Children are more likely to internalize rules, and develop true self-control, when parents encourage children to make internal attributions about their conduct. This type of moral self-concept training, combined with recognition and social reinforcement of desirable conduct, helps children learn to resist temptation.

Modelling can also assist children in learning to resist temptation. Under these circumstances models are most effective when they clearly verbalize that they are resisting an impulse, and when they provide a rationale for not undertaking the forbidden behaviour.

7. Who raises children who are morally mature?

Research into the disciplinary techniques used by parents whose children show high levels of moral reasoning indicate that induction (explaining why a behaviour is wrong and emphasizing how the behaviour affects other people) fosters the development of all three aspects of morality. In contrast, neither love withdrawal (withholding attention or approval) nor power assertion (the use of physical force or verbal commands) appears to be particularly effective at promoting moral maturity. Effective approaches to discipline are those that provide a good fit with the child's characteristics, behaviours, and temperament.

Vocabulary Self-Test

Part I: For each of the following definitions provide the appropriate term. (Answers to this portion of the self-test are provided at the end of the chapter.)

1. ________________ A home in which family members often annoy one another and use aggressive or other antisocial tactics as a method of coping

2. ________________ Piaget's stage of moral development in which children realize that rules are arbitrary agreements that can be challenged and changed with the consent of the people they govern

3. ________________ A genuine selfless concern for the welfare of others that is expressed through prosocial acts such as sharing, cooperating, and helping

4. ________________ A form of discipline in which children who misbehave are removed from the setting until they are prepared to act more appropriately

5. ________________ The process of adopting the attributes or standards of other people

6. ________________ Kohlberg's term for the two stages of moral reasoning in which moral judgments are based on social contracts and democratic law or universal principles of ethics and justice

7. ________________ Children who display high levels of hostile, retaliatory aggression because they overattribute hostile intent to others and can't control their anger long enough to seek nonaggressive solutions to social problems

8. ________________ The notion that unacceptable conduct will invariably be punished and that justice is ever present in the world

9. ________________ Parent-child relationship characterized by mutual responsiveness to each other's needs and goals and shared positive affect

10. ________________ A viewpoint which holds that moral affect, moral reasoning, and moral behaviour may depend as much on the situation one faces as on internalized moral principles

11. ________________ The theory that empathy may promote altruism by causing one to reflect on altruistic norms and consequently feel an obligation to help others who are in distress

12. ________________ A nonpunitive form of discipline in which an adult explains why a behaviour is wrong and emphasizes the effect of the behaviour on others

13. ________________ Aggressive acts for which the perpetrator's major goal is to harm or injure a victim

14. ________________ Kohlberg's term for the third and fourth stages of moral reasoning, in which moral judgments are based on a desire to gain approval (Stage 3) or to uphold laws that maintain social order (Stage 4)

15. ________________ The emotional component of morality that includes feelings such as guilt, shame, and pride in ethical conduct

Part II: For each of the following terms provide the definition.

Love Withdrawal: a disciplinary technique

Morality of Care:

Proactive Aggressors:

Oedipal Morality:

Self-oriented Distress:

Inhibitory Control:

Instrumental Aggression:

Preconventional Morality:

Moral Reasoning:

Negative Reinforcer:

Power Assertion:

Sympathetic Empathic Arousal:

Situational Compliance:

Hostile Attributional Bias:

Heteronomous Morality:

Short-Answer Study Questions

THE DEVELOPMENT OF AGGRESSION

1. Differentiate between hostile and instrumental aggression and provide an appropriate example to illustrate each form of aggression.

   a.

   b.

2. Outline how the nature and frequency of aggression changes during the preschool and early elementary-school years.

3. Describe sex differences in the nature of aggressive acts.

4. Outline how the nature of aggression continues to change over adolescence in both males and females.

5. Differentiate between proactive and reactive aggressors and discuss the different types of social information processing each type of aggressor displays.

   a.

   b.

6. Differentiate between passive and provocative victims and describe the typical home environment that is associated with each of these patterns.

   a.

   b.

7. Identify three factors that may contribute to social class differences in levels of aggression and antisocial conduct.

   a.

   b.

   c.

8. Describe the typical pattern of interactions that are seen in coercive home environments.

9. List and describe three ways in which parents and teachers might reduce aggressive behaviours in children.

   a.

   b.

   c.

ALTRUISM: DEVELOPMENT OF THE PROSOCIAL SELF

10. Outline how the nature and frequency of altruistic behaviour changes during the preschool and elementary-school years.

11. List the five stages of prosocial moral reasoning identified by Eisenberg, and describe the nature of the reasoning that is evident at each of these stages.

   a.

   b.

   c.

   d.

   e.

12. Differentiate between sympathetic empathic arousal and self-oriented distress.

a.

b.

13. Outline basic age trends in the relationship between empathy and altruistic responding.

14. Identify and describe three cultural and social factors that can influence the development of altruistic behaviour.

a.

b.

c.

15. List three reasons why rational, affectively oriented discipline might promote altruistic behaviour in children.

a.

b.

c.

WHAT IS MORALITY?

16. List three components of morality.

a.

b.

c.

PSYCHOANALYTIC EXPLANATIONS OF MORAL DEVELOPMENT

17. Briefly outline the key aspects in Freud's theory of Oedipal morality.

18. List two key criticisms that have been raised with respect to Freud's theory of moral development.

    a.

    b.

COGNITIVE-DEVELOPMENTAL THEORY: THE CHILD AS MORAL PHILOSOPHER

19. According to Piaget children progress through two key stages in the development of moral reasoning: the heteronomous stage and the autonomous stage. Contrast the types of cognitive reasoning that are evident in each of these two stages.

    Heteronomous stage:

    Autonomous stage:

20. List three criticisms that have been raised with respect to Piaget's theory of moral development and briefly describe the research evidence that is relevant to each of these points.

    a.

    b.

    c.

21. List the six stages of moral development outlined by Lawrence Kohlberg and describe the type of reasoning that is evident in each of these six stages.

    a.

    b.

    c.

    d.

    e.

    f.

22. Evidence from a number of different research studies supports three aspects of Lawrence Kohlberg's theory of moral development. Identify each aspect of his theory that has been supported by subsequent research and briefly describe the results from these research studies.

a.

b.

c.

23. Criticisms of Kohlberg's theory have centred on three aspects: the possibility that the theory is biased against certain groups, the possibility that the theory underestimates the moral sophistication of young children, and the fact that the theory focuses on a single aspect of morality (moral reasoning). Briefly describe the research evidence that relates to each of these criticisms.

a.

b.

c.

MORALITY AS A PRODUCT OF SOCIAL LEARNING (AND SOCIAL INFORMATION PROCESSING)

24. Identify three ways in which parents can help their children learn to act in moral ways by learning to resist temptation.

a.

b.

c.

WHO RAISES CHILDREN WHO ARE MORALLY MATURE?

25. Describe three different parental disciplinary techniques identified by Martin Hoffman.

    a.

    b.

    c.

26. List three reasons why inductive discipline might be effective in promoting moral maturity in children.

    a.

    b.

    c.

27. The results of Kochanska's research on temperament, discipline, and moral internalization suggest that parenting practices and children's temperaments must "fit" in order to foster adaptive outcomes. Briefly summarize the research and the results.

28. Siegal and Cowen asked children to evaluate four different disciplinary strategies that parents could use after a transgression by a child. Briefly summarize the key results from Siegal and Cowen's study.

Multiple-Choice Self-Test

For each of the following questions select the best alternative. (Answers and explanations for this self-test are provided at the end of the chapter.) Once you have selected your answer, provide a brief explanation for why the answer you selected is the best choice and why the remaining answers would not be correct.

1. Heidi purposely hit Susan with a ball during a school activity. After school, Susan attacked Heidi with her fists. Susan is engaging in:

   a. instrumental aggression
   b. retaliation
   c. hostile aggression
   d. prosocial aggression

   Rationale: ______________________________

2. Dodge found that aggressive children were more likely than nonaggressive children to respond with aggression when another child:

   a. clearly aggressed against them with hostile intent
   b. caused harm and the intentions were ambiguous
   c. clearly intended to be helpful but accidentally caused harm
   d. caused no harm and the act was unambiguously accidental

   Rationale: ______________________________

3. The results of over 100 cross-cultural studies on aggression in males and females show:

   a. greater physical and verbal aggression among males
   b. no evidence of sex differences in aggression
   c. greater physical aggression among males and greater verbal aggression among females
   d. greater physical and verbal aggression among females

   Rationale: ______________________________

4. Zahn-Waxler and associates found that mothers of compassionate toddlers were more likely to respond to their child's harmdoing with statements such as:

   a. "I said, 'stop that.'"
   b. "You made Doug cry; your biting hurt him."
   c. "Go to your room, immediately!"
   d. "Don't do that; you are very naughty to bite."

   Rationale: ______________________________

5. Some kinds of prosocial responses are seen in very young children (2–3 years of age) while others are seldom seen until the elementary-school years. Two prosocial responses that typically do not emerge until the elementary-school years are:

   a. sympathy and helping
   b. compassion and sharing
   c. sharing and helping
   d. sympathy and compassion

   Rationale: ______________________________

   ____

6. According to Piaget, the moral reasoning of 10- to 12-year-olds is characterized by:

   a. the belief that accidents such as falling down or losing something are punishments for misdeeds
   b. a focus on the magnitude of the misdeed rather than the harmdoer's intentions
   c. the belief that rules are absolutes in games and in life
   d. a focus on the harmdoer's intentions rather than the magnitude of the misdeed

   Rationale: ______________________________

   ____

7. A person at Kohlberg's stage 2 of moral development might justify returning a wallet full of money by maintaining that:

   a. such actions are usually rewarded
   b. such acts help to maintain social order
   c. "nice" people perform such acts of kindness
   d. one might be punished for spending another person's money

   Rationale: ______________________________

   ____

8. During adolescence and early adulthood (14–20 years of age) the predominant form of moral reasoning, using Kohlberg's levels, is:

   a. preconventional level reasoning, stage 2 (naive hedonism)
   b. postconventional level reasoning, stage 5 (morality of contract)
   c. moral relativism
   d. conventional level reasoning, stage 3 (good boy/good girl morality)

   Rationale: ______________________________

   ____

Activities and Projects Related to this Chapter

ACTIVITY 14-1A

FAMILY VARIABLES ASSOCIATED WITH AGGRESSION: ONE CASE

INTRODUCTION: This activity is related to the material in Chapter 14 that deals with factors that may contribute to aggression. Several family variables have been found to be related to aggression, such as lack of parental monitoring, permissiveness of aggression, and coercive discipline that models aggression.

INSTRUCTIONS: For this activity think of an example of someone you have known who was/is highly aggressive and whose family you know something about.

1. Describe the behaviours and attitudes that led you to classify this person as highly aggressive.

2. Describe the family, characterizing parental practices in each of the following areas:

   a. Monitoring of child's activities and friends

   b. Parents' willingness to tolerate aggression

   c. Punishment strategies used by parents

   d. Child's relationship with the parents

   e. Parents' attitude toward the child

   f. Extent to which aggression was modelled in the home as a way to solve problems or get what was wanted

   g. Other (specify) ____

3. Were all the children in the family aggressive? If not, how might you explain why the person you have described was so highly aggressive when siblings were not?

4. What is your **personal theory** regarding the factors that are associated with aggressive behaviours in children?

5. How does your theory regarding the factors that contribute to aggression compare with the factors described in your text as being related to aggressive behaviour in children?

ACTIVITY 14-1B

FAMILY VARIABLES ASSOCIATED WITH NONAGGRESSION: ONE CASE

INTRODUCTION: This activity is an extension of Activity 14-1A dealing with family variables associated with aggression. (Activity 14-1B is not intended to be used alone, but to accompany Activity 14-1A.)

INSTRUCTIONS: For this activity think of an example of someone you have known who was/is not an aggressive individual, someone whose family you know something about. The first three parts below are the same as for Activity 14-1A, except that this time you are describing a nonaggressive child and the parents' behaviour. The fourth and fifth parts differ from those in Activity 14-1A, focusing on the parenting patterns of aggressive and nonaggressive children.

1. Describe the behaviours and attitudes that led you to classify this person as someone who is not highly aggressive.

2. Describe the family, characterizing parental practices in each of the following areas:

   a. Monitoring of child's activities and friends

   b. Parents' willingness to tolerate aggression

   c. Punishment strategies used by parents

   d. Child's relationship with the parents

   e. Parents' attitude toward the child

   f. Extent to which aggression was modelled in the home as a way to solve problems or get what was wanted

   g. Other (specify) ____

3. Were all the children in the family low in aggression? If not, how might you explain why the person you have described was not highly aggressive when siblings were?

4. How did the parenting of the aggressive child (described in Activity 14-1A) and the nonaggressive child (described in Activity 14-1B) differ?

5. How closely do the parenting patterns of the two children match the "profile" of the parents of aggressive children and (by inference) the parents of nonaggressive children described in the text? If they do not match well, describe what other factors you think might have contributed to the development of each child's behaviour patterns.

ACTIVITY 14-2

TEMPER TANTRUMS AND DISCIPLINE

INTRODUCTION: This activity is related to the material in Chapter 14 that deals with the various types of disciplinary strategies that parents may use in the face of misbehaving children. For example, what form of discipline would you advise a parent to use if he or she is faced with a screaming, kicking toddler in the midst of an out-of-control temper tantrum. Think of the different types of discipline discussed in your text. What would be the easiest strategy to use if, and picture yourself in this situation, your child is having one of his or her tantrums in the middle of a crowded mall or grocery store. This activity is applied and clearly involves a situation faced by many, if not most, parents at one point in their parental career. What factors should parents keep in mind (e.g., situational factors, child characteristics, etc.) when deciding on a disciplinary approach? What does your text book say is the best approach? Do you believe it would work in all situations and with all types of kids?

WEBSITES OF INTEREST

For more information on moral development research, visit the Association for Moral Education web page: www.wittenberg.edu/ame/ame3.html

REFERENCES OF INTEREST

Fung, H., Lieber, E., & Leung, P.W.L. (2003). Parental beliefs about shame and moral socialization in Taiwan, Hong Kong, and the United States. In K. Yang & K. Hwang (Eds.), *Progress in Asian social psychology: Conceptual and empirical contributions* (p. 83–109). Westport, CT: Praeger Publishers/Greenwood Publishing Group.

Lamb, S., & Zakhireh, B. (1997). Toddlers' attention to the distress of peers in a day care setting. *Early Education and Development, 8(2)*, 105–118.

Lollis, S., Van Engen, G., Burns, L., & Nowack, K. (1999). Sibling socialisation of moral orientation: "Share with me!" "No, it's mine!" *Journal of Moral Education, 28,* 339–357.

Matsuba, M.K., & Walker, L.J. (2004). Extraordinary moral commitment: Young adults working for social organizations. *Journal of Personality, 72,* 413–436.

Pratt, M., Arnold, M.L., & Hilbers, S.M. (1998). A narrative approach to the study of moral orientation in the family: Tales of kindness and care. In, E.E. Aspaas Skoe & A.L. von der Lippe (Eds.), *Personality development in adolescence: A cross-national and lifespan perspective* (p. 61–79). London: Routledge.

Schonert-Reichl, K.A. (1999). Relations of peer acceptance, friendship adjustment, and social behavior to moral reasoning during early adolescence. *Journal of Early Adolescence, 19,* 249–279.

Walker, L.J. (2003). Morality, religion, spirituality—The value of saintliness. *Journal of Moral Education, 32,* 373–384.

Walker, L.J. (2002). Moral exemplarity. In W. Damon (Ed.), *Bringing in a new era in character education* (pp. 65–83). Stanford, CA: Hoover Institution Press.

Walker, L.J., & Hennig, K.H. (2004). Differing conceptions of moral exemplarity: Just, brave, and caring. *Journal of Personality and Social Psychology, 86,* 629–647.

Walker, L.J., & Taylor, J.H. (1991). Family interactions and the development of moral reasoning. *Child Development, 62,* 264–283.

Wark, G.R. (2000). Personality, gender, and the ways people perceive moral dilemmas in everyday life. *Journal of College and Character, 1,* 1–13.

Wark, G.R., & Krebs, D.L. (1997). Sources of variation in real-life moral judgment: Toward a model of real-life morality. *Journal of Adult Development, 4,* 163–178.

Wark, G.R., & Krebs, D.L. (2000). The construction of moral dilemmas in everyday life. *Journal of Moral Education, 29,* 5–21.

Wilson, A.E., Smith, M.D., & Ross, H.S. (2003). The nature and effects of young children's lies. *Social Development, 12(1),* 21–45.

ACTIVITY 14-3

KOHLBERG'S STAGES OF MORAL DEVELOPMENT

INTRODUCTION: This activity relates to the material in Chapter 14 on Kohlberg's stages of moral reasoning. Kohlberg's stages characterize a developmental sequence in the types of reasons that individuals give for their moral decisions. This activity is intended to give you some exposure to the kinds of reasons that different individuals give to back up their positions on moral issues and to give you practice in applying Kohlberg's stage definitions.

INSTRUCTIONS: Select two individuals to interview. These individuals can be adults or children, same age or different age, same sex or different sex. If they are the same sex and age category, try to select one individual whose principles and behaviour you admire and one who is less admirable. If the individuals are under 18 years of age, be sure to obtain parental permission to interview their child.

Part A: The Interview

Two possible dilemmas and probes are presented below. Select one to present to both individuals or make up one to present to the two individuals you interview. Be sure to write down each probe you present and each response given.

Part B: Classification of Responses

Classify each response given according to Kohlberg's levels of moral reasoning: preconventional, conventional, or postconventional. See the text for descriptions of each level. Then answer the following questions.

Part C: Questions to Answer

1. Was it easy or difficult to classify individuals' responses? Describe any problems you encountered.
2. How many different levels did each individual use? What was the highest level used by each individual?
3. Were the responses that were given by the two individuals consistent or inconsistent with your expectations of how they would respond? Explain.

DILEMMA 1 INTERVIEW

1. "The **abortion** issue has been a pretty hot one. What is your position?"

2. "Why do you feel that way?"

3. "Any other reasons you can think of?" (Keep probing with this to encourage multiple reasons.)

4. (if pro-choice) "Anti-abortionists argue that it is not our right to take the life of a child, even one that is in the early stages of development. What would you say to an anti-abortionist to justify your position that it is sometimes appropriate to terminate the life of an unborn child?"

5. (if pro-choice) "Are there any circumstances under which you think the mother has the moral obligation to carry the child to term?"

6. (if anti-abortion) "Pro-choicers argue that the mother should have the right to decide what happens to her body and whether she wants to mother a child. What arguments could you give to justify ignoring the mother's viewpoint?"

7. (if anti-abortion) "Are there any circumstances under which you think it would be morally right for a mother to abort her developing child?"

8. (Question of your choice; specify)

DILEMMA 2 INTERVIEW

1. "The **temptation to cheat** is something that plagues all students and income tax payers. Do you think there are any circumstances when an individual would be justified in cheating to get a higher grade or a more favourable tax return?" (Adapt to age of interviewee.)

2. (if against cheating) "What justifications can you give for your position, i.e., why do you feel a person should not cheat for personal gain?"

3. (if against cheating) "Are there any circumstances when you think it would be justifiable to cheat?"

4. (if cheating is OK) "What justifications can you give for your view, i.e., why do you feel that it is OK for a person to cheat?"

5. (if cheating is OK) "Are there any circumstances when you think it would not be morally appropriate to cheat?"

6. (Question of your choice; specify)

ANSWERS TO SELF-TESTS

VOCABULARY SELF-TEST (The answers may be found on the pages in parentheses.)

1. coercive home environment (p. 525)
2. autonomous morality (p. 542)
3. altruism (p. 530)
4. time-out technique (p. 529)
5. internalization (p. 538)
6. postconventional morality (p. 547)
7. reactive aggressors (p. 520)
8. immanent justice (p. 542)
9. mutually responsive relationship (p. 540)
10. doctrine of specificity (p. 554)
11. "felt-responsibility" hypothesis (p. 535)
12. induction (p. 557)
13. hostile aggression (p. 517)
14. conventional morality (p. 546)
15. moral affect (p. 539)

MULTIPLE-CHOICE SELF-TEST (The answers may be found on the pages in parentheses.)

1. **b** (p. 517) Retaliation is aggression in response to a previous aggressive act. Instrumental aggression would involve some objective other than simply harming the child or revenge (a). Hostile aggression (c) would be aggression solely intended to harm. Prosocial aggression (d) is a contradictory term, and does not exist.

2. **b** (p. 521) When aggressive children are harmed and the intent is ambiguous they are more likely than nonaggressive children to retaliate. If there is clear hostile intent (a) either aggressive or nonaggressive children may show retaliation. If there is clear intent to be helpful (c), or when actions do not cause harm (d), aggressive children are not likely to show aggressive retaliation.

3. **a** (pp. 517–518) Males are more physically and more verbally aggressive, on average, than females are. Males are more likely to engage in overt aggression, and females are more likely to engage in covert aggression (b). Compared to men, women are less likely to use verbal aggression (c and d), and less likely to use physical aggression (d).

4. **b** (p. 531) This type of a response is an affective explanation that may foster sympathy or remorse; it can help a child see the link between his or her actions and the distress those actions cause. Alternatives (a) and (c) show power assertion, and alternative (d) is an example of a verbal rebuke; none of these types of responses are likely to foster the development of compassion.

5. **c** (p. 531) Sharing and helping become more and more common from the early elementary-school years onward. Helping (a) is rarely seen in preschool children. Spontaneous sharing (b) is relatively infrequent among toddlers and young preschool children. Sympathy and compassion (d) are evident as early as 2 or 3 years of age.

6. **d** (p. 542) By this age children are likely to be in the autonomous stage, and they will focus on the intent more than the consequences of the actions. The belief that bad outcomes are punishments (a) reflects immanent justice, which is seen in younger children. A focus on the consequences rather than the intent (b) is typical in the heteronomous stage (5 to 10 years of age). The belief in absolute rules (c) is also seen in the heteronomous stage of moral development.

7. **a** (p. 546) A focus on the possibility of reward reflects stage 2 (naive hedonism). A focus on maintaining social order (b) would reflect stage 4 (social order maintaining). At stage 3 children are concerned with being "good" or being "nice" (c). A focus on punishment (d) would reflect stage 1 (punishment and obedience).

8. **d** (p. 548) Stage 3 moral reasoning peaks at age 16, but it is the dominant form of reasoning from just past age 12 through to approximately age 22. Stage 2 moral reasoning (a) is dominant before the age of 12. Stage 5 moral reasoning (b) typically doesn't emerge until early adulthood, and is only evident in 10% of the population during the adult years. Moral relativism (c) is not one of Kohlberg's stages of moral reasoning.

Chapter Fifteen
The Family

Learning Objectives

By the time you have finished this chapter you should be able to:

1. Define socialization and identify three functions of the socialization process.
2. Differentiate between direct and indirect effects in family systems.
3. Contrast nuclear and extended family systems.
4. Outline some social changes over the past 50 years that have affected family systems.
5. Identify the two dimensions of parenting found to be most influential on a child's overall development.
6. Compare and contrast the four parenting styles that researchers have identified, and discuss the developmental outcomes that have been associated with each of these parenting styles.
7. Discuss research evidence that relates to social class differences in parenting style.
8. Discuss research evidence that relates to ethnic and cultural differences in parenting style.
9. Describe the process of developing autonomy during adolescence and discuss what it means for the emotional bond between parent and child.
10. Discuss how the nature of the relationship between siblings typically changes from childhood through adolescence.
11. Describe some of the ways in which siblings can influence development.
12. Discuss the characteristics of children who grow up without siblings.
13. Discuss research evidence related to developmental outcomes for adopted children.
14. Discuss research evidence related to developmental outcomes for children raised in gay or lesbian families.
15. Discuss the immediate and long-term effects of divorce on children, focusing on the factors that can influence these effects.
16. Discuss the impact of parental remarriage on adjustment in both boys and girls.
17. Describe some of the factors that can influence the overall impact of maternal employment on children's development.
18. Identify some characteristics in parents that may increase the likelihood that they will abuse their children.
19. Identify some characteristics in children that may increase their risk for becoming a target of abuse.
20. Identify some of the social and contextual triggers that have been linked to child abuse.
21. Discuss the typical consequences for children who are abused or neglected.
22. Discuss some ways in which neglect and abuse might be prevented or controlled.

Chapter Outline and Summary

1. Understanding the family

Socialization is the process through which children acquire the beliefs, values, and behaviours that are deemed significant and appropriate by older members in a society. The socialization process serves at least three functions: (1) it is a means of regulating children's behaviour, (2) it promotes individual growth and development, and (3) it perpetuates the existing social order. The family plays a pivotal role in the socialization of children, and the family is where the socialization process first begins.

2. The family as a social system

Families are complex social systems in which relationships are reciprocal. Parents influence their children, but children also influence their parents, and the family (as a whole) is affected by community and cultural influences.

a. *Direct and indirect influences*

When any two members within a family system interact they influence each other. These influences are called direct effects. However, the interactions between two family members are also influenced, to some extent, by the presence of other family members. Influences of this type are called indirect effects.

Traditional nuclear families consist of a mother, a father, and their children. More complex family systems emerge in extended family households where, in addition to the parents and their children, there may also be grandparents, aunts or uncles, nieces or nephews, or other relations living within the same home. In some cases, the additional social support that is typically available in extended family households can be beneficial.

b. *Families are developing systems*

Families are also dynamic systems. As each individual within the family structure develops, the nature of the interactive, reciprocal relationships within the family will change. In many cases these changes are planned, or can be anticipated, but in other cases the changes are unplanned or unforeseen.

c. *Families are embedded systems*

Families are not isolated social systems. They are embedded within broader subcultural and cultural systems. In understanding family interactions it is also necessary to consider factors such as community norms and values, the family's religious beliefs and affiliations, and the socioeconomic status of the family.

d. *A changing family system in a changing world*

Social changes also affect the character of family life and the norms for family structures. Since the 1950s an increasing proportion of adults are postponing marriage or choosing to remain single. Those adults that do marry are waiting longer to have children and are having fewer children. The number of mothers who work outside the home has increased significantly. The divorce rate is increasing, and there are more single-parent families. Approximately 20% of Canadian families are headed by a lone parent. The high divorce rate has led to an increase in the number of reconstituted (blended) families. There has also been an increase in the number of children who live in families that are below the poverty line.

3. Parental socialization during childhood and adolescence

a. *Two major dimensions of parenting*

Two key dimensions of parenting are parental acceptance or responsiveness and parental demandingness or control. The acceptance dimension is a measure of the amount of affection a parent displays, as well as the amount of support the parent provides. The acceptance dimension also includes how sensitive parents are to their children's needs, and how willing the parents are to provide attention and praise when their children meet their expectations. The control dimension is a measure of the amount of regulation and control that parents provide for their children. The control dimension includes how much parents set rules and expect their children to follow them, and how closely the parents monitor their children's activities.

b. Four patterns of parenting

The two major dimensions of parenting can combine to produce four parenting patterns: authoritarian, authoritative, permissive, or uninvolved. Authoritarian parents are restrictive parents (high in control) who expect strict, unquestioning obedience to rules that they impose (low in responsiveness). Authoritative parents also show a high level of control, but they have a flexible parenting style; they are responsive and encourage their children's participation in family decisions. Permissive parents set few restrictions on their children (low in control), and they encourage their children to express their feelings and impulses (high in responsiveness). Uninvolved parents set few restrictions on their children, and they may ignore their children or be generally nonresponsive to their children.

Children who have authoritative parents seem to show the best developmental outcomes. They tend to do better academically and socially, and they typically have high self-esteem and a strong moral character. Children who have authoritarian parents generally have average academic and social skills; as preschoolers these children may be more moody and unfriendly, as adolescents they may be more conforming than their peers. Children who have permissive parents show poor self-control and academic competence, and they tend to be more impulsive and less independent. Children who have uninvolved parents tend to perform very poorly in school and are often high in aggression, often displaying conduct disorder; as adolescents these individuals are more likely to display delinquent or antisocial behaviour.

Authoritative parents utilize a sensitive, responsive style in interacting with their children, and they also use inductive discipline. This is the type of parenting that is associated with committed compliance, self-reliance, and high self-esteem in children. Authoritative parents also promote the growth of autonomy in their children by adjusting their level of regulation and supervision as children develop self-reliance. Permissive and uninvolved parents fail to set reasonable limits for their children, and without reasonable limits children often fail to develop adequate self-control. Authoritarian parents, on the other hand, are overly restrictive and inflexible; under these conditions children may fail to develop a sense of self-reliance and they may lack self-confidence.

c. Parent effects or child effects?

According to the parent effects model, parents influence the development of the child, such as when authoritative parenting fosters positive developmental outcomes. This is the type of model espoused by Diana Baumrind and, in fact, is supported by longitudinal research. However, other theorists and researchers point out that children, themselves, have a major influence on their parents. According to the child effects model, authoritative parenting looks adaptive because easygoing, manageable, and competent children evoke authoritative parenting from their parents.

d. Social class and ethnic variations in child-rearing

On average, economically disadvantaged and working-class parents are less likely to display an authoritative style of parenting, when compared to middle-class or upper-class parents. These overall group differences in parenting styles are evident across a number of racial and ethnic groups and have also been observed in cross-cultural studies.

There are at least two potential explanations for the observed differences in parenting styles across different social classes. First, the economic hardships that lower-SES parents are forced to deal with create psychological stress. This high level of continuing stress can make adults more anxious and irritable, leading to marital conflict, and therefore may reduce their capacity to be warm and responsive to the needs of their children. Consequently, economically disadvantaged parents are more likely to show evidence of an uninvolved style of parenting. Second, working-class parents are often blue-collar workers. Blue-collar workers typically work for a supervisor or boss and they must defer to authority if they are to be successful in their jobs. Consequently, working-class parents may emphasize respect for authority (through an authoritarian approach to parenting) because they see this as an important attribute for their children's future success.

There are also differences in child-rearing across different cultural groups. Aboriginal and Hispanic parents are both inclined to maintain close family ties and tend to teach respect for and politeness toward others and authority. Whereas Aboriginal parents are very indulgent and rarely resort to punishment, Hispanic parents are more likely to use scoldings. Asian and Asian-American parents tend to stress self-discipline and are more likely to use an authoritarian style of parenting. However, unlike children whose parents are from European ancestry, Asian and Asian-North American children who are exposed to an authoritarian parenting style tend to show high levels of academic achievement. As well, the no-nonsense style of parenting seen in African-American families may be adaptive for their children, as they tend to be cognitively and socially competent with few emotional or behavioural problems.

e. The quest for autonomy: Renegotiating the parent–child relationship during adolescence

It is important for adolescents to develop a healthy and mature sense of autonomy—the capacity to make one's own decisions and to manage life tasks without being overly dependent on other people. As children reach puberty and become adolescents conflicts with parents over issues of autonomy become more frequent, and then gradually decline in frequency (though not necessarily in intensity) over the teenage years. Parents and adolescents often have different perspectives on the role of parenting during the adolescent years. Parents may feel they still have a social or moral responsibility to regulate their child's conduct; adolescents may see parental control as an infringement on personal rights. The highest levels of psychological adjustment are evident in adolescents who are able to achieve autonomy while maintaining close attachments to their family members. This outcome is most likely when parents use an authoritative approach.

4. The influence of siblings and sibling relationships

a. Changes in the family system when a new baby arrives

First-born children have an "exclusive" relationship with both their parents. When a new baby is born into the family the parents will typically direct less playful attention toward the older child, at least temporarily. This can cause the older sibling (especially if he or she is over the age of 2) to become resentful over the loss of parental attention. However, sibling rivalry can be minimized if parents continue to provide love and attention to the older child, and also if the older child is encouraged to assist in the care of the new infant.

b. Sibling relationships over the course of childhood

Most older siblings adjust quickly to having a new brother or sister; however, conflict between siblings is common, even in the closest sibling relationships. In general, siblings are much more likely to get along if their parents exhibit good marital relations. Sibling relationships are less conflictual if parents respond sensitively to all their children; it seems that younger siblings are particularly sensitive to situations in which they perceive the older sibling(s) as being treated more favourably. Sibling conflicts, however, are not necessarily entirely negative experiences. Depending on the quality of the sibling relationship, conflicts may provide opportunities for constructive problem solving with minimal hostility.

c. Contributions of siblings to development

Siblings contribute to one another's development in a number of ways. First, siblings are a source of emotional support for each other. Second, older siblings often assist in caring for younger siblings. Third, younger siblings often look to older siblings as models and learn from them through observation. Fourth, interacting with siblings can foster a child's general psychosocial development, promoting competency in interpersonal interactions.

d. Characteristics of only children

Only children tend to be relatively high in self-esteem and achievement motivation. On average, they are also slightly more intellectually competent and more obedient than age-mates with siblings. Finally, they are likely to have good interpersonal relationships with their peers. Evidence from differing cultural settings suggests that only children are not disadvantaged by having no siblings.

5. Diversity in family life

a. *Adoptive families*

The clear majority of adoptive parents develop strong emotional ties to their children. Because adoptive parents and their children share no genes, the rearing environment that these children experience may not be as good a match for the child's genetic predispositions as is the case for biological children. However, adoption generally has positive results for adopted children, relative to long-term foster care. Preliminary research into the impact of open adoptions shows that children are more satisfied when they learn information about their biological roots, and there is no evidence to suggest that providing this type of information undermines the children's self-esteem, as some critics of these policies had feared.

b. *Gay and lesbian families*

More than 90% of adult children who had lesbian mothers or gay fathers develop a heterosexual orientation; this figure does not differ significantly from the percentages among adult children raised by heterosexual parents. Also, children of gay or lesbian parents show cognitive and psychosocial maturity and adjustment equivalent to that of age-mates raised by heterosexual parents. In other words, there is no scientific evidence that would justify denying parental rights to individuals on the basis of their sexual orientation.

c. *The impacts of family conflict and divorce*

As many as 60% of all children born in the 1980s and 1990s will spend some time in a single-parent household as a result of parental divorce. When children are exposed to marital conflict in the home they are more likely to have hostile or aggressive interactions with siblings and peers. In addition, children may experience anxiety, depression, and conduct disorders.

The lives of all family members in a divorce are often disrupted for a year or more. In the majority of divorcing families the children are placed in the mother's custody. Custodial mothers often become edgy, impatient, and less sensitive to their children's needs, and they may adopt a more restrictive, authoritarian style of parenting. At the same time, the noncustodial father may become more permissive, which can undermine the mother's attempts at maintaining discipline.

The most visible signs of distress during a divorce are seen in preschool children and children in early elementary school. In some cases they think they are somehow responsible for the break-up of the family. Older children and adolescents are better able to understand the reasons behind the divorce, but they may withdraw from family interactions; they are at an increased risk for engaging in delinquent behaviours that are endorsed by their peer group. Children who have difficult temperaments display more adjustment problems, both at the time of the divorce and in the long term.

Many investigators also report that boys are more likely to show continuing signs of emotional stress and relationship problems following a divorce. However, these sex differences may reflect a tendency by investigators to focus on overt behavioural problems that are easier to detect. Several studies suggest that girls experience more covert distress. In addition, girls from divorced families often lack self-confidence in their relationships with members of the other sex.

Compared to adolescents from nondivorced families, adolescents from divorced families are more likely to fear that their own marriages will be unhappy. This concern may be justified to some extent. Compared to adults from intact families, adults who experienced a parental divorce when they were children are more likely to divorce.

d. *Remarriage and blended (reconstituted) families*

In approximately 75% of single-parent families, the custodial parent remarries or cohabits with a partner within three to five years of a divorce. Remarriage often improves the quality of life for the custodial parent, but these reconstituted families present another set of challenges to children. The children must adjust to the parenting style of an unfamiliar adult and may have to establish relationships with stepsiblings. In fact, according to Hetherington and colleagues, the restabilizing of family roles takes longer than was true after divorce!

When a stepfather joins a single-parent family in which the mother has custody of the children, boys seem to benefit more than girls. Under these circumstances boys often show an increase in self-esteem and a decrease in previous adjustment problems. However, stepdaughters often remain cool and aloof toward their stepfather. It may be that under these circumstances the girls see the stepfather as disruptive to the relationship they had established with their mother.

It is less common to have a stepmother join a single-parent family in which the father has custody of the children. However, the research that has investigated these types of blended or reconstituted families suggests that this arrangement may be slightly more disruptive for the children. This may be because fathers who are granted custody often develop very close relationships with their children, and the stepmother may be seen as weakening that relationship. It may also be that stepmothers are more likely than stepfathers to take an active role in monitoring stepchildren's behaviour and in disciplining the children.

Children's adjustment depends to a large degree on the composition of a stepparent family. More problems are associated with complex stepparent homes, where each parent brings at least one biological child to the new family unit, than with simple stepparent homes. Research by Hetherington suggests that children's adjustment to life in stable stepparent families generally improves over time. Some believe that joint custody is the preferred arrangement; however, as long as children are permitted to maintain close ties to both parents and if the relationship between the parents is non-conflictual, the outcome for the children is more likely to be positive.

Younger children adjust better to life in reconstituted families than preadolescent or adolescent children do. Adolescents show evidence of more favourable adjustment outcomes when an authoritative parenting style is used, but nearly one-third of adolescents simply disengage from their reconstituted families. Compared to adolescents from nondivorced families, adolescents from reconstituted families are more likely to engage in delinquent behaviour. However, it is important to recognize that disengagement from a reconstituted family may have long-term benefits, if the time away from home is spent in activities that foster supportive social relationships outside the family.

e. *Maternal employment*

Research with older children suggests that children from families in which the mother works outside the home tend to be more independent, to show higher self-esteem, to hold higher aspirations regarding occupations and education, and to have less stereotyped views of men and women. This is especially true for daughters of mothers who work outside the home. Maternal employment can also be beneficial if it promotes sensitive and supportive fathers to be more involved in their children's lives.

Compared to mothers who do not work outside the home, employed mothers are more likely to encourage autonomy and independence in their children, and they are more likely to use an authoritative style of parenting. Boys in dual-career families show some evidence of lower overall academic achievement, but only when the parents fail to adequately monitor their son's behaviour. When children's activities are well monitored and parents ensure that children devote sufficient attention to their schoolwork, boys from dual-career families show levels of academic achievement that are equivalent to those seen in families where only one parent works outside the home.

High-quality daycare can be one of the strongest supports for dual-career families, or for single parents who must work outside the home. Unfortunately, many Canadian workers have a difficult time finding and financing the kind of alternative care that is most likely to optimize the development of their children.

In addition to concerns over finding high-quality daycare for infants, toddlers, and preschool children, working parents must also be concerned about the after-school care of their children. Research shows that children who participate in high-quality organized after-school care that includes enrichment and learning activities such as theatre, music, and dance, demonstrate positive emotional and academic outcomes. In Canada, an increasing number of the 2.1 million children between the ages of 10 and 14 are latchkey children; this means they care for themselves after school, with little or no adult supervision. The most optimal outcomes for these children occur when their parents utilize an authoritative parenting style, and when the children's after-school time is regularly monitored by telephone.

6. When parenting breaks down: The problem of child abuse

Child abuse includes physical and sexual abuse, psychological abuse, or neglect by caregivers. The effects of physical abuse and battering are clear; however, many researchers believe that recurrent psychological abuse or neglect by caregivers can be even more harmful to children in the long run. Research indicates that reports of child abuse have increased over the past two decades.

a. Who are the abusers?

In some cases abusive parenting is passed from generation to generation; 30% of children who are abused by their caregivers go on to abuse their own children when they become parents themselves. In addition, mothers who become child abusers are often women who are battered by their own partners. Twenty to forty percent of child abusers have an alcohol or drug problem. Other factors that increase the risk of parents becoming child abusers are poverty, poor education, emotional insecurity and low self-esteem, reliance on an authoritarian style of parenting, and little social support.

b. Who is abused?

Children who have difficult temperaments appear to be at the highest risk for abuse. In addition, being emotionally unresponsive or being hyperactive or irritable can increase the risk that a child will be abused by his or her parents. Still, many "difficult" children are never abused, and many easy-going children are mistreated by their parents. When a family situation combines a high-risk parent and a high-risk child, there is an even higher risk that a pattern of child abuse will develop.

c. Social-contextual triggers: The ecology of child abuse

When the social or emotional relationships within a family are disrupted in some way, the risk for child abuse increases. In addition, neighbourhoods that have limited community services and few informal support systems tend to have higher rates of child abuse. Finally, the prevalent attitude toward violence in general may contribute to the high rate of child abuse in this country. Results from cross-cultural studies indicate that the rates of child abuse are much lower in societies that advocate nonviolent methods for resolving interpersonal conflicts.

d. Consequences of abuse and neglect

Children who experience neglect are more likely to show intellectual deficits and academic difficulties and are unlikely to have close friends. In contrast, children who experience physical abuse are more likely to be hostile and aggressive, and are also more likely to be rejected by their peers. Children who are sexually abused may show evidence of a variety of problems, including anxiety, low self-esteem, withdrawal, or academic difficulties. In addition, there are two problems that appear to be uniquely associated with sexual abuse. Approximately one-third of children who are sexually abused begin to engage in "sexualized behaviours," and about one-third show evidence of post-traumatic stress disorder.

Some children who experience abuse or neglect are resilient. One of the major factors fostering resiliency is the establishment of a warm, secure, and supportive relationship with a nonabusive significant other. This, in addition to avoidance of severe stress, also helps prevent abused children from growing up and abusing their own children.

e. How might we solve the problem?

Early identification of infants who are at a high risk for abuse due to their temperament can be beneficial. Parents of children who are particularly unresponsive or irritable can be taught effective parenting techniques designed to increase the parents' understanding of their child's temperament and increase their ability to interact positively with their child. Parents who are at risk for becoming child abusers can be taught a variety of stress-management skills. Home-visitor programs are particularly effective if they address the parents' material needs, psychological needs, and educational needs. At the community level, policies designed to maintain or establish healthy, stable, low-risk, family-oriented neighbourhoods are also beneficial.

Parents who are already abusing their children need emotional support and the opportunity to learn more effective parenting and coping skills. Specialized programs designed to overcome the cognitive, social, and emotional problems that stem from abuse need to be made available to children who are victims of abuse or neglect. Finally, developmentalists generally agree that the health and safety of mistreated children should be a priority, even when it means that abusers' legal rights of parenthood are terminated.

Vocabulary Self-Test

Part I: For each of the following definitions provide the appropriate term. (Answers to this portion of the self-test are provided at the end of the chapter.)

1. ________________ A dimension of parenting that describes how restrictive and demanding parents are

2. ________________ Instances in which the relationship between two individuals in a family is modified by the behaviour or attitudes of a third family member

3. ________________ Children who care for themselves after school or in the evening, while their parents are working

4. ________________ A restrictive parenting pattern in which adults set many rules for their children and rely on power rather than reason to elicit compliance

5. ________________ Circumstance in which parents mutually support each other and function as a cooperative parenting team

6. ________________ The capacity to make decisions independently, serve as one's own source of emotional strength, and otherwise manage life tasks without depending on others for assistance; an important developmental task for adolescence

7. ________________ The process by which children acquire the beliefs, values, and behaviours considered desirable by the society to which they belong

8. ________________ A pattern of parenting in which otherwise accepting adults make few demands of their children and rarely attempt to control their behaviour

9. ________________ Family consisting of two married (or cohabitating) adults, each of whom has at least one biological child living at home

10. ________________ Tendency of parents in complex stepparent homes to favour and be more involved with their own biological children than with their stepchildren

11. ________________ Model of family influence in which parents are believed to influence their children rather than vice versa

12. ________________ Mixture of authoritative and authoritarian parenting styles that is associated with favourable outcomes in African-American families

Part II: For each of the following terms provide the definition.

Uninvolved Parenting: ____________________

____

Traditional Nuclear Family: ____________________

____

Sibling Rivalry: ____________________

____

Extended Family: ____________________

____

Single Parent Family: ____________________

____

Direct Effect: ____________________

____

Authoritative Parenting: ____________________

____

Family Social System: ____________________

____

Blended or Reconstituted Family: ____________________

____

Child Abuse: ____________________

____

High-risk Neighbourhood: ____________________

____

Simple Stepparent Home: ____________________

____

Child Effects Model: ____________________

____

Transactional Model: ____________________

____

Acceptance/Responsiveness: ____________________

Short-Answer Study Questions

FUNCTIONS OF THE FAMILY

1. List three ways in which the process of socialization serves society.

   a.

   b.

   c.

THE FAMILY AS A SOCIAL SYSTEM

2. Contrast direct effects and indirect effects within a family system, and provide an appropriate example to illustrate each type of effect.

   a.

   b.

3. Contrast the composition of traditional nuclear family households with the composition of extended family households.

   a.

   b.

4. List eight social changes that have taken place since the 1950s and have affected the makeup of the typical Canadian family.

   a.

   b.

   c.

   d.

   e.

   f.

   g.

   h.

PARENTAL SOCIALIZATION DURING CHILDHOOD AND ADOLESCENCE

5. Describe the two dimensions of parenting that are especially important throughout childhood and adolescence.

   a.

   b.

6. Identify four different patterns of parenting and describe the discipline style associated with each of these parenting patterns.

   a.

   b.

   c.

   d.

7. Describe the general characteristics (personality and behavioural) that are evident in children who experience each of the four different parenting patterns.

   a.

   b.

   c.

   d.

8. Identify three reasons why an authoritative parenting style is likely to be associated with positive developmental outcomes in children.

   a.

   b.

   c.

9. Discuss the general social class differences in child-rearing that research studies have identified.

10. Discuss two possible explanations for differences in general parenting style across social classes.

    a.

    b.

11. Discuss some of the ethnic and cultural variations that have been identified in parenting styles.

12. Describe the two components that are part of a mature sense of autonomy, and identify the ways in which parents can promote a sense of autonomy during their children's adolescent years.

    a.

    b.

    Parents can encourage adolescent autonomy by:

THE INFLUENCE OF SIBLINGS AND SIBLING RELATIONSHIPS

13. Describe some ways that parents can reduce rivalry between an older sibling and a new baby.

14. Discuss how sibling relationships typically change and develop from the preschool years through to adolescence.

15. List and describe four positive roles that siblings might play in one another's development.

    a.

    b.

    c.

    d.

16. Describe three characteristics that are often associated with being an only child.

a.

b.

c.

DIVERSITY IN FAMILY LIFE

17. Discuss what the research evidence suggests about the impact of moving toward a more open system of adoption.

18. List three concerns that have been raised in opposition to the granting of child custody to gay or lesbian parents, and discuss what the research evidence suggests about the validity of these concerns.

Three concerns that are often raised are:

The research evidence that is available suggests:

19. Describe the changes in parenting style that often emerge following a family divorce, focusing on the patterns typically seen in custodial mothers and noncustodial fathers.

Custodial mothers:

Noncustodial fathers:

20. Discuss how a child's age, temperament, and sex can increase the stress the child experiences following a family divorce.

21. List and describe five factors that often make the adjustment process easier for members of divorcing families.

a.

b.

c.

d.

e.

22. Describe the sex differences that are seen in children's adjustment to being part of a blended or reconstituted family.

Adjustment in boys:

Adjustment in girls:

23. Discuss the general characteristics (personality, behavioural, academic) of older children from families in which the mother is employed outside the home.

WHEN PARENTING BREAKS DOWN: THE PROBLEM OF CHILD ABUSE

24. Identify three factors that increase the risk of a parent engaging in child abuse.

 a.

 b.

 c.

25. List four characteristics that appear to place infants at a higher risk for being abused by their parents.

 a.

 b.

 c.

 d.

26. Identify three social or contextual factors that might trigger child abuse.

 a.

 b.

 c.

27. Children who experience abuse or neglect tend to display a variety of serious problems. Identify the behavioural correlates of physical abuse, neglect, and sexual abuse.

Physical abuse:

Neglect:

Sexual abuse:

28. Identify some of the methods that have been developed to prevent child abuse and neglect.

29. Identify some of the methods that have been developed to control or eliminate abuse in families in which abuse has already occurred.

Multiple-Choice Self-Test

For each of the following questions select the best alternative. (Answers and explanations for this self-test are provided at the end of the chapter.) Once you have selected your answer, provide a brief explanation for why the answer you selected is the best choice and why the remaining answers would not be correct.

1. Belinda believes that parents have the only influence on children's development and that children themselves have little influence over their parents' responses. This type of belief is consistent with which model of family interaction?

   a. parent effects model
   b. child effects model
   c. transactional model
   d. socialization

   Rationale: ____

   ____

2. The best description of the family systems approach to understanding family relationships is that:

   a. parent–child relationships within the family affect parental relationships with individuals outside the family system
   b. every person and relationship within the family affects every other person and relationship within the system
   c. sibling relationships within the family affect children's relationships outside the family system
   d. parent–child relationships within the family affect children's relationships outside the family system

   Rationale: ____

   ____

3. In comparing families today with families of 40 years ago, the least accurate statement would be:

   a. adults are waiting longer after marriage to have children and are having fewer children
   b. divorce is more common
   c. fewer children now live in poverty
   d. more adults are deciding not to marry

   Rationale: ____

   ____

4. The authoritative pattern of parenting is:

   a. a warm pattern where children are free to express themselves; few demands are made and little control is exerted
   b. a fair but reserved pattern in which the child knows the rules and the consequences for breaking the rules; no input is sought from the child and the parents remain the sole authority
   c. a reserved and aloof pattern; few demands are made and little control is exerted
   d. a warm pattern that allows considerable freedom within guidelines that are firmly enforced; the child's input is sought/allowed but the parents retain the final say

   Rationale: ____

   ____

5. Children who experience a permissive style of parenting in the home tend to be:

a. bossy, impulsive, aggressive, and low in achievement
b. self-reliant, socially responsible, cheerful, and achievement-oriented
c. unfriendly, moody, easily annoyed, and aimless
d. aggressive, hostile, selfish, and rebellious

Rationale: ____

____

6. Compared to high-SES parents, low-SES parents are more likely to:

a. be permissive parents who stress independence
b. be authoritarian parents who stress obedience
c. be permissive parents who stress happiness
d. be authoritative parents who stress ambition

Rationale: ____

____

7. Children are most likely to assume that they are the cause of the divorce when they are:

a. elementary-school age
b. high-school age
c. preschool age
d. infants

Rationale: ____

____

8. Jay lives in a reconstituted family home consisting of his mother, his stepfather, his brother, and his stepsister. This type of family is known as a(n):

a. complex stepparent home
b. simple stepparent home
c. owness effect
d. nuclear family

Rationale: ____

____

Activities and Projects Related to this Chapter

ACTIVITY 15-1

THE IMPACT OF DIVORCE FROM THE CHILD'S PERSPECTIVE

INTRODUCTION: There is considerable concern and much is written about the impact of divorce on children. Generally, it is assumed that it will be a negative experience that will have both short-term and long-term consequences for children. Your text reviews the research literature in Chapter 15. This literature suggests that divorce does affect children—how much and how long depends on many factors. Two factors found to be particularly related to developmental outcomes are (a) the extent the child was and continues to be exposed to high levels of conflict between the parents and (b) the adequacy of the parenting provided for the child (authoritative versus either coercive, lax, or inconsistently lax and coercive). In addition, a recent article suggests that there is evidence that living with one parent, even a well-functioning one, may be associated with some different—but not necessarily worse—developmental outcomes than two-parent rearing.

INSTRUCTIONS: Interview two friends/acquaintances from divorced families (one can be yourself, if you have parents who are divorced). Word questions as you wish, but be sure to write down the question just as you asked it and the exact answer. Attempt to ask both individuals the same set of questions. (Note—if the answer to one of the early questions includes sufficient information to answer a question you had planned on asking later in the interview, you do not need to wait until later to ask the question. Instead, you might follow up the individual's response with an appropriate probe to elicit further information.) Suggested questions:

1. How old were you at the time of the divorce? (also write down individual's age now)

2. What were the general circumstances at the time of the divorce? What else was happening in your life and within the family?

3. What was it like for you being a _____ -year-old whose parents were splitting up? More specifically:

   a. What were your feelings/reactions during the months prior to the divorce itself, the first 1–2 years after the divorce, and now?

   b. Were there any positive outcomes of the divorce—then and now?

   c. Were there any ways in which the divorce had a negative impact—then and now?

4. Were there any factors that made coping with the divorce easier or more difficult for you than it might have been otherwise?

5. Is there anything that you wish your parents or others had done or said (at the time of the divorce, or later) to make the experience easier for you?

6. Was there a remarriage? (if yes) How did the remarriage affect you?

7. Any additional questions you think might be appropriate and informative. (Be sure to include the question(s) in your write-up <u>exactly</u> as asked.)

WRITE-UP:

1. Present and discuss specific responses of both individuals to each question. Summarize the responses of the two individuals by <u>characterizing</u> their experience (what was the overall experience for the individual).

2. Discuss how your "findings" relate to the generalizations about the short-term and long-term impact of divorce on children, and the factors found to influence children's adjustment to the divorce presented in the text. Also see related references below.

3. Present some ideas of things parents, relatives, family friends, schools, and individual teachers could do to help children cope with the stresses of a parental divorce.

4. In terms of Canadian policy, what would you present to the appropriate ministries/officials? For example, what would you recommend in terms of custody? What factors would you have to consider?

RELATED REFERENCES

1993 issue of *Journal of Family Psychology, 7(1)*, for seven articles on families in transition.

Amato, P. R., & Keith, B. (1991). Parental divorce and the well-being of children: A meta-analysis. *Psychological Bulletin, 110*, 26–46.

Barber, B. L., & Eccles, J. (1992). Long-term influence of divorce and single parenting on adolescent family- and work-related values, behavior, and aspirations. *Psychological Bulletin, 111*, 108–126.

Ford-Gilboe, M. (2000). Dispelling myths and creating opportunity: A comparison of the strengths of single-parent and two-parent families. *Advances in Nursing Science, 23*, 41–58.

Grych, J. H., & Fincham, F. D. (1990). Marital conflict and children's adjustment: A cognitive-contextual framework. *Psychological Bulletin, 108*, 267–290.

Hetherington, E. M., & Clingempeel, W. G. (1992). Coping with marital transitions. *Monographs of the Society for Research in Child Development, 57, Serial No. 227.*

Hetherington, E. M., Hagan, M. S., & Anderson, E. T. (1989). Marital transitions: A child's perspective. *American Psychologist, 44*, 303–312.

Jenkins, J. (2000). Marital conflict and children's emotions: The development of an anger organization. *Journal of Marriage and the Family, 62*, 723–736.

Jenkins, J., & Buccioni, J. M. (2000). Children's understanding of marital conflict and the marital relationship. *Journal of Child Psychology and Psychiatry and Allied Disciplines, 41*, 161–168.

ACTIVITY 15-2

YOUR FAMILY AS A COMPLEX SOCIAL SYSTEM

INTRODUCTION: Chapter 15 emphasizes the view of the family as a complex social system, a network of reciprocal relationships and alliances that is constantly evolving. Put simply, a child's interaction with a sibling will be different when someone else (e.g., the mother, another sibling, a grandparent) is present. How a child is treated by parents and siblings will, in part, be a function of how he or she behaves toward them, and vice versa. As a child becomes more competent, expectations change and so does the way others interact with the child. Also, as parents mature their behaviour toward others, including their children, changes.

The family is truly a complex, evolving social system in which parental behaviour affects child behaviour, child behaviour affects parental behaviour, and both work interdependently to determine child development outcomes. This theme, reiterated throughout the text, reflects the views of developmentalists in the 1990s regarding the role of the family in development. This activity is intended to give you a "feel" for the interdependence and reciprocity of relationships within the family system by having you recall ways in which interactions changed in your family, depending on who was present.

INSTRUCTIONS—Part A:
Drawing on your own family experiences, select two of the following situations and write down examples of how an interaction changes/changed between the individuals when a third person is/was present.

1. Mother and child together—father enters
2. Father and child together—mother enters
3. Mother and father together—child enters
4. Two children together—mother enters*
5. Two children together—father enters*
6. Whole family is together vs. any two members alone
7. Other (specify)

* If you are an only child, the second child could be another relative such as a cousin, or one of your friends.

INSTRUCTIONS—Part B:

1. Describe two ways you treat your parents differently today than you did at an earlier point in your development.
2. How has your change in behaviour affected their reaction to you?
3. Describe two ways your parents treat you differently than they did at an earlier point in their/your life.
4. How has the change in the way they treat you affected your reaction to them?

REFERENCES OF INTEREST

Alaggia, R., Chau, S., & Tsang, K.T. (2001). Astronaut Asian families: Impact of migration on family structure from the perspective of the youth. *Journal of Social Work Research and Evaluation, 2(2),* 295–306.

Buhrmeister, D., Camparo, L., Christensen, A., Gonzalez, L. S., & Hinshaw, S. P. (1992). Mothers and fathers interacting in dyads and triads with normal and hyperactive sons. *Developmental Psychology*, *28*, 500–509.

Gjerde, P. F. (1986). The interpersonal structure of family interaction settings: Parent-adolescent relations in dyads and triads. *Developmental Psychology*, *22*, 297–304.

Hall, W.A. (1994). New fatherhood: Myths and realities. *Public Health Nursing, 11(4),* 219–228.

Kuczynski, L., Lollis, S., & Koguchi, Y. (2003). Reconstructing common sense. In L. Kuczynski (Ed.), *Handbook of dynamics in "parent-child" relations*. Thousand Oaks, CA: Sage.

Lollis, S. (2003). Conceptualizing the influence of the past and the future in present parent-child relationships. In L. Kuczynski (Ed.), *Handbook of dynamics in "parent-child" relations*. Thousand Oaks, CA: Sage.

Lollis, S., Kuczynski, L. (1997). Beyond one hand clapping: Seeing bidirectionality in parent-child relations. *Journal of Social and Personal Relationships, 14(4),* 441–461.

Lytton, H. (1980). *Parent-child interaction: The socialization process observed in twin and singleton families.* New York: Plenum Press.

Maccoby, E. E., & Martin, J. A. (1983). Socialization in the context of the family: Parent-child interaction. In P. H. Mussen & E. M. Hetherington (Eds.), Handbook *of child psychology: Vol. 4. Socialization, personality, and social development*, pp. 1–101. New York: Plenum Press.

Minuchin, P. (1985). Families and individual development: Provocations from the field of family therapy. *Child Development, 56,* 289–302.

Peters, R.D., Petrunka, K., & Arnold, R. (2003). The Better Beginnings, Better Futures Project: A universal, comprehensive, community-based prevention approach for primary school children and their families. *Journal of Clinical Child and Adolescent Psychology, 32(2),* 215–227.

Pettit, G.S., & Lollis, S. (1997). Introduction to special issue: Reciprocity and bidirectionality in parent-child relationships: New approaches to the study of enduring issues. *Journal of Social and Personal Relationships, 14(4),* 435–440.

Ross, H., Filyer, R.E., Lollis, S., Perlman, M., & Martin, J.L. (1994). Administering justice in the family. *Journal of Family Psychology, 8(3),* 254–273.

Ross, H., Woody, E., Smith, M., & Lollis, S. (2000). Young children's appraisals of their sibling relationships. *Merrill-Palmer Quarterly, 46(3),* 441–464.

Speirs, C.C., Duder, S., & Grove, J. (2003). Adoptable but still in limbo: The forgotten children in Canada. *Child and Youth Care Forum, 32(2),* 75–88.

Symons, D. K. (2001). A dyad-oriented approach to distress and mother-child relationship outcomes in the first 24 months. *Parenting: Science and Practice, 1,* 101–122.

ACTIVITY 15-3

TEENAGE EMPLOYMENT DURING THE SCHOOL YEAR

INTRODUCTION: This activity relates to the text material on teen employment and to Chapter 16 material on extrafamilial influences. In Chapter 15 the text mentions teen employment as a potentially positive influence on the development of a healthy sense of autonomy. Many parents and professionals have long assumed that having a job as a teenager would have positive consequences, e.g., help teach responsibility, an appreciation for the value of money, interpersonal skills, etc.—all of which should support the development of healthy autonomy. Your text authors point out, however, that research by Steinberg, Greenberger, and others, has raised some provocative questions about whether these assumptions are warranted. They report that any positive benefits of working are accrued in 10–14 hours per week of work, and that past 20 hours of work per week there is a negative relationship between number of hours worked and grades, work attitudes, school attendance, staying drug free, etc. Steinberg and Greenberger have suggested that the stress of working in unchallenging dead-end jobs promotes negative, cynical attitudes toward working and employers, and leads to greater use of drugs and alcohol. Questions have also been raised about the impact of premature affluence. Bachman has suggested that it can breed self-indulgence rather than financial responsibility.

Note—It should be kept in mind that the research on teen employment involves quasi/natural experiments (i.e., it utilizes existing groups rather than randomly assigning teens to working and nonworking conditions). For this reason interpretation is open to question. It could be argued that teens who are struggling in school, are using drugs, etc., are more likely to choose to invest more time in work and less time in school and school-related activities. In other words, working may not be the cause of negative outcomes, as some researchers have suggested. Prospective studies that gather information on teens before they begin working and after they have been working are needed to better understand the role that working during the school year plays in the negative outcomes that have been identified. Clearly, this is a controversial subject that is a difficult one to research. The final word is not yet in.

The purpose of this activity is to obtain information about the teen work experiences of two young adults and then relate their experiences to the text material.

INSTRUCTIONS:

Part 1

Interview two or more individuals (one can be yourself) about their work experience during high school.

Suggested questions:

Please tell me about your employment during high school:

1. Number of hours worked/week during school year? 10th grade _____ 11th grade _____ 12th grade _____
2. Types of jobs?
3. What would you say you gained from the experience of working during high school?
4. What were the "costs" to you of working during high school (e.g., not being able to participate in sports, too much stress, no time for family and friends, etc.)?
5. On balance, would you say your work experience during high school was a positive or negative influence in your life?
6. What will be your position regarding working during the school year for your own children when they are teens?

Part 2

Prepare a write-up of your interviews. In your write-up:

1. Present a summary of the responses given by your two interviewees.

2. Contrast their experiences and conclusions about working.

3. Compare your interviewees' experiences and conclusions with the concerns discussed in the text.

4. If there are discrepancies in the responses you obtained from your interviewees and the conclusions presented in the text, attempt to explain why these discrepancies might exist.

5. Present your own views on how teens can benefit from working during high school while, at the same time, minimizing the costs of working.

6. Include your protocols (questions that you asked and the responses you obtained) as an attachment.

Part 3

In Canada, some are arguing to change the legal minimum age for employment to 12 years. Why do you think this is? How has the changing cultural face of Canada influenced this? Prepare a write-up of an argument for and against such a policy.

RELATED REFERENCES

Bachman, J. (1983). Premature affluence: Do high school students earn too much? *Economic Outlook USA, Summer*, 64–67.

Bachman, J. G., & Schulenberg, J. (1993). How part-time work intensity relates to drug use, problem behavior, time use, and satisfaction among high school seniors: Are these consequences or merely correlates? *Developmental Psychology, 29*, 220–235.

Greenberger, E., & Steinberg, L. (1986). *When teenagers work: The psychological and social costs of adolescent employment.* New York: Basic Books.

Steinberg, L., & Dornbush, S. M. (1991). Negative correlates of part-time employment during adolescence: Replication and elaboration. *Developmental Psychology, 27*, 304–313.

Steinberg, L., Fegley, S., & Dornbusch, S. M. (1993). Negative impact of part-time work on adolescent adjustment: Evidence from a longitudinal study. *Developmental Psychology, 29*, 171–180.

Steinberg, L., Greenberger, E., Garduque, L., Ruggiero, M., & Vaux, A. (1982). Effects of working on adolescent development. *Developmental Psychology, 18*, 385–395.

ANSWERS TO SELF-TESTS

VOCABULARY SELF-TEST (The answers may be found on the pages in parentheses.)

1. demandingness/control (p. 570)
2. indirect, or third-party, effect (p. 565)
3. self-care (latchkey) children (p. 594)
4. authoritarian parenting (p. 571)
5. coparenting (p. 565)
6. autonomy (p. 577)
7. socialization (p. 563)
8. permissive parenting (p. 571)
9. complex stepparent home (p. 591)
10. ownness effect (p. 591)
11. parent effects model (p. 573)
12. no-nonsense parenting (p. 576)

MULTIPLE-CHOICE SELF-TEST (The answers may be found on the pages in parentheses.)

1. **a** (pp. 573–574) The parent effects model is a model of family influence in which parents are believed to influence their children rather than vice versa. The child effects model, in contrast, is a model of family influence in which children are believed to influence their parents (b). The transactional model of family influence is a model in which parent and child are believed to influence one another reciprocally (c). Socialization refers to the process by which children acquire the beliefs, values, and behaviours considered desirable or appropriate by the society to which they belong (d).

2. **b** (pp. 564–565) The family systems approach looks at the way each family member influences and is influenced by other members of the family. It is less concerned with the way relationships within the family affect relationships outside the family (a, c, and d).

3. **c** (pp. 567–568) More children are living in poverty than was the case 40 years ago. Couples are waiting longer to have children after marriage and are having fewer children (a). Divorce is more common (b), with up to 60% of new marriages ending in divorce. More adults are choosing to stay single (d), although 90% of young adults do eventually marry.

4. **d** (p. 571) Authoritative parenting is a responsive style in which limits are set and rules are enforced. Alternative (a) describes a permissive parenting style. Alternative (b) describes an authoritarian parenting style. Alternative (c) describes an uninvolved parenting style.

5. **a** (p. 572) Children of permissive parents are often impulsive, aggressive, bossy, self-centred, lacking in self-control, and low in independence and achievement. The characteristics in (b) are seen in children who experience authoritative parenting. The characteristics in (c) are seen in children who experience authoritarian parenting. The characteristics in (d) are seen in children who experience uninvolved parenting.

6. **b** (p. 574) Low-SES parents tend to stress obedience and adopt an authoritarian style of parenting. There are no differences in levels of permissive parenting (a or c) that relate to the parents' socioeconomic status. High-SES parents are more likely to stress ambition and adopt an authoritative style of parenting (d).

7. **c** (p. 587) Preschool and early elementary-school children may not understand the reasons for a divorce and may think they are somehow responsible for the break-up. Older children (a) and adolescents (b) are better able to understand personality conflicts and better able to understand reasons for dissolving relationships. Infants (d) lack the social understanding to comprehend the concept of divorce; therefore, they are unlikely to see themselves as the "cause" of the break-up.

8. **a** (p. 591) A complex stepparent home is a family consisting of two married (or cohabiting) adults, each of whom has at least one biological child living at home. In contrast, a simple stepparent home is a family consisting of a parent and his or her biological children and a stepparent (b). The owness effect is the tendency of parents in complex stepparent homes to favour and be more involved with their own biological children than with their stepchildren (c). A nuclear family home is a unit consisting of a wife/mother, a husband/father, and their dependent child(ren) (d).

Chapter Sixteen

Extrafamilial Influences: Television, Computers, Schools, and Peers

Learning Objectives

By the time you have finished this chapter you should be able to:

1. Explain what is meant by television literacy and trace the typical development of television literacy across childhood and adolescence.
2. Describe some of the potential effects of viewing television violence.
3. Discuss how television can influence social stereotypes.
4. Discuss the research evidence that relates to children's reactions to television commercials.
5. Identify some ways in which television can have a positive influence on children's development.
6. Identify some of the potential benefits that have been linked to children's use of computers.
7. Identify some of the potential drawbacks of children's increasing access to computer technology.
8. Discuss the advantages and disadvantages associated with early entry into school-like settings.
9. Identify some factors that have been shown to have a negligible impact on overall school effectiveness.
10. Identify some factors that do contribute to overall school effectiveness.
11. Discuss how parental attitudes and peer influences can interact to affect a child's academic success.
12. Explain what is meant by a self-fulfilling prophecy, and discuss how teacher expectations may influence a child's overall level of academic achievement.
13. Explain what is meant by inclusion and identify the teaching methods that can enhance the effectiveness of inclusion.
14. Identify some of the cultural differences that may explain the achievement gap between American and Asian students.
15. Outline some of the important functions that peer interactions have in a child's socialization.
16. Discuss how peer group interactions change as children move from preschool through adolescence.
17. Describe the four categories of play identified by Parten, and discuss how play activities change from infancy through preschool.
18. Discuss how parents can influence their children's peer sociability.
19. Describe five categories of peer acceptance identified through sociometric research, and discuss the factors associated with acceptance, neglect, or rejection by a child's peer group.
20. Discuss how friendship patterns change as children move from preschool through adolescence.
21. Outline some of the roles that friends play in a child's socialization.
22. Discuss the differences between interactions with peers and interactions with parents, and describe differences in the influence of parents and peers.

Chapter Outline and Summary

1. Early windows: Effects of television and computer technologies on children and adolescents

More than 98% of Canadian homes have at least one television set. Television viewing often begins in infancy, and it increases until adolescence; children between the ages of 2 and 11 are watching an average of 14.2 hours of television a week. During adolescence television viewing declines somewhat, but by the time a child is 18 he or she will have spent more time watching television than in any other activity (except sleeping).

Results from studies that have investigated the impact that the introduction of television has on children suggest that children who have access to television substitute television viewing for other leisure activities, such as listening to the radio or reading. However, in general there are no significant cognitive or academic deficiencies associated with television viewing, as long as it does not become excessive.

a. Development of television literacy

Television literacy involves the ability to construct a story line from the activities of characters and the sequencing of scenes, and the ability to accurately interpret the form of the message. Preschool children and children in the early elementary-school years have trouble constructing coherent story lines from television programs. They focus more on the actions or voices of the characters, and may fail to attend to the story during slower scenes with quiet dialogue. Young children also often fail to recognize that television programs are fictional. Young children's strong focus on the actions in television programs increases the likelihood that they will attempt to imitate the behaviours they have seen television characters perform.

During the later elementary-school years and adolescence, television literacy increases significantly. Children become more capable of accurately interpreting the form of the message in television programs, and they are also able to draw inferences between scenes that are separated in time.

b. Some potentially undesirable effects of television

American television programs are extremely violent. Although the violence index for Canadian shows is significantly lower than for American shows, Canadian children (and adults) watch a significant amount of American programming. Over half the programs in a typical broadcast day (6 a.m. to 11 p.m.) contain repeated acts of overt aggression, and nearly three-quarters contain violence in which the aggressor displays no remorse and experiences no negative consequences for his or her actions. Unfortunately, the most violent television programs are those directed toward children. Nearly 40% of the violence in children's programs is initiated by a hero or an attractive role model, and nearly two-thirds of the violence in these programs is portrayed as being humorous.

Cross-cultural, cross-sectional studies have found a consistent positive correlation between overall levels of hostile, aggressive behaviour and the amount of televised violence that individuals view. This is particularly true when children identify with the violent television characters. Longitudinal studies also suggest that the link between the viewing of television violence and the display of aggressive behaviour is reciprocal.

Even when children do not imitate the televised acts of aggression they have observed, they can still be influenced by the aggressive acts. Children may begin to view the world as a violent place, and they may be less emotionally upset by real-world acts of violence.

Television can also reinforce social stereotypes. Sex-role stereotyping and stereotyped views of minorities are common in television programs. The number of African-Americans who appear on American television programs equals or exceeds the proportion of African-Americans in the general population; however, other minority groups are underrepresented in television programming, and members of these minority groups are often portrayed in an unfavourable light. Although the representation of Aboriginal populations and other visible minorities on Canadian television has increased, they tend to play supporting roles rather than main characters. The evidence that is available suggests that children's ethnic and racial attitudes are influenced by television portrayals of minority groups.

Children are also influenced by the televised commercials they see, and their understanding of commercials shows age-related changes. Preschool children and children in early elementary school rarely understand that the intent of television advertising is to sell a particular product. They often view ads as informative announcements. By the later elementary-school years children recognize that advertisements are designed to sell a product, but they may still fail to recognize that ads can misrepresent product features. Adolescents are more likely to view product claims with skepticism, but they can still be persuaded by the advertisements they see, especially if the ads include an endorsement by a popular celebrity.

c. *Television as an educational tool*

Children are likely to show growth in their prosocial behaviour when they view television programs that emphasize the benefits of prosocial activities and when their parents encourage them to practise the prosocial lessons they have learned. Television can also promote cognitive development. When preschoolers watch *Sesame Street* on a regular basis they show increases in both their vocabularies and prereading skills, and even show better academic performances later in high school.

Other educational programs designed for school-age children have also shown some success in fostering children's cognitive growth. However, for some shows the gains in cognitive skills only appear when the child watches with an adult who encourages the child to apply what he or she has learned.

d. *Child development in the computer age*

In 2000, nearly 90% of Canadian youths had access to a computer at home and 70% had access to the Internet from home. Eighty-eight percent of elementary students and 97% of secondary-school students had access to the Internet and computers in school for instructional tools. The results from a large number of studies show that the use of computers in classroom settings is beneficial. Computers can be integrated into the learning experience in a number of ways. Computer-assisted instruction (CAI) utilizes drills or guided interactive tutorials to improve children's basic skills.

Computers can also enhance basic writing and communication skills when children are introduced to word processing packages that increase the likelihood of young writers revising and editing their written assignments. Finally, children can learn to program computers using programs such as Logo. Experience with programming appears to develop mastery motivation and self-efficacy, as well as general metacognitive skills.

Some early critics feared that the use of computers in the classroom would impede peer interactions and have an overall negative impact on children's interpersonal skills. Results from research that has investigated the social impact of computers suggests that children often collaborate with peers in solving computer-programming challenges, thereby promoting peer interactions.

The three concerns that have been raised most frequently with respect to children's exposure to computer technology relate to (1) the impact of video games, (2) the potential for social inequalities in access, and (3) exposure to information over the Internet. Early research evidence suggests that heavy exposure to violent video games can foster aggression, in much the same way as exposure to televised violence. Children from economically disadvantaged families are less likely to have access to computers in the home and may only have exposure to computers in school settings. These children may fall behind other children in acquiring the skills that will be necessary in a society that is becoming increasingly computer dependent. The impact of Internet access on children's development is an area where more research is needed. Early research suggests that unrestricted and unsupervised access has the potential for harmful effects.

2. School as a socialization agent

Schooling promotes cognitive and metacognitive growth in children. A number of studies have shown that children at any given grade level perform at higher levels on a variety of intellectual tasks, compared to age-mates who are in the next lower grade. In addition, schools promote the socialization of children by teaching them how to "fit into" their culture.

a. *Determinants of effective (and ineffective) schooling*

The effectiveness of schools has little to do with the level of monetary support that a school has; as long as a school has qualified teachers and a reasonable level of support, the actual amount of money spent per student has only a minor impact on final student outcomes.

In typical elementary- and secondary-school classrooms, with classes that range in size from 20 to 40 students, class size has little, if any, impact on academic achievement. However, prior to Grade 3, smaller classes are beneficial. The overall size of a school may have an impact on participation in extracurricular activities, and consequently on students' socialization. In larger schools there are often more activities to choose from, but students who attend smaller schools are more likely to be heavily involved in extracurricular programs.

In schools that utilize ability tracking, students are grouped by their level of academic achievement and taught with students who are of similar overall ability. This type of experience can be beneficial to high-ability students, if the curriculum is tailored to their learning needs. However, students with lower academic abilities are less likely to benefit from the implementation of ability tracking. In contrast, there seems to be no effect on the academic achievement of students in schools that implement split-grade classrooms.

In effective schools there is a clear focus on academic goals. The teachers in effective schools have good classroom management skills and the staff firmly enforces rules as soon as infractions occur. In an effective school the teachers and the principal work together as a team; they jointly plan the curriculum and monitor student progress. Finally, the "goodness of fit" between students and the classroom environment is a crucial aspect in a school's overall effectiveness.

b. *Do our schools meet the needs of all of our children?*

In Canada, Aboriginal children have lower school achievement levels than other Canadian children. In the United States, compared to European-American students, African-American, Latino, and Native-American students earn poorer grades in school and do less well on standardized achievement tests. In contrast, Asian-American students tend to outperform their European-American peers. Minority parents appear to place a high value on education, but they are often less involved in school activities. When minority parents become highly involved in school activities, their children tend to do better in school.

Results from studies that have investigated the influence of parenting style and peer groups on overall academic achievement suggest that the best outcomes are seen when students are exposed to an authoritative parenting style and to a peer group that values academic achievement. This last component appears to be particularly influential. Asian-American children often experience a more authoritarian style of parenting, and yet these children show high levels of academic achievement. This may occur because Asian-American students are more likely to be part of a peer group that encourages academic success.

Teacher expectancies for student success can also become self-fulfilling prophecies. A number of studies have found that students do better when teachers have high expectations for the success of those students; in the same way, when teachers expect students to be less successful, their expectations are often borne out.

When school districts use inclusion (or mainstreaming), they integrate special-needs students into regular classrooms, either for the entire school day or for large portions of the school day. In some instances special-needs students do better, academically and socially, in inclusive classrooms, but often their achievement levels do not differ from those seen in students placed in segregated classrooms. In addition, because they may be rejected by peers, special-needs students often show a significant decline in their overall levels of self-esteem when they are integrated into regular classrooms. Inclusion seems to have the most benefits when the curriculum incorporates cooperative learning methods.

c. *How well-educated are our children? A cross-cultural comparison*

Surveys of Canadian students reveal that most of them learn to read during elementary school and most acquire basic mathematical skills by the end of high school. Although nearly one-quarter of Canadian adolescents show weaknesses in reading and math, research indicates that Canadian students' achievement in comparison to other countries has improved recently. Educators in the United States are particularly concerned. The average scores obtained by American school children in mathematics, science, and verbal skills are consistently lower, and sometimes much lower, than those obtained by students in many other industrialized countries. The gap in performance between American children and Asian children is particularly pronounced in math, where 90 to

95% of Asian students outscore the average American child of the same age. These differences in achievement are already evident in the first grade, and they grow more pronounced at each subsequent grade level.

This achievement gap seems to reflect cultural differences in attitudes toward education as well as differences in educational techniques. First, Asian students spend more time in school and more time "on task" when they are in class. Second, Asian parents have higher academic achievement expectations for their children. Third, Asian students have a larger amount of homework assigned, relative to their American counterparts. Finally, Asian parents, teachers, and students appear to have an incremental view of academic achievement. The general belief is that all students have the potential to succeed, but that the child must work hard to achieve success.

3. Peers as agents of socialization

a. *Who or what is a peer, and what functions do peers serve?*

Peers are individuals who operate at similar levels of behavioural complexity. Peer interactions are equal-status interactions in the sense that peers are not subordinate to each other. Peers do not oversee or direct each other's activities, except by mutual consent. Peers do not have to be the same age, and the presence of younger peers can promote the development of both prosocial skills and leadership skills in older children. From the time they are toddlers until the time they reach adolescence, children's time with peers increases while the time they spend with adults decreases.

In peer interactions children are more likely to play with same-sex companions than with companions of the other sex; this is evident from the early toddler years. Boys and girls form different types of social relationships; boys often play in groups or teams, whereas girls are more likely to play in pairs.

Harlow's work with monkeys suggests that peers and parents are both important in the socialization process. When rhesus monkeys were raised with no peer contact and were only allowed to interact with their mother, they failed to develop normal patterns of social behaviour. They typically avoided monkeys who were their own age, and when they did approach age-mates they tended to be highly aggressive. However, rhesus monkeys separated from their mothers and raised exclusively with peers also showed evidence of abnormal patterns of social behaviour. They became highly agitated over minor stressors, and they were highly aggressive to age-mates from outside their peer group.

b. *The development of peer sociability*

Prior to 6 months of age, infants do not really interact with other infants. Past this point infants often babble to other infants, and they may offer toys or gesture to age-mates. However, during the first year friendly gestures are often not reciprocated. By 18 months of age toddlers are beginning to show evidence of coordinated interactions with other toddlers their own age. By the time they are 24 months old their social interactions are more likely to involve complementary roles, such as engaging in a game of tag or cooperating to achieve a shared goal.

Preschoolers' playful interactions can be placed into four categories of increasing social complexity: nonsocial activity, parallel play, associative play, and cooperative play. As children grow older, solitary and parallel play tend to decline, and associative and cooperative play become more common. However, children of all ages show evidence of all four types of play. Recent research by Coplan and colleagues has shown that preschoolers who frequently engage in particularly physical solitary play may be at risk for later academic and social problems.

A different categorization scheme has been developed by Howes and Matheson to describe the cognitive complexity of children's play, rather than its social complexity. Their classification scheme includes parallel play, parallel aware play, simple pretend play, complementary and reciprocal play, cooperative social pretend play, and complex social pretend play. The first type of play is evident in infants who are 6 to 12 months of age. Subsequent levels of play emerge across infancy and the preschool years, with complex social pretend play first appearing in children who are $3^1/_2$ to 4 years of age. According to Howes, pretend play fosters communication skills, negotiation skills, and emotional understanding.

Peer interactions continue to increase in sophistication and complexity throughout the elementary-school years. By ages 6 to 10, children are more likely to be participating in games that are governed by formal sets of rules.

The nature of peer contacts also changes during middle childhood and true peer groups are likely to form. The individuals in these peer groups typically interact on a regular basis, identify themselves with their peer group, follow peer group norms, and develop a hierarchical organization within the peer group.

By the time they are adolescents, individuals spend more time with peers than with parents or siblings. Early in adolescence cliques typically consist of approximately half a dozen same-sexed peers who share similar values. By mid-adolescence heterosexual cliques form, and several cliques may form a more loosely organized "crowd" organized around shared attitudes and activities. Cliques and crowds are important in helping adolescents develop a sense of personal identity, and early dating often occurs within an adolescent's clique or crowd. In later adolescence cross-sex friendships develop and adolescents begin to interact more as "couples." As this occurs the cliques and crowds begin to disintegrate

Parents can influence the amount of peer contact their children experience in a number of ways. When children are raised in neighbourhoods in which the houses are widely separated, they may have few opportunities to interact with peers outside of school. By encouraging their children to participate in organized activities, by involving their children in high quality daycare or nursery schools, or by hosting visits by their children's peer group, parents can increase their children's opportunities for peer interactions. Parents can also foster the development of their children's sociability by indirectly monitoring peer interactions and by allowing their children some freedom in structuring their peer activities. Lastly, parents who are positive and supportive and who use prosocial strategies tend to have children who also demonstrate positive social skills.

c. Peer acceptance and popularity

Peer acceptance is a measure of the extent to which a child is viewed by his or her peers as being a likable companion. Children may be popular (liked by many and disliked by few), rejected (liked by few and disliked by many), neglected (neither liked nor disliked by peers), controversial (liked by many peers but also disliked by many peers), or average status (liked or disliked by a moderate number of peers). In a typical elementary classroom two-thirds of the children will fall into one of the first four categories, with the remainder being classified as average-status children.

Children who are popular tend to have parents with an authoritative style of parenting. Rejected or controversial children often experience either authoritarian or uninvolved parenting. In terms of academic achievement, rejected children tend to score lower on measures of IQ than popular, average, or neglected children. Children who have difficult temperaments or who are behaviourally inhibited may be at risk of being rejected or neglected by peers. Children who are physically attractive are often more popular than their less attractive classmates. Popular children tend also to have relatively well developed role-taking skills.

Children who are cooperative and who engage in prosocial behaviours are more likely to be popular. Neglected children are often shy or withdrawn, and they are unlikely to make attempts to enter play groups. Rejected children can be placed into one of two categories, based on their behavioural interactions with their peers. Rejected-aggressive children often use forceful proactive means to dominate play groups, and they show low levels of prosocial behaviour. In contrast, rejected-withdrawn children are individuals who display immature or unusual behaviours and may react negatively to criticism by peers. These children recognize that they are not liked by their peer group, and they are at risk for experiencing depression or other emotional or internalizing disorders.

It is important to note that the criteria for popularity and unpopularity change with age and with context. For example, during preadolescence and early adolescence, aggression, especially by boys, may lead to popularity. Further, whereas consorting with opposite-sex age-mates in young childhood may violate a norm, relationships with the opposite sex during adolescence may increase popularity.

d. Children and their friends

Before the age of 8 friendships tend to be based on common activities. Children who are between the ages of 8 and 10 are beginning to see friends as people who are psychologically similar and who are cooperative and sensitive to each other's needs. By the time they are adolescents individuals see friendships as reciprocal emotional commitments.

Beginning in infancy and toddlerhood children respond differently to friends than they do to other playmates. During the preschool years children are more likely to share with friends and more likely to respond to a friend's distress. Even during the preschool years friendships are fairly stable. In preschool children friendships can often last for more than a year, and during middle childhood close friendships tend to remain relatively stable from year to year. However, the size of a child's friendship network tends to shrink as he or she approaches adolescence.

Having a close relationship with one or more friends may provide school-aged children and adolescents with emotional security that can help them deal with stressful situations. As children grow older they increasingly look to friends as sources of social support. Close friendships also contribute to the growth of mature social problem-solving skills. Finally, individuals who are able to form close same-sex friendships during the middle childhood years and early adolescent years often forge closer ties with members of the other sex in later adolescence and adulthood.

e. *Parents and peers as influence agents*

Peers, especially close friends, become more important contributors to child development with age. Some theorists claim that peers are a more important contributor than parents. Others argue that the influence of and choice of friends is governed to a large extent by parental influence.

Throughout the elementary-school years there is very little change in children's conformity to peer pressure with respect to prosocial behaviours. However, there is an increase in conformity to peer pressure that encourages antisocial behaviour. This type of peer conformity peaks in Grade 9 (around age 15) and then declines through the high-school years. Interestingly, cross-cultural research on misconduct in early adolescence suggests that early adolescent misconduct may not necessarily stem from peer pressure to misbehave.

Parents and peers tend to exert their influences in different areas. Peers are more influential than parents with respect to social issues, such as clothing styles and recreational activities; parents are more influential when it comes to occupational goals, or future-oriented activities. In addition, during childhood and adolescence, children are often part of peer groups that reflect the values they have learned at home, decreasing the potential for cross-pressures between peer influences and parental influences.

Vocabulary Self-Test

Part I: For each of the following definitions provide the appropriate term. (Answers to this portion of the self-test are provided at the end of the chapter.)

1. ________________ The belief, fostered by televised violence, that the world is a more dangerous and frightening place than is actually the case

2. ________________ Children who receive many nominations by peers as a liked individual and many as a disliked individual

3. ________________ Social agencies other than the family that influence a child's or adolescent's cognitive, social, and emotional development

4. ________________ True social play in which children cooperate or assume reciprocal roles while pursuing shared goals

5. ________________ Two or more people who are operating at similar levels of behavioural complexity

6. ________________ Tendency to go along with the wishes of peers or to yield to peer-group pressures

7. ________________ The notion that people who watch a lot of media violence will become less aroused by aggression and more tolerant of aggressive acts

8. ________________ Procedures that ask children to identify those peers who they like or dislike or to rate peers for their desirability as companions

9. ________________ The educational practice of integrating students with special needs into regular classrooms rather than placing them in segregated special education classes (formerly referred to as mainstreaming)

10. ________________ Tangible and intangible resources provided by other people in times of uncertainty or stress

11. ________________ The educational practice of grouping students according to ability and then educating them in classes with students of comparable intellectual standing

12. ________________ A large, loosely organized peer group made up of several cliques that share similar norms, interests, and values

13. ________________ A person's willingness to interact with others and seek their attention or approval

14. ________________ Method of social-skills training in which an adult displays and explains a variety of socially skilled behaviours, allows the child to practise them, and provides feedback aimed at improving the child's performance

15. ________________ A study in which the suspected causes or contributors to a developmental outcome are assessed earlier to see if they accurately forecast the developments they are presumed to influence

Part II: For each of the following terms provide the definition.

Parallel Play: ____________________

Cross-Pressures: ____________________

Computer-Assisted Instruction (CAI): ____________________

Peer Acceptance: ____________________

Aptitude-Treatment Interaction (ATI): ____________________

Social Problem-Solving Training: ____________________

Informal Curriculum: ____________________

Clique: ____________________

Cooperative Learning Methods: ____________________

Rejected-Aggressive Children: ____________________

Mother-Only Monkeys: ____________________

Peer Group: ____________________

Television Literacy: ____________________

Rejected Children: ____________________

Associative Play: ____________________

Short-Answer Study Questions

EARLY WINDOWS: EFFECTS OF TELEVISION AND COMPUTER TECHNOLOGIES ON CHILDREN AND ADOLESCENTS

1. Explain what is meant by the term "television literacy."

2. Describe the aspects of television programming that children in preschool and the early elementary years attend to the most.

3. Identify three potential effects that can result from exposure to violence in television programs.

   a.

   b.

   c.

4. Explain how children's understanding of and reaction to television commercials changes from the preschool years through to adolescence.

5. List five strategies parents can use to regulate their children's exposure to television.

   a.

   b.

   c.

   d.

   e.

6. Describe the impact that educational programs (such as *Sesame Street*) have on cognitive development, and discuss the key criticisms that have been raised regarding programs of this type.

   Impact:

   Criticisms:

7. Identify three ways that computers can be integrated into classroom settings, and describe the benefits of each form of computer usage.

   a.

   b.

   c.

8. List three concerns that have been raised concerning children's exposure to computer technology (inside and outside classroom settings).

   a.

   b.

   c.

SCHOOL AS A SOCIALIZATION AGENT

9. Identify four misconceptions about factors that affect a school's overall level of effectiveness.

   a.

   b.

   c.

   d.

10. List four values and practices that characterize effective schools.

a.

b.

c.

d.

11. Explain what is meant by a "goodness of fit" between a student and a school, and identify the teaching methods that are generally most effective with high-ability and low-ability students.

"Goodness of fit":

Effective teaching method for high-ability students:

Effective teaching method for low-ability students:

12. Explain what a self-fulfilling prophecy is, and use an illustrative example to show how a self-fulfilling prophecy might lead to low academic achievement in some students.

A self-fulfilling prophecy is:

Illustrative example:

13. Explain what "inclusion" is, and describe the methods that have been most effective in successfully integrating students with special needs.

Inclusion is:

It is most effective when:

14. List four cultural differences in educational attitudes and practices that might explain the achievement gap between American and Asian students.

a.

b.

c.

d.

15. Discuss Adams' research on the relations among family processes, school-focused parent–child interactions, the child's characteristics, and school success. What do the results of this research suggest for school–parent involvement?

16. Discuss the rationale underlying efforts to make school experiences more culturally relevant. What are some of the ways that educators might make school activities more culturally relevant?

PEERS AS AGENTS OF SOCIALIZATION

17. Describe basic age-related changes in the proportion of time that children spend with adults and other children.

18. In two separate studies Harlow raised groups of rhesus monkeys so that the monkeys (a) either had no contact with peers, or (b) had continuous exposure to peers, but no exposure to their mothers. Describe the types of socialization patterns that emerged in each group of monkeys ("mother-only" and "peer-only").

The "mother-only" group:

The "peer-only" group:

19. List and describe the four levels of social complexity that have been identified in children's play.

a.

b.

c.

d.

20. List and describe the five levels of cognitive complexity identified in children's play.

a.

b.

c.

d.

e.

21. Identify the four characteristics that are typically found in "true" peer groups.

a.

b.

c.

d.

22. Describe how the nature of peer group contact and the composition of peer groups change from early adolescence through to late adolescence.

23. List five categories of peer acceptance that have been identified through sociometric data analysis, and describe the typical peer ratings given to children in each of these categories.

a.

b.

c.

d.

e.

24. Children who are rejected by their peers can be categorized as having one of two distinct behavioural profiles. List each of these profiles and describe the types of behaviour that are typically seen with each profile.

a.

b.

25. Popular, rejected, and neglected children each show different patterns of behaviour when first interacting with unfamiliar peers. Describe each of these behavioural patterns.

Popular children:

Rejected children:

Neglected children:

26. List and describe six techniques that have been shown to be effective in improving the social skills of unpopular children.

a.

b.

c.

d.

e.

f.

27. List three roles that friends play in the socialization process.

a.

b.

c.

28. Identify three ways in which peers can exert an influence on each other's behaviour.

a.

b.

c.

Multiple-Choice Self-Test

For each of the following questions select the best alternative. (Answers and explanations for this self-test are provided at the end of the chapter.) Once you have selected your answer, provide a brief explanation for why the answer you selected is the best choice and why the remaining answers would not be correct.

1. Recent research on the impact of *Sesame Street* on intellectual and academic measures (e.g., Rice et al.) has shown that regular viewing of *Sesame Street*:

   a. primarily benefits advantaged children
   b. primarily benefits disadvantaged children
   c. has actually widened the intellectual and academic gap between advantaged and disadvantaged children
   d. benefits both advantaged and disadvantaged children, even if they view alone

   Rationale: ______________________________

   ____

2. Some have feared computer use would turn kids into passive, social recluses. Research that was reviewed in your text suggests that:

   a. this has indeed happened, and peer interactions decrease dramatically when computers are introduced into the classroom
   b. computer use has little impact on social interaction
   c. computer use has been associated with increased peer interaction and an increase, rather than a decrease, in cooperation
   d. computer use tends to create a subgroup of computer "nerds" who are rejected by their peers

   Rationale: ______________________________

   ____

3. According to Rutter and other researchers, one factor that has been found to be highly predictive of "effective" schooling is:

   a. higher levels of monetary support
   b. a clear focus on academic goals
   c. the introduction of ability tracking
   d. the use of an "open" classroom design

   Rationale: ______________________________

   ____

4. In general, inclusion of children with special needs:

   a. often results in declines in self-esteem because they are socially rejected
   b. typically results in improved academic performance and self-esteem
   c. has no particular advantages or disadvantages for physically or mentally challenged children
   d. increases their acceptance by normal children

   Rationale: ______________________________

   ____

5. In natural settings, the peer interactions of 6- to 10-year-olds more often occur in:

a. peer groups
b. cliques
c. crowds
d. confidential pairs

Rationale: ____

____

6. Nine-month-old Censari is "playing with" her ten-month-old friend Ellie. Each of the girls is playing with brightly coloured blocks. The girls are in the same room, playing with the same set of blocks, but don't seem to even notice what the other is doing. These two children are displaying:

a. cooperative play
b. parallel play
c. complementary play
d. simple pretend play

Rationale: ____

____

7. Rejected children are children who are:

a. actively disliked by most of their peers
b. liked by their peers but disliked by their teachers
c. liked by many of their peers and disliked by many of their peers
d. neither liked nor disliked by their peers

Rationale: ____

____

8. An investigator is interested in assessing children's popularity in school and relating it to later career aspirations and achievements. The best research design for this study would be:

a. a retrospective study
b. a case study
c. an ethnographic study
d. a prospective study

Rationale: ____

____

Activities and Projects Related to this Chapter

ACTIVITY 16-1

TELEVISION AGGRESSION

INTRODUCTION: This activity relates to the text presentation in Chapter 16 on potentially undesirable effects of television. It also relates to material on observational learning presented in Chapter 8. This activity can be an eye-opener if you have never given any thought to what messages might be coming across to children when they view television—messages about sex roles, ethnic and racial minorities, how to solve problems, how to be happy, etc.

INSTRUCTIONS: Identify the assumption(s) about children and the nature of their development that underlie each of the following practices.

1. Develop behavioural definitions of verbal aggression and physical aggression. What exactly do you mean by aggression—a slap, a kick, a put-down ... or what? Must actual harm be done, or is intent to harm sufficient to count an act as aggression? Coming up with behavioural criteria is an important step because "aggression" is an abstract concept that cannot be measured until it is defined behaviourally. (You may need to watch a part of some programs to help you decide on what you will count as an example of aggression. It may also be useful to discuss criteria with a classmate and see if you can arrive at a consensus.)

   Note—One of the purposes of this assignment is to give you first-hand experience that will build your appreciation of the difficulty in developing coding categories and in actually using them. The adequacy of these behavioural definitions can markedly affect the strength of conclusions that a researcher can make. Inconsistencies in behavioural definitions can also be an important factor behind inconsistencies in the results and conclusions of various studies, a possibility that you will more fully appreciate after completing this activity.

2. Choose four different television programs that children might watch. Select one program from each of the following four categories:
   a. Educational program (e.g., *Zoboomafoo, Bill Nye the Science Guy, The Magic School Bus, The Nature of Things,*)
   b. Cartoon (e.g., *Blue's Clue's, Caillou, Dora the Explorer, Creep School, Dudley the Dragon, Pokemon, Pumper Pups, Sponge Bob, Totally Spies, Wumpa's World*)
   c. Early-evening program aimed at older children and families (e.g., *Degrassi Next Generation, Joey, Simpsons, The Gilmore Girls, Malcolm in the Middle*)
   d. Evening program aimed at youth and adults (e.g., *CSI, Da Vinci's Inquest, Fear Factor, Law & Order, Survivor*)

3. Record the title and length of each program. While viewing each program tally the number of instances of verbal and physical aggression using the behavioural definitions that you developed to aid in your identification of an aggressive incident.

   Make note of the typical consequences of the aggression in each program (i.e., the aggressor gets something; the aggressor is punished; there is laughter suggesting the aggressive action was funny; the problem gets solved; the aggressor is treated like a hero; the aggression is portrayed as justified revenge, etc.).

4. Prepare a write-up that includes:

   a. Your definitions of verbal and physical aggression.
   b. A summary of your results for each program and a comparison of the programs.
   c. A discussion that includes your results, your reactions to the programs, a brief overview of the findings of studies reported in your text on the impact of televised violence on children, and your recommendations regarding children's television viewing.

5. Research current Canadian policy on regulations for children's television programming. Are networks responsible for broadcasting a certain number of hours each week of children's programs? What are they responsible for, if at all, in terms of advertising during children's programming?

6. Discuss the potential barriers to implementing strict guidelines, for example, in terms of regulating the frequency and nature of violence on both children's and adults' television programming. Do you think the V-Chip is effective, and why or why not?

7. You could do this same activity only identify positive role models and behaviours. Which TV programs rate the highest or most positively? Similarly, you could do this same activity for children's or family movies (Beauty and the Beast, Brother Bear, Finding Nemo, Harry Potter, Ice Age, The Little Mermaid, Shrek, Sleeping Beauty, Snow White, Stuart Little).

RELATED REFERENCES

Josephson, W. L. (1987). Television violence and children's aggression: Testing the priming, social script, and disinhibition predictions. *Journal of Personality and Social Psychology, 53,* 882–890.

Liebert, R. M., & Sprafkin, J. (1988). *The early window: Effects of television on children and youth.* (3rd ed.). New York: Pergamon Press.

MacBeth, T. M. (2001). The impact of television: A Canadian natural experiment. In C. McKie & B. D. Singer, *Communications in Canadian society* (5th ed., pp. 196–213). Toronto: Thomson Educational Publishing.

WEBSITES OF INTEREST

For more information on Canadian research on adolescent peer relations and adolescent health issues, visit, for example, the McCreary Centre Society web page: www.mcs.bc.ca

For information about a Canadian school-based prevention program, visit the "Roots of Empathy" program web page: www.rootsofempathy.org

REFERENCES OF INTEREST

Funk, J.B., Baldacci, H.B., & Pasold, T. (2004). Violence exposure in real-life, video games, television, movies, and the internet: Is there desensitization? *Journal of Adolescence, 27(1),* 23–39.

Griffiths, M. (1997). Friendship and social development in children and adolescents: The impact of electronic technology. *Educational and Child Psychology, 14(3),* 25–37.

Huesmann, L.R., Moise-Titus, J., & Podolski, C. (2003). Longitudinal relations between children's exposure to TV violence and their aggressive and violent behavior in young adulthood: 1977–1992. *Developmental Psychology, 39(2),* 201–221.

Johnson, L.C. (2003). Patchwork quilt or seamless day? Parent, teacher and child care staff views on early childhood education programs for kindergarten-age children in Canada. *Early Education and Development, 14(2),* 215–232.

Koh, Y., Mendelson, M.J., & Rhee, U. (2003). Friendship satisfaction in Korean and Canadian university students. *Canadian Journal of Behavioural Science, 35:2,* 239–253.

Kohen, D.E., Forer, B., Hertzman, C., & Brooks-Gunn, J. (2003). Children's school readiness. Applied Research Branch, HRDC.

Kohen, D.E., & Hertzman, C. (2001). The importance of neighborhood and family socio-economic conditions on school aged children's competencies. Final report prepared for the BC Ministry of Education and Applied Research Branch, Human Resources Development Canada.

Krcmar, M., & Cooke, M. (2001). Children's moral reasoning and their perceptions of television violence. *Journal of Communication, 51(2),* 300–316.

Larson, M.S. (2003). Gender, race, and aggression in television commercials that feature children. *Sex Roles, 48(1–2),* 67–75.

Maggi, S., Hertzman, D., Kohen, D., & D'Angiulli, A. (in press). Neighborhood and class climate effects on school performance: The case of highly competent children. *Journal of Educational Psychology.*

Mendelson, M.J., & Aboud, F.E. (1999). Measuring friendship quality in late adolescents and young adults: The McGill Friendship Questionnaires. *Canadian Journal of Behavioural Science, 31,* 130–132.

Mendelson, M.J., & Aboud, F.E., & Lanthier, R.P. (1994). Personality predictors of friendship and popularity in kindergarten. *Journal of Applied Developmental Psychology, 15,* 113–135.

Mendelson, M.J., & Kay, A.C. (2003). Positive feelings in friendship: Does imbalance in the relationship matter? *Journal of Social and Personal Relationships, 20,* 101–116.

Mounts, N.S., & Steinberg, L. (1995). An ecological analysis of peer influence on adolescent grade point average and drug use. *Developmental Psychology, 31(6),* 915–922.

Rosenkoetter, L.I., Rosenkoetter, S.E., & Ozretich, R.A. (2004). Mitigating the harmful effects of television violence. *Journal of Applied Developmental Psychology, 25(1),* 25–47.

Schonert-Reichl, K., & Hymel, S. (1996). Promoting social development and acceptance in the elementary classroom. In J. Andrews (Ed.), *Teaching students with diverse needs* (pp. 152–200). Scarborough, Ontario: Nelson.

Schwartz, K.D., & Fouts, G.T. (2003). Music preferences, personality style, and developmental issues in adolescents. *Journal of Youth and Adolescence, 32(3),* 205–213.

Subrahmanyam, K., Greenfield, P., & Kraut, R. (2001). The impact of computer use on children's and adolescents' development. *Journal of Applied Developmental Psychology, 22(1),* 7–30.

ANSWERS TO SELF-TESTS

VOCABULARY SELF-TEST (The answers may be found on the pages in parentheses.)

1. mean-world belief (p. 608)
2. controversial children (p. 637)
3. extrafamilial influences (p. 605)
4. cooperative play (p. 633)
5. peers (p. 629)
6. peer conformity (p. 646)
7. desensitization hypothesis (p. 608)
8. sociometric techniques (p. 637)
9. inclusion (p. 624)
10. social support (p. 644)
11. ability tracking (p. 619)
12. crowd (p. 635)
13. sociability (p. 632)
14. coaching (p. 641)
15. prospective study (p. 644)

MULTIPLE-CHOICE SELF-TEST (The answers may be found on the pages in parentheses.)

1. **d** (pp. 610–611) Regular viewing of *Sesame Street* is associated with impressive gains in preschoolers' vocabularies and prereading skills. It is not primarily a benefit for children from either advantaged (a) or disadvantaged (b) backgrounds; it is a benefit to children, no matter what their background. And it has not widened the academic gap (c) between these two groups; both groups are equally likely to watch the show.

2. **c** (p. 614) Students who are working with computers are more likely to seek collaborative solutions; therefore, peer interactions are increased. The level of peer interactions has not decreased (a), but there has been a positive impact on the level of social interactions (b). Computers are typically used by all the students, not just a subgroup (d).

3. **b** (p. 617) A clear focus on academic goals is one factor that is highly predictive of a school's overall effectiveness. High levels of monetary support (a), the use of ability tracking (c), and the use of nontraditional classroom styles (d), have little impact on the effectiveness of schooling that is provided to students.

4. **a** (p. 624) Self-esteem often declines because classmates tend to ridicule students with special needs and are less likely to choose them as playmates. Sometimes academics improve (b), but often they do not. There are disadvantages if a child's self-esteem declines following inclusion (c). Acceptance by "normal" children is not enhanced simply because students with special needs are present in the classroom (d).

5. **a** (p. 635) The peer interactions of 6- to 10-year-old children more often occur in peer groups. In peer groups, children interact regularly, define membership in the group, and formulate norms that specify how members are supposed to look, think, and act. In early adolescence, cliques are small groups of friends that interact frequently (b). Crowds are large, loosely organized peer groups made up of several cliques that share similar norms, interests, and values (c). Confidential pairs is not a term used (d); however, pairs of friends based on intimacy and confidentiality usually do not occur until adolescence.

6. **b** (p. 633) These two children are performing similar activities without paying attention to each other. Cooperative play (a) would occur if they were engaging in play that involved complementary pretend roles. Complementary play (c) would involve action-based role reversals. Simple pretend play (d) would require interactions and sharing of toys.

7. **a** (p. 637) Children who are actively disliked by many of their peers are rejected children. Children who are liked by their peers (b) are popular (it really doesn't matter what the adults think). Controversial children are children who are liked by many and disliked by many (c). Children who are neither liked nor disliked (d) often appear to be "invisible" to their peer group and are neglected.

8. **d** (p. 644) A prospective study is a study in which the suspected causes or contributors to a developmental outcome are assessed earlier to see if they accurately forecast the developments they are presumed to influence. A retrospective study is a study in which individuals are asked to recall past events to see if they are related in any way to present events (a). A case study is a research method in which the investigator gathers extensive information about the life of an individual and then tests developmental hypotheses by analyzing the events of the person's life history (b). An ethnographic study is a research method in which the researcher seeks to understand the unique values, traditions, and social processes of a culture or subculture by living with its members and making extensive observations and notes (c).